DRESS
AND
SOCIETY

Jane E. Workman

Southern Illinois University

Beth W. Freeburg

Southern Illinois University

Fairchild Books, Inc.

New York

DRESS
AND
SOCIETY

Director of Sales and Acquisitions: Dana Meltzer-Berkowitz
Executive Editor: Olga T. Kontzias
Acquisitions Editor: Joseph Miranda
Senior Development Editor: Jennifer Crane
Art Director: Adam B. Bohannon
Associate Art Director: Erin Fitzsimmons
Production Director: Ginger Hillman
Senior Production Editor: Elizabeth Marotta
Project Management: Fair Street Productions
Line Editor: Jeannine Ciliotta
Copyeditor: Candie Frankel
Photo Research: Photosearch, Inc.
Cover Design: Adam B. Bohannon
Text Design: Chris Welch
Typesetter: Tina Henderson
Packaging: Chris Fortunato

Library of Congress Catalog Card Number: 2007932771

ISBN: 978-1-56367-626-0

GST R 133004424

Printed in the United States of America

TP09

CONTENTS

PREFACE

Careers in the fashion industry are challenging because of the continual change that is an essential feature of fashion. Fashion careers include one or more jobs related to fashion over the course of a person's life. The growth in fashion-related occupations is rooted in a growing population that demands an increasing quantity and variety of clothing appropriate for different social situations. Understanding the societal expectations associated with dress is critical to success in fashion careers. Also critical to fashion career success are research techniques that may be used to capture the past, present, and future trends in fashion.

As a result of the demands of the fashion industry, many colleges, universities, technical centers, and proprietary schools offer undergraduate and graduate programs that prepare students for fashion-related careers. Programs include lecture and studio-based courses that facilitate the development of fashion content knowledge and skills. In addition, more and more institutions are advocating increased research learning beginning at the undergraduate level.

This textbook has a twofold purpose for students pursuing careers in the fashion industry: (a) to present a sociological perspective on the way people dress and (b) to present research perspectives that will help students develop an appreciation for the value of research skills in their academic and professional careers. What more exciting topic to study and research than dress and society!

Organization

The emphasis throughout *Dress and Society* is on the fundamental process of social control that permeates all social behavior. Concepts that provide a framework for understanding the process of social control are used to organize the chapters: norms, violation of norms, recognition of violation, report of violation, sanctions, and enforcement of sanctions. The process of social control is a means to ensure compliance with norms, including dress norms. Dress is broadly defined as "an assemblage of body modifications and/or supplements displayed by a person in communicating with other human beings" (Eicher & Roach-Higgins, 1992, p. 15). Dress norms are acceptable ways to look in specific situations.

In preparing this book, we chose material that allows students to appreciate the power of research to illuminate and explain fundamental social facts about dress and society. Pairs of chapters (14 in all) fulfill the twofold purpose of the book. The first chapter in a pair gives students a selective and representative exposure to sociological concepts associated with each step of the process of social control. The second chapter in the pair presents content designed to strengthen students' grasp of research in the field. Sociological concepts are presented and accompanied by research that demonstrates the practical application of the concept. Contemporary multidisciplinary research studies are used to relate to students' experience and interests. Recent and classic research by scholars in the field of dress and society is featured. The research is presented and explained in a way that creates an understanding of the research process for dress and society. The content is selected to give a balance between body modifications and body supplements, while providing diversity related to gender, age, occupation, and multidisciplinary perspectives.

Features

Pedagogical features encourage the learner to engage in active and collaborative learning. Each chapter emphasizes the analysis of dress and social behavior within the framework of basic sociological concepts, such as culture, deviance, gender, norms, and socialization.

Opening vignettes—stories from the popular press—begin each chapter and are referred to throughout the chapter to engage students' interest and establish the value of using sociological analysis to explain everyday social behavior. These stories, taken from actual newspaper articles, are examined from the perspective of dress and society. The stories illustrate how fashion scholars think and how the knowledge in our discipline can be applied to understanding social behavior. A chapter introduction, questions to answer as you read, and a graphic organizer give students an overview of the chapter content and the anticipated outcomes. Summaries at the end of each chapter revisit the questions to answer as you read. Key terms shown in bold in the text are listed at the end of the chapter. Discussion questions are used to relate the terms, concepts, and procedures of each chapter back to the opening vignette to reinforce the value of using sociological analysis to explain everyday social behavior. Suggested readings provide additional resources for students to expand their learning and interests. Research activities at the end of each chapter give learners the chance to apply and expand their knowledge of dress and society as well as practice using research methods and tools to collect data.

Our Hope for Students

Our hope is that through reading *Dress and Society* and being engaged in the learning activities developed for use with the textbook, students will further the knowledge and skills they need to achieve vital and effective careers in the fashion industry. For students who are pursuing careers in other industries, we hope that the problem-centered approach of the book will provide insights about how sociological analysis can generate valuable information about individual and group behavior regarding dress. Finally, we hope the content and approach appeal to varied learning styles, are motivating, and are versatile in many academic settings.

Acknowledgments

We would like to thank the reviewers selected by Fairchild Books to evaluate our manuscript for their constructive criticism and helpful suggestions:

Kathleen Rees, of Texas A&M Kingsville; Carolyn Robertson, of the Fashion Institute of Design & Merchandising (Los Angeles); and Dana Legette-Traylor, of American Intercontinental University (Atlanta, GA). Every effort was made to incorporate their suggestions into the text.

Thank you to the staff at Fairchild Books (Olga Kontzias, Joe Miranda, Jennifer Crane, Elizabeth Marotta) and Photosearch Inc. (Susan Wechsler, Deborah Anderson, Jeannine Ciliotta, and Candie Frankel).

Thanks to our students, who have been an inspiration to us through the years. Thanks to our network of support at Southern Illinois University Carbondale: Sally Arnett, doctoral student, who provided research assistance; the research librarians at Morris Library; and our teaching and research colleagues in the School of Architecture and the Department of Workforce Education and Development.

Thanks to Bill, who read the book more than once and offered helpful insights (Bill, you are the wind beneath my wings—Jane). Thanks to Brian, who did some of the legwork and provided enthusiastic support for the project (Brian, I'm so proud you are my son—Beth).

To God be the glory; great things He has done!

Jane E. Workman
Beth Winfrey Freeburg
Southern Illinois University Carbondale

DRESS
AND
SOCIETY

Chapter One

DRESS, SOCIETY, AND SOCIAL CONTROL

FROM THE HEADLINES

A website (www.ModestyZone.net) was designed by Wendy Shalit as an answer to the vulgarity prevalent on magazine covers, television, radio, movies, and even T-shirts. The following remarks were found on a blog at the website and reported by Charen. "Waiting to meet an old friend for lunch the other day, my eye fell on the young woman at the table across the aisle. She was attractive, nicely put together in a casual way: T-shirt, jeans, Eskimo-style boots, and a neat ponytail. The lady with her appeared to be her middle-aged mother. Ultimately I noticed that her T-shirt had some strange and lewd writing on it. Hmmmmm? . . . What could this young woman have been thinking? And how on earth could her middle-aged companion sip her soup and not be mortified at the outrageous slogan proudly displayed across the table?"

Source: Charen, M. (2005, December 10). A modest backlash against the trash culture. *Southern Illinoisan,* p. 4A.

The situation described in this excerpt from a newspaper column illustrates several concepts we will cover in this chapter. Why was the viewer shocked to see a woman wearing a T-shirt with a lewd slogan? Was it because of the incongruity between the woman's otherwise conventional appearance and the vulgar slogan? The slogan was the type of language one would not expect to see in a public place. The viewer also questioned the reaction (or rather nonreaction) of the woman's mother. Did the mother condone the behavior? Why was the mother not ashamed and why did she not refuse to be seen with her daughter dressed in such a fashion? The woman broke one of society's rules; the daughter's nonconformity and the lack of response from someone close to her disturbed the viewer so much that the incident was reported on a website devoted to maintaining modesty and decency in U.S. society. What do you think the young woman was thinking when she wore the T-shirt with the lewd slogan? How do you explain the non-reaction of her middle-aged companion? What does the young woman's dress tell you about her status and prestige in the United States? After reading this chapter, you will be in a better position to explain why the viewer was not only personally offended but, beyond that, was concerned about the effect of such blatant disregard for rules on society itself.

In this chapter, you'll learn about the process by which society affects the choices individuals make about dress and, conversely, how the choices individuals make about dress affect society. The study of dress and society examines the two-way interaction between societal expectations and individual choices about dress. The excerpt from a newspaper article illustrates some of the concepts you will read about. A brief introduction to sociological theories that apply to the study of dress and society follows, along with definitions of related terms so that you will be well-grounded in the basic vocabulary used throughout the rest of the text. A graphic organizer of the process of social control provides a picture to accompany this overview of the conceptual framework. The chapter ends with a list of key terms and research activities that will help you put into practice the material you have learned.

QUESTIONS TO ANSWER AS YOU READ

1. What is the sociological definition of the normative order for dress?
2. What sociological terms and concepts most closely relate to dress and society?
3. Which sociological theories provide explanations for the nature of dress within society?
4. What is the purpose of the process of social control and what are its steps?
5. How does the process of social control relate to dress?

SOCIOLOGICAL THEORIES AND CONCEPTS

This text is grounded in sociological theories that explain how society's norms influence individual behavior. Sociology is the study of social life, social change, and the social causes and consequences of human behavior. A **theory** is a collection of evidence, hypotheses, or principles used to explain social behavior.

Four Theories of Social Behavior

Four theories help to explain the behavior of members of a society regarding dress: (a) normative socialization theory, (b) social learning theory, (c) symbolic interactionist theory, and (d) social control theory. **Dress** is "an assemblage of body modifications and/or supplements displayed by a person in communicating with other human beings" (Eicher & Roach-Higgins, 1992, p. 15). See Figure 1.1.

Figure 1.2, in which a young adolescent girl is shown begging her mother for a popular brand of shirt, illustrates how reinforcement from others influences the behavior of individuals. The **normative**

FIGURE 1.1 DRESS IS A MEANS OF COMMUNICATING WITH OTHER HUMAN BEINGS. THE PEOPLE IN THE PICTURE ARE COMMUNICATING BY THEIR CHOICE OF CLOTHING AND BODY MODIFICATIONS.

FIGURE 1.2 NORMATIVE SOCIALIZATION THEORY EXPLAINS THAT LEARNING OCCURS THROUGH POSITIVE AND NEGATIVE REINFORCEMENT. THIS CARTOON SHOWS NEGATIVE REINFORCEMENT: A YOUNG ADOLESCENT GIRL BEGS HER MOTHER FOR A POPULAR BRAND OF SHIRT BECAUSE OTHERWISE NO ONE WILL TALK TO HER.

socialization theory assumes that one way individuals learn desirable behaviors in society is through a system of positive and negative reinforcements from others (Skinner, 1953).

Figure 1.3 illustrates how a young boy learns desirable behaviors such as shaving by copying his father. **Social learning theory** proposes that individuals learn desirable behaviors by imitating the actions and behaviors of those around them, who serve as role models (Bandura, 1969). In the process of imitation, individuals adopt the role models' norms and values.

The **symbolic interactionist theory** attempts to explain interactions among individuals based on symbols that are used or understood by everyone in a

FIGURE 1.3 SOCIAL
LEARNING THEORY EXPLAINS
THAT LEARNING OCCURS
THROUGH IMITATION OF
ROLE MODELS.

FIGURE 1.4 (FAR RIGHT)
EVEN YOUNG CHILDREN RECOG-
NIZE CERTAIN SYMBOLS, SUCH AS
BRAND NAME LOGOS.

We all want something better for our
children. But not *that* much better.

particular group. The term *symbolic interactionism* was coined by Blumer (1969). Symbolic interactionist theory regards socialization as the means by which individuals develop competence in interacting with others by acquiring knowledge of a culture's symbols.

The following example illustrates the last of the four theories: Prison officials in one state punish male inmates who have behaved inappropriately by making them wear pink jumpsuits ("South Carolina Prisons," 2007). Wearing a pink jumpsuit in an all-male population leads to ridicule by other inmates. The prison director is using the process of social control to encourage inmates to behave appropriately. All societies have various mechanisms of social control. **Social control theory** combines elements of the other three theories to create a more complete explanation for people's behavior regarding dress. Social control theory integrates normative socialization theory in the assumption that socialization is one form of social control. From social learning theory, social control theory integrates positive and negative reinforcement in the form of sanctions used to encourage compliance with norms. From symbolic interactionist theory, social control theory incorporates the view that appropriate behavior is learned through interaction with other people in specific situations. The focus of this text is social control theory because of its power to explain peoples' behavior regarding dress. With these theories as a base, we can begin to explain some sociological concepts.

Sociological Concepts

Sociology has a common language related to the structure of society and group behavior. This section will present some of the concepts and terms that constitute this common language. Because sociological concepts and theories are made up of terms with specialized meanings, it is important to understand the terms as a foundation for understanding the concepts. For example, understanding the terms *dress, symbol, society,* and *socialization* is necessary for understanding symbolic interactionist theory as it applies to the study of dress and society.

Normative Order

The **normative order** consists of shared **norms,** that is, shared standards or rules that specify what human beings should or should not think, say, or do, and how human beings should or should not look under given circumstances (Blake & Davis, 1964; Workman & Freeburg, 2000a). The visual aspect of dress is expressed through norms that specify how human beings should or should not look under given circumstances. The definition of the normative order is central to sociological research because it is related to the definitions of other sociological concepts such as society, culture, cultural categories, cultural principles, and the process of social control.

Society

A **society** is a large community of people tied together by geographical territory, traditions, institutions, nationality, and important cultural expectations. Society is a concept that is often considered to be broadly equivalent to the concept of country or nation; for example, people often refer to a society in the context of a geopolitical entity, as U.S. society or Korean society. Particular forms of dress are associated with particular societies: the sari is associated with Indian society, the kimono with Japanese society, the *hanbok* with Korean society, and jeans and T-shirt with U.S. society.

Culture

"**Culture** is the knowledge, language, values, customs, and material objects that are passed from person to person and from one generation to the next in a human group or society" (Kendall, 2007, p. 74). Culture is an abstract

concept that refers to a collection of shared artifacts and understandings. Within the dominant culture are many subcultures. **Subculture** refers to "the distinctive lifestyles, values, norms, and beliefs of certain segments of the population within a society" (Tischler, 2004, p. 71). Examples of subcultures are ethnic groups (Native American, Asian, African), occupational groups (teachers, firefighters, lawyers), religious groups (Amish, Buddhist, Christian), and social classes (upper, middle, lower). Two subcultures are represented by the individuals interacting in Figure 1.5.

Material culture refers to tangible artifacts or products (such as the jeans, T-shirt, and Eskimo-style boots worn by the young woman described earlier in "From the Headlines"), while **nonmaterial culture** refers to abstract concepts, beliefs, and values (as expressed in the saying on the young woman's T-shirt). Sometimes values associated with nonmaterial culture are expressed in material culture (Figure 1.6).

Cultural universals are customs and practices that are believed to exist in all known cultures (Shepard, 2005). Nearly 70 cultural universals have been identified, among them courtship, etiquette, funeral rites, jokes, language, marriage, religious rituals, and dress. Particular forms of dress (as with other cultural universals) vary from one society to another and from one time period to another within the same society (Payne, Winakor, & Farrell-Beck, 1992).

Aspects of Culture

Culture is transmitted from person to person; it is not present at birth, but must be learned. Individual members of the same culture share cultural expectations; and culture also changes, sometimes dramatically. Let's take a look at each of these aspects of culture.

Culture Is Transmitted

Both material and nonmaterial culture are transmitted, that is, passed along by members of a society. Transmission of a culture takes place as members of a society share with others their understanding of material and nonmaterial culture. Symbols are one means by which members of society communicate abstract concepts because symbols express shared meanings. A **symbol** is a visible or tangible object that represents something else. "Language is a set of symbols that expresses ideas and enables people to think and communicate with one another" (Kendall, 2007, p. 81). Language can be either verbal (spoken) or nonverbal (written, gestured, graphic).

Culture depends on symbols because symbols are the mechanism by which meaning is shared among members of a society. Symbols affect our thoughts about many aspects of life—race, ethnicity, gender, age, occupations, social class. Symbols can be a source of strong disagreement among individuals. An example is the controversy surrounding images and displays of the Confederate flag. This controversy has been played out in public schools as administrators developed dress code policies to ban Confederate flag T-shirts after determining that the symbol increased racial tensions ("Confederate Shirts Spark Fashion Fight," 2001; "T-shirt Ban Upheld," 2001; *Scott v. School Board,* 2003). The ban on the T-shirts ended up in the courts because students (and their parents) believed that their freedom of expression was being violated.

Symbols affect our beliefs about gender. In our society, both male and female gender roles have expressly stated as well as implicit expectations of dress that are understood within particular cultural and historical contexts. The color of clothing, for example, is a symbol that denotes different meanings for females and males. An analysis of infants' clothing available in the Sears catalog between 1896 and 1962 illustrates the evolution of an accepted symbol over time (Huun & Kaiser, 2001). In 1896, the first infants' clothing (a loose white dress) was offered in the catalog; in 1962, the first gender-specific clothing for infants appeared. The loose white dress, developed to allow children freedom of movement, was designated for both very young boys and girls during the eighteenth and nineteenth centuries. From 1896 to 1962, U.S. culture was "immersed in a process of renegotiating gender and age boundaries" and gender symbolism in infants' clothing became an accepted norm (Huun & Kaiser, 2001, p. 104). Prior to World War I, customs currently assumed to be true for infants' clothing (pink is a girls' color, blue is a boys' color; dresses are for girls; baseball motifs are for boys, butterfly motifs are for girls) did not apply; indeed, these customs did not become norms until after World War II (Paoletti & Kregloh, 1989). The color of clothing can send implied messages about how the child should be treated. If an infant is wearing blue, the message is sent to others that the child is a boy and should be treated like a boy.

Gender symbols affect individual and societal expectations about what females and males should think, say, do, and how they should look. After studying children's beliefs about gender norms, Blakemore (2003) concluded that "boys shouldn't look like girls and girls shouldn't act like boys" (p. 411). These expectations are pervasive and influence, often subconsciously, our perceptions of other members of our society. Traditionally, women have been considered to be the sustainers of a society's morality (Ribeiro, 1986). Therefore, the woman in our headline story who was wearing a lewd T-shirt was violating cultural expectations. However, the person observing the lewd T-shirt slogan might not have been surprised if the wearer had been a man.

Culture Is Learned

Individuals learn about culture through socialization into a society. **Socialization** is a process whereby individuals become aware of society's expectations and learn how they are expected to behave. It is a lifelong process that is accomplished through social interaction. As a result of socialization, individuals develop a self-identity and the skills (physical, mental, and social) needed for survival. Socialization is the fundamental connection between an individual and the society in which he or she lives.

Socialization is most successful when individuals conform to society's norms because they believe conforming is the best strategy. For example, Shen and Dickson (2001) found that identification with cultural norms and values influenced consumers' perceptions of ethical dilemmas such as shoplifting. If individuals do not learn society's norms and values, they may choose to engage in consumer misconduct in the acquisition of clothing or other items by shoplifting—an act that violates society's norm of conduct in exchange situations. Socialization makes it possible for a society to replicate itself by passing on its culture from one generation to the next. Individual members of a society learn society's customs, ideals, knowledge, morals, religion, and skills from their interactions with others.

Culture Is Shared

Individuals share culture as they interpret its messages and adjust their behavior to cultural expectations when interacting with others. For example, cultural expectations affect how people feel about their bodies, as well as the extent to which people diet, exercise, use cosmetics, have cosmetic surgery, and select apparel (Rudd & Lennon, 2000). "Almost everything we believe or know or do we learn from observing other people, from listening to other people, or from reading and thinking about what other people have written" (Hunt & Colander, 2005, p. 78).

Interpretation of the shared meanings of symbols such as dress is influenced by cultural codes (Kaiser, 1993). A **cultural code** represents shared cultural knowledge. It is an abstract relationship whereby the same symbol or set of symbols invokes the same or similar meanings among members of a culture.

Take a minute to look at the following statements. Do you agree or disagree with them?

1. Women should shave their legs and under their arms.
2. Men should be tall.
3. Women should have long hair.
4. People should be slim.

Many of you from the United States probably answered the questions as follows: (1) agree, (2) agree, (3) disagree, (4) agree. Why? Because you come from a shared culture. If you were from another country, your answers would likely be different. For example, when a sample of Korean respondents answered those questions, their responses were (1) disagree, (2) neutral, (3) disagree, and (4) disagree (Freeburg, Workman, & Lee, 2001).

Culture Is Transformed

In every society, both material and nonmaterial culture change. Fashion provides a perfect example of how innovations are introduced by members of a society, leading to gradual changes in the society. The fashion cycle begins when a new style is introduced to consumers and adopted by certain fashion leaders (Calasibetta & Tortora, 2003). These fashion leaders are sometimes called fashion change agents or fashion trendsetters. As the new style is adopted and worn by more and more people, it becomes highly visible and noticeable. As the style continues to grow in social acceptance and reaches its peak of popularity, it becomes a well-established fashion, and the material culture of a society is changed.

The material culture of a society, that is, tangible artifacts or products including dress, sometimes undergoes change due to technology. The Internet is one technological development that has caused profound changes in fashion—in terms of both design innovation and marketing.

The availability of technology such as the Internet (material culture) does not mean that it will be accepted by people who believe (nonmaterial culture—abstract concepts, beliefs, and values) that the Internet poses a threat to privacy and payment security (identity theft). When material culture changes faster than nonmaterial culture, a cultural lag occurs. The term *Luddite* originated in 1811 in Britain as a result of a cultural lag—some men destroyed labor-saving textile machinery (material culture) in the belief (nonmaterial culture) that such machinery would diminish employment. The term has since been applied to anyone who opposes technological change.

Technology is valuable not only because of its features and practical application but because it helps people communicate and interact in varying situations. For example, the Internet has opened up new channels for fashion marketing through online purchasing, although concerns about payment security are an obstacle to the growth of Internet shopping (Kwon & Lee, 2003). Another new technology is a device that scans the entire body to produce a three-dimensional image that can be used to create a custom pattern. Consumer interest in being scanned and in allowing use of scan data is essential to the body scanner's potential to solve issues of clothing fit (Loker, Cowie, Ashdown, & Lewis, 2004). Culture is simultaneously transformed and transmitted through processes of change and resistance to change.

CULTURAL CATEGORIES

Cultural diversity refers to differences between and within societies. Within every society, people are categorized on the basis of this diversity and society's cultural values, beliefs, and artifacts. Examples of cultural categories are age, ethnicity, gender, physical attractiveness, religion, and socioeconomic class. Each member of a society belongs to several different categories at the same time—for example, an attractive adolescent Protestant Asian female of upper socioeconomic class.

Cultural categories are made visible through artifacts such as dress and affect how people respond to one another. Categories are used to distinguish and socialize people based on relevant differences. For example, because of U.S. cultural assumptions about gender and color of clothing, if an infant is clothed in a pink dress, that infant is categorized as a baby girl. When purchasing a gift for that infant, friends and family will chose something appropriate for a girl, such as a stuffed animal. Indeed, retail clothing stores for children are often arranged into sections based on gender.

Cultural categories are recognized by cues such as appearance. Some of these cues may bring stereotypes to mind. **Stereotypes** are oversimplified images used to categorize individuals based on appearance or behavior. Stereotypes can be positive or negative, but they are more often negative. For example, cultural stereotypes applied to blonde women include innocence (depicted as angels, saints, princesses, or fairies), sexy/fun ("blonde bombshell," "blondes have more fun"), easy ("sex kitten"), and dumb ("dumb blonde," "ditzy blonde") (Heckert, 2003).

In the process of socialization, acquiring a self-identity is influenced by the combination of categories to which an individual belongs. Appearance management is a process of identity expression. Appearance can be managed to emphasize or deemphasize cultural categories because being placed in particular categories leads to unequal access to status, prestige, privileges, and power. People may resist being classified into some categories that carry less prestige in a society; for example, both men and women may dye their hair to conceal the gray (a visual symbol of old age). In this way, the cultural category of old age may be deemphasized.

Appearance perception is similarly affected by the combination of visually perceived cultural categories. Appearance perception refers to the "process of observing and making evaluations or drawing inferences based on how people look" (Kaiser, 1997, p. 7). These perceptions may determine the acceptability of individuals for various roles. For example, employment recruiters may have expectations of the role of *appearance* in the pursuit of a career. "One has an absolute right to dress in a lime green suit with red shoes and an orange tie. But one has no reasonable expectation of being treated seriously as a candidate for the executive position while so attired" (Pitts, 2005, p. 4A). A neatly groomed job candidate appearing in a conservative suit may be viewed as more acceptable than an equally qualified but less professionally dressed candidate. For example, the human resources manager for a large supermarket chain decided not to hire a perfectly qualified candidate for a senior accounting position based on a simple detail—the job candidate wore a suit but no tie (Weiss, 2006).

CULTURAL PRINCIPLES

Cultural categories are regulated by cultural principles. Cultural principles refer to the ideas or values (ideology) that provide the rationale underlying the categories. For example, why does a candidate in a conservative suit and tie seem more suitable for an executive position than a less formally dressed candidate? The human resources manager who declined to hire the candidate who did not wear a tie believed it was a reflection of the candidate's decision-making process and called his judgment into question (Weiss, 2006).

Cultural principles can also be reflected in the principles that guide the use of elements of design. Design of female clothing will more often feature curved lines and soft edges, while clothing for males will more often feature straight lines and sharp edges (Workman & Johnson, 1993). Artifacts are valuable sources of evidence for uncovering cultural principles. For example, Hawley (2005) looked at the enduring and changing cultural meanings associated with Old Order Amish quilts. The Amish quilts "are valued for their humble simplicity, quality workmanship, and appealing graphic design" (p. 102). The quilts, as material manifestations of the Amish subculture, reflect the principles of simplicity, value of women's handiwork, and low-level technology.

Whereas cultural categories can be verbalized (attractive/unattractive, old/young, male/female), cultural principles are difficult to verbalize. People may not want to acknowledge the inequities associated with social stratification (social divisions or hierarchy). Because of socialization, social inequities may be so embedded in people's thinking that they are not even consciously aware of them.

Elements of social stratification include status, prestige, privilege, and power. **Status** is a person's position in a social hierarchy. For example, a hierarchy is reflected in an organization such as a fast food restaurant using dress as a symbol. The counter workers wear one type of dress usually including a cap or hat and the managers another type of dress, thereby visually establishing the status hierarchy. Symbols of status activate widely shared societal beliefs about people in particular positions in a social hierarchy.

In a medical establishment, uniforms also indicate status. For example, in the 1970s, nurses in different specializations adopted different attire to reflect their status positions: advanced practice nurses wore lab coats, midwives wore scrubs, and nurse managers wore business suits (Houweling, 2004). Scrub suits replaced the white pantsuit in the 1980s; prior to 1980, only staff in prescribed areas such as the operating room wore scrubs. According to Houweling, the shift away from white nurses' uniforms removed this symbol of nursing status and identity, leaving patients unable to recognize the individual caring for them as a nurse, a nurses' aide, or a housekeeper. Burn (2006) reported that a new dress code mandating white uniforms for a hospital's nurses increased their visibility by distinguishing them from other hospital staff. The chief nursing officer stated that making nurses easily identifiable provides information, safety, and security for patients and family members as well as demonstrating pride in the nursing profession.

Prestige is an evaluation by others of a person's position in a status hierarchy. A high level of prestige involves such rewards as social recognition, respect, admiration, or deference (others will yield to the person's opinion or wishes). Status symbols such as dress tend to lead to different expectations of wearers' behavior and identities, resulting in different levels of prestige. Nurses are educated, skilled, and professional; when dressed in scrubs, they are sometimes mistaken for nurses' aides or housekeepers, with the resultant lack of prestige (Burn, 2006).

Privilege refers to a right or advantage enjoyed by a person or body of persons beyond the common advantages of other individuals. Privilege may be economic or social in nature. For example, some people can afford to purchase expensive brand-name products such as Rolex watches or Nike athletic shoes, while others must purchase generic brands because of limited economic resources. Some individuals who grow up in wealthy families have opportunities to attend social events such as concerts, performances, and parties that allow them to mingle with others of high social standing.

Social power is the ability to bring about a "change in the belief, attitude or behavior of a person . . . which results from the action, or presence, of another person or group of persons" (Raven, 1992, p. 218) (Figure 1.7). There are many bases for power: coercive, reward, legitimate, referent, information, and expert.

Coercive power is based on negative sanctions; punishment results from failure to comply. School dress codes are enforced through coercive power. Police uniforms symbolize coercive power (Lennon, 1999). Reward power is based on positive sanctions; compliance leads to rewards. Fashion leaders in small groups provide rewards to their followers through compliments and social acceptance. Legitimate power is based on the position held; the higher the position, the more legitimate power is attributed to a person. Military uniforms symbolize legitimate power (Lennon, 1999). Referent power is based on personal characteristics; individuals with high referent power are liked, admired, and imitated. Supermodels have referent power because they possess society's ideal physical characteristics. Information power is based on possession of valuable information. Individuals who read fashion magazines, watch fashion programs on television, attend fashion shows, and go shopping frequently possess valuable information for those interested in fashion advice. Expert power is based on possession of expertise, skill, and knowledge that gain the respect of others. For example, a physician's white coat and stethoscope are symbols of healthcare expertise.

Another base for power is connection power, which derives from associations

FIGURE 1.7 HIGH SCHOOL STUDENTS OFTEN USE SOCIAL POWER TO INFLUENCE OTHERS. THE POPULAR TELEVISION SHOW *GOSSIP GIRL* IS CENTERED AROUND SOCIAL POWER.

with influential or important persons (*Estimates of Personal Power*, 1980). When adolescents imitate the dress of a popular entertainer, they are influenced by connection power, albeit a vicarious connection.

Power is related to "life chances, the likelihood of securing the good things in life, such as housing, education, good health, and food" (Shepard, 2005, p. 211). Thus, the distribution of power has important consequences for social interactions.

THE PROCESS OF SOCIAL CONTROL

The theory of social control specifies a basic social process that is designed to maintain social order by encouraging compliance with norms. The relationship between social control and social order is revealed by the behavior that initiates social control—deviance. **Deviance** is defined as any behavior, belief, or condition that violates cultural norms (Adler & Adler, 1994; Kendall, 2007). Deviant behavior is nonconforming, nonstandard behavior. Behavior defined as deviant varies from one location to another, from one time period to another, from one context to another, and from one group to another. For example, dress codes define deviant behavior within a school context. One male student who thought it would be funny to wear a dress to the prom discovered that school officials did not share his sense of humor. When he arrived at the prom wearing a black spaghetti-strap dress and blond wig, he was issued a ticket for disorderly conduct and ultimately fined $249.00 ("Are Dress Codes a Drag?," 2005).

A process of social control operates to encourage appropriate degrees of conformity to norms, including dress norms, believed necessary for an orderly society. **Conformity** is a process whereby individuals maintain or change their behavior to act in accordance with society's norms. Through a process of social control, individuals learn to conform to the normative order—what to think, what to say, what to do, how to look. A process of social control has six steps (Figure 1.8): norms, violation of norms, recognition of violation, report of violation, response to violation (sanctions), and enforcement of sanctions (Schwartz & Ewald, 1968). We'll use the "From the Headlines" article at the beginning of this chapter to illustrate each step.

FIGURE 1.8 THE PROCESS OF SOCIAL CONTROL CAN BE USED TO STUDY DRESS NORMS.

Norms

Norms reveal specific expectations for various aspects of human behavior. Norm identification takes place in the first step of the process of social control. Identifying norms means naming or recognizing them. Identifying norms is crucial because norms are standards against which violations are measured. For example, the young woman wearing the T-shirt with the lewd slogan illustrates at least two traditional norms in U.S. society: (a) that women and children should not be exposed to vulgar and profane language and (b) that women should take responsibility for upholding the morality of their society.

FIGURE 1.9 RUDI GERNREICH'S NOTORIOUS TOP-LESS SWIMSUIT, INTRODUCED IN 1964, IS AN EXAMPLE OF DIS-OBEDIENCE OR NONCOMPLIANCE WITH A NORM.

Violation of Norms

The second step involves a member of society violating a norm. Violating a norm refers to disobedience or noncompliance with a norm—in other words, deviance (Figure 1.9). The notion of norm violation is based on the assumption that a society or group agrees on some norms from which an individual's behavior can deviate (Smelser, 1973). The young woman wearing the T-shirt with a lewd slogan violated society's norms.

Recognition of Norm Violation

The third step occurs when someone recognizes the violation (becomes aware of a norm violation). Frequently recognition occurs through visual stimuli that can be detected from a distance. Thus, violations of dress norms may be noticed even when violations of norms regarding what people should or should not think, say, or do are not noticed—and even when no social interaction occurs. The writer of the remarks on the website recognized the norm violation by the woman wearing the T-shirt with a lewd slogan.

Report of Norm Violation

The fourth step is a report of the norm violation. Reports of violations are eyewitness testimonies and can be made verbally or in writing, informally to violators, friends, or relatives or formally to authorities. The eyewitness testimony of the person observing a woman wearing a T-shirt with a lewd slogan was reported via a blog on a website.

Response to the Violation—Sanctions

The fifth step entails a response or a reaction to the violation. The response often takes the form of **sanctions,** which are rewards or punishments that affect conformity to norms with varying degrees of effectiveness (Kendall, 2007; Smelser, 1973). People conform to rules by sanctioning their own behavior; by sanctioning others' behavior, they motivate others to conform as well (Blake & Davis, 1964). The woman who wore the T-shirt with the lewd slogan may have received disapproving glances, raised eyebrows, frowns, or other signs of disapproval, but she probably was not aware of the criticism on the website of her behavior.

Enforcement of Sanctions

Enforcement of sanctions completes the process of social control. To enforce a sanction means to insist upon carrying out the sanction. The ability to enforce a sanction controls its effectiveness (Schwartz & Ewald, 1968). Effectiveness is achieving a desired end result, in this case, conformity to a given norm. A sanction would be considered effective if it convinced the woman not to wear T-shirts with lewd slogans in the future.

DRESS NORMS AND THE PROCESS OF SOCIAL CONTROL

An individual's appearance is a result of his or her choices about dress. Dress as we have defined it includes **body modifications** as well as **body supplements.** Body modifications are changes made to the body itself and can be temporary (makeup), semipermanent (hair color), or permanent (tattoos). Body supplements are items positioned on the body by wrapping (neckties), suspending (a bracelet), or preshaping (jeans). Body supplements can be inserted (earrings for pierced ears), clipped (hair clips), adhered (false eyelashes), or handheld (briefcases).

According to historical theory, dress is a visual symbol of a society's identity (Payne, Winakor, & Farrell-Beck, 1992). Remember that a symbol is used to represent something else. Members of a society may view dress as a symbol that reflects and bolsters a society's identity. Because dress communicates visually, it is a symbol that is difficult to ignore. When you read the description of the young woman with the lewd saying on her T-shirt, you probably assumed she was from the United States because of the description of what she was wearing. Jeans and T-shirt are the quintessential American style and reflect the egalitarian nature of U.S. society.

Homology implies correspondence in character and use; in other words, *what you see is what you get.* According to homology theory, dress corresponds with a group's values (Willis, 1978) whether that group is a society, a community, a family, a peer group, or any other type of group. Values are the accepted principles or standards of a society. Values legitimize and give meaning to norms by providing a basis for judgment of relative worth (right vs. wrong, good vs. bad). Some core values important to people in the United States include achievement, work, competition, courage, education, equality, financial success, freedom, health, honesty, humanitarianism, individualism, justice, materialism, morality, progress, respect for the law, respect for the rights of others, and technology (Hunt & Colander, 2005; Kendall, 2007; Shepard, 2005). Persons who deviate from **dress norms** (acceptable ways to look in specific situations) are viewed as likely to deviate from norms of acceptable thought, speech, and actions. Thus, deviance from society's dress norms is viewed as a symbol of unwillingness to accept society's values. Wearing a T-shirt with a lewd slogan undermines the values of morality and respect for the rights of others.

Conformity to norms regarding dress is a visual symbol of an orderly society. Conversely, to some, deviance in dress is a visual symbol of chaos and anarchy (rebellion or disorder).

SUMMARY

This chapter contains definitions of basic sociological terms and concepts that will be used throughout the text. The chapter has shown how these terms are useful in explaining individuals' behavior regarding dress. The six steps in the process of social control are the theoretical framework around which the rest of this text is organized.

body modifications

body supplements

conformity

cultural code

cultural universals

culture

deviance

dress

dress norms

material culture

nonmaterial culture

normative order

normative socialization theory

norms

sanctions

social control theory

socialization

social learning theory

social power

society

status

stereotypes

subculture

symbol

symbolic interactionist theory

theory

SUGGESTED READINGS

1. Huun, K., & Kaiser, S. B. (2001). The emergence of modern infantwear, 1896–1962: Traditional white dresses succumb to fashion's gender obsession. *Clothing and Textiles Research Journal, 19*(3), 103–119.

2. Rudd, N. A., & Lennon, S. J. (2000). Body image and appearance management behaviors in college women. *Clothing and Textiles Research Journal, 18*(3), 152–162.

3. Workman, J. E., & Johnson, K. K. (1993). Cultural aesthetics and the social construction of gender. In S. Lennon & L. Burns (Eds.), *Social sciences of dress: New directions* (pp. 93–109). Monument, CO: International Textile and Apparel Association.

Purpose: To analyze photographs to identify and describe the Native American material culture.

Procedure:

1. Review the definition of material culture.
2. Log on to the Library of Congress Prints and Photographs Reading Room (http://www.loc.gov/rr/print/catalog.html).
3. Search the catalog and locate three photographs depicting Native American life.
4. Identify three objects/artifacts of the Native American material culture depicted in the three photographs you selected.
5. Record your findings for each picture on the National Archives Photo Analysis Worksheet (http://www.archives.gov/education/lessons/worksheets/photo_analysis_worksheet.pdf).
6. Summarize your findings for all three photographs and submit them to your instructor.

Purpose: To analyze documents for content regarding student dress code violations and their relationship to requirements of the First Amendment.

Procedure:

1. Log on to the First Amendment Center website (http://www.firstamendmentcenter.org).
2. Review the meaning of the First Amendment to the U.S. Constitution by clicking on the U.S. flag found in the top center of the webpage.
3. Type *student dress code violation* in the search window located in the top right corner of the webpage.
4. From the results of your search, select and review one article of interest.
5. Identify and describe the norms for student dress that were violated in the article.
6. Describe how the violation(s) relate(s) to the guidelines of the First Amendment.
7. Summarize your findings and submit them to your instructor.

Purpose: To analyze Internet resources to infer the details of an historical event and its impact on current material and/or nonmaterial culture.

Procedure:

1. Review the definition of *Luddite.*

2. Search Google (http://google.com) to identify and describe the historical incident behind the term *Luddite.*

3. Identify and describe three ways in which this event affected the material and/or nonmaterial culture. Illustrate your examples with at least three pictures, maps, or other graphic data sources.

4. Use the information you find to infer how neo-Luddites affect today's material and/or nonmaterial culture.

5. Summarize your findings and submit them to your instructor.

Chapter Two

DRESS, SOCIETY, AND THE NOVICE RESEARCHER

FROM THE HEADLINES

Dockers and Slates, manufacturers of branded jeans and casual sportswear, commissioned a study to identify workers' attitudes and behaviors about business attire. This was a market analysis to identify the content of corporate dress policies and employees' preferences for work wear. Maureen Griffin, consumer marketing director for Dockers, explained that "it is significant that even companies with dressier policies are allowing employees to incorporate more personal and casual styles into their business wardrobes" (¶ 6). Findings revealed that 66 percent of those surveyed said they dress casually for work every day and that their productivity and on-the-job morale have increased as a result. Seventy-eight percent of the respondents reported that casual dress should become a permanent part of U.S. corporate culture. Results also helped Dockers and Slates expand their casual businesswear offerings.

Source: National casual businesswear survey sparks debate: What is appropriate attire for the office? (2001, May 9). Retrieved May 25, 2006, from Corporate NewsNet, http://www.bizwiz.com/bizwizwire/pressrelease/1954/8e847syyxjwek87je8j.htm

The research described in this excerpt from a newspaper article illustrates several concepts that you will read about in this chapter. An apparel manufacturer that conducted a research study chose a survey research method to collect data about two topics: corporate dress policies and employee preferences. The company expected the results to provide information that would help it make decisions about the design and manufacture of casual businesswear. On the basis of the results, the manufacturer decided to expand its line of casual businesswear.

What knowledge and skills are needed to conduct a consumer survey like the one conducted for Dockers? What research tools were used to conduct the Dockers study? How did research skills benefit the company? In this chapter, you will learn more about survey research as well as other methods and tools you can use to study issues related to dress and society.

The purpose of this chapter is to introduce the process, methods, and tools for conducting research on dress and society topics. The chapter begins with an overview of research, its basic terms, and methods for conducting research. Throughout the chapter, examples provide real-world understanding of how methods and tools are used.

QUESTIONS TO ANSWER AS YOU READ

1. How can my academic and professional careers benefit from the development of research skills?
2. What is research?
3. What are the steps in conducting research related to dress and society?
4. How is periodical literature categorized?
5. How do quantitative, qualitative, and mixed methods research differ?
6. What tools are used to collect data?

USEFUL RESEARCH SKILLS

Research is born out of our naturally inquisitive nature. *What is this? Why is it so? What is it related to?* Research is like the detective work of police and forensic specialists who examine clues and identify the time line for a crime and its perpetrators. *Did the perpetrator leave fingerprints? What are these fibers? What is the motive behind the actions of those involved?* The results of research lead to new knowledge—new fibers, new fabrics, new consumer products, and/or new approaches to working and learning. An individual's natural curiosity and appreciation for detective work can be fostered. A faculty mentor can be a valuable asset in developing a student's research skills.

How do you choose a research topic? It depends on the purpose of the research. For example, the research sponsored by Dockers was intended to provide information that would assist in planning merchandise lines. Irwin

(2001) described how she became interested in the topic of tattoos. Irwin's first visit to a tattoo shop occurred when she accompanied a friend who was getting a tattoo. During later visits to the shop to choose her own tattoos, Irwin formed friendships with the tattoo artists. Eventually, she dated and married the shop's owner. During a vacation with her husband, he mentioned that someone should do a study about changes in attitudes toward tattoos. Because Irwin was a sociology graduate student looking for a dissertation topic, she pursued the idea.

Determination, motivation, and patience are key personal attributes to successful completion of a research project. Disagreements in the literature related to a topic can be confusing (Bodi, 2002). For example, there are differences of opinion about *casual dress* for employees (Singer, 2006). It is important, however, to be persistent in locating sources with varying opinions and findings. Sources of information may seem unlimited. Using the advice of faculty mentors and research librarians to limit information sources will sustain interest in a topic and improve the value of the search results (Kuhlthau, 1993). A research strategy is similar to the strategy employed by a detective who must systematically research the crime scene to identify all related evidence and, in the process, not contaminate the findings.

In one study students were asked to rank the most important benefits they received from participating in research. The top ten benefits included enhancement of professional or academic credentials, clarification of a career path, understanding the research process in their field, learning a topic in depth, developing a continuing relationship with a faculty member, learning to work independently, learning laboratory techniques, tolerance for obstacles faced in the research process, understanding how scientists think, and understanding how professionals work on real problems (Lopatto, 2003). Additional benefits included development of personal traits such as self-confidence, independence, patience, interest in the discipline, problem-solving abilities, ability to work as a member of a team, and a sense of accomplishment (Lopatto, 2006).

Research skills can be used to increase knowledge in a discipline; in turn, increased knowledge can enhance the ability to solve problems and suggest appropriate and effective solutions. Both increased knowledge and ability to solve problems will benefit your academic and professional careers by increasing your expert credentials.

Research is a systematic approach to collecting data in an effort to answer a question or solve a problem. A **research topic** is a broad area of interest, for example, workplace dress codes. A **research question** asks what you want to learn from an investigation, for example, what is the relationship between casual dress and employee productivity? A **research problem** is an area of concern, for example, writing a clear and nondiscriminatory employee dress code. A research question is answered and a research problem is solved through collecting, analyzing, and interpreting data. **Data** are bits of information in the form of numbers (numerical), pictures (graphic), or words (narrative). Although answering a research question and solving a research problem are different, they are not mutually exclusive. Rather, they support two types of research—basic and applied.

Basic Research

Basic research adds to an existing knowledge base in a field of study by building theories, or the broad generalizations that explain phenomena (observable facts, experiences, events, trends). For example, Workman and Freeburg (1997) developed a method to identify occupational stereotypes. Stereotype theory predicts that attributes will be assigned to individuals based on recognizable features that allow individuals to be placed in cultural categories. Occupational stereotypes are overgeneralized ideas about the attributes and behaviors of individuals in occupational categories. Specifically, Workman and Freeburg examined stereotypes about automobile salespeople.

Hemmings (2002) studied senseless acts of violence by secondary students by using the theoretical framework of the youth culture of hostility. Hemmings speculated that some teenagers adapted to their lack of power by trying to claim power and control through hostile means. This theory is based on communication about money ("people who have money have the power to purchase goods, influence, status, freedom, and even more power") (p. 299); respect ("earning respect means looking and behaving in a fashion that elevates status and establishes dominance over others") (p. 301); and difference (". . . evident in groups where pressure is put on members to stick with their own kind and shun those who are not like them") (p. 303).

Both studies used a specific context to broaden their respective theoretical bases. The context for Workman and Freeburg's study was the specific occupation of automobile salesperson. The specific context for Hemmings' study was two urban high schools situated in hostile socioeconomic environments.

Different theoretical backgrounds apply in the multidisciplinary (multiple specialized subjects) study of dress and society. Various theories are based in different disciplinary perspectives, for example, psychology, sociology, social psychology, anthropology, history. These perspectives result in comprehensive coverage of research questions and problems dealing with dress and society. For example, Hansen (2004) chronicled research on dress and society by analyzing and synthesizing a selection of anthropological research on dress from the late nineteenth and early twentieth centuries. Eicher (2000) presented a chronological survey of works on dress through the nineteenth century from an anthropological perspective. Both articles provide an overview of the research related to dress and society from a theoretical perspective derived from the discipline of anthropology.

Applied Research

Applied research is conducted primarily to solve practical problems. For example, conventional hospital gown designs are lacking in both aesthetic qualities and functionality—they provide less than optimal coverage for the patient and do not easily accommodate medical procedures and equipment. Cho (2006) studied patients' perceptions of two prototype hospital gowns as compared with the conventional gown. The purpose of the research was to provide design guidelines for a hospital gown that enhanced user satisfaction, reduced embarrassment, and enabled patients to maintain their dignity (Figure 2.1). In another applied research study, customer behavior in a menswear fashion retailer was examined using video observation and individual in-depth interviews (Dodd, Clarke, & Kirkup, 1998). Analysis of videotapes provided information concerning patterns of customer movement, store atmosphere, and customer responses to store layout that could be used to redesign the store.

FIGURE 2.1 ONE EXAMPLE OF APPLIED RESEARCH IS TO PROVIDE DESIGN GUIDELINES FOR A HOSPITAL GOWN THAT ENHANCES USER SATISFACTION, REDUCES EMBARRASSMENT, AND ENABLES PATIENTS TO MAINTAIN THEIR DIGNITY.

The research process begins with identification of a research question or a research problem. The next steps are to select a research method and tool, collect and analyze data, and interpret results of the data analysis.

Identifying the Question or Problem

Research questions or problems are the starting place for all research. Examples related to dress, merchandising, design, and fashion product analysis include the following:

- ▼ *What are the dress code guidelines set forth by corporate policies?*
- ▼ *What are the businesswear preferences of corporate employees?*
- ▼ *What design characteristics of hospital gowns best match the functionality requirements of both patients and medical personnel?*
- ▼ *What are the characteristics of worn denim jeans that individualize them?*

In addition to theoretical perspectives, the source of research questions and problems can include observation of the population, personal interests, the work of other investigators, and differing results in the literature (Schneider, 1996). For example, observation of body asymmetry led one researcher to consider the role of body symmetry in designing clothing for young women with severe spinal curvature (Kidd, 2006). Atherton (1964) attributed research interest in the American cowboy to the personal interest of researchers in the cowboy as a symbol of the freedom and individualism that was characteristic of the American frontier. Further, Wilson (1991) concluded that this symbolism " . . . influenced 19th century dime novelists, proprietors of wild west shows, and eastern reporters to mold the cowboy into an heroic form" (p. 49). Because of personal interest, researchers from many different disciplines have studied the American cowboy to document dress and life during a particular historical period (Figure 2.2).

FIGURE 2.2 THIS LEVI'S AD FROM THE 1950S, FEATURING THE AMERICAN COWBOY, PLAYS ON THEMES OF MASCULINITY AND INDIVIDUALISM.

Identifying Information Sources

The work of other investigators as well as differing results in the literature can provide inspiration for further investigation. Learning to find published research related to a question or problem is an essential skill. Learning to search information sources in an organized way will make it easier to study a research topic. University libraries, staffed with research librarians, have powerful resources available to access scholarly information.

Journals, magazines, and newspapers are sources for current information in all fields of study. Periodical literature can be divided into five categories: scholarly, substantive news/general interest, special interest, popular, and sensational (*Distinguishing Scholarly Journals from Other Periodicals*, 2006) (Figure 2.3).

The main purpose of **scholarly journals** is to report on original research. Sources of information are always cited in footnotes or reference lists. Authors are scholars who have done research in the discipline. Scholarly research has been peer reviewed; experts in the same field as the author have reviewed the article and decided it was authoritative enough for publication. Peer review is a process by which articles are chosen to be included in a refereed journal. Examples include *Clothing and Textiles Research Journal, Dress,* and *Family and Consumer Sciences Research Journal.*

The main purpose of substantive news or general interest periodicals is to provide general information to a broad audience of readers. Sometimes, but not usually, sources are cited. Examples of substantive news or general interest periodicals include *Time, Newsweek,* and the *New York Times.*

Special interest periodicals provide information to an audience in a particular occupation or trade. Thus, special interest periodicals are sometimes called trade publications. Examples of trade publications include *Women's Wear Daily, California Apparel News,* and *Daily News Record.*

The main purpose of popular periodicals is to entertain readers, sell products, and promote a viewpoint. Articles are short, sources are rarely cited, information is often secondhand or thirdhand, and original sources are obscure. Popular periodicals are printed on slick paper, have an attractive appearance, and use many visual graphics such as photographs and drawings. Examples include fashion magazines such as *Vogue, Harper's Bazaar, Gentlemen's Quarterly,* and *Seventeen.*

The main purpose of sensational periodicals is to arouse curiosity and cater to popular superstitions. They often use a newspaper format and present information in a sensational manner with startling headlines. Examples include *Star, National Enquirer,* and *Globe.*

Use of publicly available Internet resources does not necessarily identify scholarly resources related to topics of interest. Examples of scholarly databases include the subscription services of *EBSCO, ERIC, SocINDEX with Full Text,* and others. Google Scholar is one publicly available scholarly database.

Identifying Research Methods and Tools

There are three basic categories of research methods—quantitative, qualitative, and mixed methods. Within each general category are more specialized methods. Each research method has specific tools that are used to collect data (Table 2.1). Tools include questionnaires, interview questions, attitude surveys, document and artifact worksheets, and published instruments.

The remainder of this chapter describes each research method, discusses the appropriate tools for each method, and gives examples of research studies that illustrate the methods and tools.

QUANTITATIVE RESEARCH

Quantitative research provides data in the form of numbers, which are then subjected to statistical analyses. The data are used for many purposes, including (a) describing situations, (b) identifying relationships, and (c) comparing groups (Glanz, 2006). Numerical data are collected through research tools such as questionnaires, attitude measures, and observation checklists. Exam-

TABLE 2.1 RESEARCH METHODS AND TOOLS

METHOD	EXAMPLES OF RESEARCH TOOLS
Quantitative	
Survey	Questionnaires, attitude measures, published tests
Observational	Observation checklists, cameras, sketchbooks
Correlational	Questionnaires, attitude measures, published tests
Group comparison:	
True experimental	Questionnaires, attitude measures, published tests
Quasi-experimental	Questionnaires, attitude measures, published tests
Ex post facto	Questionnaires, attitude measures, published tests
Qualitative	
Ethnography	Observation, interviews
Content analysis	Checklist, written or oral sources, coding worksheet
Narrative inquiry	Interviews, life stories, coding worksheet
Artifact analysis	Coding worksheet, checklist
Historical	Coding worksheet
Mixed methods	Any combination of quantitative and qualitative methods and tools

ples of questionnaires used to collect quantitative data include the Fashion Opinion Leadership Questionnaire (Hirschman & Adcock, 1978), the Tendency to Gossip Questionnaire (Nevo, Nevo, & Derech-Zehavi, 1994), and the Indirect Interpersonal Aggression Questionnaire (Beatty, Valencic, Rudd, & Dobos, 1999).

Quantitative data are analyzed and reported using statistical procedures. If the data are to be used to describe situations, three general types of statistics are appropriate: (a) measures of frequency, (b) measures of central tendency, and (c) measures of variability. Frequency refers to a count or the number of times something occurs. Frequency can be expressed in percentages (proportion of the total). Measures of central tendency include the mean (average number), median (middle number—50 percent of the data points are greater than this number; 50 percent are less than this number), and mode (most frequent number). Measures of variance report the spread of the numbers in a data set around a specific number. The range and standard deviation are often used to report variance. The range is calculated by subtracting the lowest number from the highest number. The standard deviation reflects the average difference of each number from the mean.

If the data are to be used to identify relationships, correlation coefficients are calculated to identify the strength and direction of a linear relationship between two variables. Other more complex statistical procedures are used to compare groups. Statistics coursework and software packages are available to help you develop the skills and resources needed to conduct statistical analyses.

Survey Research

Survey research gathers data at one point in time from individuals who represent groups with specific characteristics. The data are gathered to describe a situation by answering a set of questions. Trade organizations conduct survey research in order to identify trends and plan for future business. The International Mass Retail Association (IRMA)[1] is one trade organization that represents 170 mass retailers, including discount department stores, home centers, catalog showrooms, dollar stores, variety stores, warehouse clubs, deep discount drugstores, specialty discounters, and off-price stores.

IRMA conducts research to identify buying trends of American consumers. One such study queried adult consumers to identify their preferences for Halloween costumes (Halloween is reported to be second only to Christmas in holiday sales; Verdisco, 1999) (Figure 2.4). Through use of a questionnaire, researchers identified the percentage of consumers, by age group, who planned to wear costumes and the average amount of money they planned to spend. The results (the description of the situation) helped mass retailers select and stock merchandise that met the needs and preferences of their customers, resulting in increased sales.

Observational Research

Observational research methods are used when information needed to answer questions is best obtained through direct observation. Observational research gathers data for organization into categories. It is the earliest and most prevalent method of research (Best & Kahn, 2006). In the context of quantitative research, observation generates numbers through use of a research tool called a data collection worksheet. Direct observation of dress and associated behaviors, for example, allows for a more thorough understanding of individuals' behavior regarding dress (Eicher, 2000).

Observational research can be used by designers to solve a problem. According to Skaggs (2004), "observational research introduces the designer to the user(s) of the product, the environment the product is used in, how the product is used, sequences and frequency of use, patterns of behavior, gaps in processes, problems, and perceptions of the user" (p. 11). Observational research can be conducted as an outsider, that is, by observing the environment and users as unobtrusively as possible. Observational research can also be conducted as an insider, that is, by using the product and recording the experience. The outsider approach may work best for the designer because it provides more objective data. Tools for observational design research include cameras, camcorders, sketchbooks, and notebooks. Observational research can also make use of such research tools as conversations, interviews, and questionnaires.

Observational research produces descriptive results, that is, the results allow the researcher to describe a situation as it exists. A fashion count is one observational research technique that allows the researcher to describe the norm for a particular category of dress at one point in time. For example, a researcher might record the number of people at a particular location wearing particular types of shoes on one day in June.

In their observational research, Salter, Grammer, and Rikowski (2005) tested a research hypothesis. A **research hypothesis** is one way of stating a research question or research problem that includes predicting a relationship between two variables. **Variables** are "factors having two or more values or distinguishable properties or characteristics" (Glanz, 2006, p. 351), for example, acceptable and unacceptable dress. The hypothesis developed by Salter and colleagues predicted that individuals seeking admission to an exclusive nightclub use interpersonal signals, such as gestures, words, or dress to obtain admission from male doormen with authority to grant or refuse admission. One criterion doormen used to refuse admittance was unacceptable dress, including wearing sandals or unfashionable clothes. Videotapes of would-be patrons were observed and analyzed for dominance (speed in approaching doorman), affiliative behaviors (friendly, nonaggressive words and gestures) and sexual behavior (visible skin and tightness of dress). The descriptive results were used to develop guidelines for handling aggressive, domineering prospective patrons.

Correlational Research

Correlational studies examine the degree of relationship between and among variables. Demographic variables refer to individual characteristics such as gender, ethnicity, education, occupation, socioeconomic status, religious affiliation, and age. Gender is a nominal variable meaning that two or more values are assigned to categories, that is, male or female. Each person can be a member of only one category, and all other members of the category have the same characteristic. Of the other demographic variables listed previously, ethnicity, occupation, socioeconomic status, and religious affiliation are also nominal.

Education is an ordinal variable, meaning two or more values are assigned to categories with ranking from lowest to highest. A high school education is ranked lower than a two-year college education; a two-year college education is ranked lower than a four-year college education. Age is a continuous variable, meaning that within the numerical limits of the variable range—up to about 116—any value is possible ("World's Oldest Person," 2006). Age is also an interval variable, meaning it is based on equal units of measurement. Psychological tests such as the Arousal Seeking Tendency (AST) scale (Mehrabian & Russell, 1974) and Rosenberg's Self-Esteem Scale (Rosenberg, 1965) are interval in nature. Data about these variables are collected through research tools such as questionnaires or attitude measures. The correlation between variables is measured through statistical analysis of numerical data.

The relationships measured do not include cause and effect (one variable is the direct result of a second variable). Attributing cause and effect to a correlational relationship is a research mistake called the post hoc fallacy. Rather, relationships are expressed in direction (positive or negative) and strength (high, moderate, low). Correlational values range from +1.00 (a perfect positive correlation) to −1.00 (a perfect negative correlation). Positive relationships occur when, as one value rises, another value also rises; negative relationships occur when one value rises as another value decreases. High strength is ± 1.00 to ± .67. Moderate strength is ± .66 to ± .34. Low strength is ± .33 to 0.00. For example, optimum stimulation level (an individual's preferred level for environmental stimulation) had a positive correlation of .25 with willingness to try body scanning (Fiore, Lee, Kunz, & Campbell, 2001).

Wong and Li (2004) studied the relationships among physiological and psychological thermal and moisture responses in tight-fit aerobic wear. Sensors were used to measure skin surface temperature and humidity on six body locations from individuals wearing different garments. In addition, subjects' perceptions of thermal and moisture sensations as indications of overall garment comfort were collected using questionnaires. There was a high positive correlation (.96) between physical measurement of humidity and psychological ratings of moisture sensation. There was also a high positive correlation (.71) between physical measurement of temperature and psychological ratings of thermal sensations. Correlational data of relationships between physical skin temperature and humidity with subjects' psychological ratings of thermal and moisture sensations were used to improve the design of the garment for increased comfort.

Group Comparison Research

Group comparison research compares data from members of different groups who have been exposed to different conditions or treatments. Conditions or treatments are variables with different values. For example, when comparing consumer responses to items of dress, responses may be influenced by brand names, fiber content, country of origin, care label instructions, and size labeling.

Group comparison research identifies differences among and between responses of different groups. One group may be shown a garment with the care instructions of *dry clean only* and their responses compared with another group shown the same garment with the care instructions of *machine wash, tumble dry.*

Tools used to collect data in group comparison research include questionnaires, attitude measures, observation checklists, and other published tests with established reliability and validity (Glanz, 2006). One published test with established reliability and validity is the Sociocultural Attitudes Toward Appearance Questionnaire (Heinberg, Thompson, & Stormer, 1995). This questionnaire has been used to compare responses of different groups—middle school boys and girls, adolescents, and adults—to recognition and acceptance of societally sanctioned standards of appearance.

In group comparison research, variables may be manipulated. Manipulation of variables means that one group is exposed to one value of a variable (intensity, characteristic, treatment), while a second group is exposed to another value of the variable. For example, one group might be shown a picture of a model in a wheelchair while another group is shown a picture of the same model in a lawn chair. The manipulated variable is the type of chair. Group comparison research includes true experimental research, quasi-experimental research, and ex post facto research.

True Experimental Research Design

In a **true experimental research design**, groups are formed by randomly assigning individuals to different conditions or treatments. **Random assignment** means that individuals have an equal chance of being assigned to any group. Generally, an experimental group is exposed to a condition or treatment and a control group is not. Randomization allows for the equal distribution across the groups of characteristics that could influence the results, referred to as confounding variables. Results of aging, attrition (dropping out) of research study participants, environmental conditions, and historical events are examples of confounding variables.

For example, Workman, Arseneau, and Ewell (2004) examined the meanings assigned by observers to an adolescent wearing a promotional T-shirt for alcohol. Participants were randomly assigned to one of four groups. Groups One and Two gave their impressions about the personal traits of a male or a female pictured in the T-shirt using 7-point bipolar scales (healthy/not healthy, religious/not religious). These groups were the experimental groups. Groups Three and Four used the same bipolar scales but saw a photograph of a male or a female in a plain T-shirt. These were the control groups.

Data from the questionnaire research tool were analyzed to determine the effect of the promotional T-shirts on perceptions of personal traits of males and females. Among the confounding variables that were controlled via random assignment were ownership of alcohol promotional T-shirts, drinking behavior, and propensity for risky behavior. Random assignment assured that participants who owned alcohol promotional T-shirts were distributed equally among the groups. Ownership of an alcohol promotional T-shirt might influence participants' perceptions of the personal traits of another owner. However, with ownership distributed equally among the groups, the influence of this variable was also distributed equally among the groups.

Quasi-Experimental Research Design

In **quasi-experimental research design,** intact groups are randomly assigned to conditions or treatments and data are collected. Intact groups refer to naturally occurring groups such as students in classrooms, workers in a particular office, or members of a club. This research method is appropriate for the study of fashion consumer behavior. For example, two consumer groups (intact groups of university women) were shown two different advertisements (Workman & Freeburg, 1996a). One group was a class of traditional students; the other group was a class of nontraditional students. The purpose of the study was to identify the effect of a model in a wheelchair (visibly different from the traditional images in print media) on consumers' self-reported product commitment. One group was shown an advertisement that featured a female modeling spring sportswear seated in a lawn chair (Condition 1). The second group was shown an advertisement that featured the same model in the same spring sportswear seated in a wheelchair (Condition 2). Data collected provided information about the influence of the advertisement on differences between the two groups in their likelihood of purchasing the sportswear.

Ex Post Facto Research

Ex post facto research analyzes events that have already happened for the purpose of understanding differences between two or more groups. Also called causal-comparative research, the method includes analysis of data to identify potential causal connections between variables, factors, and/or constructs. For example, Reglin and Chisom (1993) studied the self-perceptions of 60 urban black male tenth graders on five domains, including physical appearance. Achievers (above 50th percentile) and potential achievers (below 50th percentile) were identified by scores on the California Achievement Test. Achievement and physical appearance were the variables of interest. Potential achievers, who did not have a realistic view of their abilities, were confident of successful careers as athletes or entertainers and viewed themselves as better-looking than achievers. The research provided insight into differences in self-perception that could influence achievement.

Qualitative research provides an understanding of an event in its natural setting from the perspective of the researcher. **Qualitative research** provides descriptive results using words (rather than numbers) because small groups of people are studied for an in-depth understanding of their behaviors and perceptions. This approach to research focuses on questions about the process (*how?*) and the rationale (*why?*) related to a particular phenomenon (Glanz, 2006). Qualitative research is appropriate for questions that can "best be answered by verbally describing how participants in a study perceive and interpret various aspects of their environment" (Crowl, Kaminsky, & Podell, 1997, p. 499).

Qualitative research methods used to study dress and society include ethnography, content analysis, narrative inquiry, artifact analysis, and historical research. Qualitative data are collected and summarized using research worksheets. Sample worksheets are available on a National Archives website (http://www.archives.gov/education/lessons/worksheets/index.html).

Qualitative data analysis procedures are much less rigid and proscribed than statistical analysis. The body of data is first organized around themes. Through data reduction the data are selected, focused, simplified, and transformed for manageability and understanding in terms of what is being studied. For example, ethnographic studies describe observed behavior in a narrative format and often include direct quotations from participants' conversations. Document analysis and narrative inquiry both analyze words to identify themes or groups of ideas presented by the data. Artifact analysis and historical research use words to describe characteristics of objects and graphic portrayals of people, events, and locations. Preparation and experience in appropriate research methods are important in interpreting qualitative data.

Ethnography

The **ethnographic method** is based on field observation in combination with face-to-face interviews. Ethnographers compare their observations and findings with the observations and findings of studies conducted in other societies. Cultural anthropology applies the comparative method and evolutionary perspective to human culture (American Anthropological Association, 2001).

The comparative method is a safeguard against ethnocentrism, which is the tendency to interpret unfamiliar customs on the basis of biases derived from one's own culture. Cultural anthropologists study humans using the ethnographic method. Virtual ethnography involves conducting ethnographic studies on the Internet. Many ethnographers study U.S. cultural groups by applying anthropological perspectives to U.S. culture and society.

Hemmings (2002) studied the senseless acts of violence committed by secondary students through field observation (an ethnographic method). The researcher went to school with six high school seniors to observe and record overt (directly observable) behavior and conversations (Figure 2.5). In addition, Hemmings tape-recorded interviews that provided information about interactions among friends and classmates. The original intent of the research was to study identity conflicts in public high schools. However, frequent discussions of school violence led the researcher to examine factors that perpetuate hostility in this population.

FIGURE 2.5 FIELD OBSERVATION IS AN ETHNOGRAPHIC METHOD WHEREBY A RESEARCHER GOES TO A SPECIFIC SETTING, SUCH AS A HIGH SCHOOL, TO OBSERVE AND RECORD OVERT BEHAVIOR AND CONVERSATIONS.

Content Analysis

Content analysis is a process in which narrative is summarized into categories—words, phrases, sentences, or themes. Narrative refers to written or oral stories or other accounts of an event. Inferences are then made about the messages, the author(s), the audience, the culture, as well as other factors. For example, Freeburg, Workman, and Lentz-Hees (2004) content-analyzed secondary school handbooks to identify stated rationales for dress and appearance codes. Using themes suggested in the literature, two raters used a coding worksheet to record these themes as well as others found in the handbooks. To establish reliability, findings were analyzed for percent of agreement between the raters. Results were used to make suggestions for clarifying vague and overbroad wording of dress codes.

Narrative Inquiry

Oral stories are one type of data obtained through a **narrative inquiry** method. Narrative inquiry is the study of social behavior based on individuals' personal experiences, expressed through stories (Clandinin & Connelly, 2000). The development of personal trust between researchers and participants is critical to obtaining broad and insightful information.

Using personal stories to support and empower others is one theme of a research study that focused on the development of positive lifestyle behaviors and attitudes (Pelican et al., 2005). Researchers gathered narratives or life stories from 103 participants related to three variables: food and eating habits, physical activity, and body image perceptions. Interview transcripts were analyzed using worksheets. The worksheet included items such as demographic characteristics of the speaker, dates of interviews, themes of the conversations, and important quotations related to the three variables. From this analysis, themes emerged related to the power of others to shape body image and sources of positive and negative influences.

Artifact Analysis

Artifact analysis is the study of things created by humans for a practical purpose and from a particular period. Specific characteristics studied include the type of artifact (shoes, hats, jewelry), material (leather, cotton, plastic, metal, other material), its special qualities (shape, color, texture, weight, messages, movable parts), use of the artifact, information about the technology of the time it was made, the lives of the people who made and used it, and related items of today.

The Federal Bureau of Investigation (FBI) analyzed characteristics of denim jeans (artifacts) to identify criminal suspects depicted in bank surveillance film (Hauser, 2004). Although the robbers' faces were invisible to the camera, garment characteristics (size, manufacturer, and style) and individual characteristics (manufacturing processes and normal wear-and-tear) of their jeans created unique features for these artifacts. The research tool was a worksheet designed to collect data about type of artifact and individual characteristics. Results revealed that each pair of jeans was "imprinted with the signature of the wearer's body, evoking or revealing the wearer's identity, character or physiognomy" (p. 299).

> The way in which an individual washes and dries his/her jeans, whether they iron them, what they carry in their pockets, the way they walk, and so on, will all result in particular patterns of fading and wear. In particular, it is at the seams and hems where unique characteristics appear.

Puckering in these areas, an unavoidable consequence of the manufacturing process, . . . causes ridges and valleys which over time are made more visible as areas of dark and light blue, as the indigo denim is abraded through wear, washing or perhaps pre-purchase stone-washing or other treatment. (pp. 294–295)

The homes and vehicles of the suspects in the bank robberies were searched and 27 pairs of jeans were found. One pair of jeans in particular matched the characteristics of the jeans worn by one of the suspects on the bank surveillance film and was used as evidence to successfully prosecute and convict the robber (Hauser, 2004).

Historical Research

Historical research methods provide information about past events and conditions from primary or secondary sources. Primary sources are firsthand accounts of events that include original written, graphic, artifactual, or otherwise depicted sources of information (Figure 2.6). Secondary sources are accounts of events that are one or more levels removed from the primary source. Secondary sources may be a synthesis of sources of information that may also be secondhand.

Historical research may be used to understand the evolution of dress within a specific population. For example, an examination of American cowboy dress led to conclusions about the function and fashion of commonly worn attire (Wilson, 2001). Primary historical sources in the form of photographs in catalogs from western suppliers and clothing items from Montana museums provided data for studying clothing materials, special qualities, and uses. In addition, conclusions were drawn about the available technology and the life and times of these American cowboys, leading to one conclusion that the focus on purely functional clothing shifted to concern for a fashionable appearance.

FIGURE 2.6 EXHIBITS LIKE THIS RETROSPECTIVE ON JACQUELINE KENNEDY PROVIDE AN EXCELLENT OPPORTUNITY TO CONDUCT HISTORICAL RESEARCH THROUGH OBSERVING PRIMARY SOURCES.

MIXED METHODS RESEARCH

Mixed methods research employs multiple methods, both qualitative and quantitative. Many researchers tend to restrict their work to either qualitative or quantitative methods. Recently, single method research has been cited as a threat to the advancement of research in the social sciences (Onquegbuzie & Leech, 2005). Scholars studying dress and society who learn to use multiple methods of inquiry can advance the discipline. Described below are two research studies that used mixed methods.

Persad and Lukas (2002) used mixed methods research to solve a problem related to individuals seeking employment. The researchers focused on increasing understanding of the barriers and discrimination experienced by Muslim women who wear the *hijab* (head scarf) when seeking employment. Data were collected using five methods:

1. Interviews with employees of community-based organizations working with Muslim women (qualitative)
2. Focus group discussions with Muslim women (qualitative)
3. Survey research with Muslim women (quantitative)
4. In-person field-testing at job sites (qualitative and quantitative)
5. Job applications placed with employment agencies (qualitative and quantitative)

The research methods were qualitative and quantitative and data came from multiple sources. Using multiple methods to collect data from multiple sources had two advantages. First, a mixed methods approach countered the limitations of a small sample. Second, it strengthened the findings that "women who wear hijab do experience barriers and discrimination when applying for work . . . are denied jobs, told they must remove their hijab, harassed in the workplace and fired from jobs as a result of wearing hijab" (p. 3) (Figure 2.7).

Workman and Freeburg (1997) used qualitative and quantitative methods to develop a method to identify occupational stereotypes. The researchers used multiple sources of data and multiple methods of analysis to determine the content of one occupational stereotype—automobile salespeople. Data were collected using:

FIGURE 2.7 MIXED METHODS RESEARCH CAN BE EMPLOYED TO SOLVE A PROBLEM. THROUGH THE USE OF QUANTITATIVE AND QUALITATIVE TECHNIQUES, RESEARCHERS FOCUSED ON INCREASING UNDERSTANDING OF THE BARRIERS AND DISCRIMINATION EXPERIENCED BY MUSLIM WOMEN WHO WEAR THE *HIJAB* (HEAD SCARF) WHEN SEEKING EMPLOYMENT. THE YOUNG WOMEN IN THIS PICTURE ARE KNEELING TO PRAY AT AN ICE RINK.

1. Content analysis of narratives from the popular press such as newspapers and magazines
2. Human subjects' responses to questionnaires
3. Content analysis of cartoons featuring automobile sales people

Clothing cues and personality attributes were identified as content of this occupational stereotype.

SUMMARY

Research is a systematic approach to collecting data in an effort to answer a question or solve a problem. Basic research advances theoretical knowledge, while applied research solves practical problems. The journals, magazines, and newspapers that are sources for information in all fields of study can be divided into five categories: scholarly, substantive news/general interest, special interest or trade, popular, and sensational. There are three general categories for research methods—quantitative, qualitative, and mixed methods. Within each general category are more specialized research methods. In addition, each research method has appropriate tools that are used to collect data. The development of research skills can benefit your academic and professional careers by developing your competence in answering questions or solving problems in an orderly, scientific way.

KEY TERMS AND CONCEPTS

applied research

artifact analysis

basic research

content analysis

correlational studies

data

ethnographic method

ex post facto research

group comparison research

historical research

mixed methods research

narrative inquiry

observational research

qualitative research

quantitative research

quasi-experimental research design

random assignment

research topic

research

scholarly journals

research hypothesis

survey research

research problem

true experimental research design

research question

variables

SUGGESTED READINGS

1. Kellsey, D. (2005). Writing the literature review. *College and Research Libraries News, 66*(7), 526–534.
2. Miller, D. C., & Salkin, N. J. (2003). Evaluating research studies. *Handbook of Research Design and Social Measurement,* 16–17.
3. Webster, J., & Watson, R. T. (2002). Analyzing the past to prepare for the future: Writing a literature review. *MIS Quarterly, 26*(2), xiii–xxiii.

Research Activity 2.1: Literature Analysis

Purpose: To develop your ability to search academic literature.

Procedure:

1. Identify two or three research topics of interest to you. The topics must relate to dress and society. Describe a problem you would like to solve or a question you would like to answer about that topic.
2. Write a one-paragraph summary explaining why you are interested in exploring each topic.
3. Search Google Scholar (http://scholar.google.com) or an academic database (EBSCO, ERIC, SocIndex) to identify literature related to each topic you identify. Don't shortcut your search; use this as a time to explore ideas. You may not be sure what you want to investigate, but you will have explored possibilities.
4. Print out a list of at least three articles found in your search that relate to each topic.

5. Print out one article and evaluate it for the following components:

    Yes   No   Does it have a reference list? If so, how many references are listed? _____

    Yes   No   Is there information about the author(s)' credentials?

    Yes   No   Are sources of data cited within the article?

    Yes   No   Are conclusions backed up with facts?

    Yes   No   Is/are the point(s) of view in the article unbiased?

    For what audience does the article seem to be written? _____

6. Review questions for which you answered *No*. How does the *No* answer affect the quality of the article?

7. Summarize your findings and submit them to your instructor.

Research Activity 2.2: *Fashion Count*

Purpose: To make a set of observations (collect data) to determine the frequency with which a clothing or accessory item is being worn by a particular group of people. It can also determine the norm.

Procedure:

1. Select an observation category for which you will collect data.

Female dress categories	*Male dress categories*
skirt or bifurcate length	trouser length
skirt silhouette	trouser width
skirt or bifurcate type	trouser type
bodice treatment	torso treatment
shoe type	shoe type
leg covering	socks
waistline placement	shirt type
dress type or combination	combinations
sleeve style	hirsuteness (hairiness)
fabric type	fabric type
color	color
hairstyle/length	hairstyle/length

2. Design and test an observation schedule.
   a. List all the possible alternatives within the category chosen. Example for skirts:
      - micro-mini—6 inches or more above knee
      - 5 to 6 inches above knee
      - mini—3 to 4 inches above knee
      - to top of knee
      - to middle of knee
      - to bottom of knee
      - mid-calf
      - below mid-calf
      - other (Include an "other" classification)
   b. If necessary, check Internet resources for current fashion magazines, *Women's Wear Daily, Daily News Record,* etc., to determine the incoming fashion within your category.
3. Select a location to collect your data. The population to be studied is the campus norm.[2]
   a. Choose a site from which you can observe people pass by slowly, such as the student union or student center.
   b. Record the dress of every individual of appropriate age and sex who passes your checkpoint. Record observations until you have observed 100 individuals of appropriate age and sex.
4. Write a brief analysis of your findings below, including the following:
   a. Determine the percentage of individuals observed to be wearing each given alternative.
   b. Analyze for a description of the mode, its relative strength or magnitude, and variability.
   c. Analyze in terms of conformity or nonconformity to the campus norm.
5. Summarize your findings and submit them to your instructor.

Fashion Count—Observation Schedule

Name of observer _____

Time and date _____

Checkpoint _____

Weather _____

Category	Number observed	Percent*
A.		
B.		
C.		
D.		
E.		
F.		
G.		
H.		
I. Other (Specify)		

TOTAL OBSERVED_____

*The percentage is determined by dividing the number observed in each category by the total number observed.

1. International Mass Retail Association (IRMA) changed its name to Retail Industry Leaders Association (RILA) in 2004.
2. If a count is made only once, it will identify the mode, yield a measure of its strength or magnitude, and demonstrate the variability within a social system at a given point in time. If a count is made every day for at least a week, a daily diffusion curve for the style can be drawn.

Chapter Three

THE RULES WE LIVE BY: NORMS

FROM THE HEADLINES

A federal appeals court ruled that a casino company's requirement for female bartenders to wear makeup does not amount to sexual discrimination. After working for 21 years as a bartender, a female bartender was fired for refusing to wear makeup. The ruling against the bartender "affirms the right of employers to adopt reasonable dress and grooming standards," according to lawyers for the casino company. The court ruled that the policy burdened women no more than men: men were required to cut their hair while women were not, and men were not allowed but women were required to wear makeup.

Source: Sonner, A. (2006, April 15). Bartenders' makeup stays on, court rules. *Southern Illinoisan*, p. 5A.

The incident described in this excerpt from a newspaper article illustrates several of the ten aspects of norms that you will read about in this chapter. A casino company established specific, detailed guidelines that required female employees to wear makeup. A female bartender refused to wear makeup and subsequently was fired. Believing that the dress code discriminated on the basis of gender, and that she was fired unjustly, the bartender sued the company. The authority of the company to have dress and grooming norms was upheld in court.

What were the casino company's reasons for the rules governing employee dress? What risks does an employee face when deciding to challenge a company dress code? Did the casino dress code burden women more than men?

In this chapter[1] we will examine the first step of the process of social control: the shared norms that specify how human beings should or should not look under given circumstances (the normative order for dress) and the ten aspects of norms, which vary. The ways in which dress norms can vary are

interrelated. Like any set of rules, the normative order for dress is only an approximation of how people should or should not look under given circumstances. Even when there is widespread societal agreement on dress norms, conformity is influenced by the ways in which norms can vary. After reading this chapter, you will be better able to analyze the casino dress code for the ten aspects of norms, their variations, and their interrelatedness.

QUESTIONS TO ANSWER AS YOU READ

1. What are norms?
2. What are the aspects of norms?
3. How does each of the aspects of norms vary?

IDENTIFYING NORMS

In Chapter 1 we presented a six-step model of a process of social control. The first step is identifying the shared norms that constitute a normative order (Figure 3.1).

We defined dress norms in Chapter 1 as "standards or rules that specify how people should or should not look under given circumstances" (Workman & Freeburg, 2000a, p. 48). "From the Headlines" spotlights one example of a dress norm: the rule that specified female bartenders must wear makeup and male bartenders must not wear makeup.

It is not always easy to identify norms, but when a norm is violated, the standard becomes obvious (Meier, 1982) (Figure 3.2). For example, a male student wore a skirt to high school. His principal told him he could not attend school if he wore a dress, kilt, or skirt and sent him home to change ("Skirting the Issue," 2006). The dress norm in this case was that males should not wear female clothing.

ASPECTS AND VARIATIONS OF NORMS

Dress norms vary because there are at least ten aspects of norms (Blake & Davis, 1964; Kitsuse, 1972; Meier, 1982; Workman & Freeburg, 2000a). Each aspect has variations that express the relative extent, amount, intensity, or level of some aspect of a norm, especially when compared with other norms (Table 3.1). Variations of an aspect may be represented as a continuum or as categories. A continuum is a continuous series, which ranges from being hidden to completely visible. Categories are formed based on defining features, for example, norms that relate to a goal or the means to a goal.

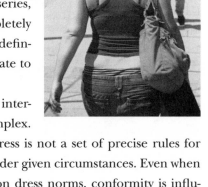

FIGURE 3.2 YOU CAN EASILY IDENTIFY THE DRESS NORMS FROM THE VIOLATION IN THIS PICTURE.

Because the aspects of dress norms are interrelated, the process of social control is complex. Furthermore, the normative order for dress is not a set of precise rules for how people should or should not look under given circumstances. Even when there is widespread societal agreement on dress norms, conformity is influenced by the aspects and variations of norms. For example, conformity with dress guidelines was mandatory (not voluntary) for bartenders who worked for the casino described at the beginning of this chapter.

SALIENCE

Based on the fact that how an individual looks is open to observation through the senses of sight, hearing, smell, and touch, dress norms are **salient,** that is, they are conspicuous and attract attention. The salience of dress norms may vary based on (a) other social cues, (b) whether witnesses are present, (c) environmental cues, (d) the operative norms for a situation, (e) the process of impression formation, and (f) group membership.

Other Social Cues

The salience of a particular dress norm may vary based on other social cues, for example, what other people are wearing (jeans, tuxedo, pajamas, kimono, Halloween costume), the physical environment (home, work, fast food restaurant, exclusive nightclub), the activity taking place (dancing, watching a movie, eating, walking, playing football), or the age of people present (infants, children, teenagers, adults). In one case, students were asked to leave a homecoming dance because they came dressed in police outfits (Ferguson,

TABLE 3.1 ASPECTS OF NORMS AND THEIR VARIATIONS

ASPECT OF NORMS	VARIATION	CATEGORY OR CONTINUUM
Salience	Salient.........Not salient	Continuum
Content	Goal	Category
	Means	Category
	Negative.........Positive	Continuum
Societal Function		
	Economic	Category
	Political	Category
	Replacement	Category
	Educational	Category
	Religious	Category
Authority	Rational	Category
	Traditional	Category
	Charismatic	Category
	Public opinion	Category
Origination	Formal.........Informal	Continuum
Realism	Ideal.........Real	Continuum
Acceptance	Voluntary.........Mandatory	Continuum
Properties	Specific.........Vague	Continuum
	Flexible.........Rigid	Continuum
	Explicit.........Implicit	Continuum
Application	Groups	Category
	Statuses	Category
Transmission	Primary socialization	Category
	Secondary socialization	Category
Sanctions	Immediate.........Deferred	Continuum
	Positive.........Negative	Continuum
	Severe.........Mild	Continuum
	Extreme.........Moderate	Continuum

2006). Another group of students came to the dance dressed as robbers with bandanas over their faces; they were also evicted from the dance. What other people were wearing, the physical environment, the activity taking place, and the age of the people present all combined to heighten the salience of the dress norm for a homecoming dance.

Witnesses

The salience of norms may also be heightened when other people are present. Norms are adhered to more faithfully when there are witnesses present (Wenegrat, Abrams, Castillo-Yee, & Romine, 1996). Compliance with trivial norms, such as wearing white shoes only after Memorial Day and before Labor Day, offers little or no advantage for an individual, yet some individuals still worry if they are not in compliance. Compliance with some norms may even result in a disadvantage, for example, spending limited resources in order to purchase the most popular brand of athletic shoes. Yet, individuals will make an effort to comply if the norms are salient to them and if they believe others are observing them. Compliance with salient norms may be particularly important if the observers are known to the individual. For example, consider potential differences in how vacationers dress when they will encounter only strangers versus when they will be with friends.

Adolescents may be especially vulnerable to compliance with salient norms because peer acceptance is such a vital concern, and because they tend to believe their peers scrutinize them closely. Adolescents live in an appearance-oriented culture that is governed by peer norms and expectations (Jones & Crawford, 2006). Among adolescents, peer teasing and remarks about appearance are everyday experiences. In addition to personal experience, adolescents also learn from the peer teasing and remarks experienced by others. Adolescents are acutely aware of the appearance teasing experienced by their peers and learn from others' experiences that appearance is often a target for explicit and critical teasing. This is one way the norms and expectations of peer appearance culture become known and shared. Teasing pinpoints appearance attributes that violate expectations and thereby aids in establishing and reinforcing norms.

Environmental Cues

Environmental cues may draw attention to certain norms. For example, in some schools, student dress codes are posted on classroom doors as a reminder

(Townsend, 2006). A sign on a restaurant door that specifies *No shirt, no shoes, no service* makes the dress norm for that restaurant salient. A sign posted at the front desk of a county jail has rules for visitor dress specifying that the dress must be appropriate and modest (Bostrom, 2006). The dress code for jail visits includes the following prohibited items: see-through clothing, tank tops, spaghetti straps, low-cut tops, tube tops, bathing suits, jeans that show underwear, bare feet, and T-shirts with inappropriate pictures, logos, or words. To ensure that the rules were obvious, they were conspicuously displayed.

Operative Norms

Norms that are signs of specific social skills depend upon the situation (Wenegrat, Abrams, Castillo-Yee, & Romine, 1996), which may specify the norm in effect for a particular situation (the **operative norm**). For example, a male candidate interviewing for an executive position should be aware that the operative dress norm is a suit and tie (Figure 3.3). The operative dress norms for teachers in high school classrooms become especially salient when a teacher violates the norm. Students do not expect to see a female teacher wearing a strapless dress or a male teacher in a bathing suit (Alexander, 2006). The salience of dress norms is **context dependent;** the social context (classroom, park, swimming pool, retail store, boardroom, restaurant, executive office) not only determines the operative norms, but how salient they are.

Impression Formation

Conformity with salient norms creates impressions of appropriateness, competence, or correctness (Wenegrat, Abrams, Castillo-Yee, & Romine, 1996). The signaling function of norms in creating impressions of competence is enhanced as norms (even trivial norms) become more salient. For example, a candidate who wore a suit but no tie to an interview for an executive position created an impression of incompetence (Weiss, 2006). The impression formation function of norms can explain the strong behavioral tendency, both cognitive and emotional, to conform to norms.

Group Membership

Some social norms are unique to groups. Dress norms communicate information about a group through their salience. For example, police uniforms signal power to enforce laws; gang dress symbolizes allegiance to gang values. "You look at how the colors are being worn, whether they're sagging (their pants), in a group together—that denotes certain types of gang activity . . . it's the look and your actions" (Eger, 2006, ¶ 13). One principal reported contacting the local Safe and Drug-Free Schools Office regularly for the latest police update on gang signs to watch for—the colors, color of the rubber bands worn on the wrists, or arches and lines shaved into the eyebrows. Another principal commented that he confronted known and suspected gang members about their conduct or appearance on a daily basis.

CONTENT

The content of norms refers to the subject matter the norms address. It includes goals and means, negative and positive expression, and societal function.

Goals and Means

The content can relate to a goal (the end an individual aims to accomplish) or to the means (measures or methods adopted) to reach a goal (Workman & Freeburg, 2000a). The norm that people should be slim relates to a goal. For example, members of the fashion industry believe that clothes look best on tall, thin females (Heller, 2006). The norm that people should not overeat relates to the means. For example, many young women believe that weight can be controlled by exercise and dieting. A survey of female undergraduates found they preferred thin fashion models to advertise products because many felt that putting on weight showed a lack of willpower ("Women Prefer Thin Models," 2006).

Negative and Positive Expression

Norms can be stated positively (should) or negatively (should not). For the bartenders described in the "From the Headlines" at the beginning of this chapter, a dress code was stated positively for females (must wear makeup) but negatively for males (must not wear makeup) (Sonner, 2006). Many public school dress codes are phrased negatively. For example, 128 students were suspended for wearing such prohibited items as baggy pants, low-cut shirts, tank tops, and graphic T-shirts ("What Not to Wear," 2006). Morsch (2006) listed ten workplace appearance norms that were stated negatively. Employees should not wear the following to work: poor-fitting clothing; too much perfume or cologne; shorts or too-short skirts; out-of-control hair; dirty, ripped, or torn jeans; clothes that show cleavage; tank tops; noisy jewelry; gym attire; and extremely high heels. A positively stated norm prescribed that in the United States women should shave their legs and under their arms (Brunner, 2006).

Some norms call for constant change, growth, and development. For example, members of the creative professions (fashion designers, fashion retailers, movie stars, entertainers) need to be up-to-date because change and innovation are part of their occupational roles. As professional change agents, they conform to positive norms that stipulate change (Figure 3.4). According to the Occupational Information Network ("Summary Report for Fashion Designers," 2004), fashion designers need the ability to come up with a number of ideas about a topic. The quality, correctness, or creativity of the ideas is not as important as the number of ideas. Further, fashion designers need to be able to generate unusual or clever ideas about a given topic or situation and to imagine creative ways to solve problems. Among the work activities engaged in by fashion designers is creative thinking about new products, applications, or relationships, including artistic combinations. Fashion designers are required to keep up-to-date technically and apply new knowledge to their job. The occupation of fashion designer requires working with form, designs, and patterns, requires self-expression, and requires working without a clear set of rules.

Societal Functions

The content of norms fluctuates in a manner that is consistent with the societal function involved. Basic social institutions function to fulfill the economic, political, replacement, educational, and religious needs of a society (Table 3.2).

FIGURE 3.4 DESIGNER ISAAC MIZRAHI, PICTURED HERE IN HIS STUDIO, IS CONSTANTLY COMING UP WITH NEW AND INNOVATIVE IDEAS RELATING TO FASHION.

TABLE 3.2 SOCIETAL FUNCTIONS

FUNCTION	DESCRIPTION
Economic	Production, distribution, and consumption of society's resources
Political	Actions by the government on behalf of its citizens
Replacement	Replacement of deceased members
Educational	Training of replacements
Religious	An organized system of beliefs, practices, rituals, and symbols that facilitates closeness to the sacred and responsibility to community

Economic Function

The economic function of a society refers to the production, distribution, and consumption of society's resources (Tischler, 2004). Individuals taking on a variety of occupational and consumer roles fulfill an economic function. Dress norms are frequently associated with occupational roles. It is easy to identify police officers, letter carriers, airline pilots, fast food restaurant workers, and medical personnel by their conformity to workplace dress norms. In Hartford, Connecticut, police officers were required to cover spiderweb tattoos with bandages or long sleeve shirts. The spiderweb tattoo had been appropriated by extremist groups as a symbol of hate and racism and was therefore considered to be offensive and to present an unprofessional appearance (Moore, 2006). The city's authority to regulate appearance was upheld by the court.

Workplace dress codes are often justified on the basis of three business-related reasons: (a) presenting or creating a professional or identifiable public appearance; (b) promoting a positive working environment and limiting distractions due to outrageous, provocative, or inappropriate dress; and (c) ensuring safety while working ("Personal Appearance," 2006). Employer dress policies presume that employees are representatives of the business, and therefore employee dress affects the public's impression of the business as well as internal morale (Figure 3.5).

One such dress code stated: "Your personal appearance is a reflection of your readiness and willingness to work. It can be a factor in the quality of your work" ("Appearance Standards," 2006, ¶ 4). Further, the dress code prohibited dreadlocks, required

FIGURE 3.5 THE PEOPLE IN THIS PICTURE ARE DRESSED AS PROFESSIONALS: THEY COULD BE LAWYERS OR BUSINESS EXECUTIVES.

tattoos to be covered, limited piercing to earlobes, and specified that hair must be neat, clean, and of normal, natural coloring.

Political Function

The political function refers to actions by the government on behalf of its citizens, for example, establishing laws and norms, providing social control, ensuring economic stability, setting goals, and protecting against outside threats (Tischler, 2004). **Laws** are norms that are formally defined and enforced by officials (Shepard, 2005). For example, governments make and administer rules to control production, distribution, and consumption of unsafe products. In the United States, a government agency—the Consumer Product Safety Commission (CPSC)—carries out this function by evaluating the safety of consumer goods. For example, the CPSC recommended that an apparel company voluntarily recall children's wear with oval-shaped zipper pulls that could come off and cause a choking hazard ("Old Navy Recalls Children's Clothing," 2004). So-called Creepy Cape Halloween costumes were recalled by the CPSC because the vinyl capes did not meet federal flammability standards, posing fire and burn hazards to consumers ("Family Dollar Recalls," 2006).

Replacement Function

The replacement function deals with the necessity of replacing each of society's members when they die or the idea that children replace current members of society (Tischler, 2004). Men and women make gender-specific contributions to the replacement function. Related to the replacement function are dress norms that reinforce these gender-specific contributions. For example, a gender-specific norm is that men should not wear women's clothing and women should not dress to look like men ("Cross Purposes," 2006), presumably because men cannot fulfill the female reproductive role and women cannot fulfill the male reproductive role. In one example, authorities accused a mother of radically changing her appearance to that of a man. When arrested for abduction of her children, she was 5 feet 9 inches tall, weighed 280 pounds, had cropped hair, a slight mustache, and stubble (Waggoner, 2006). In another instance, a woman wrote to an advice columnist concerning a problem she had never before encountered ("Man Dressed as a Woman," 2006). She was in a women's restroom when a man dressed as a woman came in. It was obvious he was a man even though he was wearing a wig, high heels, and a floral print dress because he was 6 feet tall, had a large Adam's apple, and a deep husky voice. The woman wondered if a transvestite should be allowed to use the ladies' restroom.

Educational Function

The educational function refers to "efforts, usually by more mature members of a society, to teach each new generation the beliefs, the way of life, the values, and some portion of the knowledge and skills of the group" (Hunt & Colander, 2005, p. 208). The school as an agent of cultural transmission has a twofold focus—to socialize students and to help them develop individuality. The end result of effective education is members of society who demonstrate general and specialized skills, display moral character, accept cultural values, adopt roles, and cultivate a personality or self-identity.

The two focal points of the educational function are revealed in student dress codes. Lenient dress codes give students some freedom of choice. Presumably this freedom of choice allows students to develop a personality or self-identity and learn responsibility for their choices (Townsend, 2006). On the other hand, school officials may use strict dress codes to encourage acceptance of cultural values such as respect for the rights of others or to support development of moral character. For example, most schools prohibit clothing with printed messages related to alcohol, drugs, tobacco, profanity, or gang membership (Workman & Freeburg, 2006). Some codes regulate revealing clothing such as short skirts, clothes that bare the midriff, muscle shirts, or tank tops, presumably to encourage the development of moral character. Educational goals provide a basis for prohibiting dress that may be distracting, unhealthy, dangerous, and/or that promotes values in conflict with those endorsed by the school (Workman & Studak, 2008).

Religious Function

The religious function is "an organized system of beliefs, practices, rituals, and symbols designed (a) to facilitate closeness to the sacred or transcendent (God, higher power, or ultimate truth/reality) and (b) to foster an understanding of one's relationship and responsibility to others in living together in community" (Koenig, McCullough, & Larson, 2001, p. 18). Religion functions to promote social cohesion; reaffirm a group's beliefs and values; help maintain norms, mores, and prohibitions; transmit a group's cultural heritage to the next generation; and provide emotional support during stressful times and at important life stages, such as marriage and death (Hunt & Colander, 2005).

Generally, religious bodies have authority to regulate norms related to morality. The Christian church has a long history of encouraging individuals to cover the physical body with modest dress because the body is believed to be where spiritual order resides (Rubinstein, 1995). Sometimes it is difficult to find a balance between religious and educational functions. For example, a high school student tried to adhere to religious tradition by wearing a *jilbab* or *abaya* (traditional Islamic robes) with a *hijab* (religious head scarf) to school. The school allowed the student to wear the religious dress but required her to wear a polo shirt, part of the school's uniform, over her traditional Islamic robes (Viren, 2006).

AUTHORITY

Norms gain their legitimacy from one or more sources—rational, traditional, charismatic, or public opinion (Table 3.3). Rational authority is based on a conviction that a specific individual has a clearly defined right and duty to uphold rules in an impersonal manner (Tischler, 2004). Rational authority implies trust in rules and the power of an individual in a position of authority to issue orders. Traditional authority is based on the time-honored status of ancient traditions and authorities. "Traditional authority is rooted in the assumption that the customs of the past legitimate the present" (p. 387). Charismatic authority is based on the exceptional characteristics of an individual. The authority of public opinion is based on a conviction that certain attitudes

TABLE 3.3 BASES FOR LEGITIMACY OF NORMS

BASE	DESCRIPTION
Rational grounds	Rules and the power of a person in authority to issue orders
Traditional grounds	Time-honored status of ancient traditions and authorities
Charismatic grounds	Exceptional characteristics of an individual
Public opinion	Attitudes and beliefs widespread throughout society

and beliefs are widespread among members of a society. **Opinion leaders** have publicly recognized expertise that people feel they can draw on if needed.

Rational Authority

A rational source of authority is the basis for occupational dress requirements, such as those issued by management for employees conducting work activities. These requirements are prevalent in the hospitality industry. For example, casinos can, with some restrictions, use appearance as criterion for hiring and firing (Gostomski & Kennedy, 2006). Women interviewing for cocktail server positions at one casino were required to wear bustier tops, velvet tights, and 4-inch heels. Cocktail servers at another casino signed contracts with the requirement that their weight would not vary beyond certain percentages (7 percent of their body weight).

Traditional Authority

The legitimacy of dress **taboos**—norms that are associated with moral or ethical misconduct—is based on traditional authority. For example, in 1946 when the bikini was introduced by fashion designer Jacques Heim, it was banned for being too scandalously revealing (Stohs-Krause, 2006). Historic garments, such as the cassock, clerical collar, miter, and pectoral cross, symbolize the sacred nature of religious leaders and the legitimacy of their traditional authority (*Clothing the Clergy*, 1997).

Charismatic Authority

The charismatic authority of fashion designers, supermodels, television personalities, entertainers, or athletes is responsible for many fashion norms. For example, supermodel Kate Moss was named Model of the Year at the 2006 British Fashion Awards as the model who contributed most to the global fashion world in the past year. A spokesperson commented that "Kate Moss is a fashion icon and without a doubt one of the most prolific models in the industry" ("Kate Moss Named," 2006, ¶ 4).

Each year new movies and television shows create the potential for entertainers to influence fashion. Some of these individuals reach the status of a cultural icon. A cultural icon is someone who embodies abstract cultural ideas in a tangible and visible manner (San Francisco Museum of Modern Art, 1997). Examples of abstract cultural ideas are wealth, physical attractiveness,

FIGURE 3.6 KATE MOSS: MODERN DAY CULTURAL ICON.

and success. Celebrities, professional athletes, entertainers, models, and fashion designers may become cultural icons (Figure 3.6). Cultural icons have power because they may (a) serve as symbols for a subculture, (b) transcend racial, class, and gender boundaries by promoting universal values or sentiments, and (c) challenge mainstream society and taste (Murray, 2006). Examples of cultural icons that have influenced fashion are Michael Jordan, Oprah Winfrey, Kate Moss, Calvin Klein, Ralph Lauren, and Donna Karan.

Public Opinion

The process of social control capitalizes on anticipation of evaluation by anonymous others—that is, public opinion. In 2004, 63 percent of respondents to a Gallup poll of U.S. public opinion said that buying and wearing clothing made of animal fur is morally acceptable (Walker, 2006). Although a majority of those polled shared this sentiment, a spokesperson for People for the Ethical Treatment of Animals (PETA) contended that in the United States, the trend of wearing fur is limited to two groups: (a) fashion folks who are always into the latest thing and (b) the "pimp and ho" look of rappers.

In Britain, public opinion about fur was expressed in a recent statement that 90 percent of young women surveyed said they would never wear fur (Barney, 2006). After criticizing several members of the British royal family for wearing fur, a spokesperson for PETA declared that "It is appalling that the very people who are supposed to represent the country go against what is very clearly public opinion" (¶ 8). One royal wife admitted it had been a judgment error when she had purchased a red fox-fur hat on the spur of the moment because it was so cold in St. Moritz where she was skiing. Several retailers have refrained from carrying fur products in response to public opinion (Walker, 2006).

ORIGINATION

The term *origination* refers to how the norms come into being. Norms may derive from a political function and thus have formal origination. A formally originated norm required foundry workers to wear safety shoes, gloves, and coveralls that were heat or chemical resistant ("Was Inadequate Protective Equipment," 2006). A foundry was cited and subsequently fined for violating the rule "which requires that protective equipment be provided, used, and maintained as necessary to protect against workplace hazards" (p. 9). Workers were observed wearing protective gloves and shoes with holes in them and using duct tape to repair damaged safety shoes. In a repeat violation, a worker wearing a short-sleeved shirt was observed cleaning out a pit that contained caustic chemicals; the worker was required by law to wear heat and chemical resistant coveralls.

Customs are enduring norms and refer to situations in which people always dress in a particular way because of tradition. Dress customs are practices that have informal origination—that is, the norms develop unofficially. For example, in Western wedding tradition, a bride usually wears a white dress and veil ("Wedding Dress," 2006). The origin of this custom dates to 1840, when Queen Victoria wore a white wedding gown (Bachmann, 2006). Many wedding superstitions date from the early 1900s; for example, it was considered very unlucky to wear black to a wedding. To attend a wedding as a guest, a woman in mourning could wear a deep red dress and then return to wearing her black mourning costume the next day.

REALISM

Realism is the faithful portrayal of reality. Norms may vary in a spectrum from real to ideal. Ideal norms are the norms that members of a society aspire to attain. An ideal norm is reflected in the physical characteristics of supermodels or professional athletes. According to the National Eating Disorders Association, the average American fashion model is 5 foot 11 inches tall and weighs 117 pounds, with a BMI of 16.3 (Green, 2006). Real norms refer to the norms that members of a society actually can attain. A real norm is reflected in the physical characteristics of the majority of the population (Figure 3.7).

FIGURE 3.7 As illustrated here in this cartoon about sizing, ideal norms can be manipulated to appear real.

The average American woman is 5 foot 4 inches tall and weighs 163 pounds, with a BMI of 28 (Green, 2006). The healthy range for BMI is 18.5 to 24.9.

Acceptance

Depending on the authority that legitimizes a norm, it may vary in degree of acceptance from voluntary (individuals may choose whether to abide by the norms) to mandatory (acceptance is required and enforced). For example, one rule of etiquette stipulates that white shoes can properly be worn only between Memorial Day and Labor Day ("White Shoes after Labor Day," 2006). Rules of **etiquette** are norms legitimized by an authority on manners but generally are regarded as voluntary.

Folkways are norms that allow a wide range of individual interpretation as long as certain boundaries are not exceeded (Tischler, 2004). For example, a wide range of dress is acceptable in most restaurants, but even informal eateries usually post signs requiring that patrons wear shoes and/or shirts. Similarly, six judges approved rules for attorneys in their judicial circuit: "No socks, no shoes, no litigation" ("Judges to Lawyers," 2006, ¶ 1). The rules on courtroom decorum and dress required appropriate professional attire, including a coat and tie for men. Apparently a wide range of coats and ties were acceptable, however, qualifying this norm as a folkway. The rule also specified that lawyers should advise their clients of proper courtroom attire.

"**Mores** (pronounced *more-ays*) are strongly held norms that usually have a moral connotation and are based on the central values of the culture" (Tischler, 2004, p. 61). Acceptance of mores is generally considered mandatory, and conformity is enforced by negative sanctions of extreme magnitude. An example of a mandatory norm is wearing clothing in public. A 50-year-old carpenter was arrested for indecent exposure when a client came home and found him building a set of bookcases while in the nude (Asimov, 2006). The carpenter had been cited three times since 2000 for public nudity; this time he was arrested and sentenced to two years' probation for violating the city's anti-nudity ordinance.

PROPERTIES

Norms may be stated in a vague manner or in a specific, detailed statement. **Fashion** "is a sociocultural phenomenon in which a preference is shared by a large number of people for a particular style that lasts for a relatively short time, and then is replaced by another style" (Calasibetta & Tortora, 2003, p. 154). In other words, fashion is the currently prevailing style of dress. Fashion is a vague, diffuse norm with a variety of interpretations. Each year names are assigned to the fashionable colors in clothing. For example, fashion colors for spring and summer 2006 were predicted to include rich floral shades like poppy and hibiscus (red) ("Spring into Cotton," 2006). **Fads** are fashion changes characterized by a rapid rise in popularity followed quickly by an abrupt drop (Calasibetta & Tortora, 2003, p. 152). Fads of the 1990s included baby doll dresses, backpack purses, butterfly clips, caps with the tag left on, Doc Martens shoes, double shirts, fanny packs, flannel shirts, half-heart necklaces, body piercings, plastic rubbery bracelets, tattoos, and thigh-high stockings ("Clothes of the Nineties," 2006). Fashions and fads are transitory norms—they may be widely dispersed but do not last long enough to become customs (Figure 3.8).

Some aspects of fashion may be stated specifically. For example, the White Shoe Rule stating a specific period of time during which white shoes can properly be worn. Another specific rule states that the correct width of a man's tie is about 3 inches ("The 10 Commandments of Style," 2006).

Rigid norms require exact conformity; flexible norms allow leeway in conformity. "Rigid dress norms are enacted and enforced by those in political power and may even be elevated to the status of law" (Workman & Freeburg, 2000a, p. 51). Indeed, dress norms instituted by school authorities have been challenged in court and upheld. School authorities attempt to regulate dress by stipulating rigid norms regarding skirt length (the fingertip rule specifies that a girl's skirt or dress must reach the length of her fingertips) or banning items such as baggy pants, bandanas, and camouflage (Beaudoin & Drevitch, 1998; Ridgley, 2006). Flexible norms allow some room for freedom of action. Flexible norms are obvious in specifications for a quasi-uniform: for example, a neutral-colored shirt with khaki or blue pants

FIGURE 3.8 LEGGINGS ARE AN EXAMPLE OF A CURRENT FAD.

THE RULES WE LIVE BY: NORMS

worn instead of a traditional school uniform. Any khaki or blue pants worn with any neutral-colored shirt would be acceptable under these flexible rules (Hill, 2005).

The clarity of a norm refers to whether it is explicit or implicit. Law books, regulations, and codes clearly delineate explicit norms. A dress code for an apartment complex in Minneapolis, Minnesota, contained an explicit statement of norms (Mccahill, 2006). The complex's security firm established the dress code as a preventive measure to deter gang activity. The dress regulations specified explicitly that in public areas residents were not allowed to wear pants that *have a tendency to drag up the ground* or that could *slide off the hips*, sideways baseball caps, bandanas, and Ku Klux Klan paraphernalia. If residents wore the prohibited attire, they were asked to go to their apartments or change.

Implicit norms are understood or implied without being stated. Advertising, in particular, uses implicit norms such as the law of association to transmit nonverbal messages of appropriate appearances. For example, because young, thin, attractive, perfect models advertise fashionable attire, fashion is coupled with youth, thinness, attractiveness, and perfection (Sproles & Burns, 1994).

The many books of advice on professional dress link success with a professional look. For men, a professional look consists of a suit, dress shirt, tie, and polished shoes. For women, a professional look consists of modest, conservative, unmemorable clothing.

A recent national Fashion in the Workplace survey found that 70 percent of executives surveyed perceived that employees who dressed in traditional business suits and skirts were more senior level and were taken more seriously ("Fashion Survey Reveals," 2006), revealing the implicit association between the norm of professional dress and success. A consultant on professional dress recommended that attorneys need to be concerned with their image: "In the first 30 seconds, people are usually judging big picture ideas about you—your level of education, your level of success, your level of sophistication. From then, until the end of the four minutes, they're starting to judge a little deeper. They're deciding things that have to do with your trustworthiness, reliability, honesty, compassion and confidence" (Vassallo, 2006, ¶ 7).

APPLICATION

We share many norms simply because we are all members of one society (for example, U.S. society). However, any one specific norm can apply differently to different groups. A group is made up of people sharing something in common such as interests, beliefs, or goals. Primary groups are made up of people who interact regularly face-to-face, including families or friendship groups, such as sororities. Secondary groups (support groups, church groups, hobby clubs) are more formally organized and often focus on specialized needs or goals of the members. A peer group is made up of social equals—acquaintances or friends similar to one another in age, education, social class, or interests—who interact socially on a regular basis. Every social group has its own culture—its own goals, norms, values, and ways of doing things.

Every individual belongs to many groups. One function of a group is to control the behavior of group members. When members conform to group expectations, such as ways of dressing, they are rewarded. Indeed, without conformity, there would be no groups.

For example, conformity to group expectations has allowed the Mennonite church to survive in the face of overwhelming economic and social pressures (Schmidt, 2001). But schisms developed within the Mennonite church over dress regulations and church discipline. Pants or dress, cut or uncut hair, wearing or rejecting the prayer covering are important indicators of community conformity. "In traditional Amish and Mennonite communities, small changes in appearances, such as wearing a smaller prayer covering, wearing one's hat at a jaunty angle, or worse yet, using makeup, cutting one's hair, and

FIGURE 3.9 MEMBERS OF THE AMISH COMMUNITY CONFORM TO A SPECIFIC DRESS CODE.

wearing fashionable clothing, indicate dissension from church regulations and religiously sanctioned community practices" (p. 86) (Figure 3.9).

Recall that status refers to an individual's position in a social hierarchy and prestige refers to others' evaluation of an individual's position in a status hierarchy. **Ascribed statuses** are assigned due to birth or other significant factors not under an individual's control, for example, gender and age. In a proposed dress code for teachers, a gender-specific dress norm that applied only to women was wearing dresses or skirts; a gender-specific dress norm for men was wearing neckties (Spicuzza, 2006).

Achieved statuses are obtained due to effort or choice, such as educational and occupational statuses. In economic institutions a norm may apply differently within and among status positions. The status hierarchy for employees of one hospital was made visible by a dress code that stipulated that different medical personnel have different color lab coats. Attending physicians wore gray coats, residents or house staff physicians wore blue coats, volunteers wore pink or burgundy coats, and diagnostic lab personnel wore white lab coats ("Nurses' Attire Shows No Pride," 1997). Housekeeping, engineering, and food services personnel also wore distinctive uniforms. All employees wore identification badges imprinted with name and position.

Norms that apply to upper social class men were outlined in an issue of *Gentlemen's Quarterly*, a men's fashion magazine, with the caveat that if a man follows these rules, he will possess great taste ("The 10 Commandments of Style," 2006). Among the norms were to have a tailor custom-fit your suits, to wear sneakers made for a man, to invest in the right timepiece, to match your socks with your suit, to wear a tie that is the correct width, to carry an elegant, slim leather credit card holder and a money clip instead of a wallet, to wear the right tie with the right tux, to wear brown shoes with nearly everything, to learn when pants should be cuffed, and to remember to wear an undershirt.

"**Roles** are the culturally defined rights and obligations attached to a status; they indicate the behavior expected of an individual holding that particular status" (Shepard, 2005, p. 127). Every individual has many roles deriving from various groups and statuses. Rights are behaviors that an individual in a particular status is entitled to expect from others. Alternately, obligations are behaviors that others can expect from an individual in a particular status because of legal or moral duty.

A **rite of passage** is a public ceremony that is used to validate changes in a person's status (Kendall, 2007). The white coat ceremony is a rite of passage for medical students (Huber, 2003). The white coat ceremony is an initiation ritual. Like other rites of passage, it uses symbols, its own language, and reflects an ideal. It begins the development of an identity as a medical professional. A typical white coat ceremony includes the presence of family and friends to observe the donning of the white coat and the swearing of the Hippocratic Oath (an ethical code for the medical profession). The white coat ceremony is a ritual that helps students adjust to their new status and role as medical students with all their rights, obligations, and behavioral expectations.

TRANSMISSION

Transmission or communication of norms takes place during both primary and secondary socialization. Recall that socialization is a lifelong process whereby individuals become aware of society's expectations and learn how they are expected to behave. During the socialization process, which depends on interaction with other people, individuals learn attitudes, values, and the motivation to conform to societal expectations.

Primary socialization refers to those interactions through which a child initially learns a language, adopts basic cultural norms and values, behaves in terms of these norms and values, and forms a culturally appropriate social identity (Tischler, 2004). "Norms about gender-appropriate dress are transmitted during primary socialization when children are likely to accept dress norms without questioning them—convinced that the norms are inherently right" (Workman & Freeburg, 2000a, p. 52) (Figure 3.10).

FIGURE 3.10 CHILDREN FORM A GENDER IDENTITY, INCLUDING WHAT IS GENDER-APPROPRIATE DRESS, DURING PRIMARY SOCIALIZATION. THIS CARTOON ADDRESSES BOYS' GENDER IDENTITY STANDARDS: NOTHING GIRLISH IS ACCEPTABLE.

Gender is a psychological and cultural term, referring to an individual's subjective feelings of maleness or femaleness. "In past generations, so-called sissy boys and tomboy girls were made to conform, based on the belief that their behaviors were largely products of dysfunctional homes" (Brown, 2006, ¶ 18). A mother wrote to a pediatrician and parenting expert about her four-year-old son who preferred to play with girls and was interested in dressing up in fairy gowns and being the bride (Heins, 2006). The expert replied:

Between ages 3 and 6 children develop "gender understanding" (they know gender is defined by genitals, not external appearance), "gender constancy" (they know that when a boy puts on a dress it doesn't change his gender), "gender stability" (they know their gender was there when they were born and it will stay the same when they grow up). . . . "Gender role" refers to behaviors or characteristics that are attributed to one gender or another and are culturally determined. . . . Nearly all creative and imaginative 2- year-olds go through a stage of pretending to be lots of characters including those of the opposite sex. . . . The term "core gender identity" is used to describe one's sense of belonging to one gender (and not the other) and valuing this. (Heins, 2006, ¶ 3, 4, 8, 9)

Secondary socialization refers to the processes by which individuals learn new statuses or roles (Tischler, 2004). Norms relating to workplace dress are transmitted during secondary socialization. For example, a city's taxicab regulation advisory committee proposed a dress code for cab drivers that included the following: clean shoes, no sandals, collared shirts with long or short sleeves, khaki style pants or shorts or clean neat jeans without tears or holes (Weber, 2006). The dress code also specified that drivers must be well-groomed with a clean appearance.

SANCTIONS

Norms fluctuate in keeping with the sanctions administered. Recall that sanctions are rewards or punishments that affect conformity to norms. The rewards or punishments may be immediate (take place at once, without delay) or deferred (delayed until a later time—an hour, a week, a month, years, or perhaps even until death or shortly thereafter). A norm that is stated positively (women should shave their legs and under their arms) implies a positive sanction for compliance (social acceptance or approval). A negatively stated norm (males should not wear female clothing) involves a negative sanction when it is violated (social ostracism or even arrest).

Sanctions of extreme magnitude, either rewards (being named Model of the Year) or punishments (being arrested for indecent exposure), are signs that a norm has wide acceptance in society or within a subculture, that conformity is mandatory, and that strong emotions are involved (phobias, fear, shame, reverence, admiration). Violation of a widely accepted, mandatory dress norm learned during primary socialization (wearing clothing in public) will carry severe sanctions of extreme magnitude (arrest, social ostracism).

INTERRELATIONSHIP OF NORM ASPECTS

The interrelatedness of norms refers to the interaction and interdependence of the ten aspects of norms and the variations of those aspects. Norms are the social rules that guide our behavior. The interrelationship of norms can affect social rules in three basic ways: Norms can be strengthened (increased in power or force), supplanted (replaced with something newer or more relevant), or undermined (weakened by removing or gradually diminishing the foundation for the norm).

Consider the norm that people should be slim. This norm is powerful because all four sources of authority agree on it: (a) rational authority in the form of the medical profession has declared a war on obesity because of its deleterious health effects; (b) religious authority specifies that gluttony is a sin; (c) models and movie stars with charismatic authority are thin; and (d) public opinion is reflected in the notion that if you ask people, they will say they should lose some weight. Consider the norms of fashion—they are supplanted on a regular basis by something newer or more relevant. For example, a trend among adolescents is to wear their shirttails hanging out (not tucked in) (Gelpi, 2006). School officials considered whether they should change the dress code rules to allow students to untuck their shirts and follow the latest trend. Consider the norm of professional dress in the workplace. The foundation for this norm gradually weakened during the 1990s because of an emphasis on casual dress and employees' opinion that they were more productive when dressed casually.

SUMMARY

We have examined the first step of the process of social control, that is, the shared norms that constitute a normative order for dress and the ten aspects along which they may vary. Based on the fact that how one looks is open to observation through the senses of sight, hearing, smell, and touch, identification of dress norms is open to observation.

Norms can be identified by observing the use of sanctions and inferring the existence of a norm (Meier, 1982). It is sometimes difficult to identify norms before they are violated (Kitsuse, 1972). All of the norms mentioned in this chapter had sanctions associated with violation, either explicitly stated sanctions (arrest, suspension from school, reprimand, anger, embarrassment, being fired from a job) or implied sanctions (social disapproval, censure, disrespect, criticism, guilt, and shame). Therefore, the dress norms could be inferred from the sanctions. Identifying norms is crucial in examining the normative order because norms are standards against which individuals measure violations.

KEY TERMS AND CONCEPTS

achieved statuses	mores
ascribed statuses	operative norm
context dependent	opinion leaders
customs	primary socialization
etiquette	rigid norms
fads	rite of passage
fashion	roles
folkways	salient
gender	secondary socialization
laws	taboos

SUGGESTED READINGS

1. Rubinstein, R. (1995). *Dress codes: Meanings and messages in American culture.* Boulder, CO: Westview Press.
2. Workman, J. E., & Freeburg, E. W. (2006). Safety and security in a school

environment: The role of dress code policies. *Journal of Family and Consumer Sciences, 98*(2), 19–24.

3. Workman, J. E., & Freeburg, E. W. (2000). Part I: Expanding the definition of the normative order to include dress norms. *Clothing and Textiles Research Journal, 18*(2), 46–55.

Research Activity 3.1: *Fashion Fads/Trends/Forecasting*

Purpose: To analyze fashion trade resources to identify fashion fads, fashion forecasts, and fashion trends.

Procedure:

1. Review the definition of a fad.
2. Identify fashion fads of past decades.
   a. Log on to http://www.inthe90s.com
   b. Select (click on) "Fads/Fashion" to locate fashion fads in the Clothes of the Nineties Index.
   c. Write a statement that identifies the norm for appearance identified by the fads from the 1990s.
3. Forecast fashion trends.
   a. Locate a definition for fashion forecast.
   b. Log on to the iVillage website (http://www.ivillage.co.uk/).
   c. Search iVillage to locate two fashion trends for the current season.
   d. Write two statements that identify the norm for appearance identified by the fashion trends for the current season.
   e. Search an online fashion catalog, such as one promoting products sold by Target, Eddie Bauer, Talbots, or Coldwater Creek, and compare the appearance norms for the current season with what you observe in the online catalog.
   f. Compare the appearance norms and catalog items to answer the question "Were the forecasts accurate?"
4. Describe color forecasts for the current season.
   a. Locate a definition for color forecast.
   b. Use the Google (http://google.com) search engine to locate fashion websites that forecast color. One website example is www.fashiontrendsetter.com
   c. Bookmark three websites to compare and contrast color trends.

d. Identify two color trends for the current season identified on each website. Include the website URL.

5. Submit your work to your instructor.

Research Activity 3.2 Dress Norms

Purpose: To analyze a set of pictures to identify and describe dress norms.

Procedure:

1. Review the definitions of the normative order and dress norms.
2. Log on to the Library of Congress American Memory website (http://memory.loc.gov/ammem/).
3. Select (click on) "Advertising" from the list of Collections by Topic.
4. Select (click on) one of the six collections. For example, you might select "Advertising, Multiformat, 1850–1920."
5. Browse that collection by subject to select five clothing advertisements.
6. Analyze the five clothing advertisements using the National Archives Photo Analysis Worksheet (http://www.archives.gov/education/lessons/worksheets/photo_analysis_worksheet.pdf).
7. Identify one or more norms portrayed in each advertisement.
8. Summarize your findings and submit them to your instructor.

NOTES

1. The conceptual framework for this chapter appeared as part of an article in the *Clothing and Textiles Research Journal,* Workman, J. E., & Freeburg, E. W. (2000). Part I: Expanding the definition of the normative order to include dress norms. *Clothing and Textiles Research Journal, 18*(2), 46–55.

Chapter Four

RESEARCH: DRESS CODES, GENDER NORMS, GROUP NORMS, AND MORE

FROM THE HEADLINES

More than one in three patients who filled out a questionnaire indicated that sandals, clogs, and blue jeans were inappropriate dress for medical doctors of both genders. Name badges, white coats, and dress shoes were desirable dress for doctors of both genders. Male doctors should wear dress pants and avoid open shirts, long hair or ponytails, earrings, surgical scrubs, and cologne, and female doctors should wear skirts or dresses or dress pants. One in four patients preferred traditional hairstyles for both male and female doctors. "The informal image of doctors in television shows such as *ER* is far different from that of past television physicians such as Marcus Welby, M.D., and Dr. Kildare, but apparently hasn't greatly influenced patients' preferences for their own doctors' appearances, the researchers said (¶ 5)."

Source: Tanner, L. (2002, April 14). Despite TV image, patients want docs to be well-dressed, study says. The Associated Press State & Local Wire. Retrieved May 31, 2006, from http://www.lexisnexis.com

The research described in this excerpt from a newspaper article illustrates several concepts that you will read about in this chapter. Researchers conducted a study by having patients fill out a questionnaire giving their opinions about appropriate dress for medical doctors. The research was motivated by popular television programs that depicted physicians wearing scrubs, sandals, and other casual dress items. Researchers expected the data to provide information that would help doctors make decisions about dress that would be consistent with patient expectations.

How should health care workers dress? How does the white lab coat and

RESEARCH METHOD	TOOL(S)	AUTHOR(S)	YEAR	ARTICLE TITLE
Qualitative	Observation worksheet	Arthur	1997	Role salience, role embracement, and the symbolic self-completion of sorority pledges
Theoretical paper	Literature analysis	Brandt	2003	On the value of an old dress code in the new millennium
Qualitative	Interview worksheet	Colls	2006	Outsize/outside: Bodily bignesses and the emotional experiences of British women shopping for clothes
Qualitative	Interview worksheet	Colls	2004	"Looking all right, feeling alright": Emotions, sizing, and the geographies of women's experiences of clothing consumption
Qualitative	Content analysis worksheet	Crockett & Wallendorf	1998	Sociological perspectives on imposed school dress codes: Consumption as attempted suppression of class and group symbolism
Qualitative	Ethnographic tools	Deil-Amen	2006	To teach or not to teach "social" skills: Comparing community colleges and private occupational colleges
Qualitative	Ethnographic tools	Dellinger	2002	Wearing gender and sexuality "on your sleeve": Dress norms and the importance of occupational and organizational culture at work
Qualitative	Interview worksheet	Dellinger & Williams	1997	Makeup at work: Negotiating appearance rules in the workplace
Qualitative	Conversation analysis worksheet	Freitas et al.	1997	Appearance management as border construction: Least favorite clothing, group distancing, and identity . . . not!
Qualitative	Content analysis worksheet	Suitor & Carter	1999	Jocks, nerds, babes and thugs: A research note on regional differences in adolescent gender norms
Qualitative	Content analysis worksheet	Suitor & Reavis	1995	Football, fast cars, and cheerleading: Adolescent gender norms, 1978–1989
Qualitative	Content analysis worksheet	Workman & Freeburg	2006	Safety and security in a school environment: The role of dress code policies

stethoscope symbolize the medical profession? How does the dress of health care workers affect impressions of their competence? In this chapter, you will read about research that has examined issues related to dress norms in various societal contexts.

The methods and tools used in each research study are summarized in Table 4.1. The chapter is organized into topical areas: (a) dress codes, (b) gender norms, (c) body modification norms, (d) group norms, and (e) body norms and the "sized" body. Studying dress norms is important because dress

TABLE 4.2 SUMMARY OF QUANTITATIVE RESEARCH METHODS AND TOOLS RELATED TO NORMS

RESEARCH METHOD	TOOL(S)	AUTHOR(S)	YEAR	ARTICLE TITLE
Quantitative	Survey	Freeburg & Workman	2000	An empirical test of norms related to appearance
Quantitative	Survey	Hall & Berardino	2006	Teaching professional behaviors: Differences in the perceptions of faculty, students, and employers
Quantitative	Survey	Kanzler & Gorsulowsky	2002	Patients' attitudes regarding physical characteristics of medical care providers in dermatologic practices
Quantitative	Survey	Nickson et al.	2005	The importance of attitude and appearance in the service encounter in retail and hospitality
Quantitative	Survey	Volokh & Snell	1998	School violence prevention: Strategies to keep schools safe
Quantitative	Document analysis worksheet	Workman & Lentz	2000	Measurement specifications for manufacturers' prototype bodies
Quantitative	Questionnaire	Workman & Studak	2005	Stereotypes associated with design of plus-size apparel
Quantitative	Survey	Wu & Workman	1993	Restrictive forces in clothing design for large-size women

is a sociological variable that provides information about society and the process of social control. When we study dress norms, we learn about our society and how it operates. For example, we learn what our society values and what the expectations are for various statuses and roles.

QUESTIONS TO ANSWER AS YOU READ

1. What are some specific norms that relate to dress?
2. How is research about dress norms conducted?
3. How does dress norm research incorporate the process of social control?

DRESS CODES

Dress codes make clear the norms for dress within a particular environment. Dress codes are commonly found in two situations: the workplace and school. Within limits imposed by legislation, historical precedents, concern for civil

RESEARCH: DRESS CODES, GENDER NORMS, GROUP NORMS, AND MORE

rights, and so forth, employers and school officials have a legal right to establish obligatory dress norms for employees and students.

Workplace Dress Codes

Donais (2006) described **workplace culture** as a system of shared understandings, beliefs, values, behaviors, and norms for workers in a particular workplace. Dress and appearance norms are one aspect of workplace culture. Many new employees learn about dress and appearance rules through interaction with co-workers. Some corporations have formal, written dress and appearance codes; however, many workplaces use informal methods to communicate rules about dress.

Job performance is influenced by norms or behavioral standards (Lawrence, 1996). Specifically, norms related to effective job performance include written and oral communication (what employees should or should not say), appearance (what employees should or should not look like), initiative (what employees should or should not think), and quality and quantity of work (what employees should or should not do). Appearance may be the most salient norm category, but all of the norms are interrelated.

Hard and Soft Workplace Skills

In the workplace, employees need both hard skills and soft skills (Figure 4.1). **Hard skills** refer to technological, finance, legal, strategic, and analytical skills; understanding of business dynamics; ability to make effective decisions; and ability to use evidence and data as bases for decision making (Holbeche, 2006). **Knowledge** refers to organized sets of principles and information with general relevance. **Technical skills** refer to competence in design, setup, operation, and correcting malfunctions related to machines or technological systems (*O*Net Descriptors,* 2004). **Soft skills** refer to creativity, emotional intelligence, empathy, self-awareness, flexibility, resilience, social skills, ability to cope with ambiguity and paradox, and ability to communicate effectively (Holbeche, 2006). **Social skills** fall into the category of soft skills and refer to the way people in groups behave and interact.

Nickson, Warhurst, and Dutton (2005) focused on norms for aesthetic skills in service industries. **Aesthetic skills** include attitude and appearance, and fall into the category of soft skills (Figure 4.2). Employers acknowledge the importance of employees having appropriate aesthetic skills in the retail service en-

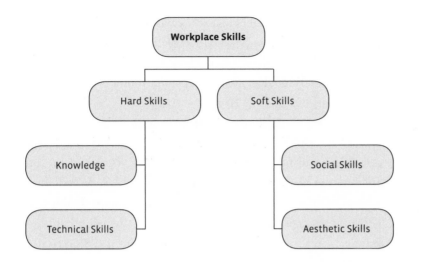

FIGURE 4.1 WORKPLACE SUCCESS INCLUDES DEMONSTRATED COMPETENCY IN BOTH HARD SKILLS AND SOFT SKILLS. AESTHETIC SKILLS ARE AMONG THE SOFT SKILLS NEEDED IN SERVICE INDUSTRIES LIKE FASHION.

counter. Employees are expected to embody the product being sold. "As part of this process of embodiment, employees are now expected to not only demonstrate soft skills with regard to their attitude, but also have the ability to 'look good' or 'sound right', or in short to draw on their 'aesthetic skills'" (p. 196). The retail product is both tangible (apparel, accessories, etc.) and intangible (customer service). Employees with particular attributes, attributes that positively influence customers' visual or aural senses, are a key aspect of quality service. Employees' appearance and speech become an integral part of the tangible product—that is, they literally embody the image of the company.

The Company Image

At the recruitment and selection stage, employers can eliminate applicants who do not embody the company image. Many young people, such as students, look for work by personally speaking with a store manager. This informal

FIGURE 4.2 AESTHETIC SKILLS INCLUDE ATTITUDE AND APPEARANCE.

RESEARCH:
DRESS CODES,
GENDER NORMS,
GROUP NORMS,
AND MORE

FIGURE 4.3 HIRING DECISIONS BASED ON PHYSICAL ATTRIBUTES—SUCH AS DREADLOCKS—ARE POTENTIALLY DISCRIMINATORY.

process enables managers to assess an applicant's aesthetic skills, such as language, dress, shape and size of body, manner, and style. The authors noted that hiring people based on physical appearance raises the question: Is **lookism** a potentially discriminatory practice, like sexism, racism, and ageism? (Figure 4.3).

Responses to questionnaires from employers in the retail and hospitality industries revealed that 93 percent considered employee appearance to be central or critical to the success of the business (Nickson et al., 2005). Over 90 percent of the surveyed companies had an employee dress code that was used to establish and refine the corporate image. Dress code components that identified aesthetic requirements included rules for general tidiness (98 percent), clothing style (74 percent), jewelry (66 percent), makeup or personal grooming (63 percent), and hair style and length (45 percent). Employers were especially looking for aesthetic skills (attitude and appearance) in their front-line personnel, not just hard technical skills. The authors concluded that workers who meet the norms of aesthetic skills have a distinct advantage in the recruitment and selection process. Once hired, companies train their employees about appearance norms through dress and appearance regulations.

Knowledge of Occupational Cultures

Hall and Berardino (2006) surveyed managers, faculty, and students (both undergraduate and graduate) about their perceptions of professional behavior. The norms for professional behavior included the soft skills of honesty, ethical decision making, regular attendance, punctuality, professional dress and appearance, participation in professional organizations, and appropriate behavior during meetings. The most distinct differences between groups resulted from perceptions of dress and appearance norms. Managers and MBA (Masters of Business Administration) students agreed that students should be required to dress in suits for major presentations, while undergraduates disagreed. Managers agreed much more strongly than other groups that students with facial piercing (eyebrow and lip piercing, jewelry in nose) should be advised about a more appropriate business appearance.

Cultural capital is "widely shared, high status cultural signals (attitudes, preferences, formal knowledge, behaviors, goals, and credentials) used for social and cultural exclusion" (Lamont & Lareau, 1988, p. 156). Teaching students occupationally relevant social skills and expectations expands their cultural capital, thereby enhancing opportunities for upward mobility (Deil-Amen, 2006). Successful upward movement in a status hierarchy involves becoming knowledgeable about the norms, expectations, and social networks in occupational cultures (Rosenbaum, Kariya, Settersten, & Maier, 1990). These norms are based on shared understandings and commonsense assumptions. Applicants from lower social classes who are not familiar with the norms of professional culture are at a disadvantage in competition for jobs, because social skills play a critical role in employers' evaluations (Heckman & Lochner, 2000). Applicants who violate the performance norms and expectations of a professional culture will not create a favorable impression even if they are otherwise qualified.

Deil-Amen's (2006) research included case studies of 14 colleges, including public community colleges and private occupational colleges. Faculty at both types of institutions agreed that workplaces require social skills and cultural knowledge that many of their students lacked. For example, one respondent remarked that students had no concept of how they should dress for the office, how they should look, what their appearance should be, how to answer the telephone, and so forth. Some faculty commented that the norms of some students' cultural background actually contradict the norms of professional culture, for example, preference for certain styles of dress.

Faculty at the occupational colleges described the need to inform students about behaviors that might seem readily apparent or common sense for middle-class people who are familiar with such norms. These taken-for-granted assumptions include knowledge about workplace conduct and appearance, such as expectations for communication, cooperation, punctuality, dress, and appearance. The norms of professional culture represent common ideas about appropriate behavior in professional work settings.

Dress is important even in occupations such as information technology (IT), where the stereotype of an IT worker is a male who is egregiously overweight, is ethically challenged, has poor personal hygiene, and is fashion-challenged (May, 2006). Research found that high-performing IT organizations managed their perception such that IT *looks like* the business (employees wear the same type of clothes as people on the organization's business side). Employees in different aspects of IT have their own implicit dress codes, that is, salespeople wear suits, break-and-fix contract employees (technical service providers) wear dress pants and golf shirts, technology consultants wear collared dress shirts and business-casual, and "security folks remain tragically out of step with sartorial norms" (p. 23). The author concluded that social and aesthetic skills are important to the evolution of the IT profession.

Wearing Makeup at Work

Dellinger and Williams (1997) interviewed 20 women in a variety of work settings to answer the question, "Why do women wear makeup to work?" Women who routinely wore makeup but forgot it one time received comments and negative attention from co-workers about appearing tired, fatigued, ill, or like they just woke up. Conversely, when they wore makeup, they received favorable comments about their appearance, resulting in increased self-confidence and productivity. "In addition to marking women as healthy and well-rested, makeup also marks women as heterosexual" (p. 159). When women refused to conform to the makeup norms at work, consequences ranged from pressure to appear more feminine to outright discrimination. One woman reported that she was denied jobs for which she was qualified because she did not look feminine enough.

Some women wore makeup because they believed it made them appear more competent (Dellinger & Williams, 1997). In an occupation where someone gives advice to others about their appearance (as in a retail store), competence as a source of advice is enhanced if the advisor looks professionally competent. Females in the fashion industry "may feel that wearing makeup is particularly important for establishing their credibility, since they are in a position of selling advice to other women about their appearance" (p. 168). Positions that require customer interaction are likely to have dress codes that encourage employees to wear makeup (Adkins, 1995).

When workplace appearance norms are internalized, the norms affect women's personal choices to wear makeup (Dellinger & Williams, 1997). **Internalized appearance norms** become personal goals and standards against which one measures the self and others. Makeup was a topic of conversation that bonded women, but women were sensitive to the negative stereotypes about women who are overly interested in cosmetics and appearance. Dellinger and Williams found that some women resisted the norm by wearing the minimum acceptable amount of makeup at work. While women acknowledged that appearance rules governed their use of makeup at work, some resisted conformity by refusing to monitor their cosmetics throughout the day. Although many women found pleasure in wearing makeup, workplace norms limited the possibilities for resistance. The authors concluded that appropriate makeup use in the workplace was associated with health, heterosexuality, and credibility.

FIGURE 4.4
PROFESSIONAL BUSINESS ATTIRE.

Accountants and Editors

Dellinger (2002) studied the occupational and organizational dress and appearance norms of men and women who worked as accountants and editors at two different types of magazines. On the basis of the comparative case study, Dellinger concluded that norms about the appropriate division between personal and work identities depended on occupational culture (what they did, editor or accountant) and organizational culture (where they worked, type of magazine). Dress norms reflected what an accountant looks like and what an editor looks like. Accountants at both magazines did not have a written dress code, but the understood code was a suit and tie for men and some kind of business attire for women. A business suit symbolized work mentality and embodied the rationality and order characteristic of accountants. Professional business attire signaled their competence to others and acted as a symbol of the split between public and private spheres—work and home, work and play, work and individual personality, work and sexuality (Figure 4.4).

The implicit dress code among editors reflected the notion that creative work requires freedom of expression and "creative people feel stifled in suits" (Dellinger, 2002, p. 12). Although there were limits to appropriateness (shorts and ragged clothes were not appropriate), dress was casual (for example, jeans were acceptable) (Figure 4.5). The workplace dress norms emphasized personal expression at work. Although a wide range of dress styles were acceptable at each organization, there was a normative line beyond which employees might be seen as not conforming to the organizational culture. Informal, unwritten occupational

FIGURE 4.5 CASUAL BUSINESS ATTIRE.

RESEARCH:
DRESS CODES,
GENDER NORMS,
GROUP NORMS,
AND MORE

and organizational norms influenced workers' definitions of appropriate and inappropriate expressions of gender and sexuality at work.

Doctors' Dress

In a study of doctors' dress, Kanzler and Gorsulowsky (2002) pointed out that the primary goals of a medical care provider—to prevent and treat disease—are accomplished through direct interactions with patients. Nonverbal cues such as appearance might influence the comfort level of patients, especially new patients, during these interactions. Increasing the comfort level of patients may improve exchange of information and patient care. Earlier studies found that patients preferred doctors to have a traditional appearance, including wearing a white coat and name tag. The authors speculated that public perception of how physicians should look may have changed as a result of the informal appearance of physicians on popular television programs. Therefore, the research question guiding the study was: Have the norms for doctors' physical appearance changed over the last generation?

To answer that question, Kanzler and Gorsulowsky (2002) distributed questionnaires to patients. The questionnaires asked for demographic data as well as preferences about items of dress and grooming of doctors. Items included name tag, white coat, sport coat/blazer, dress pants, blue jeans, surgical scrubs, dress shoes, tennis shoes, clogs, sandals, and hairstyle. The researchers concluded that there was little change in patients' attitudes from similar studies performed over twenty years ago. "Despite a general trend in Western society toward more casual attire in public, very little change has occurred in patients' preferences regarding the preferred attire of their medical care providers" (p. 466). Patients still find traditional attire such as name badges, white coats, and dress shoes preferable for doctors.

Brandt (2003) reviewed research related to dress of physicians. Using key words such as *dress code, professional attire, physician attitudes, white coat,* and *clothing,* the researcher searched several electronic databases. Thirty-one articles were found that were pertinent to the research question of whether the dress of a health care provider is important to patients. Universal symbols of the medical profession were found to be the white laboratory coat and stethoscope. Brandt concluded that the attire of health care providers was important to patients whether the patients were young or old and regardless of geographic location.

Secondary School Dress Codes

Dress codes in student handbooks are a method by which school officials establish and communicate norms for student dress and appearance. Schools have a great degree of control over student behavior and establish dress codes to ensure a safe and healthy educational environment, to discourage gang activity, and to eliminate disruption and distraction in the classroom.

Security and Dress Codes

Some students stay home or skip classes because they do not feel safe at school. Of the school districts that responded to a 1993 survey, 41 percent used dress codes as a strategy to deal with school violence (Volokh & Snell, 1998). Workman and Freeburg (2006) examined student handbooks for evidence that dress codes are used to deal with the physical and psychological security of students. Content analysis of 80 online secondary school handbooks revealed 84 percent related dress codes to safety—over twice the percentage found a decade earlier (National School Boards Association, 1993).

Physical security was defined as freedom from harm to the bodily self (Workman & Freeburg, 2006). Clothing items frequently related to physical safety were headwear, outerwear, jewelry/accessories, and footwear. Headwear was defined as anything on or around the head and included hats, caps, bandanas, picks, combs, headbands, masks, hoods, hairnets, do-rags, visors, and hair curlers. Headwear potentially obscures identification of the wearer, interferes with the wearer's vision, or identifies a student as a gang member. Outerwear was defined as garments that are usually worn over indoor clothing for protection from outside elements (coats, jackets, scarves, gloves, and warm-ups) and was banned because of a potential for concealing forbidden items. Jewelry or other accessories with spikes, studs, or chains (including chains with fishhooks or handcuffs) were most likely banned because of their potential use as weapons. Students were required to wear some type of footwear on the basis of health, safety, or protection against injury, but footwear with wheels, rollers, and/or cleats was banned because of potential damage to school property. Other prohibited items included sunglasses, backpacks, excessively large or loose-fitting or ripped clothing, pierced body parts, and expensive personal items.

Psychological security was defined as freedom from perceived threats to personal well-being (Workman & Freeburg, 2006). **Personal well-being** refers to a frame of mind that reflects comfort with existing conditions. Prohibited items related to psychological safety were items that promoted products illegal to minors (tobacco, alcohol, and drugs), promoted sexual behavior, contained vulgar language, identified gang membership, or promoted violence.

DeMitchell (2002) stated that dress codes that prohibited items not legal for students to use or possess were consistent with the in loco parentis or common law view of the legal status of minors in the public school setting. Dress that promoted covert or overt sexual behavior (sexual innuendo, promiscuity, nudity, or behavior that was suggestive, off-color, obscene, lewd, indecent, or immoral) was frequently prohibited. Some brand names associated with promotion of sexual behavior were prohibited (Hooters, Playboy, Co-Ed Naked, Big Johnson, and Big Dogs). A legitimate concern of school officials is protection of students from exposure to sexually explicit, indecent, or lewd speech (DeMitchell, 2002). Dress with vulgar, objectionable, offensive, inappropriate, or profane writings or depictions was prohibited because it created a perceived threat to personal well-being.

Dress that was evidence of gang membership or affiliation was also prohibited. Gang symbols or signs can be overt (arrows or pitchforks shaved into the hair) or covert (wearing a certain combination of colors). Gang identifiers change constantly and lead school officials to be flexible and knowledgeable in what clothing items are prohibited. Dress that promoted violence was prohibited by many schools: it included camouflage clothing, dress that displayed or made reference to weapons, insubordination, or personal threats. School violence includes implied violence, brought about without the use of weapons (Volokh & Snell, 1998). Other prohibited items were dress that denigrated or expressed prejudice toward others, promoted intolerance, promoted cults or secret societies such as Satanism/Occultism, death or suicide, or disrespect of country, school, or religion.

Rationales for Dress Code Policies

While students are in school, school officials have a duty to ensure their safety due to the in loco parentis doctrine and the legal duty of school officials to comply with state and local school board regulations (Cohen, 2000). Within these limitations, school officials have the authority, then, to establish dress norms designed to promote student safety.

Crockett and Wallendorf (1998) noted that "school dress codes will likely force students to construct other, more subtle markers to distinguish and define themselves and their group affiliations" (p. 116). In an examination of media reports of school dress codes, the authors found three primary rationales for dress code policies: (a) prevention of gang-related violence, (b) prevention of competitive dressing and clothing theft, and (c) the imposition of discipline.

Recent school violence has often been based on group affiliation and "associated with students' adoption of particular, localized clothing styles" (Crockett & Wallendorf, 1998, p. 118). By assuming that particular clothing styles are visible indicators of gang membership, the media reports implicate gangs as the key link between particular clothing styles and violence. Reports in the media identified one problem with unrestricted choice of school clothing—when clothing is used to symbolize gang affiliation, it is a cue that can prompt violence between members of rival gangs. However, adolescents in general, not just gang members, prefer to dress like their peers or in similar styles (Chin, 1996). "Dressing alike is interpreted as a marker of gang activity when done by ethnic minority youth but not when done by majority youth" (Crockett & Wallendorf, 1998, p. 128).

Clothing symbols can denote either gang membership (colors) or status group membership (brands). In either case, clothing can be a symbol of group membership and identity. Advertising that links brand names with particular desired characteristics has been so successful that certain brand logos become cultural capital as symbols of group status and social exclusion (Crockett & Wallendorf, 1998).

A second problem with unrestricted choice of school clothing is violence associated with theft. Students who wear the most current fashions or popular brand names may become targets for theft. By eliminating status symbols, dress codes not only decrease theft but potentially delay or discourage the development of materialistic values. The moral presumption underlying this benefit of school dress codes is that refusal to engage in fashion consumption connotes "positive moral virtues such as seriousness of purpose, sensibility, and rational self-directedness" (Thompson & Haytko, 1997, p. 18).

Some restriction of children's consumer choice is considered appropriate because children are cognitively and emotionally immature. Children cannot legally purchase or consume some products (alcohol, tobacco, and firearms). Certain styles of clothing worn to school produce or encourage harmful social attitudes or behaviors such as alcohol or tobacco consumption or violence.

Noncompliance with Dress Code Policies

Some students resist dress code restrictions through exemptions, variable items, and boundary challenges (Crockett & Wallendorf, 1998). Schools with voluntary dress codes exempt students who do not wish to participate by allowing them to transfer to another school. As another means to resist dress restrictions, students may manipulate those aspects of appearance over which they are allowed some choice. By varying these items, students distinguish between statuses and groups. School dress codes are based on current symbols of group affiliation, but the symbols change. When certain symbols are prohibited by dress codes, the cultural categories and principles formerly encoded in those symbols shift to aspects of appearance over which students have discretion. "Footwear has been and will continue to be a major arena for displaying distinctions. Athletic footwear is a particularly salient marker of group or status identity because brands and styles are clearly identifiable as authentic at a glance" (p. 125).

In the type of noncompliance known as **boundary challenges,** a student is technically in violation of the dress code (Crockett & Wallendorf, 1998). However, the violation is so trivial that administrators may ignore it or consider it not worth the effort to initiate the disciplinary process. When large numbers of students participate in a boundary challenge at the same time, violations may be so plentiful and frequent that administrators cannot discipline all those who are in technical violation of the dress policy. For example, some students' shirts might come untucked from their slacks over the course of a school day. When other students intentionally pull their shirttails out, this form of resistance becomes even more obvious.

Although dress codes may be designed to eliminate gang identity in schools, gang members will probably switch to more subtle symbols of membership. "Dress is only one symbolic manifestation of the roots of a much deeper culture permeated by race, class, and gender distinctions that breed markedly high levels of violence" (Crockett & Wallendorf, 1998, p. 128).

GENDER NORMS

Gender is an ascribed status. A gender role represents behavior expected of males and females. Each gender role has associated rights (behaviors they can expect from others) as well as obligations (behaviors others expect from them). Gender roles include dress norms—that is, expected behavior regarding how males and females should look.

For a class assignment, students chose gender norms to violate and the authors did a content analysis of their choices (Nielsen, Walden, & Kunkel, 2000). The dress norms that women chose to violate included going shirtless in a sports contest, trying on and buying men's suits and ties, wearing a moustache, wearing men's cologne, wearing a football uniform, wearing a Rambo outfit or army fatigues, not shaving their legs and underarms, sitting with their legs apart, having and displaying a tattoo, appearing bald, and dressing as a priest. The dress norms that men chose to violate included trying on, wearing, buying women's clothing and/or women's shoes in public; wearing makeup, lipstick, and/or having a makeover; shaving their body hair; coloring or curling their hair; wearing a flower in their hair; putting on and wearing fake fingernails; wearing fingernail polish; having a manicure; wearing earrings; doing needlepoint, crocheting, or knitting in public; carrying a purse; wearing pink shirts; having a pedicure; showing an interest in fashion; primping their hair; wearing an apron and hairnet; trying on and wearing women's underwear, halter top, nightgown or bathing suit; and performing in a male beauty pageant. The difference in the length of the two lists is noteworthy. The authors concluded that unquestioned normative expectations and proscriptions that exist in U.S. culture become obvious when traditional gender norms are violated.

Suitor and Carter (1999) measured adolescent gender norms by asking students to list five ways in which males or females could gain prestige in the high school they attended. The authors reasoned that adolescents acquire prestige by conforming to group norms; therefore, the means of acquiring prestige should indicate the operative group norms. The most common ways to gain prestige were the same for males and females: grades, sports, appearance, sociability, and popularity. Sports predominated as a way to gain prestige for males. For females, prestige could be attained about equally with grades, appearance, sports, and sociability. Clothes ranked sixth as an avenue of prestige for females and eighth for males.

Suitor and Reavis (1995) measured changes in adolescent gender norms in the 1980s. In both the early and late 1980s, boys gained prestige through sports, grades, access to cars, sociability, popularity, physical attractiveness, and participation in school activities. During the same time period, girls gained prestige through physical attractiveness, sociability, grades, popularity, clothes, participation in school activities, and cheerleading. The relative importance of these avenues to prestige differed for males and females. The authors concluded that there was little change in adolescent gender norms during the decade of the 1980s. Results from Suitor and Reavis agreed with the results of Eckert (1989), who found that physical appearance and dress were more important for adolescent females' than males' social status.

BODY MODIFICATION NORMS

Body modifications are alterations to inherent parts of the body, such as the muscular/skeletal system, hair, skin, breath, teeth, or nails. Body modifications can relate to all five senses and can be temporary, semipermanent, or permanent (Eicher, Evenson, & Lutz, 2000) (Figure 4.6).

FIGURE 4.6 NORMS RELATED TO TATTOOS ARE CHANGING, WORKPLACE DRESS CODES MAY REQUIRE THAT EMPLOYEES WITH LARGE, VISIBLE TATTOOS WEAR CLOTHING THAT COVERS THESE BODY MODIFICATIONS.

One source for information about body modification norms is the newspaper advice column. Freeburg and Workman (in press) analyzed 223 letters related to body modifications appearing in syndicated advice columns. Thirty-five possible body modification norms were identified. The norms were assumed to apply within cultural (U.S.) and historical (early 1990s) contexts and across social contexts.

In a second study, Freeburg and Workman identified the minimal proportion of agreement needed to confirm or refute as a norm a statement about how people should or should not look under given circumstances. Although most definitions of a norm depict it as a shared expectation, it is not realistic to expect 100 percent agreement (Gibbs, 1981).

A questionnaire contained demographic questions (age, gender, ethnicity, marital status, and a nine-point social class scale from lower-lower to upper-upper), a definition of norms, the context for the judgments, and the 35 statements. Sixteen statements were confirmed as norms (Table 4.3). The statement "Everyone should take a daily bath or shower, change underwear daily, and use an underarm deodorant" received the greatest propor-

- People should not expose sexual parts of the body in public.
- Women should shave their body hair.
- People should not judge other people by their outward appearance; it's what is on the inside that counts.
- Women should not attempt to imitate the body structure of men.
- Nudity in the privacy of your home is acceptable but should be kept secret.
- Women should not have facial hair.
- Men should have body hair.
- Women should not have body hair.
- Men should not attempt to imitate the body structure of women.
- Women should not be obsessive about cosmetics use.
- Everyone should take a daily bath or shower, change underwear daily, and use an underarm deodorant.
- People should not have bad breath (halitosis).
- A person should have a full set of well-cared-for teeth.
- Children should not attempt to imitate the body structure of adults.
- Men should avoid apparel that immodestly exposes the body.
- Men should enjoy looking at naked women.

tion of agreement (94 percent Yes). The statement "Men should have body hair" was confirmed with the smallest proportion of agreement (61 percent Yes).

Not one statement was endorsed by 100 percent of the participants, providing support for the notion that it is unrealistic to expect 100 percent agreement. Based on the results, the authors concluded that at least 60 percent must agree with a statement for it to be considered a norm. Thirteen statements were refuted as norms (Table 4.4). Two statements, "Old people should have gray hair" and "People should be tanned," were refuted as norms with the greatest proportion of disagreement (78 percent No). The statement "Children should not be concerned about their hair" was refuted with the smallest proportion of disagreement (64 percent No).

Participants were undecided about six of the previously identified statements (Table 4.5). The six statements on which participants were undecided meant that approximately equal numbers agreed and disagreed with the statement.

Because norms may be specific to subgroups in the population and not be shared by society as a whole, the statements on which participants were

TABLE 4.4 STATEMENTS REFUTED AS NORMS

- Men and boys should not be concerned about their hair.
- Children should not be concerned about their hair.
- Women should not have long decorated fingernails.
- People should be slim.
- Men should be tall.
- Women should be naturally endowed with full breasts.
- Stigmatizing features (e.g., scars, amputated limbs) should be corrected or concealed whenever possible.
- Women should not enjoy looking at naked men.
- Women should have long hair.
- Women should treat their hair as a "crown of glory."
- Old people should have gray hair.
- People should not be tattooed.
- People should be tanned.

TABLE 4.5 STATEMENTS ABOUT WHICH PARTICIPANTS WERE UNDECIDED

- Skin should be smooth, clear, and free of blemishes.
- A woman should be shorter than the man who accompanies her.
- Women should avoid apparel that immodestly exposes the body.
- Men should have short hair.
- Body structure should not be altered through artificial means.
- People should have a flat abdomen.

undecided were analyzed by subgroup. Subgroups based on sex, age, ethnicity, marital status, and social class differed in their expectations for appearance. For example, single participants and participants age 30 or younger confirmed that "skin should be smooth, clear, and free of blemishes."

GROUP NORMS

One function of a group is to control the behavior of members through its own normative standards. Each group creates normative standards about what group members should think (attitudes, opinions), what they should say (slang, nicknames), how they should act (walk, stand), and how they should dress (expensive jewelry, brand-name sneakers). Members must be willing to yield to group control and give up some individual choice. The continued existence of a group depends on conformity of its members.

Primary Groups: Sororities

Recall that members of primary groups, such as sororities, interact regularly face-to-face, know one another well, and seek out one another for social interaction. Arthur's (1997) qualitative study was based on the notion that people who are insecure in performing a social role use clothing to give them confidence. Arthur observed that sorority pledges used dress to validate their social role as a sorority member. The transition from the status of nonmember to pledge was difficult both for pledges undergoing the transition and for members of the sorority. Visual symbols were used to express a **personal identity** (attributes assigned to the self) because pledges wanted to look like members. Rites of passage that involved clothing helped ease the transition from one status to another. Recall that a rite of passage is a public ceremony used when a person's status changes.

Idealized images of the *sorority girl look* included visible Greek letters and expensive dress (clothing, shoes, perfume, or accessories). New members tended to spend their first few years conforming to these appearance norms as a way to show kinship with their sorority sisters and to express their social identity as sorority members. A **social identity** refers to attributes assigned to others in order to categorize them as members of a social group (a sorority). Because of the pain involved, tattoos symbolized a heightened commitment to the organization. In one sorority, a number of members had ankle tattoos of their sorority symbol (an unusual location because of the pain involved in tattooing the lower leg).

Peer Groups

Members of peer groups share similarities in age, education, social class, or interests. Some peer group dress norms may not be clear until the norms are compared with those of other groups. Even within a peer group, knowing what not to wear is just as important as knowing what to wear. Freitas, Kaiser, Chandler, Hall, Kim, and Hammidi (1997) examined everyday conversations about dress in order to explain the concept of identity (who one is) versus nonidentity (who one is not). University students were asked two questions: What is your least favorite clothing item? What groups do you intentionally avoid dressing like? The students interviewed avoided wearing styles typical of older adults, such as their parents. Looking older was associated with being out-of-date or behind the times. Some students avoided dressing like certain social groups, such as punk rockers, sorority members, rich people, girls who hang out in bars, bimbos, Republicans, white people, black people, and hippies. Some students were concerned with gender norms, for example, a male remarked that he did not want people to think he was gay so he avoided wearing an earring. Other students did not want to dress in something too feminine (males) or too masculine (females). The authors concluded that appearance management is one social force that can be used to adapt to changing social identities.

BODY NORMS AND THE "SIZED" BODY

A **sized body** refers to quantifying the physical size of the body via a numerical clothing size. Traditionally, women's clothing is sized numerically (e.g., Misses sizes 4–18; Juniors sizes 1–15). Numerical clothing sizes provide the means for the physical boundaries of the body to be quantified and its size revealed. Just as the Body Mass Index (BMI) establishes norms for women's bodies according to height and weight ratios, clothing sizing establishes norms for women's bodies according to a numerical size (Figure 4.7).

FIGURE 4.7 CLOTHING SIZING ESTABLISHES NORMS FOR WOMEN BY QUANTIFYING THE PHYSICAL BODY BY NUMERICAL SIZE. BUT SIZE, AS THIS CARTOON SHOWS, CAN BE MANIPULATED TO ALLOW WOMEN TO FEEL THEY ARE FOLLOWING DRESS NORMS.

Studies of Women's Emotions and Body Size

Colls (2004) conducted 20 group interviews and 8 individual interviews and accompanied eight women while they shopped to investigate women's emotions about the sized body. Although sizing can be used to quantify a body, this does not account for how women *feel* their own size, which may occur in the split second of a glance in a mirror or a reflection in a department store window. Women can see their reflection and feel different sizes at different points in time. A woman may connect the numerical sizing of clothes and her feelings about herself, and therefore her bodily size, either negatively or positively. Colls wondered what it felt like to "be a size." "The connotations of wearing an extra large T-shirt means that she feels her size in a way that places her body in need of reduction" (Colls, 2006, p. 536).

In addition to how women feel about their size, the boundaries of a woman's body actually do change when she loses or gains weight. The associated change in numerical sizing enables women to link past and present (Colls, 2004). For example, one woman remembered being a size 10 on her wedding day, compared with her current larger size resulting from weight gain. When other people stare at her body, a bigger woman will feel her size more acutely. However, wearing the right clothes can be a means of feeling normal by covering up the body shape and visually reducing the body boundaries; the result is she may escape the notice of other people (Colls, 2006). The type of clothes a bigger woman considers suitable for her body may be based on the notion that big bodies should be covered up.

Female consumers can attempt to conform to or resist the bodily norms of a culture (Colls, 2004). However, women are encouraged by mass media to look for flaws in themselves compared to the ideal norms of beauty and bodily size. Adam (2001, p. 41) noted that big women "by not conforming to an expectation of slenderness are in the margins of femininity." Big women can conform to experts' suggestions about what to wear, or they can choose to make their own rules about what a big body should and can wear (Colls, 2006). Colls concluded that the way bigger women dress indicates they are outside the norms of fashionable clothing.

Body Measurements and Sizes

What measurements do sizes represent? Researchers looked at body measurement specifications for fit models gleaned from advertisements in *Women's Wear Daily* and *California Apparel News* (Workman & Lentz, 2000). **Fit models** are models used by women's apparel manufacturers to fit and size their styles. In choosing a fit model to establish a company fit, a manufacturer uses body measurements, or key dimensions, including height, bust, waist, and hip measurements. "Fit, also known as cut, refers to the way a garment conforms to or differs from the body. The company fit allows a company to differentiate its products from competitors' products. For this reason, the same size garments from different companies are not likely to have the same fit" (p. 252).

Measurements of dress forms (used by designers for creating styles) also vary by manufacturer. For example, Workman and Lentz (2000) found that a size 8 dress form had an average bust measurement of 35.5 inches, waist 26.43 inches, and hips 36.86 inches, but the measurements varied (34.5 to 36.5 inches for bust, 25 to 27.5 inches for waist, and 36 to 38.5 inches for hips). Likewise, a size 10 dress form had an average bust measurement of 36.2 inches (range 35.5 to 36.5 inches), waist 27 inches (range 26 to 27.5 inches), hips 37.25 inches (range 37 to 37.5 inches).

Measurements for the 1997 size 8 fit models were: Height (average = 67.28 inches; range = 65 to 68 inches); Bust (average = 36.11 inches; range = 35.5 to 37 inches); Waist (average = 27.72 inches; range = 27 to 28 inches); and Hips (average = 37.89 inches; range = 37 to 38.5 inches). So the answer to the question "What measurements do sizes represent?" is: It depends on the manufacturer. Workman and Lentz (2000) concluded that because all size 10 measurements were encompassed within the size 8 ranges, not only was an 8 an 8 but an 8 was also a 10. The prototype garments developed from using these measurements are the basis for master production patterns from which all other sizes in that style are derived (Price & Zamkoff, 1996). The master production pattern is upgraded, downgraded, or both to obtain all sizes in the desired size range. Thus, measurements for all sizes are ultimately dependent on the measurements for the prototype size.

Vanity Sizing

As Colls (2004) noted and Workman and Lentz (2000) have shown, clothing sizing is inconsistent, making women uncertain about what size they are. Adding to the uncertainty is a practice called **vanity sizing,** in which manufacturers label garments one size smaller (Frings, 1999). Vanity sizing is designed to appeal to a customer's psychological need to feel slim. For example, a woman may feel big, and therefore upset, when a pair of size 14 slacks does not fit but previously a size 12 fit (Colls, 2004). An awareness of the inconsistency of clothing sizing allows the woman to feel all right about the size 14 slacks being too small. Women know the *real* and *unreal* sizing of their own bodies and recognize their *real* numerical size.

A woman's body can *cheat* the numerical indicators by fitting into a size that is not really hers. Numerical sizing labels are not just numbers on a hang-tag (a small paper or plastic slip attached to an item being sold that gives information about the item). Women are aware of which stores and/or brands have a generous cut so they can fit into a smaller size than they really are. Women use the inconsistency of sizing to help them to feel better about their size. Being able to buy a smaller size boosts a woman's morale (Colls, 2004). When a woman shops in large-size specialty stores, she may be able to wear a size labeled *small* (Colls, 2006).

Plus-Size Clothing

There are limited choices for large-size women when they shop for clothes (Colls, 2004). Available clothing is often baggy, unfashionable, and designed to cover up the body rather than reveal its physical form. Words used to describe *plus-size* clothing included *fat sacks*, *tents*, and *camouflage wear*. Adam (2001) commented that plus-size clothing is "very conformist and conventional, containing those bodies that threaten to break out" (pp. 50–51). Plus-size women may try to hide their body size by wearing inconspicuous clothing so nobody will notice.

But sixty percent of U.S. women wear plus-size garments (sizes 14–32). A spokesperson for a plus-size line commented: "The whole plus-size mentality and all the taboos have changed considerably. The product offered now is more fashionable and contemporary, with better quality fabrications" ("Personality Plus," 2002, p. 2). From a survey research study, Wu and Workman (1993) reported 20 norms associated with clothing for large-size women. Workman and Studak (2005) also used a quantitative survey research method to answer the research question "Do the same norms exist about plus-size clothing in 2004 as in 1993?" Using a 36-item questionnaire developed by Wu and Workman, students rated their agreement with each item on seven-point scales.

Eighteen of the 20 norms found in the 1993 study were also found in 2004. Norms stated negatively included: large-size women should not wear bikinis, halter tops, stretch pants, mini skirts, shiny fabrics, clingy knit fabrics, low-cut dresses, waist-length jackets, horizontal stripes, or anything with ruffles. Norms stated positively included: large-size women should wear overblouses or tunics, dark colors, cool colors, pleated skirts, full skirts, vertical stripes,

FIGURE 4.8
LARGE WOMEN CAN ALSO LOOK
ATTRACTIVE AND STYLISH AND
NEED NOT WEAR STEREOTYPICAL
CLOTHING.

and jackets that are longer than hip-length and should dress to minimize their size (Figure 4.8).

Some norms had not changed since 1993 (large-size women should not wear mini skirts); other norms had relaxed slightly (large-size women should not wear bikinis); other norms had strengthened (large-size women should not wear stretch pants). Since 1993 the norms that large-size women should not wear clothing that reveals or visually enlarges the body had not changed. The findings of Workman and Studak (2005) confirmed the findings of Colls (2004).

SUMMARY

Research about dress norms is diverse and its relationship to the process of social control is complex. Most of the research articles do not explicitly acknowledge the process of social control, but the process is implicit in the description of the norms. Recall that the process of social control begins with a norm (makeup at work), the norm is violated (a woman refuses to wear makeup at work), the violation is recognized (by her supervisor), the violation is reported (the supervisor speaks with the woman regarding her noncompliance), sanctions are applied (the woman is reprimanded), and finally the sanction is enforced (the woman is fired if she does not comply after being reprimanded).

KEY TERMS AND CONCEPTS

aesthetic skills

boundary challenges

cultural capital

fit models

hard skills

internalized appearance norms

knowledge

lookism

personal identity

personal well-being

physical security

psychological security

sized body

social identity

social skills

soft skills

technical skills

vanity sizing

workplace culture

SUGGESTED READINGS

1. Brandt, L. J. (2003). On the value of an old dress code in the new millennium. *Archives of Internal Medicine, 163,* 1277–1281.

2. Freitas, A., Kaiser, S., Chandler, J., Hall, C., Kim, J., & Hammidi, T. (1997). Appearance management as border construction: Least favorite clothing, group distancing, and identity . . . not! *Sociological Inquiry, 67*(3), 323–335.

3. Workman, J. E., & Freeburg, E. W. (1996b). The newspaper advice column as regulatory device for normative standards of dress. In C. M. Ladisch (Ed.), *Proceedings of the International Textile and Apparel Association, Inc.* (p. 55). Monument, CO: ITAA.

Research Activity 4.1: *Literature Analysis*

Purpose: To analyze research literature related to dress norms, identifying the purpose, research method, and results.

Procedure:

1. Describe the characteristics of a research article.

2. Use the Google Scholar (http://scholar.google.com/) search engine or an academic database (EBSCO, ERIC, SocIndex) to locate one research article related to dress norms. For example, you might use the key words *dress norms* or *appearance standards* to search for a research article.

3. Print a copy of the research article.

4. Highlight and label the purpose of the study, the research method used, the results of the study related to its purpose, and the dress norm(s) studied.

5. Submit your work to your instructor.

Research Activity 4.2: *Occupational Search on the O*Net*

Purpose: To investigate workplace skill requirements for jobs in the fashion industry.

Procedure:

1. Review the definitions of workplace skills, hard skills, and soft skills.

2. Log on to O*Net Online (http://online.onetcenter.org/).

3. Select (click on) "Find Occupations" and insert a fashion industry job key word in the Quick Search window, for example, *fashion merchandising* or *fashion design*.

4. Review and select (click on) one of the occupations matching your key word search.

5. Print the Summary Report for the occupation you selected.

6. Highlight and label the hard skills and soft skills within the Summary Report.

7. Summarize your findings and submit them to your instructor.

Chapter Five

VIOLATION OF NORMS

FROM THE HEADLINES

A young man learned an important lesson about what is and what is not proper attire for a court proceeding. The man showed up for a court hearing wearing a T-shirt that had graphic text on the front. According to the judge, "We had a busy setting Tuesday afternoon, probably a dozen or more cases, and this guy shows up for court with this obscene shirt on with bright yellow writing on the front. We had a lady deputy circuit clerk, a lady court reporter and a very crowded courtroom and he walks in wearing a shirt like that. It was inappropriate, to say the least." The man tried to make a joke out of it but the judge considered the shirt openly contemptuous and stated the man should have known better. The judge commented that people think they can show up in court wearing anything, for example, tank tops and shorts. "It says on the summons that proper attire is required" (p. A2).

Source: Muir, J. (2003a, June 12). Judge dresses down man over T-shirt.
Southern Illinoisan, pp. A1–A2.

The incident described in this excerpt from a newspaper column illustrates a blatant norm violation and the consequences of that violation. The T-shirt with an obscene slogan violated the dress norms for a court appearance. The man thought the slogan was humorous, but the judge thought the man should have known better. Why did the man wear the T-shirt to court? What reason(s) might have motivated him? Are there situations where wearing an obscene T-shirt would not be considered a norm violation? Is there a temporal incompatibility between the statuses of the young man and the judge? Why or why not? After reading this chapter, you will be better able to explain the reasons for violations of norms and why norm violations are sometimes considered threatening.

Norm violations are the second step in a process of social control (Figure 5.1). In this chapter[1] we will identify reasons for violations of dress norms and

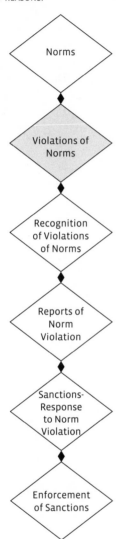

FIGURE 5.1 THE SECOND STEP IN THE PROCESS OF SOCIAL CONTROL INVOLVES VIOLATION OF NORMS. PEOPLE VIOLATE DRESS NORMS FOR A VARIETY OF REASONS.

Norms

Violations of Norms

Recognition of Violations of Norms

Reports of Norm Violation

Sanctions-Response to Norm Violation

Enforcement of Sanctions

examine how norm violations differ. The social control process ensures appropriate degrees of conformity to dress norms believed to be necessary for an orderly society. However, the process is imperfect and violations of norms occur for a variety of reasons: culture change, location, transmission, values and motives, physical conditions, environmental conditions, demands on resources, temporal incompatibilities between statuses, the normative system itself, and internalization. We'll discuss each in turn.

QUESTIONS TO ANSWER AS YOU READ

1. Why are dress norms violated?
2. What are some specific examples of dress norm violations?
3. How can dress norm violations vary?

DEVIANCE AND SOCIAL CONTROL

Identifying norms is the first step in examining the process of social control, because norms are standards against which individuals measure violations. Norm violation is based on the existence of societal or group norms from which an individual's behavior can deviate. Recall from Chapter 1 that deviant behavior is any behavior, belief, or condition that violates cultural norms. For several reasons, deviant behavior is dysfunctional, that is, it fails to perform the function that is normally expected (Tischler, 2004). It threatens the social order by making social life difficult and unpredictable. It causes uncertainty about society's norms and values. It undermines trust in the idea that people will behave according to certain rules of conduct. Finally, it diverts valuable resources in order to control the deviant behavior. A norm violation can serve a useful function when it teaches normal behavior by providing an example of deviance.

When deviant behavior goes beyond a limit tolerated by a society or group, the process of social control begins. Deviant behavior likely to exceed a tolerable limit includes violation of dress norms appropriate for specific situations. The man who wore an obscene T-shirt to court exceeded the tolerable limit and consequently was sentenced to seven days in jail for contempt of court.

TABLE 5.1 REASONS FOR VIOLATION OF NORMS

REASON	DESCRIPTION
Culture change	Modification of norms at different periods of time
Location	Geographical locality
Transmission of norms	Diffusion of information
Values and motives	Principles and motivation underlying actions
Physical conditions	Bodily state
Environmental conditions	Ecological state
Demands on resources	Requirements for time, facilities, finances, or action
Temporal incompatibilities	Relating to time as a quality that renders something incompatible with something else (i.e., statuses)
The normative system itself	The combination of related norms organized into a complex whole
Internalization	Adoption of others' attitudes, beliefs, and values, either consciously or unconsciously

There are at least ten reasons for norm violations. These reasons include culture change, location, transmission, values and motives, physical conditions, environmental conditions, demands on resources, temporal incompatibilities between statuses, the normative system itself, and internalization (Blake & Davis, 1964; Gibbs, 1981; Schwartz & Ewald, 1968; Smelser, 1973; Workman & Freeburg, 2000b) (Table 5.1).

CULTURE CHANGE

One of the characteristics of culture is that it changes. **Culture change** refers to the modification of norms at different periods of time. What is a violation of a dress norm at one period in time may be conformity at another period in time. Dress norms are modified as society changes. Remember that norms can be strengthened (increased in power or force), supplanted (replaced with something newer or more relevant), or undermined (weakened by removing or gradually diminishing the foundation for the norm). For example, wearing casual dress to church services may be a reflection of a general trend toward a more casual lifestyle in U.S. society (West, 2006). However, there is controversy over appropriate dress for church. "Whether it's because societal norms have changed or simply because some churchgoers can't afford nicer clothes, the term 'Sunday best' . . . now refers less to your attire and more to your state of mind and heart" (¶ 4). Those who support dressing up for church believe it is a sign of respect and an acknowledgment that church is a special environment. Those who support casual dress for church believe it will encourage people to attend services and that people should not judge others by their outward appearance. They question the motives of those who dress up for church—are they dressing to show respect or are they dressing to impress other parishioners? Most churches have issues with immodest clothing, which can be a distraction. Increasingly casual dress at weddings and funerals is an outgrowth of casual dress at church.

Another example of culture change and its effect on norm violation relates to males wearing earrings. Historically, earrings on males were associated with pirates, gypsies, and sailors. During the time period from 1975 to 1990 the cultural meaning of males wearing earrings changed (Nielsen, Walden, & Kunkel, 2000). In the 1970s, one or two earrings worn by a male was considered a symbol for homosexuality. In the 1980s, it was not uncommon for straight men to wear an earring in the left ear (to help people remember the meaning of an earring in the left or right ear, a phrase was coined—"Left is right and right is wrong"). In the 1990s, the meaning attached to males wearing earrings was ambiguous, although it was still unusual for straight men to wear earrings in both ears. Violation of dress norms must therefore be considered within a specific but constantly changing cultural context (Figure 5.2).

"Sorry...I just can't marry a man who wears prettier earrings than I do."

FIGURE 5.2 CULTURE CHANGE IS THE MODIFICATION OF NORMS AT DIFFERENT PERIODS OF TIME. IN THE 1990S, THE MEANING ATTACHED TO MALES WEARING EARRINGS WAS AMBIGUOUS.

LOCATION

Location refers to a geographical locality. Different parts of the country have local norms that apply to dress.

Regional Norms

In New York City, businessmen are expected to wear dark business suits, conservative ties, and dress shoes with dark socks ("Etiquette and Local Customs in New York City," 2006). White socks are worn only with sneakers and are reserved for playing sports. The New York City Etiquette Guide also advises that businesswomen wear business suits or conservative dresses, comfortable dress shoes with moderate heels, and jewelry. At upscale New York restaurants, a tie and jacket are usually required; sneakers, shorts, and T-shirts are never acceptable.

Contrast that advice with the description of a business suit in Honolulu, Hawaii: "In Hawaii a business suit is a tucked-in aloha shirt, and there is no shortage of executives hurrying (admittedly in Hawaiian fashion, which is a stroll) along city streets, briefcase in hand and bright, flower-splashed shirt tucked in" (Loomis, 1988, ¶ 1). Many tourists buy aloha shirts. However, what seemed right to wear on vacation in Hawaii apparently shows a lack of taste or judgment in aesthetic matters back home. "People realized they'd be a laughing stock if they wore them on the mainland so they put their shirts in the closet and there they stayed for years, in vintage condition" (¶ 8).

There are fashions associated with certain regions of the country. "Who says Central Florida's all flip-flops and Hawaiian shirts?" (Wheatt, 2006, p. 44). The head of a trend, color, and forecasting division of The Doneger Group (a New York-based company that consults for retailers and designers all over the world) was asked how to look New York-chic when you live in Florida. He replied: "I think all the trends are applicable in warm-weather climates, but obviously it has to be comfortable and practical" (p. 44). "I think the way to do it is to think about the season's color, because you can wear very light-weight fabrics in the fashionable colors of fall and look like you've changed seasons without having to suffer" (p. 44).

Tourist Dress

Tourists who travel abroad sometimes dress like slobs bound for the local mall—baggy shorts, stretched out T-shirts, and sandals (Borcover, 2006). The image is reminiscent of the sculptor Duane Hanson's lifelike *Tourists II*. The sculpture depicts an overweight middle-aged couple; he is wearing a loud Hawaiian shirt, baggy Bermuda shorts, athletic shoes with Velcro fastening and white socks; she is wearing a pair of red slacks, a loose blue and white striped polo shirt and flip-flops; both are carrying cameras and tote bags. Security specialists advise U.S. citizens traveling abroad to blend in with the locals. "Wearing faux athletic department T-shirts, cargo pants, fanny packs and flip-flops in foreign capitals is like wearing a bulls-eye on your back"

(Borcover, 2006, ¶ 3). It is easy for pickpockets and scam artists to spot tourists from the way they are dressed.

TRANSMISSION OF NORMS

All societies and social groups transmit norms to incoming generations. Recall from Chapter 1 that both material and nonmaterial culture are transmitted by members of a society through the process of communication. But not everybody receives the same training and social modeling of appropriate dress and information about the consequences of inappropriate dress.

Parenting Styles

The parenting styles of some adults are not effective for transmitting societal norms to their children. The style called **laissez-faire** (the practice of letting children do as they wish with no interference) is an inadequate system for socializing children. Parents need to set boundaries and to communicate with their children, not as friends, but as sources of valuable information (Rowbotham, 2002). The combined socializing influences of images portrayed via the media and the marketing of the fashion industry adds to the problem of socialization by sexualizing young children in the way they look and dress.

Socialization within a particular culture results in the transmission of knowledge about dress norms. However, there is a difference in the extent to which children receive normative transmissions. Children must be taught to dress appropriately, and it is the parents' job to teach them and to set a good example. Parents must begin the training process by doing a task for their children (such as tying their shoes), talking about the importance of the task, and then teaching children how to do the task for themselves. Some parents do not expend the time and energy to train and/or correct their children's behavior.

Gender Socialization

The extent of transmission can affect norm violation. In the United States, boys are socialized differently than girls with regard to dress norms. Traditionally, males have been allowed, indeed encouraged, to be oblivious to rules of dress. Thus, men are less knowledgeable about dress norms and, as a result, more likely to violate them than women. Masculinity has traditionally been defined by what it is not—not feminine, including not being effeminate in physical appearance or mannerisms. **Effeminate** refers to a male who is similar to or imitates the behavior, appearance, or speech traditionally associated with females. Effeminate men may be perceived negatively because they violate traditional gender role stereotypes.

Changes in cultural views of masculinity have resulted, for some men, in less avoidance of femininity and more acceptance of customs and attitudes once reserved for women. The term *metrosexual* was coined by a British journalist in 1994 (Simpson, 2002) to describe an urban male who has a strong aesthetic sense and spends a substantial amount of time and money on his appearance ("Metrosexual," 2007). Metrosexual men display feminized masculine aesthetics (such as color coordination), good grooming (such as exfoliation), and a stylized appearance. They are concerned with style and prettiness (modern manifestation of a nineteenth-century dandy) and distaste for macho masculinity (Figure 5.3).

FIGURE 5.3
METROSEXUAL MEN DISPLAY GOOD GROOMING, AND A STYLIZED APPEARANCE.

Social Position

Individuals in various social positions (age, gender, social class) and contexts (historical, social, cultural) understand and interpret norms differently. Although cultural categories change over time, some individuals' stereotypes remain the same—they have a mental file folder for each cultural category in which they file dress cues. For example, *white trash* has been considered to be a derogatory label with racist undertones that denotes rural poverty and a lack of education (Mui, 2006). The term white trash is still used as a negative comment in many communities. However, the term is now being marketed as a symbol representative of the average American. The fashion look is variously called white trash chic, redneck couture, poor chic, blue-collar vogue, or trailer park chic. Examples of the trend include trucker hats, big belt buckles, flip-flops, and tasteless, loud, tacky, cheap T-shirts.

From punk to grunge to hip-hop to trailer park chic, mainstream fashion consumers have a long history of seeking innovative designs from lower social classes. A professor of sociology described the white trash movement as a **frame transformation** (Reed, 2006), a process whereby groups take a negative concept like white trash and try to turn it into something positive in order to create a sense of belonging and pride (Figure 5.4). According to the

FIGURE 5.4 HIPPIE CHIC
IS ONE EXAMPLE OF FRAME
TRANSFORMATION, ILLUSTRATED
BY BRITISH SINGER JOSS STONE.

sociologist, the frame transformation may work for a time, but over the long term, the concept usually remains an insult.

Sanctions and Conflicting Signals

Examples of sanctions against people who have not conformed may reinforce the warnings of consequences of norm violation; however, not everyone is exposed equally to the examples (Workman & Freeburg, 2000b, p. 92). In the United States, newspapers and other mass media report violations and sanctions daily in news stories, cartoons, comic strips, human interest stories, and advice columns. For example, a newspaper article reported on students who violated a school's dress code (A. Garza, 2006). Students who wore clothing in colors prohibited by the school's dress code policy (black, blue, and red) were given an opportunity to change. Those who refused were suspended.

In complex societies such as the United States, conflict between agencies of socialization is unavoidable (Shepard, 2005). The school and the family sometimes have contradictory purposes, as evidenced when parents support and even encourage their children to sue the school over sanctions for dress code violations ("6th Cir. Upholds," 2005). A student and her father sued a school district claiming that the dress code prevented self-expression and parental control. The 6th Circuit noted that the list of fundamental rights "does not include the wearing of dungarees" (¶ 13). According to the decision handed down by the court, "The First Amendment does not protect such vague and attenuated notions of expression—namely, self-expression through any and all clothing that a 12-year-old may wish to wear on a given day" (¶ 8). The court decided that the school district's dress code did not prevent the student from expressing herself, and it did not interfere with the father's right to control his daughter's dress.

Parents may blame the **mass media** for promoting values contrary to those they have taught their children regarding appearance, behavior, and/or possessions. Societal expectations are influenced by multimedia lifestyles: "Television and print advertisements, plus the focus on teen celebrity behavior, can lead to unrealistic personal expectations" (Awosika, 2006, p. E1). The physical and emotional changes that occur during adolescence make adolescents particularly vulnerable to media messages in spite of parental guidance.

Attachments to significant others (parents, teachers, peers) help children accept norms and values linked to a conventional lifestyle. "Without these attachments and acceptance of conventional norms, the opinions of other people do not matter and the individual is free to violate norms without fear of social disapproval" (Tischler, 2004, p. 150). Violation of norms is discouraged by the anticipated disapproval of others. Parents who do not properly transmit society's norms to their children raise children who are not influenced by the anticipated disapproval of others. For some individuals, the socialization process was not what it should have been—they did not learn to function effectively according to society's norms and values.

For example, in past generations, self-professed sissy boys and tomboy girls were forced to conform because their behavior was believed to be a product of dysfunctional homes. "Children who did not conform to gender norms in their clothing or behavior and identified intensely with the opposite sex were steered to psychoanalysis or behavior modification" (P. L. Brown, 2006, ¶ 1). Now, some young parents, educators, and mental health professionals are supporting children as young as five who display tendencies to dress like the other sex. However, a first-grade teacher recalled that other teachers were upset when a young boy arrived at school dressed in a skirt. Common reactions were "This is not normal [and] It's the parents' fault" (¶ 6). One five-year-old boy, who strongly identified as a girl, asked to be called *she* and to wear pigtails and pink jumpers to school. The mother commented that she felt the insecure nature of the daily reality of her son's decision. "It's hard to convey the relentlessness of it, every social encounter, every time you go out to eat, every day feeling like a balance between your kid's self-esteem and protecting him from the hostile outside world" (¶ 13).

One psychologist maintained that because 80 percent grow out of this trans-gendered behavior, the correct approach is to help these children be more content in their biological gender until they are older and can determine their gender identity. Families are caught in an underlying force that runs in the opposite direction to the normative one. One mother said she drew the line on dress and tried to provide masculine activities for her six-year-old son, but worried about him becoming a social outcast. At one elementary school, an eight-year-old boy perceived as effeminate was thrown into a large trash bin by a group of boys. In response to the incident, the principal suggested the mother was to blame because she had not taught her son how to be tough enough.

Peer Groups

Some socialization takes place in secondary groups such as peer groups (Figure 5.5). Deliberate violation of conventional norms of dress may be one way for groups to distinguish themselves. Students may push the limits of a school's dress code as a way of expressing allegiance to a group. Recently, two different groups of students attended school; members of one group wore matching white bandanas and members of the other group wore black and gray clothes (Madden, 2006). Administrators asked each student to remove the

FIGURE 5.5 GROUPS OF HIGH SCHOOL STUDENTS MAY SEEK TO DISTINGUISH THEMSELVES THROUGH DELIBERATE VIOLATION OF CONVENTIONAL NORMS OF DRESS.

bandana and to not display colors, as these acts violated a dress code ban on gang-affiliated clothing. The students "with the white bandanas said that they had agreed ahead of time to wear them to school, just as they would agree to wear any number of things—types of shirts, skirts, color combinations—but that it was done in fun and meant nothing" (¶ 6).

The students who wore black and gray were male and female, lower and upper middle class, black, white, and mixed race. These students denied their dress choices were premeditated, denied they belonged to a gang, and said gray and black were merely color trends. One student explained the colors as an example of students trying things out in their cliques or groups. The bandanas and clothing were group markers, just like other symbolic dress choices such as members of the football team wearing their jerseys to school or members of a group who wear Carhartt brand pants.

VALUES AND MOTIVES

People with different values and motives interpret the legitimacy of norms in different situations and for different people. Have you ever heard someone say, "That rule doesn't apply to me" or "That rule doesn't apply in this situation?" Recall from Chapter 1 that values are broad cultural principles most people in a society consider desirable. A **motive** is that which causes an individual's action. Individuals face situations involving choice between personal and collective values. In New York, a Sikh transit authority employee protested a dress code requiring employees to wear an MTA logo on their turbans (Goldstein, 2006). The turbans are religious headwear and the employee believed the dress code violated his religious freedom. He "regularly flouts the dress code, pinning the logo to his blue turban only when a supervisor orders him to do so" (p. 4).

Body Modification

The social acceptability of certain body modifications is determined by culture. Body modifications such as using cosmetics, tanning, orthodontics, cosmetic surgery, body building, and dieting may be motivated by the desire to conform to a culture's ideal of beauty (S. Thomas, 2006). A contrasting motivation is to violate society's norms by engaging in extreme forms of body modification such as tongue slitting, ear shaping, skin implants, scarification, branding, piercings, and tattoos. For example, "ear lobe stretching is practiced in the punk scene and is often greeted with disapproval in the mainstream culture" (¶ 20). Indeed, punk styles were intended to violate conventional norms and offend members of the mainstream culture (P. W. Thomas, 2006). Likewise, part of the ideology of the Goth subculture is individual defiance of social norms (Hodkinson, 2002). Goth fashions reject mainstream values, emphasize freedom of expression, defy conventions, and challenge taboos by emphasizing transformation of the body, conscious eroticism, and otherness.

Rebellion and Conformity

A search for novelty, uniqueness, individualism, excitement, and a way to escape boredom may be motives that cause individuals to rebel against social norms by adopting new and innovative fashions. In particular, merchandise targeted to adolescents emphasizes novelty and individualism, such as sexually suggestive styles or T-shirts with questionable messages (Troller, 2006). "Although middle school is an environment where students may be doing the most to push the boundaries of what's acceptable, there are sometimes concerns at the elementary school level, and obvious examples of clothing are a clear distraction at the high school level, too" (p. A1). "As middle schoolers, it's their job to push the limits, but it's our job, gently but sternly to push back," one principal commented (p. A1).

Conversely, conformity to current fashion norms may satisfy an individual's need for gaining the friendship and companionship of others while reducing the fear of ridicule or social disapproval. Conformity to fashion norms may be a way to maintain or increase a feeling of personal security. For example, adolescents want to be popular and think having the right clothes will help them become part of a certain popular group. To accomplish this, some adolescents insist on wearing clothing with certain brand labels or from certain stores such as Abercrombie & Fitch and American Eagle Outfitters (Awosika, 2006).

According to the normative socialization theory, people modify their behaviors in response to the rewards and punishments their actions produce. In a fairly traditional environment, individuals are rewarded for conformity, such as dressing in a conventional way. Nonconventional dress may be rewarded in a nontraditional environment, for example, a gang. A gang is a group of young people who socialize and may engage in antisocial and delinquent behavior. Norm violation is relative, however. Gang members who reject conventional cultural dress norms may conform routinely to a gang dress code (Figure 5.6).

Indeed, keeping up with constantly changing gang signals is a challenge for many school districts (Hsuan & Melton, 2006). One student was suspended for wearing knee socks because the "fashion statement too closely resembled the latest styles sported by local gang members" (p. B1). In some schools, items with religious or cultural meaning (such as rosaries) have been banned because gangs are appropriating the items for their own use. Gang members may be the first to adopt new styles, for example, baggy clothes or knee socks, but other students pick up on the trend and soon everyone is wearing baggy clothes and knee socks; in the process, the styles lose the ability to be a gang symbol.

The church and the adolescent peer group may hold incompatible values. For example, a Christian educator's homeschool group planned a prom for its adolescents that re-

FIGURE 5.6 THIS PICTURE SHOWS MEMBERS OF THE LOS ANGELES CRIPS DISPLAYING GANG SIGNS ALONG WITH THEIR DRESS.

flected the organization's morals and family values (Copeland, 2006). Instead of blaring hip-hop music, the prom featured folk dances, waltzes, and jigs. Instead of risqué styles, girls chose their floor- or tea-length dresses to comply with the dress code, to appeal to their individual sense of style, and to satisfy their parents' ideas of modesty and affordability. The dress code for the dance specified no strapless dresses so some girls bought ribbon or used extra fabric to create straps for their dresses. The whole family attended the formal dance: grandparents, parents, and siblings.

PHYSICAL CONDITIONS

A physical condition is a bodily state over which an individual has no control, such as age, body build, facial structure, or physical disability. Some physical conditions may result in an inability to comply with norms. "If an individual is old, has inherited a large bone structure, has facial features which are not symmetrical, or has a physical disability, he or she would be unable to achieve the normative demands to look young, slim, beautiful, and perfect, even if he/she wanted to" (Workman & Freeburg, 2000b, p. 93).

Standards of Beauty

People with symmetrical facial features are perceived as beautiful (Snead, 2003). A *golden ratio* of 1:1.618 has been found to occur in beautiful things both natural and manufactured. A plastic surgeon designed a mask that applies this ratio to the face. The closer a face fits the mask, the more attractive the face is perceived to be.[2] People who have asymmetrical features can have cosmetic surgery to create symmetry through such procedures as face-lifts, nasal refinements, eyelid lifts, collagen injections, liposuction, and breast implants. In lieu of surgery, women can use makeup to create the illusion of a more symmetrical face—larger eyes, higher cheekbones, narrower nose, fuller lips. "Creating symmetry is all about using light, dark, and reflection" according to a Hollywood makeup artist (¶ 11).

Disabilities

People with disabilities have special difficulties in finding comfortable, attractive, fashionable clothing. For example, one quadriplegic woman commented that she used the pinky test to decide whether to try on low-rise jeans, that is, the fly on a pair of jeans had to be longer than her pinkie finger (Henry, 2006). Low-rise jeans are not designed for someone who sits in a wheelchair all day. Another woman, who was born with one leg shorter than the other, commented that she would like to wear high heels but she walks with the aid of crutches and settles for athletic shoes.

For people in wheelchairs, there are many barriers in everyday life (*Americans with Disabilities*, 2007) For example, a nine-year-old girl with spina bifida who used a wheelchair wanted to participate in a retail store's modeling program—a four-session course in fashion modeling for children ages 8 to 17. The instructor said the girl could not participate because a runway that was 12 inches off the ground was used for the models and the girl would not fit in with the other children. A settlement was reached with the retailer that ensured the girl and any other child with a disability would be allowed to attend the modeling program.

Color blindness is an inherited physical condition that is more common in men than women. Two basic types of color deficiency are red-green and blue-yellow. One out of every 12 men is red-green color deficient. For the color-blind individual, the most daunting, frustrating problem is selecting and coordinating clothing items (Bridge, 2006). One man explained that his wife did not dress him every morning, but she did pick out his clothes. Another person developed an efficient method for avoiding criticism by memorizing what could be worn together. A color-blind athlete had difficulty distinguishing one jersey from another if they were not light and dark; it was not easy to tell who was a member of his team and he wanted to avoid passing the ball to a member of the other team. A color-blind teacher wrote numbers on each item of clothing, ensuring that items with the same number matched, and then matched numbers when getting dressed.

The Special Problems of Blindness

Blindness is another physical condition that presents an obstacle to selecting and matching items of clothing. One solution is a product called Do-Dots, which are clear clothing markers with Braille symbols that snap onto the hem, cuff, or collar of clothing to identify it ("Do-Dots," 2007). On one side, the buttons have Braille symbols for the clothing's design (light or dark, print, plaid, stripes or plain) and on the other side there is one of 45 Braille symbols for color. A Braille-coded key to the abbreviations accompanies each package of buttons.

The Secretary of the National Federation for the Blind of Idaho wrote about color and the blind (Walhof, 2000). She recalled that when she was a child people told her that red dresses looked good on her but that she should not wear a pink hair clip with a red dress. As she grew older and began to make and buy her own clothes, she sought advice from her mother about what colors looked right together. When she was away from home at the school for the blind and her mother was not available, she memorized which blouses and sweaters went with certain skirts. After she had children of her own, she checked her son's choice of clothes closely because she knew that if he wore clothes that did not match, people would say she did not know it. She recalled one Christmas when her son received a pair of pants with an orange stripe. He wanted to wear a plaid flannel shirt that had purple stripes with the pants. She told her son he could not wear those two garments together. Walhof concluded that children are not born knowing what is attractive; they learn that from their culture.

The editor of the National Federation for the Blind (NFB) monthly publication, the *Braille Monitor*, offered some insight into clothing, grooming, and social acceptability for the blind (Pierce, 2003). Pierce noted that blind children do not have the luxury of being oblivious to social expectations because if they choose to disregard convention or flout social expectations, they are not excused but condescendingly dismissed on the grounds of blindness. They are presumed not to know any better or to be doing the best they can. Pierce stressed the importance of parents and other family members teaching blind children to care for themselves, to make a good appearance, and to behave in ways that will not embarrass them.

Blind children need to learn how to recognize items of clothing by touch as well as what items go together. Similarly, children who have severely impaired vision and cannot distinguish colors, or do not see some colors well, need to memorize the rules of color coordination: "[P]laids and stripes don't go together; different prints should be kept apart unless they have been designed to go together; check with someone reliable to be sure that different shades of the same color are harmonious; some colors go together and some do not" (Pierce, 2003, ¶ 7). Children of either sex who are blind or have significant visual impairment need to develop skill in applying these rules.

Benson (2004), who is blind, commented that his mother's instructions regarding clothing and the need to look nice were based on tradition and social convention, not as blindness-related issues. Benson recalled that joining the Boy Scouts was a turning point in managing his own clothing and grooming because the meetings required members to wear a properly fitted and pressed uniform with polished shoes. He considered his mother's caution "You always want to look nice" as sage advice (¶ 12).

His mother and other adults instilled in him the notion that clothing is a visible statement of who one is, so he paid particular attention to what he wore. Benson advised parents that they should not be tolerant of inattention to good grooming and proper hygiene because these are highly valued attributes in our society. "The stereotype of the obese, slovenly dressed blind person with gravy stains down the front of his shirt is an image that still haunts us" (¶ 22). "We are changing what it means to be blind, and improving image is an important—no, an essential part—of that change" (¶ 22).

ENVIRONMENTAL CONDITIONS

Environmental conditions refer to an ecological state such as temperature, humidity, and precipitation. Office workers may be tempted to change their professional attire for something more comfortable when summer arrives (Salerno, 2006). Changing professional attire to adapt to warmer weather is acceptable as long as the changes are reasonable. However, a recent survey found that 81 percent of employees believed work attire affected their professional image and nearly half said clothing appreciably affected how an employee is perceived on the job (Salerno, 2006). So what changes are acceptable adaptations to temperatures in the triple digits? One unacceptable type of footwear is flip-flops. In 2005, a university's women's lacrosse team received widespread criticism when team members wore flip-flops to the White House for a photograph with the president. The incident illustrated a growing division between older adults, many of whom still abide by the rule of no-toes showing, and younger adults who wear flip-flops almost everywhere, including the workplace.

Experts advise that collared polo shirts are acceptable for business casual offices, but Hawaiian shirts (unless one is in Hawaii) or clothes with bright colors and designs should be avoided. Workers can wear layers that can be removed when walking to lunch or to the car but replaced inside air-conditioned offices.

In one county, the county commissioners voted on a resolution to relax the dress code because of summer temperatures (Schultz, 2006). The proclamation read "All citizens of Martin County are hereby freed of all neckties, long sleeves, suits and other similar climate-hostile fashions from Memorial Day through Labor Day, both indoors and outdoors" (p. B1). A commissioner remarked that "If you step outside in August in a suit and tie, you are going to be soaked" (p. B1).

When the weather is hot outside, it may be too cold for workers inside offices with air-conditioning ("Four in Ten Toronto Workers," 2006). Four out of ten workers said they dressed differently because their workplace air-conditioning was set too cold. In some offices, there are long-standing battles over a couple of degrees on the thermostat (Murray, Plumb, & Murray, 2006). One solution is for employees to keep sweaters in their offices or dress in layers. Summer is the prime time for dress code abuse in the office, for example, large tattoos that show only because bare legs and shoulders are visible and bra straps that show under lingerie-style tops. Some dress guidelines are necessary to ensure professional attire.

"In the late 19th century, Oscar Wilde was ridiculed for his views on fashion, specifically that men should follow the enlightened example of women in the Victorian era: lighter fabrics, brighter colors, and generally more comfortable clothes. A parody of Wilde in *Punch* caricatured a man wearing shorts as effeminate and wimpy" (Wilson, 2006a, Section 9, p. 1). Wilson (the male author of this article) decided to wear a dressy pair of knee-length navy shorts, a white dress shirt, brown loafers (no socks), and a gray jacket to work one day in New York City. On the street, people stared and took pictures. One man asked "What country are you from?" (p. 1) and added that if he looked around, he would see that all the men were wearing long pants, so it should be obvious that is what men have to wear. On Wall Street, Wilson discovered that everyone was dressed alike in trousers and a dress shirt, either white or cobalt blue with the top button open. He observed two men pointing at his shorts and laughing. Wilson concluded that there are lines that men will not cross and, for the immediate future, wearing shorts is stepping over that line. The next day he wore pants.

Attempts to comply with competing norms is another source of norm violations, that is, claims on time, facilities, money, or energy are incompatible (Workman & Freeburg, 2000b). Individuals who occupy favorable positions in the social class structure have many resources at their disposal. On the other hand, those who occupy unfavorable positions lack sufficient resources. Unequal access to important resources creates a situation in which norm violation is likely to occur.

The high school prom is an extravagant display of consumerism and a reflection of social status (Mansfield, 2006). For example, when some girls can spend $2,000 or more on a dress, they are in a position to demand exclusivity (Bentley, 2006). It is a **fashion faux pas** (a mistake) to wear the same style dress to the prom as another girl. Because exclusivity is as important as fit when choosing a prom dress, some retailers have started a registry in which they keep track of each dress sold for each area prom. On the other hand, many teens struggle to pay for prom expenses—some pay for the prom with money they earn working part-time (Nardi, 2006). A national organization called Becca's Closet asks girls to donate their prom dresses. The dresses are then given to students who cannot afford to purchase a dress and do not object to wearing a secondhand dress. "Buying a used prom gown at Goodwill [resale thrift shop] would send most teenage girls into hyperventilation" (Mansfield, 2006, p. D1).

Prom night is a big event in the lives of most high school students (Reese & Strauss, 2004). But the cost of this rite of passage has escalated in recent years, with costs ranging from $400 to $3,000. *Your Prom* magazine estimated that the average teenager spends $638 on the prom and that prom-related spending totals $4.1 billion a year (Wood, 2006). For example, renting a limousine can cost from $90 to $1,500; prom tickets $10 to $125; professional photographs $25 to $100; tuxedo rental $70 to $250; prom dress $150 to $500; accessories $10 to $400; hair $15 to $150; grooming $25 to $100; and flowers $20 to $30.

Some schools, parents, and teens have responded to media coverage of out-of-control spending. Indeed, some religion-associated

FIGURE 5.7 A UNIVERSITY OF SOUTHERN MISSISSIPPI SCHOOL OF SOCIAL WORK GRADUATE STUDENT FROM SEMINARY, MISS., SORTS THROUGH MORE THAN 100 PROM DRESSES DONATED TO THE STUDENT ASSOCIATION OF SOCIAL WORKERS PROM DRESS DRIVE.

schools have cancelled the prom, citing the "flaunting of affluence, exaggerated expenses and a pursuit of vanity for vanity's sake" (Wood, 2006, p. 1). Prom dresses are being monitored for modesty, with some schools prohibiting low-cut backs, plunging necklines, leg-revealing slits, and other sexy styles. "Teens are trapped by cultural expectations of extravagance—fed by TV shows and fanned by prom marketers, fashion magazines, peer pressure" (Wood, 2006, p. 1).

Temporal Incompatibilities Between Statuses

A **temporal incompatibility between statuses** exists when time as a quality renders something incompatible with something else. Temporal incompatibilities between statuses are another source of norm violation (Workman & Freeburg, 2000b, p. 93). This type of incompatibility occurs when children take on adult behaviors and dress before they are ready; "An individual may not be prepared—psychologically, socially, and technically—to make a change from a status at one life stage to a later status (from child to preteen)" (p. 93). Parents and children's advocacy groups have protested the sexy, imitation-adult fashions marketed to girls, expressing concern about the adult messages (sex and body image) being sent by such fashions. What was marketed to eight-year-olds in the past is now being marketed to five- and six-year-olds. "Today many of those same fashions have been further miniaturized and are now filtering down to size 4 to 6X" (Deam, 2006, p. 3).

Just as older styles are filtering down to younger girls, so is the peer pressure to wear them. "And [peer pressure], as any parent knows, is a mighty force to be reckoned with" (Deam, 2006, p. 3). However, parents control spending within a family, so it is not clear if the situation is about fashion or about parenting. Admittedly, adults can become desensitized to marketing messages when exposed to a product over an extended period of time.

Adolescents may not be prepared—psychologically, socially, physically, or emotionally—to make the transition from adolescence to emerging adulthood. A classic conception of **adolescence** characterizes it as consisting of two stages of development: early adolescence (ages 12 to 18) and late adolescence (ages 18 to 22) (Erikson, 1997). Arnett (2000) characterized late adolescence as **emerging adulthood**. During early adolescence, developmental tasks include physical maturation, emotional development, peer group membership, and heterosexual relationships. Developmental tasks of emerging adulthood include autonomy from parents, internalized morality, and career choices (Newman & Newman, 1987). Ranking high among the criteria defining the transition to adulthood is compliance with social norms (Arnett, 2001).

During adolescence, some teens will push the limits, for example, by wearing message T-shirts that have double meanings, promote drugs and alcohol, or make subtle references to violence or sex (McGee, 2006). Teachers and parents may be unaware of the meanings associated with current teen lingo and jargon. **Lingo** is a specialized set of terms requiring that it be learned like a language. **Jargon** is a language that is used by a particular group, especially when the words and phrases are not understood or used by other people. That is why adolescents invent lingo and jargon. For example, according to one teacher, "a Pillsbury Doughboy means you are a [drug] seller. I thought the doughboy just laughed" (p. B1). If school officials do not know the meaning of the term, they do not know they need to do something about it.

Transitions between statuses sometimes may temporarily cause errors in judgment about appropriate behavior (adulthood to old age). "Age-appropriate dressing is a fine concept but tricky to pull off" (Glentzer, 2006, p. 4). Older women who try to look well-put-together, taller, and slimmer have an aging body to consider: wrinkles at the neck, a thickening middle, bulges around the bra line, veins in the legs, and flabby arms. Many older women dress to conceal their body; but, as Glentzer noted, there is a fine line between *modest* and *matronly*. As a woman gets older and fuller, trying to cover it up only makes her look like a sack of potatoes, advised the owner of a boutique. The owner commented that as women age, nothing will make them look older than dressing too young. "Fashion maven Clinton Kelly of TLC's *What Not To Wear* strongly cautions women who dress much younger than their age" (*5 Tips to Look Younger Longer*, 2006, ¶ 10). A **fashion maven** is somebody who is an expert or knowledgeable enthusiast in the field of fashion. According to Kelly, dressing much younger than your age sends the message that you are trying too hard. Kelly suggested dressing stylishly but age-appropriately by choosing clothes that fit in colors that flatter, resulting in a look of confidence and sophistication.

The Normative System Itself

The **normative system** is the combination of related norms organized into a complex whole. In a certain situation an action might be considered deviant, whereas in another context, it will not. Individuals who take on competing statuses at the same time may experience role conflict with regard to dress norms.

Statuses and roles allow society to be predictable and orderly. However, each individual has many statuses and each status has associated roles. **Social roles**, by definition, tend to be highly standardized sets of expectations. The variety of statuses and roles results in conflict and strain. "**Role conflict** occurs when the performance of a role in one status clashes with the performance of a role in another status" (Shepard, 2005, p. 131). **Role strain** takes place when roles associated with a single status are in opposition to one another. The fulfillment of one role may interfere with the performance of others.

For example, a pregnant police officer whose request for limited duty was denied had to tolerate patrol duty without wearing a bulletproof vest because the vest did not fit over her pregnant stomach (Kelleher, 2006). Another female police officer asked for a desk job without revealing she was pregnant and was given the position; when she began wearing maternity uniforms, she was ordered back on patrol. The three roles associated with the statuses of female, mother-to-be, and police officer caused role conflict. Both gender roles and occupational roles have expectations about dress that sometimes are perceived as incompatible and can inadvertently lead to violation of norms with regard to dress.

Role strain can occur within an occupational role. For example, the role of teacher has expectations for dress and appearance that generally include professional dress (Berghom, 2006). However, the job duties of teachers sometimes require working with messy materials (art) or physical exertion (physical education classes) where the demands are incompatible with requirements for professional dress. Because many public schools have student dress codes, school boards sometimes expect teachers, principals, and other staff to set an example of appropriate dress. The requirement to be a role model for students may cause role strain when employment duties would be better served with another type of dress.

INTERNALIZATION

Internalization of norms occurs during the process of socialization. **Internalization** refers to adoption of others' attitudes, beliefs, and values, either consciously or unconsciously. Internalization results in norms becoming part of an individual's motivational system, resulting in a commitment to the norms as being appropriate, reasonable, and therefore mandatory. Although it is the express purpose of socialization, not all individuals accept the norms and values of their culture to the same degree—not all individuals internalize the norms.

If socialization proceeds as expected, individuals conform to norms not just because they know what the norms are, but also because they have internalized the norms. Internalization of norms results in feelings of guilt or discomfort when norms are violated (Figure 5.8). For example, those who are members of the group People for the Ethical Treatment of Animals (PETA) have internalized the norm of humane treatment of animals (Doniach, 2006). Members do not believe in wearing fur, leather, or wool because they contend that "the fur, leather, and wool industries use animals to maximize profit at the expense of animal welfare" (p. B7). Recently, PETA volunteers handed out tickets to people in various cities across the United States in an attempt to make them feel guilty or uncomfortable for wearing fur, leather, or wool. The point they were trying to make was their internalized belief that "It is against fashion law to wear leather" (p. B7).

For the normative order to function properly, the norms must become an integral part of each individual's emotional life and thought processes. As a result, each individual learns to judge his or her own actions. An individual's internal control operates even when reactions by others are missing. When tempted to deviate from norms, an individual's conscience may provide moral reasons to resist temptation. Internalization of norms motivates an individual

FIGURE 5.8 NORMS BECOME A PART OF AN INDIVIDUAL'S MOTIVATIONAL SYSTEM. THIS CARTOON DEPICTS A STRONGLY HELD NORM: POLITICAL CORRECTNESS.

to regard violations as immoral and inappropriate. Internalization is what makes people decide not to wear fur even when they do not anticipate any protest if they do.

Summary

Violation of dress norms occurs because of the complex nature of the process of social control. In this chapter, we looked at some of the reasons why norm violations occur, including culture change, location, transmission, values and motives, physical conditions, environmental conditions, demands on resources, temporal incompatibilities between statuses, the normative system itself, and internalization.

Key Terms and Concepts

adolescence	laissez-faire
culture change	lingo
effeminate	mass media
emerging adulthood	motive
fashion faux pas	normative system
fashion maven	role conflict
frame transformation	role strain
internalization	social roles
jargon	temporal incompatibility between statuses

Suggested Readings

1. Blakemore, J. E. O. (2001, April). *First, third, and fifth grade children's attitudes about gender norm violations.* Poster session presented at the Biennial Meeting of the Society of Research in Child Development, Minneapolis, MN.
2. Nenga, S. K. (2003). Social class and structures of feeling in women's

childhood memories of clothing, food, and leisure. *Journal of Contemporary Ethnography,* 32(2) 167–201.

3. Nielsen, J. M., Walden, G., & Kunkel, C. A. (2000). Gendered heteronormativity: Empirical illustrations in everyday life. *Sociological Quarterly, 41*(2), 283–297.

Research Activity 5.1 *Dress Norms and New York*

Purpose: To identify potential dress norm violations by comparing and contrasting your hometown norms with the dress norms of New York City.

Procedure:

1. Log on to CitiDex.com, Etiquette and Local Customs in New York City (http://www.citidex.com/342.htm).
2. Review the section "Dress in New York."
3. Compare dress customs in New York with dress customs in your hometown. Which of your hometown dress norms violate the dress norms of New York City? Why?
4. Summarize your findings and submit them to your instructor.

Research Activity 5.2 *Violations of Dress Norms*

Purpose: To identify reasons for dress norm violations as reported in the newspaper.

Procedure:

1. Review the reasons that dress norms are violated.
2. Log on to a website from a daily newspaper. Examples in addition to your local newspaper include the *New York Times* (http://www.nytimes.com/), the *Chicago Tribune* (http://www.chicagotribune.com/), or the *Los Angeles Times* (http://www.latimes.com/). As an alternative, you may also use the LexisNexis database if it is available through your college or university library.
3. Use the newspaper's or LexisNexis' search engine to locate two articles about a dress norm violation. You may use key words such as *dress code violation.*
4. Print a copy of the articles; highlight the dress norm violation reported and the reasons that may be associated with the violation.
5. Summarize your findings and submit your work to your instructor.

Notes

1. The conceptual framework for this chapter appeared as part of the following article: Workman, J. E., & Freeburg, E. W. (2000). Part II: Testing the expanded definition of the normative order. *Clothing and Textiles Research Journal, 18*(2), 90–99.
2. If you would like to see how your face fits the mask, go to http://www.beautyanalysis.com

Chapter Six

Tattooers, Body Piercers, Cross-Dressers, Punks, Goths, and More

FROM THE HEADLINES

A national survey by the Employment Law Alliance revealed disagreement over regulating appearance in the U.S. workplace (weight, clothing, hairstyles, body piercing). Employer-employee disputes have been increasing, and the disputes sometimes escalate into lawsuits. One such lawsuit challenged a national superstore chain's prohibition on "visible facial or tongue jewelry (earrings excepted)" (¶ 3).

The "America at Work" poll questioned a representative national sample of 1,000 adults about their views on appearance-based discrimination. The poll has a confidence interval of +/− 3.1%. Results revealed that more than half of the respondents indicated there was no employee dress or appearance policy in their workplace. Two out of five respondents indicated that employers should be able to refuse to hire someone based on the applicant's appearance (weight, clothing, piercing, body art, or hairstyle). About one-third indicated that attractive people were more likely to be hired or promoted in their workplace. About one-third responded that unattractive, overweight, or unconventionally dressed people need legal protection similar to protection given to persons with disabilities. Finally, about one in six felt they had experienced discrimination because of their appearance.

Source: Hirschfeld, S. (2005, March 22). National poll shows public opinion sharply divided on regulating appearance—from appearance to tattoos—in the workplace. Retrieved October 31, 2006, from http://www.hrmguide.com/diversity/appearance-at-work.htm

The research described in this excerpt from a newspaper column illustrates several concepts you will be reading about in this chapter. Researchers conducted a national survey to gather opinions about appearance-related discrimination. The research was motivated by employee norm violations resulting in an increase in employer-employee disputes over appearance. Researchers expected the data to provide information that would help companies formulate dress code policies and handle dress code violations in a nondiscriminatory manner.

Should employers have the right to refuse to hire an applicant based on appearance, including weight, clothing, piercing, body art, and hairstyle? Should employees who are not physically attractive, who are overweight, or who look or dress in an unconventional manner be given special government legal protection against discrimination or retaliation? Should employers have the right to give preference in hiring or promoting to attractive workers? In this chapter, you will read about other research that has been used to study issues related to dress norm violations. The methods and tools used in each research study are summarized in Table 6.1.

Each group creates its own normative standards for group members, so some social norms are specific to particular groups. The normative order includes norms regarding what group members should think (attitudes, opinions), what they should say (slang, nicknames), how they should act (walk, stand), and how they should dress (punk or Goth fashion, tattoos, body piercings). What members of one group consider conformity to norms may be considered norm violations by members of another group.

Recall from Chapter 5 that there are many reasons for norm violations including culture change, location, transmission, values and motives, physical conditions, environmental conditions, demands on resources, temporal incompatibilities between statuses, the normative system itself, and internalization. This chapter examines research studies related to: (a) norm violations of social class groups; (b) body modifications such as tattoos and body piercings; (c) gender norm violations; and (d) subcultural styles associated with such groups as punks, Goths, and skateboarders.

QUESTIONS TO ANSWER AS YOU READ

1. How do I recognize violations of norms?
2. What are some research topics concerning dress norm violations?
3. What research methods can be used to conduct research related to norm violations?
4. What tools can be used to collect data for research related to norm violations?

RESEARCH METHOD	TOOL(S)	AUTHOR(S)	YEAR	ARTICLE TITLE
Qualitative	Ethnographic tools	Bennett	2006	Punk's not dead: The continuing significance of punk rock for an older generation of fans
Qualitative	Interview worksheet	Blakemore	2003	Children's beliefs about violating gender norms: Boys shouldn't look like girls and girls shouldn't act like boys
Quantitative	Survey	Carroll & Anderson	2002	Body piercing, tattooing, self-esteem and body investment in adolescent girls
Quantitative	Survey	Ceglian & Lyons	2004	Gender type and comfort with cross-dressers
Qualitative	Observation and interview worksheets	Davis	2006	Growing up punk: Negotiating aging identity in a local music scene
Quantitative	Survey	Frederick & Bradley	2000	A different kind of normal? Psychological and motivational characteristics of young adult tattooers and body piercers
Qualitative	Interview worksheet	Irwin	2001	Legitimizing the first tattoo: Moral passage through informal interaction
Qualitative	Ethnographic tools	Irwin	2003	Saints and sinners: Elite tattoo collectors and tattooists as positive and negative deviants
Qualitative	Interview worksheet	Kelly, Pomerantz & Currie	2005	Skater girlhood and emphasized-femininity: 'You can't land an ollie properly in heels.'
Qualitative	Content analysis worksheet	Kunkel & Nielsen	1998	Gender, residual deviance, and social control
Qualitative	Interview worksheet	Nenga	2003	Social class and structures of feeling in women's childhood memories of clothing, food, and leisure
Qualitative	Content analysis worksheet	Nielsen et al.	2000	Gendered heteronormativity: Empirical illustrations in everyday life
Qualitative	Interview worksheet	Pomerantz et al.	2004	Sk8ter girls: Skateboarders, girlhood and feminism in motion
Qualitative	Interview worksheet	Szkryhalo & Ruble	1999	"God made me a girl": Sex-category constancy judgments and explanations revisited

SOCIAL CLASS AND VIOLATION OF NORMS

Social class refers to societal subgroups with similar origins, upbringing, education, and occupations and whose members share personal circumstances

TATTOOERS,
BODY PIERCERS,
CROSS-DRESSERS,
PUNKS, GOTHS,
AND MORE

and experiences. It is commonly assumed that there are five social classes in the United States: upper class, upper middle class, lower middle class, working class, and lower class (Tischler, 2004). Members of the upper class (about 1 to 3 percent of the population) are wealthy, educated, and have occupations related to politics, corporate ownership, or honorific positions in government and the arts.

Members of the upper middle class (10 to 15 percent of the population) are affluent, successful business and professional people, with a college education (Figure 6.1). Members of the lower middle class (25 to 30 percent of the population) have a high school education or some college and work in clerical and sales positions, are small-business semiprofessionals, or farmers (Figure 6.2).

Members of the working class (25 to 30 percent of the population) have adequate financial resources but little money available for luxuries, have a grade school or high school education, and work in skilled and semiskilled manual labor, factories, and other blue-collar work (Figure 6.3).

FIGURE 6.1 (ABOVE LEFT) MEMBERS OF THE UPPER-MIDDLE CLASS ARE AFFLUENT, SUCCESSFUL BUSINESS AND PROFESSIONAL PEOPLE, WITH A COLLEGE EDUCATION. THIS LAWYER IS DRESSED IN UPPER-MIDDLE CLASS STYLE

FIGURE 6.2 (ABOVE RIGHT) MEMBERS OF THE LOWER-MIDDLE CLASS HAVE A HIGH SCHOOL EDUCATION OR SOME COLLEGE. SOME WORK IN CLERICAL AND SALES POSITIONS, LIKE THE SECRETARY SHOWN HERE.

FIGURE 6.3 (LOWER LEFT) MEMBERS OF THE WORKING CLASS HAVE ADEQUATE FINANCIAL RESOURCES BUT LITTLE MONEY FOR LUXURIES, HAVE A GRADE SCHOOL OR HIGH SCHOOL EDUCATION, AND WORK IN SKILLED AND SEMISKILLED MANUAL LABOR, FACTORIES, AND OTHER BLUE-COLLAR WORK, LIKE THE MINERS SHOWN HERE.

FIGURE 6.4 (LOWER RIGHT) MEMBERS OF THE LOWER CLASS ARE AT THE BOTTOM OF THE ECONOMIC LADDER, HAVE LITTLE EDUCATION OR OCCUPATIONAL SKILLS, AND ARE OFTEN UNEMPLOYED OR UNDEREMPLOYED IN UNSKILLED LABOR AND SERVICE WORK. THE FAST FOOD WORKER PICTURED HERE EXEMPLIFIES THIS SOCIAL CLASS.

Members of the lower class (15 to 20 percent of the population) are at the bottom of the economic ladder, have little education or occupational skills, and are often unemployed or underemployed in unskilled labor and service work (Figure 6.4).

Status disparities result from the unequal distribution of money, power, and prestige among these social classes. Recall from Chapter 1 that status is a person's position in a social hierarchy, in this case, a social class hierarchy; disparity refers to the notion that the statuses are unequally valued.

Social Class and School Uniforms

Subtle symbols can distinguish and define members of different social classes. Certain brands of clothing can be symbols of social class membership and status disparities. In the public school environment, students use clothing to symbolize class and status disparities.

Public school uniform specifications usually stipulate style and color but not a particular manufacturer (Crockett & Wallendorf, 1998). For example, one school specified khaki pants and white shirts; another school gave students a choice between khaki, navy, or black bottoms and any solid-colored top with a collar; another school specified khaki or black pants with a white or green collared shirt (Rauh, 2006). One rationale for such dress codes was to eliminate status disparities; one principal was quoted as saying uniforms blurred the line between students from wealthy and poor families.

Status disparities become obvious because of where students purchase their uniforms. Wealthy students can purchase high-quality shirts made of fine fabrics and pants that are tailored to an individual fit. Lower-income students are likely to purchase similar items (but of comparatively lower quality) at national department or discount stores. For example, at one discount outlet store, a pair of navy pants sold for $13 and a collared uniform top for $7 (Rauh, 2006). In an upscale catalog, a pair of navy pants sold for $24.50; a collared uniform top for $14.50; and a pair of wool blend pants for $32.50. One thing that differentiates upscale uniforms, then, is their price.

Quality differences in fabric and tailoring also differentiate high-quality uniforms. For example, in the upscale catalog, the pants were described as "tailored to the hilt" and made of a softer "peached" fabric (*Lands' End*, 2006). The wealthiest students are able to demonstrate their elite status through subtle distinctions in quality. The subtle price and quality distinctions in an otherwise identical uniform illustrate the strength of a consumer culture that marks individual identity, status, and social position through consumption.

Social Class and Childhood Memories of Clothing Norm Violations

In terms of social class, social and material resources shape everyday life and culture. People dress to communicate their social class identity and to allow others to place them in the class hierarchy (Kaiser, 1997). Nenga (2003) interviewed 27 working-class and middle-class women about their childhood memories of clothing norm violations. The memories revealed emotional responses (feelings such as anger, pride, shame, embarrassment) that varied by social class. When asked to tell about a memory that had something to do with clothing, the women told about clothing norm violations.

Most of the clothing norm violations recalled by working-class women were violations of their peers' clothing norms (Nenga, 2003). For example, a 52-year-old woman told how she normally wore anklets and saddle shoes to school, but on field trip days girls were allowed to wear nylons and flats. She remembered showing up to school for a field trip wearing anklets and saddle shoes as "the most mortifying experience of my whole life" (p. 178). She recognized the norm violation as soon as she saw the other girls. Some of the other working-class women recalled that as children they were not aware of their norm violations until their peers notified them. A 21-year-old recalled wearing a bright royal purple shiny stretch sleeveless jumpsuit to seventh grade. On top of the jumpsuit she wore purple and white vertical striped short shorts and a lavender shirt with white lace. Her classmate's laughter notified her that her outfit violated clothing norms. She said, "I didn't know how to dress" (p. 178). Obviously, she was not aware her outfit violated her peers' clothing norms when she put the items together. She felt angry, hurt, ashamed, and embarrassed.

Some of the working-class women reported not being able to afford current fashions (Nenga, 2003). A 39-year-old woman recalled wearing her brother's hand-me-down dress clothes to the first day of high school. Even 25 years later, she was so ashamed of that outfit, she would not describe it to the researcher. A 24-year-old remarked that she lied rather than reveal the discount and thrift store source of her clothes. A 29-year-old remembered an exciting shopping trip to a factory outlet mall where she bought some designer jeans for fifteen dollars.

Once working-class women were aware of the clothing norms that they could not or did not meet, they made an effort to either conform to the clothing norms or conceal their nonconformity (Nenga, 2003). A 75-year-old, who wore hand-me-downs until she began sewing her own clothes, recalled how anxiously she tried to be fashionable. She remembered being very particular about colors and whatever styles were in fashion. She recalled that a woman's purse, gloves, and shoes were supposed to match. In a few cases working-class women happily remembered being able to meet clothing norms. For example, a 41-year-old remembered shopping in a nice department store and buying just one expensive outfit with the money her mother had given her to buy a number of clothing items. In summary, working class women remembered peers notifying them of clothing norm violations and of being anxious to conform to peer clothing norms.

Middle-class women recalled violating their mothers' clothing norms (Nenga, 2003). Their mothers insisted on plain, sensible, and moderately priced clothing. Many of the women wanted fancy and expensive clothes or shoes. One woman remembered wanting a pair of expensive Capezio shoes that a lot of girls were wearing, but that her mother thought were not sensible. A 29-year-old wanted to wear fancy ballgowns to pageants and photo shoots, but her mother insisted she wear childlike pedal pushers and plain Jane dresses. The middle-class women were proud of their ability to conform to their peers' clothing norms. Mothers warned their daughters when their taste in clothes was a norm violation of femininity and/or appropriateness (too expensive, too masculine, or too risqué).

All of the women offered childhood memories of clothing norm violations (Nenga, 2003). Working-class women had fewer material resources with which to buy fashionable clothing. They reported wearing secondhand clothing and clothes bought at discount department stores. Lack of material resources contributed to an inability to conform to peers' clothing norms. Conversely, middle-class women generally had ample material resources to conform to their peers' clothing norms.

BODY MODIFICATION NORM VIOLATIONS

The mass media provide coverage of the innovative individuals who are among the first to adopt a new trend. Models, athletes, rock stars, and other celebrities who display tattoos and body piercings serve as role models for young, impressionable individuals (Burger & Finkel, 2002; Gunter & McDowell, 2004; Kinnon, 2000). "Given the media's glamorous portrayal of fashionable elites who flaunt their tattoos and body piercings, it is not surprising that many of today's youth consider getting some type of body modification" (Burger & Finkel, 2002, p. 203). As noted earlier, norm violation is determined by the definition and responses of others (sanctions).

Tattoos

A **tattoo** is a "permanent design made on skin by the process of pricking and ingraining indelible pigment" (Calasibetta & Tortora, 2003, p. 448). Tattoos are a modification of the color and texture of the skin. They are a violation of conventional values and norms regarding hygiene (tattoos are dirty and dangerous), beauty (especially female beauty norms; clear, unblemished skin), decision making (image of first tattoos as the product of reckless, impulsive, and drunken decisions), and self-presentation (reactions of others that might threaten future employment or social opportunities). Tattoos and other forms of appearance deviance are ways to project a disassociation with mainstream or conventional culture (the artifacts and understandings shared by the majority of members of a society).

Long associated with low social class, criminals, gangs, sailors, bikers, punk rockers, skinheads, renegades who thumb their nose at society, and social outcasts (and, at the other end of spectrum, military personnel), tattoos became increasingly popular in U. S. society in the 1990s. Advertisements featured models with tattoos, entertainers and athletes had highly visible tattoos, and even Barbie, the fashion doll, was featured with a tattoo (Kuntzman, 1999). All these sources reinforced the idea that a tattoo no longer symbolizes a social outcast but a rock star, a model, or a fashionable, trendy young person. Despite the increasing popularity of tattooing, many conventional members of society continue to view tattoos as inconsistent with the norms of a conventional social network (Figure 6.5).

In interviewing first-time tattooees to investigate their motivations, fears, and reasons for choosing particular designs, Irwin (2001) found that many first-time clients were concerned with getting a tattoo that would be acceptable in conventional society. They feared the negative images associated with tattoos and feared that getting a tattoo might

FIGURE 6.5 MANY CONVENTIONAL MEMBERS OF SOCIETY CONTINUE TO VIEW TATTOOS NOT AS AN INDICATION OF A FASHIONABLE, TRENDY PERSON, BUT AS AN INDICATION OF SOMEONE WHO IS ALIENATED FROM CONVENTIONAL NORMS AND SOCIAL NETWORKS. SOMEONE LIKE KAT VON D, WHO IS A FEATURED TATTOO ARTIST ON THE POPULAR TELEVISION SHOW *MIAMI INK*, COULD BE VIEWED AS A NORM VIOLATOR.

damage relationships with family members, friends, and employers. Conversely, they believed that becoming tattooed symbolized liberation, independence, and freedom from conventionality. Fashion-conscious tattooees conformed to conventional aesthetics by selecting small, discreet tattoos with conventional themes like butterflies or flowers.

Many people consider tattoos to be dirty, dangerous, and lower class and view the heavily tattooed as freaks. Irwin (2003) collected data about professional tattooing and tattoo collection during a five-year ethnographic study. Heavily tattooed individuals embraced norms and values that contrasted glaringly with core standards of conventional society and with conventional appearance norms. "Collectors and producers of large, visible tattoos violate many core mainstream appearance norms" (p. 34). In U.S. society, clear skin is an enduring beauty norm; blotchy, blemished, and marked skin is perceived as unhealthy, impure, ugly, or low-class.

Just as conventional appearance norms are reinforced through informal and formal social networks, appearance norms among tattoo collectors were reinforced through interactions with other tattoo collectors and tattoo artists. However, in mainstream society, heavily tattooed individuals were often denounced, shunned, and insulted. Negative reactions varied according to whether an individual was able and willing to cover the tattoos with clothing. Many wore long-sleeved shirts and pants in conventional interactions.

Although all individuals with large tattoos violate conventional norms, for females, having many large tattoos is an extreme violation of conventional female beauty norms. For violating these norms, female tattoo collectors and artists were sometimes sanctioned by accusations of being masculine, ugly, or slutty.

Body Piercing

One reason for violation of norms is motivation. Individuals who modify their body via tattoos or body piercing tend to report a high level of internal motivation for the behaviors (Frederick & Bradley, 2000). Major reasons given for body piercing were self-expression and personal identity rather than deviance or rebellion (Armstrong, Roberts, Owen, & Koch, 2004; Ceniceros, 1998; Stirn, 2003). **Body piercing** is defined as an insertion of jewelry into openings made in the body, for example, ear lobes and cartilage, eyebrows, genitals, lips, navel, nipples, nose, and tongue (Armstrong, 1996; Armstrong, Ekmark, &

Tattooers,
Body Piercers,
Cross-Dressers,
Punks, Goths,
and More

137

FIGURE 6.6 ONE INDIVIDUAL'S MOTIVATION FOR A NORM VIOLATION.

Brooks, 1995). In this chapter, body piercing refers to multiple piercings and to piercings other than traditional (normative) pierced ear lobes (Figure 6.6).

Presence of body piercings appears to be a reliable predictor of risky and reckless behaviors (Colman & Colman, 2004). Risky behaviors are socially approved adventurous or thrill-seeking acts and reckless behaviors are non–socially approved acts where precautions could easily be taken, but are not, to avoid potentially negative consequences (Arnett, 1992). Body piercing has been found to be associated with higher levels of sexual activity, smoking, marijuana use, truancy, running away from home, suicide attempts, and affiliation with a peer group who engaged in substance use (Roberts, Auinger, & Ryan, 2004).

Adolescents with tattoos and/or body piercings (compared to those without) were more likely to have engaged in risk-taking behaviors and greater degrees of involvement in the areas of gateway drug use, hard drug use, sexual activity, suicide, and disordered eating (Carroll, Riffenburgh, Roberts, & Myhre, 2002). Grief and Hewitt (1999) found body modifications, including piercing, were associated with risky behaviors such as drug use, cigarette smoking, and alcohol use. Body modifications such as piercing were found to predict unsafe sexual practices and alcohol use (Burger & Finkel, 2002).

Individuals with body piercings (compared to those without) are more likely to be violent. Carroll and Anderson (2002) found a significant correlation, among adolescent girls, between number of tattoos and body piercings and a predisposition to react with anger, especially verbal expression of anger. Ceniceros (1998) discovered that young adults with body piercing (compared to those without) reported greater levels of violent behavior and were more involved in the risky activity of Russian roulette.

Likewise, young adults with tattooing and body piercing experience behavioral problems. Compared to those without, young adults with tattooing and body piercing reported higher anxiety and more dysfunctional social behavior (Ceniceros, Brown, & Swartz, 1998). Age of piercing was a factor in that the younger individuals were when they began body piercing, the higher their self-reported antisocial attitudes (Frederick & Bradley, 2000). Further, body piercing is a form of self-mutilation, that is, deliberate, nonsuicidal destruction of one's own body tissue (Armstrong & Kelly, 2001; Koenig & Carnes, 1999).

There appears to be no difference between pierced and nonpierced individuals on some demographic and psychological measures. For example, pierced (those who violated the norm) and nonpierced (those who did not violate the norm) students did not differ in church attendance, strength of faith, closeness to God, and daily prayer (Armstrong, Roberts, Owen, & Koch, 2004). Frederick and Bradley (2000) discovered no significant differences between individuals with body piercing and those without body piercing on any of five psychological scales including depression, anxiety, vitality, psychopathology, and self-esteem. These authors found that the average age at which multiple piercing began was 15, and the earlier the age at which piercing began, the greater the tendency to psychological disturbance. "The most common background for piercing in teenagers is peer pressure and the wish to fit into a group" (Armstrong, 1996, p. 237). Armstrong and Kelly (2001) speculated that if an adolescent wanted to pierce his or her body, he or she would do it regardless of regulations, risks, financial cost, or sanctions.

GENDER NORM VIOLATIONS

One cultural universal is that females and males are visually differentiated by gender-appropriate dress (Hegland, 1999). Based on cultural definitions of normality (what is customary, common, or ordinary), individuals observe and interpret others' gender role behavior.

Gender Role Socialization

Through the socialization process, members of both sexes learn the cultural definition of femininity and masculinity, along with gender-appropriate behavior and appearance. **Sex** is a biological term; individuals are either male or female depending on their sex organs and genes. Recall from Chapter 3

TATTOOERS,
BODY PIERCERS,
CROSS-DRESSERS,
PUNKS, GOTHS,
AND MORE

139

that gender is a psychological and cultural term, referring to an individual's subjective feelings of maleness or femaleness (their **gender identity**). Gender role refers to society's evaluation of behavior as masculine or feminine. Femininity and masculinity are revealed through dress, facial features, body shape, mannerisms, voice, and gestures.

Through **gender role socialization**, members of society learn how males and females ought to look, and therefore dress is a key factor in communication of an individual's gender. Gender role socialization not only teaches individuals what gender-appropriate dress is but also what responses individuals should have toward the gender-appropriate or gender-inappropriate dress of others (Figure 6.7).

Norms that govern gender-appropriate dress are powerful, and individuals are sanctioned (rewarded or punished) for clothing choices that conform to or violate conventional norms. These sanctions contribute to development of a gender identity. Choosing gender-appropriate dress is a demonstration of an individual's willingness to comply with cultural gender role norms. In the United States, expected male and female physical characteristics, behaviors, and personality traits are classified according to a binary gender system (a system divided into two distinct groups—male and female).

FIGURE 6.7 EVEN AS BABIES INDIVIDUALS ARE DRESSED IN GENDER-APPROPRIATE CLOTHING TO ENSURE APPROPRIATE SOCIETAL RESPONSES—FOR EXAMPLE, GIRLS IN PINK, WITH HIGH HEELS, RUFFLES, AND FEATHERS.

College Students and Gender Norm Violations

Nielsen, Walden, and Kunkel (2000) analyzed students' written narratives of gender norm violations gathered in class projects over a 15-year period. **Gender norm violations** were defined as doing the unexpected or not doing the expected for a given gender. Students' narratives included their gender norm violation, their own reactions, and others' reactions. Students were accompanied by a partner who observed and recorded others' verbal and nonverbal reactions. The most common reaction to male norm violators was being labeled homosexual or potentially homosexual. Male norm violators were blatantly, overtly, and derogatorily labeled homosexual, made fun of, and subjected to implications that they appeared or acted gay. For example, two men who wore dresses to a bar were told "fairies aren't allowed in here." A man with red fingernail polish felt compelled to tell onlookers that it was for a class project and reported that they appeared relieved that he was not gay.

Sanctions against women were principally in terms of the norm violation's effect on their attractiveness and availability to men (whether she was pretty, cute, or would be nice to kiss) (Nielsen, Walden, & Kunkel, 2000). Women expressed concern that others might think they were gay when they tried on men's suits, wore men's suits and ties to a sorority dinner, or failed to shave their legs and underarms. A woman who violated gender body language by sitting with her legs apart reported that observers seemed to interpret the position as promiscuous instead of masculine. Students' gender norm violations brought sanctions that revealed taken-for-granted and compulsory gender norms. The results illustrated the interconnected nature of society and individual experience.

Kunkel and Nielsen (1998) used a societal reaction approach to examine gender norm violations. A societal reaction approach to deviance employs a qualitative methodology to measure public reactions and responses to single, transitory, gender-specific norm violations. These authors noted that little is known about gender-specific informal means of social control in everyday, routine social interaction. Residual deviance was defined as "violations of those unwritten, unarticulated but taken for granted rules that govern the mass of society in everyday life" (p. 340). Scheff (1984) identified dress (clothing, appearance, and the body) as one area subject to informal social control. Underlying normative assumptions were brought into the open when students did not do what was expected (women not shaving their underarms) or did the unexpected (men wearing nail polish). Data came from student gender norm violation projects.

One methodological problem identified by Kunkel and Nielsen (1998) was defining and measuring informal (vs. formal) means of social control in the form of sanctions and thus identifying residual deviance. Social control is "largely informal—unstated, unseen, and unacknowledged" (Scheff, 1984, p. 25). Prior studies had used self-reports, reactions to hypothetical scenarios, and anecdotal and common knowledge about gender norms, rather than specific reactions to specific norm violations.

Gender norms were defined as "rules or standards of behavior held for one sex or the other and shared by most members of society" (Kunkel & Nielsen, 1998, p. 344). Students stated explicitly the gender norm they chose to violate. Norms identified were an integral part of students' perceived everyday reality, indicated by such phrases as "women can dress like men, so why can't men wear skirts?" Gender norm violations related to appearance included women wearing mustaches and men wearing makeup or fingernail polish. Women defined a wide range of actions as norm violations, reflecting their perceptions of wide-ranging social control. Males had a harder time choosing or finding a gender norm to violate—they perceived little that they could not already do, hence their selection of appearance norms: looking like a woman in some way or another. Based on an analysis of the gender norms selected by students, the authors concluded gender norm boundaries remained unchanged over the 15-year period of the study.

Reactions to the norm violations were categorized, ranging from no reaction, nonverbal double take, strong expression of disapproval, to overt action (calling the police) (Kunkel & Nielsen, 1998). The category of norm violation made a difference in terms of societal reaction—appearance norm violations generated the most negativity. Female norm violators were sanctioned more than men as targets of verbal and sexual remarks—47 percent of women compared to 29 percent of men reported sexual responses to norm violations. Reactions to the women's projects had a specific content—female norm violators were talked at (rather than with), and the content of the talk was often sexual in nature.

Male norm violators were sanctioned more than female norm violators in terms of negativity, strength of reaction, laughter, and homophobia. The findings suggested that men were strongly censured through concern and fear of being labeled homosexual and that this is primarily through informal means in everyday life. Homosexuality constitutes a sex-orientation norm violation (Kunkel & Nielsen, 1998). These findings indicate a strong role for informal means of social control for men. The authors concluded that men experience fewer restrictions about what they can do and where they can go but stronger reactions both internally and externally when they challenge gender boundaries.

Children and Gender Norm Violations

Children can distinguish males and females shortly after two years of age and acquire basic knowledge about gender norms between ages two and five years (O'Brien, Peyton, Mistry, Hruda, Jacobs, Caldera, et al., 2000). Blakemore (2003) examined children's knowledge of and beliefs about violating gender norms including hairstyles, clothing, and toys. Blakemore measured 3- to 11-year-old children's knowledge of gender norms, their judgments about whether it was possible to violate these norms, and their evaluations of children who did so. She compared age and gender differences in evaluations. Among the 16 gender norms were four norms related to appearance: boys' hair, girls' hair, boys' clothes, and girls' clothes (all accompanied by pictures).

Both older and younger children identified girls' clothes as norms, including 80 percent of the youngest children (Blakemore, 2003). When children were asked if it was possible to violate these norms, first graders expressed the least degree of belief that norm violation was possible, less than both preschoolers and the older children. Girls were more likely than boys to say that it was possible for girls to wear boys' clothes and for boys to have girls' hairstyles. Knowledge of the norms and flexibility about the possibility of violating them generally increased with age.

Girls evaluated norm violations more positively than boys in all cases (Blakemore, 2003). Boys with feminine hairstyles or clothing were evaluated more negatively than girls with masculine hairstyles or clothing. Among the gender norms, boys wearing girls' clothing were evaluated almost as negatively as children who steal. Boys playing with Barbie dolls were also negatively evaluated; this norm is related to appearance because Barbie dolls involve hairstyles, clothing, and makeup. Violation of appearance norms can be seen as related to basic gender identity.

A study by Szkrybalo and Ruble (1999) showed that young children were more likely to incorrectly identify a child's actual sex when the child wore clothing of the other gender than when other kinds of gender norms (activities or traits) were violated. Children were asked questions about changes in sex identity accompanying changes in stereotypic clothing, activities, and traits, for example, "If Jack wore a dress, would Jack be a boy or a girl? [or asking girls] If you went into the other room and put on clothes like these [boy's clothes card], would you then really be a girl or really be a boy?" (p. 395).

Questions about changes in gender-typed clothing were assumed to be more difficult for children to resolve than questions about activities or traits because gender-typed clothing is salient. Salient cues such as clothing might accentuate conflicts between gender norms and gender identity. Children sometimes used gender norms to explain their responses, for example, a girl who responded that she would really be a girl explained "Because I won't be wearing boys' clothes" (p. 397). The authors speculated that children may learn strong cultural taboos early, for example, the taboo against cross-dressing. Children may mistakenly believe that violations of gender-appropriate dress are likely to change a person's sex identity.

Cross-Dressers

Cross-dressers violate the culturally prescribed and proscribed dress norms for males and females. Hegland (1999) defined **cross-dressing** as "those occasions when a male puts on feminine dress or a female adopts masculine dress for whatever purpose or to whatever effect" (p. 195). Although some authors suggest that there are no female cross-dressers because women can easily wear men's clothing, there is a powerful taboo against male cross-dressing. In a fieldwork study, Hegland considered three types of male-to-female cross-dressers: the transsexual, the transvestite, and the drag queen. Within each category, a male cross-dresser modifies and supplements his appearance to create a feminine image.

A **transsexual** is someone who identifies himself or herself as a member of one sex, but has the reproductive organs of the other sex. Feminine dress seems natural to the male transsexual because he feels trapped in the wrong body. In creating the illusion of a female, the transsexual removes all telltale body hair, grows the hair on his head into a feminine hairstyle, uses padding to create the illusion of breasts and hips, expertly applies makeup, buffs and polishes his fingernails and toenails, wears earrings in his pierced ears, and decorates his body with other jewelry such as necklaces, bracelets, and rings. He wears currently fashionable women's clothing.

The male **transvestite** is a male who dresses in feminine attire and emulates the female form, but never forgets he is a male (Hegland, 1999). The transvestite's cross-dressing might not be publicly visible; it may be limited to wearing women's undergarments under men's clothing. **Exhibitionism** is deliberately behaving or dressing in a way that attracts attention. Exhibitionism plays a big role in transvestism, but most transvestites suffer immense anxiety—they feel guilty when they cross-dress but experience uneasiness and depression when they are unable to cross-dress. They create a feminine image that is a bit old-fashioned: "a few curls, perhaps a string of pearls, a tweed skirt, sensible shoes, and stockings" (p. 197). Usually, it is obvious that they are wearing wigs.

The **drag queen** is defined as "a homosexual male who cross-dresses in the spirit of satire" (Hegland, 1999, p. 198). The drag queen tends to break the rules by creating an appearance comparable to a showgirl or a prostitute. The drag queen may dress in spiked heels, a dress of reflective fabric (sequins, lamé, black vinyl), bouffant hairstyle, or slinky provocative clothing that clearly defines the curves of the body. Hair, makeup, breasts, gestures, carriage, and vocal intonation are all exaggerated.

Male-to-female cross-dressing is considered a violation of norms in our culture. However, cross-dressers provide an example of norm violation and, by contrast, serve to highlight how males and females should or should not look in our society.

Ceglian and Lyons (2004) investigated the comfort level of individuals interacting with cross-dressers. The Bem Sex Role Inventory (Bem, 1974) was used to categorize participants' gender role type as masculine, feminine, or androgynous. According to Bem, masculinity and femininity are distinct dimensions of an individual's personality rather than opposite ends of a continuum. Individuals (males and females) who depict themselves as having traits congruent with male gender role expectations are gender-typed as masculine. Likewise, individuals who depict themselves as having traits congruent with female gender role expectations are gender-typed as feminine. Individuals who have incorporated masculinity and femininity equally in their personality and behaviors are androgynous.

Ceglian and Lyons (2004) used the Comfort with Cross-Dressers Scale to measure participants' comfort before and after interacting with cross-dressers. The feminine group experienced the least change and the masculine group experienced the most change in comfort after interacting with cross-dressers. The authors concluded that attitudes toward individuals who violate gender-role norms can be changed through interaction with the violator.

SUBCULTURAL STYLES AS NORM VIOLATIONS

"Youth subcultures are conspicuous features of Western and other societies of the world" (Holme, 2005, p. 43). A **youth subculture** is a subdivision within a society with a distinctive lifestyle, values, norms, and beliefs that attract young people as members. A subculture may be organized around music (punk, grunge, Goth), sports (skateboarders, surfers), art, literature, or poetry (Beatniks), religion, and so forth. Adolescents' search for identity can

TATTOOERS,
BODY PIERCERS,
CROSS-DRESSERS,
PUNKS, GOTHS,
AND MORE

145

be one motivation for their interest in a subculture. To become a part of a subculture requires effort; prospective members need to learn the unspoken rules and acquire various things that symbolize the subculture's ideology.

Davis (2006) noted that if subcultures are all style and no substance, their symbols are suitable for adoption by the very consumer culture that they are critiquing or abandoning. Subcultures can lose control of the symbols that give meaning to their subcultures, and those symbols can actually be transformed into their opposite meaning through commodification. **Commodification** refers to the process by which a product is developed for commerce, for buying and selling.

Subcultures can survive because the dominant culture, through commodification, has managed to fit them into the normative order (Davis, 2006). Subcultural styles can provide inspiration for designers and become fashion innovations in conventional clothing (P. W. Thomas, 2006). For example, companies such as Nike and Adidas have devoted design and marketing resources to developing their image of a skateboarder, which comprises expensive sneakers, brand-name clothes, and flashy accessories (Pomerantz, Currie, & Kelly, 2004). Subsequently, these companies promote and sell their commodities not only to skateboarding enthusiasts, but to mainstream consumers as well.

Punk Fashion

Punk was a British subculture of the 1970s epitomized by the look and attitude of The Sex Pistols (a short-lived and infamous band). Hebdige (1979) interpreted punk style as a visual response to the socioeconomic crisis in Britain at the time. The **punk look** is characterized by clothing that has been destroyed and put back together, is inside out, unfinished, or deteriorating (Bell-Price, 2006). The most recognizable punk fashions are bondage trousers (with leg straps), boots, ripped T-shirts with anarchic slogans, spike bands (neck or wrist), brightly dyed hair standing up on end, and facial piercing (de la Haye & Dingwall, 1996). Indeed, a focal point of the punk look was hair colored pink or green with food dyes and spiked into a Mohican hairstyle by sugar and water solutions, soap, gelatin, glue, hair sprays, and hair gel (P. W. Thomas, 2006). An alternative look was to shave areas of the scalp.

Punks pierced facial parts such as eyebrows, cheeks, noses, or lips and inserted studs and pins. "Self-mutilation, rejection of prettiness and body piercing were not the norms" in the 1970s (P. W. Thomas, 2006, ¶ 6). These styles were intended to violate conventional norms, create an intimidating look, startle the onlooker, attract attention, and offend traditional members of society (Figure 6.8). Some punks think the term punk fashion is an oxymoron because punk is the antithesis of fashion (*Punk Fashion*, 2006).

Punk fashion was commodified (adapted to mass marketing) in less than three years (Bell-Price, 2006). In the twenty-first century, punk and hip-hop, another subcultural style, merged into a standard look for contemporary youth (Bell-Price, 2006). In fashion, hip-hop has been associated with baggy jeans, gold jewelry, baseball caps, and certain designer brands like Tommy Hilfiger (Kitwana, 2002). Elements of fashion that emerged from punk style are clothing and imagery that appear "dirty, ripped, scarred, shocking, spectacular, cruel, traumatized, sick, or alienating" (Bell-Price, 2006, ¶ 11). Punk fashion was a do-it-yourself anti–mass culture ethic and aesthetic (Leblanc, 1999).

FIGURE 6.8 PUNK ROCKER, COMBINING THE PUNK LOOKS OF THE SHAVED HEAD AND SPIKED HAIR, AS WELL AS ACCESSORIES DESIGNED TO INTIMIDATE.

Punks designed garments to attract attention; they cut up old clothes from charity and thrift shops, destroyed the fabric, and deconstructed the garments into new forms characterized by torn fabrics, frayed edges, and defaced prints (P. W. Thomas, 2006). Prior to punk fashion, fabric had been a material to keep as pristine, new-looking, and beautiful as possible. Trousers, deliberately torn to reveal dirty legs or tights with runs in them, were worn with heavy Doc Martens footwear; safety pins and chains held bits of fabric together. Neck chains made from padlocks and chains emerged later as mainstream fashion status symbols when produced in gold.

Punk fashion included black leather, studs, chains, grayed sweated-out black T-shirts, and leg straps. Punk body piercing entered mainstream fashion with the three-stud earlobe, progressing to the outline of the whole ear embedded with studs. Blatant and obvious sexual references in written form, on dyed and destroyed vests, became a norm in the mass market production of T-shirts with obscene phrases.

Davis (2006) conducted six months of participant observation and 20 interviews with members of the local punk scene in Colorado and examined archival data of punk community publications, song lyrics, and other punk-scene cultural products. Things that may stimulate interest in the punk subculture are the lively young people, the fashion, the music, and the shows. Even within the punk scene, fashion trends come and go . . . "it used to be kids with fat pants and big t-shirts . . . . and now everyone's wearing tight clothes" (p. 10). Older punkers were criticized for inappropriate displays of youth by continuing to dress and cut their hair like young people. Subcultural members create a group identity as punk. From the group identity, they create a personal identity that is an achieved status. The group identity changes as the membership of the group changes—leading to a changing definition of *punk*.

Based on qualitative research using ethnographic interviews, Bennett (2006) examined how fans of punk rock articulate their attachment to the music and its associated visual style. Punk fashion, a highly visible subcultural style, is a protest against the obsessive consumerism of the dominant society (Bennett, 2006). Commitment to the punk ideology was symbolized by display of spectacular visual attire, a form of visual shock tactics. The punk image was used to express youthful anger, directed at the older generation and its dominant institutions. Punk visual style included reworking domestic utility items, such as safety pins and dustbin liners, as items of clothing. Selected items with obvious punk associations included nose rings, multiple earrings, metal studs, sew-on patches, tattoos with the name and/or logo of a favorite band, or all-black clothing. The hairstyle of older punks was often a subtle variation of the original, visually striking punk hairstyles of the 1970s. "A typical style was to have the hair cut very short, or shaven, with a slightly longer strip of hair following the shape of the classic punk Mohican style" (p. 225). One punk noted that because punks were visually different, they risked getting beaten up, people laughing at them, or people questioning why they wanted to look like that. Older punks toned down their visual punk image because of domestic and/or work commitments. However, the moderated outward display of punk style was offset with internalized punk ideology that eliminated the need for striking visual display of commitment to punk.

Reddington (2004) described the fishnet stockings, spiky dyed black hair, and dramatic eye makeup of female punks: a "threatening sexual style that is most associated with what have been disparagingly labeled 'punkettes'" (p. 440). An exhibition that opened in May 2006 explored the music, clothing, designs, and images of punk, through the work of three key individuals—Vivienne Westwood, Malcolm McLaren, and Jamie Reid ("Via Makes Noise," 2006).

Vivienne Westwood was acknowledged as British Designer of the Year in 1990 and 1991 for her history of creating original and outrageous fashions (Cardell, 1996). Westwood was one of the creative forces behind punk rock fashion and "continues to break rules and taboos with revolutionary looks" ("Vivienne Westwood," 2006, ¶ 3). Westwood is credited with popularizing "the bustier, the Westwood tartan, and the 10-inch platform shoes from which Naomi Campbell famously toppled mid-catwalk strut" (*Biography: Dame Vivienne Westwood*, 2006, ¶ 5).

GOTH STYLE

Goth style commonly includes black hair and clothes, horror-style makeup (white facial foundation, black eyeliner, and dark lipstick for both women and men), and symbols of death (crucifixes). Part of the ideology is individual defiance of social norms. Many who are drawn to the culture have already failed to conform to the norms of existing society. The Goth subculture provides a way to gain status through enthusiastic participation and creativity such as making clothes, designing, or creating art. Based on participant-observation and interviews, Hodkinson (2002) concluded that subcultural themes included "horror, death, misery, and gender ambiguity" (p. 61).

Like the punk subculture it grew out of, early Goth fashion had a strong emphasis on the do-it-yourself (DIY) ethic (*Gothic Fashion*, 2006). The simplicity of the style lends itself to variation, and it is often combined with elements of other subcultural styles. Hair is often dyed blue-black and sometimes backcombed to give it a large, ratty appearance. The core of Gothic fashion is individual taste, as the Gothic culture is opposed to conventions of how one must look. Borrowing from punk fashion, sometimes Goths will tear or cut their clothes apart (usually with scissors), then repair their clothes with safety pins, buckles, or similar fastenings to create a style associated with punk or industrial music cultures. Goths reject mainstream values, emphasize freedom of expression, and challenge taboos—making it difficult to define the aesthetic principles of Goth fashion. Goth fashions defy conventions by emphasizing transformation of the body, conscious eroticism, and otherness (Figure 6.9).

Lolipop Goth (Hirano, 2004) is a new fashion category emerging from Japan. It is a cross between Gothic and Lolita and combines elements of Gothic with a sweet childishness. Goth-Loli style involves an abundance of

FIGURE 6.9 THREE GOTH TEENAGERS, EXHIBITING GOTH TENDENCY TOWARD OTHERNESS WITH RATTED HAIR AND BODY TRANSFORMATION THROUGH TATTOOING AND MAKEUP, WAIT OUTSIDE BEFORE A MARILYN MANSON CONCERT.

TATTOOERS,
BODY PIERCERS,
CROSS-DRESSERS,
PUNKS, GOTHS,
AND MORE

decorativeness, incorporating lots of frills and layers. Goth-Loli fans want to distinguish themselves from the masses. What makes the fashion different from punk fashion is that there is no larger message of unrest or disquiet.

Skateboarder Style

Skateboarders are individuals who demonstrate an interest in, and technical knowledge of, skateboarding. The values associated with skateboarding culture include individual self-expression, authenticity, nonconformity, and disdain for mass consumerism. Kelly, Pomerantz, and Currie (2005) interviewed 20 girls who participated in skateboarding culture by wearing the casual, comfortable clothes that allowed them to move with ease on their skateboards.

> The girls came to be seen—both by themselves as well as their friends and peers—as skaters by: expressing particular beliefs, values and feelings; using a skateboard and demonstrating technical knowledge about skateboarding; displaying physical risk-taking and enduring bodily pain; dressing in certain ways; using skater and other in-group slang; avoiding behavior associated with emphasized or dominant femininity; and engaging in activities closely allied with skater culture, such as listening to alternative or punk rock music. (p. 232)

Among the emerging norms of skater girlhood were fun, adventure, confidence, and nonconformity (Kelly, Pomerantz, & Currie, 2005). Every skater girl interviewed said she valued nonconformity, that is, being different, alternative, unique, not normal, weird, an original, freaky, creative, artistic, standing out from the crowd, or trendy.

Skateboarding stereotypes are associated with nonconformity (Kelly, Pomerantz, & Currie, 2005). The pothead stereotype refers to violation of prevailing mores against drug use; the punk or hooligan stereotype refers to violation of prevailing mores of respect for private property; the slacker stereotype refers to nonconformity with the dominant work ethic; and the laid-back and underground stereotypes refer to nonconformity with consumer culture.

In general, the girls liked the casual, comfortable (baggy) look of skater clothes and disliked the revealing, brand-name clothes (tight, expensive designer jeans or skirts, tight tank tops, and lots of makeup) they associated with a certain type of popular, boy-hunting girl (Kelly, Pomerantz, & Currie, 2005). Some of the skater girls expressed through their style that they wanted to "be their own person," to "stand out" (by wearing safety pins as earrings), or to be funky (by dying their hair blue). In an act of nonconformity with consumerism, some skater girls shopped at secondhand clothing stores. There was concern that skater style had become increasingly popular; anyone could wear expensive skate shoes and skate clothing without being an authentic skater.

Using skater slang to describe the skateboard or skateboarding tricks was another way girls came to be seen as skaters (Kelly, Pomerantz, & Currie, 2005). Different groups of skaters developed inside jokes, invented funny names for each other, and made up words. Skater girlhood was full of contradictions and tensions—expressing a unique personal style while adhering to group norms, disavowing fashion and popularity even as skateboarding itself became more expensive and trendy, and valuing an easygoing demeanor while distancing oneself from those who pretended to be skaters.

Pomerantz, Currie, and Kelly (2004) contrasted skater girls (girls who were members of the skateboarding culture) as a social category with what Connell (1987) called **emphasized femininity**—a kind of traditional femininity based on subordination to men and boys. These authors interviewed eight girls who were members of a group of skateboarders called the Park Gang.

Some of the male skateboarders accused members of the Park Gang of being posers. "A poser wears the right clothes, such as wide sneakers with fat laces, brand-name pants and hoodies, and, of course, carries a skateboard. But posers do not really skate" (Pomerantz, Currie, & Kelly, 2004, p. 552).

Some of the popular girls at school had boyfriends and money to spend on the right clothes. These girls were described by one of the skater girls as annoying people who lived by an image—skinny, thin, pretty, makeup, lots of money, shoes, spoiled, and living their life for a boy. The so-called Bun Girls dressed to be popular with boys and had a ditzy reputation because they spent so much energy worrying about clothes, looks, and boyfriends. The nickname of Bun Girls derived from the fact that they often wore buns in their hair. "Bun Girls wore tight, low-cut tank tops and tight, low-cut jeans from expensive, brand-name stores. Their appearance was coiffed, polished, and en vogue" (p. 553).

Skater girls described a Bun Girl as a carbon copy with no defining characteristics, except caring what other people think. Members of the Park Gang believed this kind of self-conscious behavior was all too typical and gave girls a bad name. Bun Girl femininity, based on physical appearance, money, clothing, and inactivity, was giggly, ditzy, and purposefully subordinate to boys.

The Park Gang dressed casually and comfortably as a means of differentiation from the Bun Girls femininity. They avoided wearing makeup and did not engage in sexual display through style. They saw themselves as individuals with unique personalities who took pride in being different, fun, and alternative.

Skate culture has been continuously redefined since its original incarnation in the 1970s Californian surf culture. Many elements remain the same today—a dedication to punk rock (now splintered into pop punk, old school punk, hardcore, and Goth), a love of baggy clothes, and a slacker reputation. The Park Gang did not buy expensive skater clothes, opting instead for an alternative secondhand look—for example, men's dress shirts and black gloves with the fingers cut off. A well-known teen pop singer, Avril Lavigne, was called a *skate punk* for her style and connections to skateboarding (Pomerantz, Currie, & Kelly, 2004).

SUMMARY

This chapter explored research related to violation of norms. We examined research studies related to (a) norm violations of social class groups, (b) body modifications such as tattoos and body piercings, (c) gender-norm violations, and (d) subcultural styles associated with such groups as punks, Goths, and skateboarders.

KEY TERMS AND CONCEPTS

body piercing	Goth style
commodification	punk look
cross-dressing	sex
drag queen	skateboarders
emphasized femininity	social class
exhibitionism	status disparities
gender identity	tattoo
gender norms	transsexual
gender norm violations	transvestite
gender role socialization	youth subculture

1. Armstrong, M. L., Roberts, A. E., Owen, D. C., & Koch, J. R. (2004). Contemporary college students and body piercing. *Journal of Adolescent Health, 35*, 58–61.

2. Burger, T., & Finkel, D. (2002). Relationships between body modifications and very high-risk behavior in a college population. *College Student Journal, 36*(2), 203–213.

3. Morgado, M. A. (2007). The semiotics of extraordinary dress: A structural analysis and interpretation of hip-hop style. *Clothing and Textiles Research Journal, 25*(2), 131–155.

Research Activity 6.1: *Literature Analysis*

Purpose: To analyze research literature related to violations of appearance norms, identifying the purpose, research method, and results.

Procedure:

1. Describe the characteristics of a research article.

2. Use the Google Scholar (http://scholar.google.com/) search engine or an academic database (EBSCO, ERIC, SocIndex) to locate one research article related to the violation of appearance norms. For example, you might use the key words *dress norms violation* or *appearance standard violations* to search for research articles.

3. Print a copy of the research article.

4. Highlight and label the purpose of the study, the research method used, the results of the study related to its purpose, and the violations of appearance norm(s) studied.

5. Submit your work to your instructor.

Research Activity 6.2 *Culture and Dress Norm Violations*

Purpose: To analyze videos to understand how a cultural context influences perceptions of dress norms.

Procedure:

1. Log on to the *National Geographic* magazine website (http://www. nationalgeographic.com/).

2. Select (click on) "People and Places" and "Countries."

3. Select (click on) a country or region other than the United States.

4. Select (click on) and view a "Featured Video" or "Photo Gallery" for that country or region.

5. Identify one dress norm portrayed in the video or photographs. Compare and contrast that norm to dress norms in Western society.

6. Submit your work to your instructor.

Chapter Seven

RECOGNITION OF NORM VIOLATIONS: THE FASHION POLICE

FROM THE HEADLINES

Glamour magazine's feature called "Dos and Don'ts" has become a pop culture institution. Recently, Blip.tv publicized its licensing agreement with
Glamour to create a consumer-generated fashion photograph gallery in the
online magazine, Glamour.com. Online readers who visit the Dos and Don'ts
site (http://www.glamourdosanddonts.com/) can have an interactive experience by contributing photographs of fashion Dos and Don'ts they notice
on the street. People everywhere can document and share the fashions they
see on the street, from the well-dressed to the worst faux pas. "Don't" spot-
ting turns people-watching into a shared experience. *Glamour* readers can
take the part of fashion editor, critically assess street fashion, and even select
the best and worst examples. *Glamour,* with an average monthly circulation of
more than 2.4 million copies, reaches one in every ten women in the United
States, or more than 14 million monthly readers.

Source: Blip.tv and Conde Nast's *Glamour* team up as fashion police: Company lets
anyone with a camera submit fashion dos & don'ts to Glamour.com
(2006, October 4). *PR Newswire US.* Retrieved January 9, 2007
from http://www.lexisnexis.com

This news story announces a method for people to document and share
the norm violations they notice. It is no accident that readers of *Glamour* magazine notice dress norm violations; they embody many of the
characteristics of those who are likely to notice norm violations. How are people who are likely to recognize dress norm violations influenced by a magazine feature such as "Dos and Don'ts"? Can the designation of *fashion police* be
attributed to knowledge gained from exposure to a magazine feature such as
"Dos and Don'ts"? Why or why not? How are submissions to *Glamour*'s fashion
photograph gallery influenced by the characteristics of those who are likely to

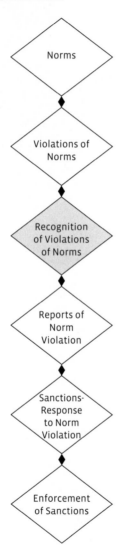

FIGURE 7.1 THE THIRD STEP IN THE PROCESS OF SOCIAL CONTROL IS TO RECOGNIZE NORM VIOLATIONS. WE HAVE ALL RECOGNIZED DRESS NORM VIOLATIONS. WE NEED TO LOOK AT WHEN, WHERE, WHAT, AND WHY DRESS NORM VIOLATIONS ARE RECOGNIZED.

recognize dress norm violations? In this chapter, you will read about the characteristics of people who are likely to notice norm violations. We will look at recognition of norm violations from a journalistic tradition: who, what, when, where, and why norm violations are likely to be recognized (Figure 7.1).

Among the factors affecting *who* will be most likely to recognize dress norm violations are fashion knowledgeability, status, sensitivity to aesthetic rules, self-monitoring, fashion involvement, fashion interest, fashion innovativeness, and fashion opinion leadership. Among the factors affecting *what* norm violations are most likely to be recognized are visibility, egregiousness, and incongruity. Among the factors affecting *when* norm violations are most likely to be recognized are publicity and celebrity status. Among the factors affecting *where* norm violations are most likely to be recognized are explicit and implicit dress codes. Among the factors affecting *why* particular norm violations are likely to be recognized are unpredictability and uncertainty.

QUESTIONS TO ANSWER AS YOU READ

1. How do I recognize norm violations?
2. Why are some people more likely than others to recognize norm violations?
3. What, when, where, and why are certain norm violations likely to be recognized?

THE FASHION POLICE

Knowledge of the shared rules of the normative order for dress is a necessary but insufficient condition for a violation to be recognized. Because of their subjective, emotional, and ethical character, norms are difficult to identify with certainty (Blake & Davis, 1964; Gibbs, 1981; Workman & Freeburg, 2000a). By extension, then, violations of norms are also difficult to identify with certainty. On the other hand, because visual stimuli such as dress can be detected from a distance, violations of dress norms may be recognized even when violations of other norms are not recognized, and even when no social interaction occurs.

Fashion police is a term that refers to an imaginary police force that ensures people dress in accordance with fashion ("Fashion Police," 2006). The term can refer to self-appointed individuals or to individuals who by virtue of their position are placed in an enforcement role (school administrators, business managers). The term is used humorously to refer to self-appointed individuals who notice and critique the outfits other people wear in order to point out their norm violations (Figure 7.2). The term is used disapprovingly to imply that the fashion police have a narrow, rigid, or uncreative sense of style or propriety.

Alternately, the term can be used approvingly with regard to the assumed personal judgment of the fashion police if an individual believes someone has committed a fashion faux pas. A faux pas is a violation of accepted, albeit unwritten, social rules or norms. In French, the term means *false step* ("Faux Pas," 2006). *US Weekly* magazine reports regularly on celebrities who have committed fashion faux pas. For example, a photograph and critique of a female actor, Sienna Miller, wearing sheepskin Ugg booties in the summertime appeared in *US Weekly* (Hancock, 2006).

FIGURE 7.2 *GLAMOUR'S BIG BOOK OF DOS AND DON'TS* IS A GUIDE TO NORM VIOLATIONS.

WHO RECOGNIZES NORM VIOLATIONS?

A number of social and psychological qualities characterize members of the fashion police force. Factors that influence who is likely to recognize norm violations are outlined in Table 7.1 and explored in detail below.

Fashion Knowledgeability

Fashion knowledgeability refers to the amount of fashion information obtained and used by individuals. Fashion knowledgeability is related to recognition of norm violation; individuals who are knowledgeable about fashion are more likely to recognize a norm violation than those who are less knowledgeable. Understanding the meanings associated with dress is a complex process because meanings stem from a blend of aesthetic rules with social rules and cultural customs (Kaiser, 1997).

Aesthetic rules refer to the principles of design (rhythm, emphasis, balance,

TABLE 7.1 FACTORS THAT INFLUENCE WHO IS LIKELY TO RECOGNIZE NORM VIOLATIONS

FACTOR	DESCRIPTION
Fashion knowledgeability	The amount of fashion information obtained and used by individuals
Status	A person's position in a social hierarchy
Ascribed: Gender	Male/female
Ascribed: Age	Young … old
Achieved: Occupation	A job regarded as a long-term or lifelong activity
Sensitivity to aesthetic rules	Responsiveness to aesthetic stimuli
Self-monitoring	Individuals' monitoring and controlling self-presentations in harmony with social cues
Fashion awareness	Recognition of fashion objects and their meanings
Fashion involvement	The extent to which an individual views the activities surrounding fashion as a meaningful and engaging part of her/his life
Fashion interest	The amount of time, energy, money, and personal commitment an individual expends in the pursuit of fashion
Fashion innovativeness	Willingness to try new products relatively early in the product life style
Fashion opinion leadership	Influencing others in purchase decisions, giving advice, and being an information source

FIGURE 7.3 THIS YOUNG MAN WEARS PLAID, STRIPES, AND A TIE WITH A CASUAL SHIRT; HE VIOLATES A NUMBER OF AESTHETIC RULES.

scale, proportion, and unity) that are used to manipulate the aesthetic elements (the basic components used to create a visual design, such as color, pattern, line, shape, form, texture, light) during the design process (Figure 7.3). For example, a seven-year-old girl won a Design a Dress Contest sponsored by a children's dress company (Israelsen, 2006). The dress she designed was pink (color), decorated with roses (emphasis), floor length (proportion), big (scale), poofy (form) with a princess line bodice and square neckline (line), made of shantung silk (texture).

Social rules are norms that govern groups and situations (Figure 7.4). For example, a bride-to-be wrote for advice concerning appropriate dress for wedding guests ("A Dress Code," 2006). The country club where the reception was to be held had a rule about men wearing jackets after 5 PM and she wondered how to inform the guests. The columnist suggested that the invitation contain a note that jackets are required by the country club. Otherwise, the guests without jackets might have difficulty getting into the club. Invitations for other types of social gathering can specify rules for dress, such as "white tie" or "cocktail attire."

FIGURE 7.4 (LEFT) CAN YOU POINT OUT SOME OF THE NORM VIOLATIONS HERE IN THIS PICTURE OF WEDDING ATTENDEES?

FIGURE 7.5 (RIGHT) ONE CULTURAL CUSTOM IS THAT BASE-BALL COACHES AND PLAYERS WEAR THE SAME UNIFORM.

Cultural customs are the traditions associated with a particular society or subcultural group within a society (Figure 7.5). For example, even in 97-degree heat, a young Cayuse Indian woman riding in a Julyamsh Powwow wore a full-length buckskin dress and wool blanket around her legs (Lutey, 2006). The dress she wore was a third-generation heirloom given to her at a formal recognition ceremony of becoming a woman when she was in her teens. In American Indian families, children were carefully taught the traditions associated with ceremonial dress. Children were told the story of the buckskin dress they would someday wear, who made it, and who had worn it proudly.

Codes are a system of rules relating to one subject. An **aesthetic code** is a combination of aesthetic rules, social rules, and cultural customs regarding dress. The aesthetic code includes the type of fabric, the texture of the material, the color and pattern of the material, the volume and silhouette of the structure, the occasion for which it is worn, the meanings associated with each element making up an outfit, the characteristics of the wearer (age, body type, coloring, height), the culture in which it is worn, and its historical background. Aesthetic rules, social rules, and cultural customs provide the background needed to interpret information conveyed by dress. Interpretation may be influenced by the culturally subjective nature of some design principles (what is considered harmonious or in proportion) (Davis, 1994). For example, South Korea recently removed the mini skirt rule from its list of minor offenses ("It's Official," 2006). The rule dated back to the military dictatorship of the 1970s, when showing too much skin in public places was considered indecent exposure.

Fashion symbols are created using an aesthetic code and can be thought of as a collection of signs (for example, dresses with or without sleeves) that convey ideas (modesty or immodesty) or information (a sacred ceremony) in a particular context (a child's First Communion). Every spring over 800,000 U.S. children accept the sacrament of First Communion ("Buy Early to Beat," 2006). Because some parishioners, priests, and nuns have been shocked by inappropriate dress, many parishes have adopted dress codes. Parents searching for the perfect dress for their little girls to wear are advised to research the First Communion dress codes established by their parish, because guidelines vary among parishes. Some churches prohibit sleeveless dresses, others do not. Modesty is the foremost First Communion dress code rule. The dresses the girls wear should meet the guidelines, look beautiful, and fit perfectly so they can focus on the sacred meaning associated with the day. The aesthetic code allows a message to be created and selectively understood (McCracken & Roth, 1989).

The aesthetic code is not the same as codes in other areas. First, messages transmitted through the aesthetic code can be used to create fashion symbols. These messages are often emotional impressions such as professionalism, modesty, physical attractiveness, femininity, masculinity, power, status, or prestige. For example, the Board of Supervisors for a California county debated a dress code for county employees (Troha, 2006). The dress code prohibited the wearing of denim jeans, required tattoos to be covered, and prohibited facial piercing, including nose, tongue, eyebrow, and lip piercing. The Human Resources Director commented that supervisors were going to be the fashion police to ensure employees presented a professional appearance.

Second, messages are transmitted through fashion symbols without using words or language. A writer for *GQ* [*Gentlemen's Quarterly*] commented on messages sent by people wearing baseball caps—for example, wearing the bill sideways or backwards makes the wearer look like an idiot (McCloud, 2006). Wearing the caps with dress shirts and ties is incongruous because of the combination of casual and dress items, and shows a lack of fashion savvy. A message of disrespect is conveyed when baseball caps are worn in class, church, the cafeteria, when the color guard passes in a parade, or when the national anthem is played. Similarly, women who wear an adjustable baseball cap with a ponytail sticking out above the tab send a message about their lack of fashion sense.

Third, the aesthetic code used to transmit fashion symbol messages is determined by convention and is most effective in communicating culturally defined categories, principles, and processes (age, sex, social class). The white dinner jacket, which first became popular during the 1920s, has elements of ostentation, formality, and one-upmanship (Birkner, 2006). During the 1940s, it was a favorite with Hollywood's leading men. The white dinner jacket is perceived as the "black blazer's wealthy, uppity, distantly related cousin" (p. 13). Because of its legacy, people perceive a white dinner jacket as expensive, upper-class, and something worn by wealthy people.

Finally, the aesthetic code is always changing. The meanings of fashion symbols emerge and change over time and among individuals—creating a symbolic life cycle for fashion symbols (Davis, 1994). A state health department launched an antitobacco campaign that used the symbolic life cycle of fashions as a cornerstone for their promotion (Welling, 2006). Absurd fashions from past decades were used to highlight the absurdity of past smoking trends. Fashions that changed in meaning over time and among individuals included the zoot suit (a man's suit, popular in the 1940s, with baggy high-waisted trousers tapering to a narrow hem and a long jacket heavily padded at the shoulders), the mullet (a hairstyle that is long at the back and short at the front and sides), knee-high white patent leather go-go boots, flower children hippie attire, and denim overalls with one unfastened strap.

Aesthetic knowledge is required to recognize coordination (or lack of coordination) of colors, fabrics, and styling of fashion items. Recognizing quality in fabric, construction, and fit also requires knowledge. Knowledge is gained from many sources, including study, training, observation, and reading. The creative director of a men's bespoke tailoring company, who is extremely knowledgeable about fashion, commented that he is "part chiropractor, part designer, part bespoke tailor, part illusionist, part psychiatrist" (Banks, 2006, p. 25). *Bespoke tailoring* is a British term for custom-made garments such as men's suits and coats. Bespoke tailoring is characterized by dedication to the tiniest detail—the inside of the garment is as beautiful as the outside.

Status

Recall from Chapter 1 that status refers to a person's position in a social hierarchy and that there are ascribed statuses and achieved statuses. Recall also that symbols of status activate widely shared societal beliefs about people in particular positions in a social hierarchy.

Ascribed Status: Gender

Socialization within a particular culture results in the transmission of knowledge about, recognition of, and respect for dress norms. However, as noted in Chapter 6, individuals differ in the extent to which they have received normative transmissions. Parents in the United States spend little time socializing boys with regard to dress norms and allow boys to be oblivious to the aesthetic code. Therefore, men are likely to be less knowledgeable about and consequently less likely to recognize violations of dress norms than women. For example, a fashion-challenged software programmer commented that the deciding factor in what he wore to work was whatever outfit was the least wrinkled (Pacio, 2006). His low-maintenance clothing philosophy showed in his typical choices for work—a rumpled mint green button-down shirt and a pair of oversized jeans with dirty, stringy hems dragging on the ground. His girlfriend had nominated him for a fashion makeover, where he received some style advice. Afterward he commented that he had never before had so much attention given to how he looked, including from himself.

During gender role socialization, an interest in achieving a fashionable appearance is transmitted as a feminine gender role expectation. McDowell (2006) typified the feminine interest in fashion when she reported that for as long as she could remember, she had been obsessed with the dos and don'ts of fashion. In high school, she kept a record of what she wore every day in order to avoid the teenage fashion faux pas of wearing the same article of clothing within six weeks of the last time she wore it. In college, when she was assigned to teach the class a skill, she taught about fashion faux pas. Her interest in fashion faux pas extended to her career as a staff writer for a newspaper, where she recognized and reported on the following faux pas: wearing too much bling at once, professional clothes with sneakers, orange fake tans, big hair, visible lipliner, scrunchies, banana clips, overly tweezed brows, and hair done over the top of a visor (about which she commented that this was the dumbest thing ever).

Because of gender role socialization, gender affects recognition of dress norm violations. Females are more conscious than males of both clothing function (use for which clothing is suited or designed) and clothing image (a characteristic or distinctive impression created by the clothing) (Auty & Elliott, 1998; Elliott, 1994). According to Traud (2006), copyright law has traditionally considered clothing a utilitarian item and not an artistic expression, but clothing is both. Clothing function and clothing image are so tightly entwined they are impossible to separate.

Women more readily recognize a **look** (appearance, style, or fashion, especially dress or hairstyle) and are more sensitive to fashion cues than are men. Parker (2006) recalled what a member of a baseball team wore to the prom—a white linen outfit with his last name and jersey number on the back accessorized with a white baseball cap turned to the side. Another young man wore cowboy boots and a Stetson hat with his tuxedo. Smith (2006a) provided prom tips for high school boys, advising them to get a haircut about two weeks prior to the prom and to wear dress socks with their tuxedo, dress shirt, tie, and vest or cummerbund.

Ascribed Status: Age

An individual's age group affects interpretation of fashion symbols and, by extension, recognition of dress norm violations. Different age groups respond differently to popular brands and to certain looks, such as tattoos and body piercings. For example, a customer wrote to a business columnist to complain about companies that "hire people who look like idiots" (DeBare, 2006, p. C1). The customer described a bank teller who had her tongue pierced with a metal spike and a photocopy technician with dreadlocks. The business columnist replied that because Generation Y is a pierced and tattooed generation, employers who rely on young workers to fill entry-level jobs often cannot eliminate applicants with tattoos and piercings without drastically reducing their pool of qualified applicants. Younger people are more conscious of fashion trends than older groups, and many people now interpret a pierced tongue as a youthful fashion statement rather than evidence of drug addiction or a "loser" mentality.

Fashion consultants recommend that if an individual is old enough to remember wearing a style the first time around, he or she should avoid wearing the trend again (Roberts, 2006). Recognizing a style from a previous decade also increases the possibility of recognizing a norm violation of the way it is worn.

Achieved Status: Occupation

Individuals with different occupational statuses and roles use different criteria to interpret the same information provided by fashion symbols. **Clothing** is a generic term that refers to garments, especially outer or decorative clothing. Recall from Chapter 3 that fashion refers to the currently prevailing style of dress. Clothing is a means of communicating social identity as well as personal identity, and so clothing is symbolic of the values advocated by the group identity. Individuals who belong to different groups make different judgments about the same clothing item. For example, designers, retailers, journalists, fashion editors, and fashion students use criteria that differ from those the average person uses in labeling a style fashionable or unfashionable (Kaiser, 1997).

The following article about one of the hottest fashion trends for the summer of 2006 mentions several occupational statuses that are recognized as requiring knowledge about fashion (the occupations are *italicized*). "As reimagined for the contemporary woman, shorts have lost their casual and athletic connotations. *Designers* are showing them as key components in sophisticated looks for work and evening, not just a day in the park" (Sullivan, 2006, p. C1, ¶ 5). An *assistant director of a college's women's business center* speculated that shorts are not going to be acceptable in the workplace. According to the assistant director, shorts are not a professional look and only the young, thin body type looks good in shorts. A *manager of a women's retail clothing store* remarked that cropped pants are acceptable in the workplace. The *owner of a women's boutique* agreed that cropped pants and long shorts are acceptable in a casual workplace. In the June 2006 issue of *Glamour* magazine, Bermuda shorts were cited as the *fashion-editor* obsession. Bermuda shorts were first designed in Bermuda in the mid-twentieth century when government regulations prohibited women from appearing in public in short shorts. According to the *reporter* (Sullivan), knee-length Bermudas represent the shortest length anyone should even consider wearing to work.

FIGURE 7.6 INDIVIDUALS WHO ARE ENGAGED IN A FASHION CAREER CAN USE THEIR KNOWLEDGE AND SKILLS TO RECOGNIZE VIOLATIONS OF DRESS NORMS.

Individuals who are engaged in a fashion career gain an in-depth knowledge of the aesthetic code and learn to recognize quality, fiber and fabric characteristics, and variations of the principles of design (Figure 7.6). Such knowledge and skills can lead to a sense of self-confidence in recognizing conformity to and violation of dress norms.

A fashion career involves one or more jobs over the course (or a distinct portion) of a person's life that relate to the fashion industry. A fashion career implies that someone is trained for and expects to work in a fashion-related occupation for his or her entire working life. Fashion-related occupations include the entire product chain from fiber to fabric to clothing production to retail. Individuals who have been trained in fashion are sensitive to variations of the aesthetic code in dress. As individuals become better trained and organized—that is, more professional—their sensitivity increases.

Sensitivity to Aesthetic Rules

Individuals vary in sensitivity to aesthetic rules (responsiveness to aesthetic stimuli). Seamstresses and tailors are extremely sensitive to the countless aesthetic variables to be considered in altering garments for a good fit (Bass, 2006). For example, the variables to consider in altering a skirt include style, lining, layering, zipper, darts, waistband, and length. Innovative and creative individuals are able to detect small changes in levels, conditions, or amounts of the aesthetic elements and are sensitive to changing aesthetic rules.

Yet even fashion insiders may disagree about the specific rules that govern aesthetic codes of dress. A fashion reporter recalled being stopped in October by a woman who reminded her that she should not wear white shoes after Labor Day (Crow, 2006). The reporter commented on the changing rules of fashion. For example, fashion rules that have changed over the years include the following: women over 40 should not have long hair; black and blue should never be worn together; handbags and shoes must match; black should not be worn to weddings; and velvet should only be worn for evening. Such rules make fashion choices more predictable and stem from a fear of others recognizing our fashion mistakes. The reporter's colleague mentioned a fashion rule that he considered outdated—do not wear white socks with sandals. The reporter disagreed, saying that the rule is still valid.

Fashion awareness refers to recognition of fashion objects and their meanings. A reader asked a newspaper staff writer how one could know the ins and outs of fashion trends (Junkin, 2006). The writer responded that one way is to read fashion magazines such as *Harper's Bazaar* and *In Style* every month from cover to cover. Fashion awareness depends not only on sensitivity to aesthetic rules, but also requires knowledge of the meanings associated with aesthetic elements. Some apparel attributes associated with the image or symbolic aspects of the product include color, attractiveness, fashionability, and brand name. One customer commented that the young salesclerks at

RECOGNITION
OF NORM
VIOLATIONS:
THE FASHION
POLICE

165

Abercrombie & Fitch looked and acted like the Abercrombie image that teens desire to emulate ("Abercrombie and Fitch," 2006). A heightened awareness of the variability of meanings of fashion apparel allows such individuals to recognize norm violations more readily than others.

Self-Monitoring

Self-monitoring reflects the degree to which individuals monitor and control their self-presentations in harmony with social cues (Peluchette, Karl & Rust, 2006; Snyder, 1979). Self-monitoring is an indication of an individual's sensitivity to the expression and self-presentation of others in social situations and the use of these cues as guidelines for monitoring his or her own verbal and nonverbal self-presentations (Snyder, 1974). For example, students in fifth and sixth grade are quick to imitate what they observe middle school students wearing, and middle school students are quick to imitate what they see high school students wearing (Pasciak, 2006). Many tweens, teens, and college students monitor what their classmates are wearing before they purchase new clothes for school (Hajewski, 2006).

High self-monitors have a heightened awareness of the impressions or messages that products such as clothing send to others (Peluchette, Karl & Rust, 2006). For example, different fashion colors send different messages (Critchell, 2006). The meaning of black has changed over time; in the 1800s men wore black to show conservatism and reliability, but in the twentieth century, black symbolized society's rebels (beatniks, punks, and Goths). Blue is associated with tranquility or serenity, while white is associated with purity and innocence.

Because high self-monitors are aware of the impressions or messages that dress sends, social approval is a strong motive when self-monitors choose clothing (O'Cass, 2001). High self-monitors are sensitive to the social cues around them and want to conform to social norms. "Only low self-monitors will risk expressing an indifference to the judgment and taste of their peers by wearing jeans with no social meaning" (Auty & Elliott, 1998, p. 119). When shopping for back-to-school clothing, purchasing the latest styles and the right brands are important to children (Podsada, 2006). According to a retail trend analyst, "The age-old conflict between parents and children over brand-name purchases has been on the wane for the last five years" (p. E1). Contemporary parents and children exchange information and learn from one another about brands to the point that parents often embrace their children's brand preferences.

Fashion Involvement and Fashion Interest

Fashion involvement is the extent to which an individual views the activities surrounding fashion as a meaningful and engaging part of his or her life. "The importance of involvement in the domain of fashion clothing can be seen via the defining role of fashion clothing in society" (O'Cass, 2001, p. 48). Fashion results from cultural changes in the style and tastes of individuals and groups. For example, the rules of fashion have changed since 1939, when *Glamour* magazine first began showing readers the dos and don'ts of fashion (Mosley, 2006). Some rules that have changed are, for example, shoes and handbags do not have to match; two patterned pieces can be worn together; black and brown, black and navy, red and pink can be worn together. Some of the worst don'ts in recent fashion history included low-rise jeans that revealed thong underwear, muffin tops (the ooze of a person's belly over the waistband of their pants), and rear cleavage. Fashion involvement is relevant in the interpretation of aesthetic codes and, by extension, in the recognition of norm violations.

Fashion interest refers to the amount of time, energy, money, and personal commitment an individual expends in the pursuit of fashion. An individual with more interest in fashion is more likely to notice norm violations. One way to measure fashion interest is to assess how well an individual keeps informed on current fashion trends and keeps his or her wardrobe up-to-date. Another indication of fashion interest is voluntary exposure to fashion, such as reading fashion advertisements, reading fashion magazines, discussing fashion with others, window shopping, observing fashions in stores, or observing what others are wearing.

These are all ways to express an interest in fashion as well as to increase knowledge, awareness, and sensitivity to fashion norms. A professional tennis player, Bethanie Mattek, dressed in skimpy gym shorts, over-the-calf socks, a tight-fitting top, headband, and chandelier earrings for her match against defending champion Venus Williams (Elmore, 2006). Mattek had prepared for the tournament by going shopping. Williams commented that her opponent was "always coming out with some kind of new little outfit" (p. C8).

Fashion Innovativeness and Fashion Opinion Leadership

Because of the multisensory imagery involved in fashion apparel, it is capable of stimulating and requiring extensive mental activity (Hirschman & Holbrook,

RECOGNITION
OF NORM
VIOLATIONS:
THE FASHION
POLICE

167

1982). Fashion products and shopping are more interesting and stimulating to some individuals than others. Recognition of dress norm violations is influenced by willingness to invest resources of time, money, and both mental and physical energy in the pursuit of fashion. Two applicable concepts are those of fashion innovativeness and opinion leadership.

Fashion innovativeness is defined as willingness to try new products relatively early in the product life cycle. Traud (2006) recalled that her first attempt at fashion innovativeness occurred when she was in ninth grade. When cleaning her room, she found her Girl Scout sash with a row of six gold star pins. She took the pins off the sash and fastened three along each of the pocket edges of her hip-hugging, bell-bottom Landlubber jeans. Within a week, anyone at her school who had ever earned a Girl Scout longevity pin was copying the look.

Fashion opinion leadership is defined as influencing others in purchase decisions, giving advice, and being an information source. Men's capris are an example of a fashion trend that spread because of fashion opinion leadership. Men's capris are not the same as women's capris but are the long, wide shorts called *Baltimore shorts* after the city where they first became popular (White, 2006). The shorts start at the waist, are free-flowing, roomy, wide-legged, boxy, and end just above the ankle. "It seems oxymoronic, but in the eyes of the long-short wearer, longer is always better" (p. D1). A New York fashion insider commented, "I've seen them, and I think they're just one of those goofy trends that emerge and somehow get adopted" (p. D1).

Fashion innovators and fashion opinion leaders tend to have a psychological (or want-based) perspective on fashion problem recognition, while fashion followers have a utilitarian (or need-based) perspective on fashion problem recognition (Workman & Studak, 2006). **Fashion problem recognition** refers to the tendency of some individuals to buy clothing simply because they *want* something new, while other individuals shop primarily when they *need* something to replace what wears out or for a specific context. For example, a nine-year-old *wanted* just one thing from his back-to-school shopping spree—Air Jordans (Jones, 2006). The boy's father acknowledged the peer pressure children face even at a young age. A ninth-grade high school student *needed* a new school wardrobe, because she previously wore uniforms at a middle school. A 12-year-old's grandmother suggested that it was better to extend clothes buying over a longer period of time because children grow so fast they *need* new clothes regularly.

What Norm Violations Are Recognized?

Some violations of dress norms stand out more than others. For example, when supermodel Elle Macpherson wore an acid-green strapless gown to the annual Costume Institute gala, her violation of the norm was salient because almost everyone else was dressed in a Chanel-inspired theme of black and white (Wilson, 2006b). Her faux pas of wearing beaded flip-flops with the dress might have gone unnoticed if people had not already been staring at her because of the color of her dress. Another salient norm violation occurred when "First Lady Laura Bush experienced every woman's worst nightmare when she turned up at a White House gala wearing the exact same $8,500 outfit as not one—but three—other women" (de Kretser, 2006, p. 3). A celebrity fashion reporter commented that for women of a certain age and social class, wearing the same dress to an event as another woman is virtually unavoidable.

In order for violations of dress norms to be recognized, the violation must be visible. For example, some heavily tattooed individuals cover their tattoos by wearing long-sleeved shirts and pants when interacting in conventional society (Irwin, 2003), thereby preventing their norm violation from being visible. Body art can be a distraction in the workplace. Similarly, most piercings on the face can be removed; the rest can be covered by clothing. As one commentator noted: "Do whatever you want to your body, but I don't want to be subjected to it in the workplace. . . . It's a visibility issue. No one cares what you have on your body as long as they don't have to look at it" (Read, 2006, ¶¶ 9, 12). In traditional suit-and-tie companies with frequent face-to-face client interaction, it is especially important for employees to cover their body art. At firms targeting younger clients (retailers, design firms, salons), it is not uncommon for employees to have body art. One design firm CEO commented that a young woman actually used her tattoos as part of her application portfolio and was hired.

Egregious violations, that is, bad, blatant, or ridiculous to an extraordinary degree, are likely to be noticed. Rock musicians and fans have historically been **avant-garde** (ahead of their time) and have been known for egregious violations of fashion norms. For example, indie rockers strive to send a "message of independence in a mass media, mass-produced culture" (Laue, 2006,

RECOGNITION
OF NORM
VIOLATIONS:
THE FASHION
POLICE

169

p. E1). Indie rock music is characterized by its reliance on independent record labels rather than major record labels ("Indie Rock," 2007). Indie fashion is exemplified by a pair of form-fitting jeans worn with a band T-shirt and blazer; hair is shaggy and unkempt (Gabay, 2006). Indie rock has influenced mainstream fashion, as evidenced by the many department and specialty stores that stock clothing inspired by indie fashion.

A major fall 2006 fashion trend was skinny jeans, a style that derived from indie rocker guys wearing girls' jeans (Laue, 2006). There is no one indie look—the indie look is a do-it-yourself, be-yourself aesthetic. Indies customize clothing items they find at thrift stores with such techniques as writing on ripped shoes, exposing garment seams, and using embellishments such as grommets and *grandma jewelry* (Laue, 2006). Guys wear girl jeans; girls wear old-man pants. One indie rocker described her favorite outfit as consisting of brown old-man pants, canary yellow shirt, grass-green jacket (all polyester thrift store finds) with mismatched shoelaces—one in rainbow colors, one in black—holding together four-year-old Chuck Taylor sneakers. On the left toe of one shoe, she had written the lyrics to an indie rock song "Reality is truly scaring me" (Laue, 2006, p. E1). Another indie rocker wore a pair of jeans topped by a floral thrift store dress and a black hoodie. A male indie wore girls' jeans—tight and white—with a T-shirt modified using a vintage silk screen of a reggae band.

Incongruous dress, that is, dress that is unsuitable, strange, or out of place in a particular setting or context, is likely to be noticed. For example, a police officer became suspicious when he noticed a man dressed in a coat during an August heat wave (Baker & Mannion, 2006). The man had just left a store and was holding both arms in front of him as if he was shivering in the 90 degree heat. Police officers stopped the man to question him and noticed the man's coat appeared to be stretched to the limit. When the coat was opened, 43 boxes of toothpaste fell out.

WHEN ARE NORM VIOLATIONS RECOGNIZED?

The average person has too little time or interest to be effective in recognizing violations of dress norms, except perhaps during periods of heightened publicity about some form of norm violation. For example, at the beginning of each new school year, changes made in public school dress codes resulting from unacceptable fashion trends are publicized (Cates, 2004). In 2004, many schools changed their dress codes to prohibit risqué fashions such as skimpy tops, short skirts, and spiked dog collars (Figure 7.7).

Celebrities who attend well-publicized events are subject to scrutiny about what they wear. Every year there are critiques of dress worn to awards ceremonies such as the Golden Globes, Grammys, and Oscars (Salas, 2006). The so-called red carpet fashion faux pas are posted to such websites as http://www.people.com or http://www.eonline.com/index.jsp. The websites allow readers to comment and vote for fashion dos and don'ts. More than 70 percent voted that Madonna's corset-leotard combination at the 2006 Grammys was a fashion don't.

FIGURE 7.7 AT THE START OF EACH SCHOOL YEAR, MANY SCHOOLS CHANGE THEIR DRESS CODES TO PROHIBIT RECENT FASHION TRENDS THAT ARE INAPPROPRIATE IN THE SCHOOL SETTING.

WHERE ARE NORM VIOLATIONS RECOGNIZED?

Norm violations are likely to be noticed in environments that have explicit or implicit dress codes. Explicit dress codes are likely to be present in settings such as the workplace, restaurants, courtrooms, jails, and schools. Maraghy (2006) reported that sometimes in the school environment, teachers have to be fashion police. "Some students—mainly girls—come to school dressed appropriately and then change in the restroom and their parents are none the wiser" (p. M1). Some teachers believe that being the clothing police detracts from their educational duties. Some students admitted they avoided teachers they knew would notice their dress code violations.

While teachers are monitoring students' dress, students are also noticing teachers' dress (Levenson, 2006). "When you are a teacher . . . you have the constant scrutiny of hundreds of pairs of eyes, checking out whether you're cool, have street cred or are just plain square" (p. 30). Levenson remembered an elementary school teacher who wore a see-through blouse. For the rest of the day and for weeks after, the students talked about having seen their teacher's bra.

Implicit dress codes are likely to be present in settings such as graduations, confirmations, weddings, or funerals (Figure 7.8). As societal norms relating

RECOGNITION OF NORM VIOLATIONS: THE FASHION POLICE

FIGURE 7.8 CAN YOU POINT OUT SOME OF THE NORM VIOLATIONS HERE IN THIS PICTURE OF FUNERAL ATTENDEES?

to appropriate dress have become less rigid, these implicit codes have been weakened. Thus, at a twenty-first-century funeral, mourners might see a girl with bare shoulders and hot pants, a woman in a demure black dress, a man in a Brooks Brothers suit, and a man in a short-sleeved shirt and baggy jeans (Gustafson, 2006). However, most people would consider the bare shoulders, hot pants, and baggy jeans inappropriate in this setting.

Image consultants typically recommend that funeral attire emphasize timeless style and elegance, not be attention-getting. Mourners attend funerals to pay their respects to the deceased and support the deceased's family—not to attract attention to themselves. Black is the traditional color of mourning, and although it is not necessary to wear black, it is safe. However, even with black, the fabric can make a difference; a black wool skirt would be appropriate, while a black leather skirt would not. Among funeral faux pas are backless outfits, short outfits, fur, bold jewelry, flip-flops, sneakers, bold color (a head-to-toe outfit of fire-engine red), and bare bodies (breast cleavage or rear cleavage exposed by low-rise pants and skirts).

WHY ARE NORM VIOLATIONS RECOGNIZED?

Persons who violate dress norms are viewed as likely to also violate norms of acceptable thought, speech, and actions. Thus, violation of society's dress norms is viewed as a symbol of unwillingness to accept society's values and an attempt to undermine the values considered important to conventional members of a society. For example, the values associated with a punk-rock clique included premarital sex, drug abuse, and rebellion against authority (Maragh, 2006). Cliques are social groups often formed on the basis of similar values and interests such as fashion, wealth, status, acceptance, or education.

The desire for certainty and predictability are basic human motives. Norm violations cause uncertainty about society's norms and uncertainty leads to anxiety. Hahn (1988) coined the term **aesthetic anxiety** to describe the "fears engendered by persons whose appearance deviates markedly from the usual" (p. 42). Aesthetic anxiety results in a tendency to avoid those with unattractive bodily attributes and a tendency to pursue an ideal body. Aesthetic anxiety derives from a widespread cultural emphasis on physical attractiveness. **Existential anxiety** refers to a feeling of personal identification with another person. Existential anxiety is expressed in thoughts such as "There, but for the grace of God [or luck or fate or other fundamental beliefs], go I" (p. 43) or verbalized in statements such as "I would give up a year of my life rather than be fat" ("Obesity Research," 2006, p. 101). Existential anxiety results from internalization of the threat posed by a norm violation and projection of those feelings onto the norm violator.

FIGURE 7.9 THE APPEARANCE OF THE MOTORCYCLE CLUB MEMBER IN THIS PICTURE COULD BE INTERPRETED AS INTIMIDATING.

Individuals have a need for control—pragmatic control (power over events) and predictive control (being able to foresee what will happen or being able to predict a threat's occurrence and consequences) (Miceli & Castelfranchi, 2005). Goths, punks, emos, indies, and metalheads are subcultural groups who dress in distinctive styles, such as black, skintight clothes, black eyeliner, Mohawk or spiked hairstyles, and multiple piercings (Wight, 2006) (Figure 7.9). Some business owners complained that the intimidating look of members of these groups frightened customers. Business owners had observed customers hesitate before entering a store when the teens were hanging around outside and complained that the teens scared away tourists and local customers alike.

Because society is "organized and made possible by rules of behavior" (Blake & Davis, 1964, p. 457), members of a society may view a violation of dress norms as an indefinite threat and question whether they are correct in their assessment of society's norms. An indefinite threat refers to uncertainty about what the possible danger is; the uncertainty arouses anxiety (Miceli & Castelfranchi, 2005). A perceived threat may be indefinite because (a) many events are ambiguous, (b) change is rapid and complex, and (c) cognitively complex systems (such as the normative order for dress) are abstract and symbolic (Miceli & Castelfranchi, 2005). For example, a reader wrote to a columnist wondering if the normal duration of fashion cycles was still seven years (Luther, 2006). The reader speculated that the time span was shorter because she had purchased some trendy clothes and felt that the "expiration date had come and gone, leaving [her] frilly and silly" (p. E6). The columnist confirmed that fashion has experienced an accelerated cycle of change.

By making social life unpredictable, norm violations jeopardize the normative order. The need for predictive control is a need to recognize, with the highest degree of certainty, factors affecting the current situation as well as future situations (Miceli & Castelfranchi, 2005). Predictive control works to alleviate anxiety. People are on the alert for other people breaking the rules because norm violation undermines trust in the idea that people will behave according to certain rules of conduct. This vigilance concerning rule breaking is aimed at reducing uncertainty.

The popularity of *Glamour*'s Dos and Don'ts feature takes advantage of people being on the alert for other people who break the rules, that is, commit fashion faux pas (Harris, 2006). The feature has become a reader-generated Internet photo gallery to which anyone can contribute. Everyone has an equal chance to be a fashion editor; the power is in the hands of the public to expose inappropriate fashion. Photo categories include overexposed, pantylines, editor's choice, see-through, and muffin tops. It is an Internet community assembled by a common interest in recognizing inappropriate fashion.

SUMMARY

This chapter examined some issues that affect recognition of norm violations. Among the factors affecting who will be most likely to recognize dress norm violations are status position, sensitivity to aesthetic rules, self-monitoring, fashion awareness, fashion interest, fashion knowledgeability, fashion involvement, fashion innovativeness, and fashion opinion leadership. Factors affecting what, when, where, and why norm violations are likely to be recognized are visibility, egregiousness, incongruity, publicity, status, explicit and implicit dress codes, unpredictability, aesthetic anxiety, existential anxiety, and uncertainty. Violations of dress norms must be recognized before the process of social control can continue.

KEY TERMS AND CONCEPTS

aesthetic anxiety

aesthetic code

avant-garde

clothing

existential anxiety

fashion innovativeness

fashion knowledgeability

fashion opinion leadership

fashion police

fashion problem recognition

incongruous dress

look

self-monitoring

SUGGESTED READINGS

1. O'Cass, A. (2001). Consumer self-monitoring, materialism and involvement in fashion clothing. *Australasian Marketing Journal, 9*(1), 46–60.

2. Workman, J. E., & Studak, C. M. (2006). Fashion consumers and fashion problem recognition style. *International Journal of Consumer Studies, 30*(1), 75–84.

3. Peluchette, J. V., Karl, K., & Rust, K. (2006). Dressing to impress: Beliefs and attitudes regarding workplace dress. *Journal of Business and Psychology, 21*(1), 45–63.

Research Activity 7.1 *Egregious and Avant-Garde Fashion*

Purpose: To analyze web resources to describe egregious and avant-garde fashion.

Procedure:

1. Review the definitions of *egregious* and *avant-garde*.

2. Log on to the *Glamour* magazine website (http://www.glamour.com/).

3. Select (click on) "Dos & Don'ts" from the navigation bar across the top of the page.

4. Select (click on) and view one slideshow.

5. Print the slide that represents the most egregious fashion; explain why you chose that slide.

6. Print the slide that represents the most **avant-garde** fashion; explain why you chose that slide.

7. Submit your work to your instructor.

Research Activity 7.2 Materialism

Purpose: To analyze sound recordings to understand how materialism is conveyed in the words of a song and its relationship to recognition of norm violations.

Procedure:

1. Review the definition of *materialism.*

2. Look up and review the words to the song *Material Girl* (http://homepage. ntlworld.com/alan.stuart/music/madonna/material.html).

3. Locate another song that conveys materialism and listen to a recording of the song. For example, solo artists such as Michael Jackson, Phil Collins, and Lionel Richie and rap artists such as The Notorious B.I.G. and Snoop Dogg sang about a materialistic culture.

4. Write your findings for the recording on the National Archives Sound Recording Analysis Worksheet (http://www.archives.gov/education/lessons/worksheets/sound_recording_analysis_worksheet.pdf).

5. Write a few sentences predicting how materialism might affect recognition of norm violations.

6. Submit the completed Sound Recording Analysis Worksheet to your instructor.

Chapter Eight

RESEARCH ABOUT
RECOGNITION OF NORM
VIOLATIONS

FROM THE HEADLINES

A woman described an experience in which she went shopping dressed in
shorts, no makeup, and her hair in post-workout disarray. She intended to
spend a couple of hundred dollars but she left the store without purchasing
anything because she was ignored and provided incompetent service by the
sales associate. She attributed the poor service to how she was dressed. In
a recent study, researchers observed 90 shoppers and 13 sales associates at
three women's clothing stores. They rated the appearance of customers from
poor to good in ten areas such as fashionable clothing, handbag, hair, and
makeup. They also recorded how much time it took sales associates to greet
a customer and how friendly the associates were. Researchers confirmed that
well-dressed shoppers received friendlier and more prompt service than poorly
dressed shoppers. One explanation for the results was that dress is an indication of how much money a customer has to spend.

Source: Hood, M. (2006, March 12). Appearances matter: Shoppers who are
well-dressed get better service, study confirms. *The Columbus Dispatch.* Retrieved
February 14, 2007, from http://www.lexisnexis.com

The research reported in this news article illustrates the potential consequences of noticing a norm violation. An in-store observational
study was used to document reactions of sales associates to customers
who did and did not violate dress norm expectations for shoppers. Did sales
associates assume poorly dressed shoppers did not have money to spend?
What norms were recognized as being violated by each of the individuals in
the department store shopping scenario? What are some characteristics of

the individual(s) who recognized the norm violations? How do the questions *what, when, where,* and *why* influence recognition of the norm violations? Building on the recognition of norm violations discussed in Chapter 7, in this chapter you will read about research that explores who notices norm violations, what they notice, and when, where, and why they notice what they do.

The methods and tools used in each research study are summarized in Table 8.1. A number of research studies relate to the social and psychological qualities characterizing individuals who are likely to recognize norm violations. A cultural universal among members of any particular society is recognition of which clothing styles are widespread, contemporary, and appropriate, as well as which are inappropriate. However, the acuteness of that recognition differs among individuals of various statuses.

Research studies have addressed both achieved statuses (fashion designers, fashion consumers) and ascribed statuses (gender, age). Other research has examined *what* norm violations are most likely to be recognized (visibility); *when* during the innovation diffusion process the norm violations are most likely to be recognized (publicity); *where* norm violations are most likely to be recognized (explicit and implicit dress codes); and *why* particular norm violations are likely to be recognized (power and status issues).

QUESTIONS TO ANSWER AS YOU READ

1. What is the nature of research related to recognition of norm violations?
2. What research methods are used to investigate recognition of norm violations?
3. What tools are used to collect data for research about recognition of norm violations?

RESEARCH ABOUT WHO IS LIKELY TO RECOGNIZE NORM VIOLATIONS

Fashion research is a systematic approach to collecting data to answer a question or solve a problem related to fashion. By conducting fashion research,

TABLE 8.1 SUMMARY OF RESEARCH METHODS AND TOOLS RELATED TO THE RECOGNITION OF NORM VIOLATIONS

RESEARCH METHOD	TOOL(S)	AUTHOR(S)	YEAR	ARTICLE TITLE
Quantitative	Questionnaire	Auty & Elliott	1998	Fashion involvement, self-monitoring and the meaning of brands
Qualitative	Interview worksheet	Blakemore & Russ	1997	Preschool children's attitudes about deviations from gender-role behaviors
Theoretical paper	Literature analysis	Cholachatpinyo et al.	2002	A conceptual model of the fashion process—part 1: The fashion transformation process model
Theoretical paper	Literature analysis	Crane	1999a	Diffusion models and fashion: A reassessment
Theoretical paper	Literature analysis	Crane	1999b	Fashion design and social change: Women designers and stylistic innovation
Quantitative experimental design	Questionnaire	Dahl et al.	2003	Does it pay to shock? Reactions to shocking and nonshocking advertising content among university students
Qualitative ethnography	Worksheets	Eckert & Stacey	2001	Adaptation of sources of inspiration in knitwear design
Law review	Literature analysis	Fisk	2006	Privacy, power, and humiliation at work: Re-examining appearance regulation as an invasion of privacy
Quantitative	Questionnaire	Goldsmith	2002	Some personality traits of frequent clothing buyers
Quantitative	Questionnaire	Goldsmith	2000	Characteristics of the heavy user of fashionable clothing
Law review	Literature analysis	Hicks et al.	2006	Reasonable dress and grooming requirements survive court scrutiny
Quantitative	Observation worksheet	Kim & Lennon	2005	The effects of customers' dress on salesperson's service in large-sized clothing specialty stores
Quantitative	Questionnaire	O'Cass	2004	Fashion clothing consumption: Antecedents and consequences of fashion clothing involvement
Law review	Literature analysis	Post et al.	2001	Prejudicial appearances: The logic of American antidiscrimination law
Qualitative	Ad worksheet	Thompson	2000	Gender in magazine advertising: Skin sells best
Quantitative	Questionnaire	Workman	2003	Alcohol promotional clothing items and alcohol use by underage consumers
Quantitative	Questionnaire	Workman & Studak	2006	Fashion consumers and fashion problem recognition style

FIGURE 8.1 FASHION
RESEARCH PROVIDES DESIGNERS
WITH THE STRUCTURAL FEATURES
TYPICAL OF A PARTICULAR FASH-
ION TREND. THE OUTFIT IN THIS
ILLUSTRATION SHOWS A NUMBER
OF STRUCTURAL FEATURES, FROM
COLLAR TO SLEEVES TO BUTTONS
TO POCKETS TO HEM.

FIGURE 8.2 A LOOK FROM
THE SEAN JOHN SHOW AT NEW
YORK'S FASHION WEEK (2008).

designers and others who work in the field of fashion explicitly verify the perceptual impressions they have implicitly recognized: (a) what is and is not fashionable, (b) what cultural connotations a garment will have, and (c) how a design needs to be modified in order to conform to fashion. Fashion research provides designers with a set of concepts (layering), memories needed to create new designs (the decade of the 1980s), the points at which a fashion ends and beyond which it becomes something else (what looks dated and what is too fashion-forward), key looks (skinny jeans) and structural features (pleats) that characterize a particular fashion trend (Eckert & Stacey, 2001) (Figure 8.1).

The fashion research process begins with explicit recognition of current fashion trends, including proportions (oversized, cropped), styles (miniskirts, capris), and overall appearance (casual, glamorous). One method of conducting fashion research is to study the clothes presented in couture designer collections. Catwalk fashion in magazines and forecasting materials can be examined for themes (romance), colors (red), styles (leggings), prevalent features (layering), and novel features (metallic gold fabrics) (Eckert & Stacey, 2001).

Another method of conducting fashion research is to study clothes in the stores, particularly **bellwether stores** known for being indicators of future developments or trends. Another method of conducting fashion research is to travel to fashion capitals (Milan, Paris, London, or New York) to attend fashion shows or watch people on the streets (Figure 8.2).

As a result of fashion research, designers and other fashion experts recognize the boundaries of what is acceptable, what appears relatively moderate, what looks daring, and what exceeds the boundaries of prevailing social norms. Garment designs that exceed the desirable limits of deviation from the norm will be rejected as worthless and irrelevant (Eckert & Stacey, 2001).

Achieved Status: Occupation Fashion Designers

If we examine research about one occupation—fashion designer—some of the traits that exemplify individuals who are likely to notice norm violations will become clear. Recall that fashion designers are in the business of violating current fashion norms in a positive way (Figure 8.3).

Using ethnographic worksheets as their research tool, Eckert and Stacey (2001) studied 80 clothing designers and technicians in 25 companies in three countries to examine the design process. These authors uncovered several social and psychological qualities that characterize designers, an occupational category composed of individuals who are likely to recognize norm violations. Through training or inherited abilities, designers come to possess technical understanding of garment structure, excellent visual memory for garments, and spatial visualization skills.

Structure

Structural design refers to the way parts of a garment are put together (seams, darts, gores, yokes) and how they work together (where and how it will open). Because designers are able to focus on a particular structural area or structural detail, they develop a vocabulary for garment features (dolman sleeve, pagoda sleeve). Designers recognize styles and developing trends in the many garments they see during the process of fashion research. In order to create garments that appear new and different, designers use novel structural features or variations or combinations of structural features to create aesthetic effects that appear novel in appropriate ways, while remaining within the acceptable limits in other ways.

FIGURE 8.3 BETSEY JOHNSON CONSTANTLY PUSHES THE BOUNDARIES OF ESTABLISHED FASHION NORMS.

Memory

Fashion designers see large numbers of garments and report being able to remember them in vivid detail. Designers' memories include details of both structure and context. As part of the design process, designers summarize similarities among garments, interpret information (written descriptions), and associate styles with remembered times and situations. The content of long-term memory contributes to design ideas. Designers often describe a new design as a modification of another design, suggesting that memories of a wide variety of garments play a key role in their thinking. The shared context of remembered designs provides a language to communicate design ideas. It is difficult to describe significant features of garments except in terms of variations from other designs.

Designers have a vocabulary for garment features that includes verbal labels for garment categories. Designers use reference-based descriptions; they report vivid and detailed memories of large numbers of garments they have seen. Designers' mental representations of possible garment designs are composed of a variety of garments that serve as **exemplars** (prime examples) of subcategories that can only be referred to by their origins.

Designers' long-term memory includes information about the context of a garment, such as who wore it, what it was, when it was worn, where it was worn, and why or how it was worn. How different clothing styles are interpreted depends on their context—for example, where the style was seen (on the streets of a fashion capital or on the streets of a small town in the United States). Remembered experiences with similar clothing styles affect interpretation of current styles and recognition of norm violations.

Spatial Visualization

Spatial visualization is the "ability to mentally manipulate an entire spatial configuration, to imagine the rotation of depicted objects, to imagine the folding and unfolding of flat patterns, and to imagine the relative changes of position of objects in space" (McGee, 1979, p. 17). An important attribute of a good designer is the ability to visualize designs mentally as detailed, realistic images of garments, similar to photographs (Eckert & Stacey, 2001). Being able to mentally translate the recognized trends into garments is a vital skill.

The designers studied by Eckert and Stacey used visual/spatial mental representations of **types** (category of things whose members share some qualities, such as types of skirts or types of sleeves), **trends** (a general tendency, movement, or direction of fashion change), and **spaces** (the boundaries within which creative interpretation of the fashion can occur). Category membership was recognized perceptually rather than through the use of logical thinking—for example, recognizing that a *skort* is a type of miniskirt/short combination.

The creative skill of expert designers is displayed in the complexity and subtlety of their perceptual evaluation of designs as much as in their ability to generate design ideas. Expert designers understand what visual/spatial properties of the garments within a fashion trend must be held constant and what properties can be varied, so that new garments appear new and different while remaining within the boundaries of acceptability.

Achieved Status: Fashion Consumer Groups

Recognition of norm violations by ordinary individuals, nonexperts, is strongly influenced by implied (not expressed in words) perceptual learning. The average person does not think explicitly about garment structure or visualize garment designs in detail. The cultural connotations of individual garments—that is, their meaning—depend on remembered experiences with similar garments.

However, the meanings of garments are actively manipulated by the people who present them in runway shows, in magazines, in advertisements, by how garments are combined (with other garments, situations, and images). All convey cultural meanings, and the combinations create new meanings. A combination of deliberate and chance cultural communication embeds individual garments in contexts influencing how consumers perceive them (Eckert & Stacey, 2001). For example, the cover of *Women's Wear Daily*, September 21, 2007, featured a photograph of a model wearing a silk hand-painted above-knee length dress from a designer collection. The dress was worn with beige-colored knee-high hose with the stretch elastic comfort band showing. The deliberate use of visible knee-high bands (which most women remember as a fashion faux pas) combined with an elegant dress was an attempt to actively manipulate the cultural connotations associated with the combination.

Fashion Innovators, Opinion Leaders, Innovative Communicators, and Followers
An individual's personality influences the level of her or his interest in a particular subject or activity such as fashion. The first consumers to buy and wear new clothing fashions are called fashion innovators; fashion opinion leaders influence other consumers to buy and wear new fashions. **Innovative communicators** are among the first to buy and wear new fashions and also influence others to follow the fashion trend. Fashion followers are by far the largest group of fashion consumers; they follow the example of the fashion change agents (fashion innovators, fashion opinion leaders, and innovative communicators). The four groups of fashion consumers differ in many characteristics—for example, self-monitoring, materialism, fashion knowledgeability, fashion involvement, and fashion problem recognition style.

Self-Monitoring
According to Auty and Elliott (1998), clothing is susceptible to differences in consumption stereotyping, and therefore to differences in ability to decode a range of messages. In an effort to further our understanding of how people interpret clothing and how different groups of people make different judgments about the same brand of clothing, Auty and Elliott looked at the meanings associated with jeans by high and low self-monitors. Recall from Chapter 7 that self-monitoring is the degree to which individuals monitor and control their self-presentations in harmony with social signals. Self-monitoring is an indication of a person's (a) sensitivity to the self-presentation of others, and

(b) subsequent use of others' self-presentations as (c) standards for scrutinizing his or her own self-presentations.

Participants in the study were 335 men and 334 women from three age groups (14–17; 18–24; 25–34). Participants filled out a three-part questionnaire, including demographic questions, a self-monitoring scale (18 true-false questions), and a scale consisting of 27 bipolar adjectives that might be used to describe jeans. **Bipolar adjectives** are presented with both the positive and negative ends of the scale, for example, individual/not individual, associated with cowboys/not associated with cowboys. Participants were shown a pair of either branded or unbranded jeans.

The 14- to 17-year-old age group viewed the branded jeans more favorably than the older groups, leading to the conclusion that the meaning of fashion brands differs between age groups. Women had more favorable attitudes than men toward branded jeans—specifically, image, modernity, practicality, quality, and trendiness. Men perceived unbranded jeans to convey an image, be more American, and be more original than women did, suggesting that men were not noticing and processing the cues as accurately as women. High self-monitors regarded unbranded jeans more negatively than low self-monitors, specifically the functional qualities, such as less well cut, less hard-wearing, less comfortable, low-quality, and not individual. Low self-monitors had more favorable attitudes toward the functional qualities of unbranded jeans.

The authors concluded that self-monitoring scores, which depend on the extent to which a person desires to stay in tune with other people, appeared to have an effect on the perceptions of unbranded jeans in particular. Jeans are high-involvement fashion items that are used as *code* by wearers to send messages about their self-presentations. Meanings of fashion items are interpreted with surprising consistency, depending on differing levels of self-monitoring, especially for unbranded products (Auty & Elliott, 1998). Recognition of norm violation is a critical feature of self-monitoring—that is, recognizing the social signals that indicate conformity or deviance, social approval or disapproval.

Materialism, Fashion Knowledgeability, and Fashion Involvement
Consumers differ in how much they pay attention to other consumers and how much others influence their behavior. Fashion clothing puts a consumer in a vulnerable situation relative to the judgment of others who may notice when they have made an inappropriate choice.

O'Cass (2004) examined the relationships between gender, age, materialism, fashion knowledgeability, and fashion involvement. A self-administered mailed questionnaire was used to collect data from 478 respondents. **Materialism** is a value that reflects the importance people attach to owning worldly possessions (Solomon, 1996) and the importance of recognizing norm violations that will reflect poorly on impressions of wealth and prosperity. Materialism as a value is reflected in such phrases as "shop till you drop" and "he who dies with the most toys wins" and in the rise in credit card usage and consumer debt. Results indicated that fashion involvement was affected by materialism—that is, the higher the materialistic tendencies, the higher the fashion involvement.

Females and younger respondents were more involved in fashion than males and older respondents. Those who scored high on fashion involvement also scored high on fashion knowledgeability. Respondents high in fashion knowledgeability were more confident in making purchase decisions about fashion. Fashion knowledgeability includes recognition of socially approved and disapproved fashions (norm violations).

Goldsmith (2002) replicated an earlier study of personal characteristics of frequent clothing buyers by using data from a survey of 533 adult consumers including college students and nonstudents. To **replicate** a study means to repeat it. In the earlier study, Goldsmith (2000) found that more frequent buyers of clothing were more innovative, involved, knowledgeable, and higher in opinion leadership than less frequent buyers. In the replication of the study, Goldsmith added some items dealing with social and personal identity in order to gain insight into the motives of frequent clothing buyers. As conceptualized by Goldsmith, self-concept had two aspects: (a) external or social concern with perspectives and feedback from other people (social identity) and (b) internal or self-directed thoughts, beliefs, and attitudes (personal identity). Both aspects of self-concept are influenced by clothing choices that help individuals express who they are, who they want to be, and how they want others to see them. Social identity in particular would require attention to recognition of norm violations.

Consistently for both men and women of all ages, more frequent buyers of clothing described themselves as involved, innovative, and knowledgeable opinion leaders. They were also more likely to view new fashions as a means of expressing social and personal identity than less frequent buyers. Women reported buying more frequently than men and younger consumers more frequently than older ones. Psychological traits were more strongly associated with frequency of purchasing clothing than were demographic traits such as age, education, and income (Goldsmith, 2000).

Fashion Problem Recognition Style

The fashion consumer groups differ in fashion problem recognition style. For example, Workman and Studak (2006) found that fashion followers reflected a need-based approach to problem recognition and both fashion innovators and fashion opinion leaders reflected a want-based approach to problem recognition.

Being exposed to advertisements of the latest fashions can trigger recognition of a norm violation when an individual decides that the clothing he or she has is out-of-date and wants something more fashionable. Thus, one influence on recognition of dress norm violations is advertising of new products by the fashion industry. Some consumers recognize a norm violation because they have seen the new fashions advertised and concluded that their current fashions are out-of-date. Other consumers recognize norm violations only when what they have no longer fits or is no longer serviceable (Figure 8.4).

FIGURE 8.4
THIS CARTOON SHOWS THE
SECOND FASHION PROBLEM REC-
OGNITION STYLE: WHAT THEY
HAVE NO LONGER FITS.

Ascribed Status: Gender Boys and Girls

Because of the evolving nature of fashion and culture, which items of dress and ways of behaving are masculine and which are feminine will change. Regardless of this propensity for change, children are socialized to consider some items of dress as masculine and other items as feminine.

Blakemore and Russ (1997) interviewed 3- to 7-year-old children to examine their knowledge about gender roles and norms, their beliefs about violating these roles and norms, and their attitudes about children who violate these roles and norms. Gender role norms were grouped into seven categories, including toys, hairstyles, and clothing. Feminine gender-role violations included a girl playing with G. I. Joe, a girl with a boy's hairstyle (short, dark hair cut above the ear and to the top of the neck in back), and a girl wearing a suit, shirt, and tie with laced dress shoes. Masculine gender-role violations included a boy playing with Barbie, a boy with a girl's hairstyle (long, curly hair that hangs down past the shoulders), and a boy wearing a dress (ruffled skirt, socks with ruffles, and dress flats).

FIGURE 8.5 YOUNG GIRLS SHOPPING AT BARBIE STORE IN ARGENTINA.

Aspects of the feminine gender role recognized by the 3- to 7-year-old children were Barbie dolls, toy kitchens, girls' hairstyles, and girls' clothes (Figure 8.5). Male items were recognized and stereotyped more strongly than female items. Children's recognition of gender norms increased between ages 3 and 7. Boys' gender-role violations involving physical appearance (clothing and especially hair) were recognized and judged more negatively than similar violations by girls.

RESEARCH ABOUT WHAT NORM VIOLATIONS ARE LIKELY TO BE RECOGNIZED

Research related to characteristics of norm violations that are more likely to be recognized focuses on several general characteristics. Norm violations that are more prominent are easily detected through the senses—that is, the violation must be visible. Violations that are egregious or blatant are more likely to be noticed than those that are covert.

Shock advertising is advertising that intentionally startles and offends its audience by deliberating violating norms for societal values and personal ideals (Dahl, Frankenberger, & Manchanda, 2003). Shocking messages are created using norm violations of law or custom (indecency, obscenity), of a moral or social code (profanity, vulgarity), or of a moral or physical nature (gratuitous violence, disgusting images). "Advertising, as a social object, is evaluated by norms and is considered offensive when its content breaches norms for decency, good taste, aesthetic propriety, and/or personal moral standards"

FIGURE 8.6 CALVIN KLEIN JEANS AD.

(p. 269). Some of the most widely publicized advertising campaigns involving shock advertising were produced by clothing manufacturers such as Calvin Klein and Benetton (Figure 8.6). Advertisers typically justify shock appeals in advertising for their ability to break through the clutter, get noticed, and get people's attention (Vagnoni, 1999).

One experimental design employed three different advertising appeals—shock, fear, and information (Dahl, Frankenberger, & Manchanda, 2003). A greater percentage of subjects chose the shock advertisement as the one that drew their attention the most, compared with the fear and information advertisements. The reason given for why the shock advertisement attracted the most attention was that a specific norm violation drew their attention. Norm violation was the key to heightened awareness of shocking advertising content. Shock tactics are often used in advertising that involves a new product or new brand ("The Media Business," 2007). The attention-grabbing ability of a shock appeal can be used to gain an awareness level of the greatest intensity. Adolescents and emerging adults are often targeted with shock advertisements because shock tactics are consistent with the stereotypical youth need for rebellion against societal norms.

Suggestively clad, partially clad, or nude models are used to sell all types of products in all types of magazines to all segments of U.S. consumers. Thompson (2000) analyzed fashion advertisements published in *GQ* [*Gentlemen's Quarterly*] and *Vogue* between 1964 and 1994 to determine if there were changes in the use of sexual attire and nudity during that time period. Advertisements were rated in terms of the following descriptors: revealing, nude, disclosing, clinging, showing, divulging, displaying, exposing, exhibiting, or baring (display of cleavage, visible bra or no bra, bare legs, plunging necklines, skin). These norm violations are related to impropriety (violations of social conventions of dress) or sexuality (references to sexually suggestive nudity or partial nudity).

No sexually explicit images of men were found in *GQ* before 1984, but corresponding with the appearance of Calvin Klein advertisements in which men's bodies were displayed (Faludi, 1999), there was a dramatic increase in sexually explicit fashion ads featuring male models after 1984. A dramatic increase in women's sexual images in *Vogue* occurred between 1964, when there were only 4 images, and 1974, when there were 53. This increase coincided with the influence of the sexual revolution—an influence that apparently applied only to women's bodies until the 1980s. Fashion advertising in the 1990s became more sexually explicit and provocative for both men and women. Overall, the number of sexual appeal images was higher in *Vogue* than in *GQ*, consistent with the more traditional objectification of women's bodies (Thompson, 2000).

RESEARCH ABOUT WHEN NORM VIOLATIONS ARE LIKELY TO BE RECOGNIZED

Research related to when dress norm violations are likely to be recognized focuses on time issues. During periods of changing fashions, publicity is heightened and recognition of norm violations is under intense inspection or analysis. In U.S. culture, fashion changes rapidly and with extensive publicity. During times of especially dramatic fashion changes (the extremely low-cut jeans in fashion during the early to mid-2000s), part of the evaluation process seems to be ridiculing new fashions as norm violations (low-cut jeans gave rise to the fashion terminology *muffin top*, which was widely acknowledged as a fashion faux pas). The changing boundaries of popular tastes can be traced by media coverage of new fashions. As the new fashion becomes well known, commonly seen, and easily recognized, recognition of the fashion as a norm violation and media coverage decline.

Fashion is one of the most visible media of change and progress in modern society. Cholachatpinyo, Padgett, Crocker, and Fletcher (2002) proposed the *fashion transformation process model* as a theoretical foundation for research on fashion diffusion. The fashion and lifestyle of a particular time symbolize the **Zeitgeist** or *spirit of the time*—that is, the thought and feeling of a particular period of time. It is not always easy for individuals to understand which fashions are appropriate and which are inappropriate, resulting in feelings of uncertainty. Individuals respond to uncertainty in four ways, all of which require recognition of norm violations: (a) conformity—dressing according to dominant social norms; (b) anticonformity—dressing to show one is violating the norm; (c) concealment—easily and frequently changing appearance in order to create an appearance that escapes notice; (d) modification—adapting dress.

Emerging fashion trends provide consumers with fashion ideas. When individuals become involved with fashion clothing in the retail marketplace, they select some fashions in order to conform to the social concepts of the time and reject others as violations of the norm. Decisions related to acceptance or rejection of changing trends in fashion require recognition of acceptable and unacceptable norm violations.

In a theoretical paper, Crane (1999b) commented that avant-garde and postmodern designers violate norms to create styles that exhibit *the shock of the new*. For example, avant-garde designers violate (a) norms of perfection inherent in designer clothing, (b) aesthetic norms, (c) norms associated with construction and design of clothing, (d) norms associated with materials that are appropriate for clothing, (e) norms concerning combinations of themes and motifs, (f) the normative meaning attributed to specific items of clothing, (g) the normative meanings associated with other types of objects in order to redefine them as being appropriate for apparel, or (h) norms concerning the expression and enhancement of female sexuality. The intent of avant-garde designers is to disrupt normal thought processes, to subvert conventional meanings, and to stimulate new and possibly irrational associations. Because fashion consumers recognize these newly introduced clothing styles as norm violations, many of them are not immediately accepted, may never be accepted, or may be accepted by only a fraction of fashion consumers (Figure 8.7).

FIGURE 8.7 ALEXANDER McQUEEN DESIGN.

In another theoretical paper, Crane (1999a) examined the diffusion of fashion as "a succession of changes that occur over time in the use of fashionable or fad items" (p. 15). Avant-garde and postmodern fashions are designed with little concern for wearability or practicality—innovation is emphasized at the expense of usefulness. Newly introduced avant-garde fashions are coded; the meanings are likely to be understood by some groups in the population but not others. Recall from Chapter 7 that an aesthetic code is a combination of aesthetic rules, social rules, and cultural customs regarding dress that provide the meanings conveyed by dress. Consumers who do not understand changed meanings will interpret the unconventional styles as norm violations. Fashion targeted to adolescents tends to be more heavily coded than fashion targeted to older customers; therefore, fashion styles targeted to adolescents are likely to be interpreted as norm violations by older adults.

Research About Where Norm Violations Are Likely to Be Recognized

Research regarding where norm violations are likely to be recognized focuses on environments with explicit dress codes. Recall from Chapter 7 that examples of these environments include office settings, hospitals, restaurants, and schools. Likewise, norm violations are more likely to be recognized at events that have implicit dress codes, including interview situations, weddings, funerals, and even shopping in retail stores.

Explicit Norms for Dress

In Chapter 4 we discussed the notion of lookism, which is the basis of screening for employees who embody the company's image. Recruiters and interviewers can eliminate candidates who do not embody the company image. For example, "The appearance of casino employees is central to a gaming establishment's ability to project a successful image" (Hicks, Hall, & Westbrook, 2006, p. 342). Dress and grooming standards are one way to ensure employees project a desired image. When a company has a dress and appearance policy, violations of the policy will be noticed by a manager or supervisor because there is no point in having a policy if it is not monitored.

In a case study presented in a law review, sanctions against a female bartender were detailed (Fisk, 2006; Hicks, Hall, & Westbrook, 2006). After refusing to sign a statement promising to comply with the casino's appearance policy requiring female bartenders to wear makeup and nail polish, the bartender was fired. As part of the casino's Personal Best Program, each employee was given a makeover and then a photograph was taken. Supervisors were asked to use the photograph as an *appearance measurement tool*. The supervisor was empowered to scrutinize the details of employees' appearance on a daily basis, to compare each employee to a photograph, and to reprimand the employee if on a particular day the supervisor decided that the employee did not look enough like the idealized image in the photograph. In this situation, violations of norms are extremely likely to be noticed.

Workman (2003) looked at the visibility of alcohol promotional items being worn in school settings in violation of dress code policies. Participants were 154 females and 106 males in grades 7–12 who filled out a questionnaire.

Student recognition of norm violation the day of the survey was high, with over 50 percent of students indicating they had seen someone wearing an alcohol promotional item that day. For every student who wore an alcohol promotional item in violation of the school dress code policy, 10 students recognized the norm violation.

Implicit Norms for Dress

One situation for which there is an implicit dress code is the interview situation. Employers may explicitly or implicitly use recognition of norm violations as a basis for hiring decisions. For example, interviewers may screen candidates to eliminate undesirable employees and keep desirable employees in the pipeline. **Screening** is using clothing and appearance to assess a prospective employee for certain traits and then using these implied traits as a basis for hiring or not hiring (Figure 8.8). Interviewers may screen prospective employees by not hiring individuals when they recognize the individuals have violated widely accepted societal norms, such as having visible tattoos or appearing for the interview in inappropriate dress.

An advocate of a proposed ordinance that would have prevented employers from screening on the basis of employee appearance described the unfair treatment she received. She remarked that employers seemed to feel threatened by her appearance (shaved head, except for a single bit of bright pink hair, and a tattooed stripe on her face). Post, Appiah, Butler, Grey, and Siegel (2001) commented on the inconsistency between the woman's awareness and endorsement of the shock value of her appearance and her belief that she should not be overlooked for employment because of the reactions her appearance provoked. It is a paradoxical idea that individuals use their appearance to communicate meanings, including messages of threat, and simultaneously expect others to ignore these messages (Fisk, 2006, p. 36–37).

Shoppers in a retail store may be treated differently as a function of how they are dressed (Kim & Lennon, 2005), as spotlighted in the "From the Headlines" story at the beginning of this chapter. In a retail setting, a customer's dress is one indicator of status and how much money he or she has to spend. Sales associates may unconsciously notice the norm violations of poorly dressed customers and conclude they are simply browsing. Such an assessment made as a result of implicit dress expectations affects the treat-

FIGURE 8.8 IN THIS PHOTO OF THE LEAD CHARACTER OF THE SITCOM *UGLY BETTY*, CLOTHING AND APPEARANCE SUGGEST CERTAIN TRAITS.

ment customers receive. Kim and Lennon conducted structured observations during which they rated customers' dress as well as friendliness of salespeople and promptness of service. Well-dressed meant attractive, fashionable, formal, feminine, overall well-groomed, well-groomed hair, clothing made of high-quality fabric, makeup, high-quality accessories, and high-quality purses. Poorly dressed meant unattractive, unfashionable, informal, not feminine, poorly groomed overall, poorly groomed hair, clothing made of poor-quality fabric, poor makeup, poor-quality accessories, and poor-quality purses.

Two criteria for assessing service quality, friendliness, and promptness of service were affected by customer dress (Kim & Lennon, 2005). As compared with poorly dressed customers, well-dressed customers received friendlier and more prompt service from salespersons. Customer dress characteristics that affected salesperson friendliness included attractive, fashionable, and formal clothing; well-groomed overall, well-groomed hair; clothing of high-quality fabrics, wearing makeup, high-quality accessories, and high-quality purses. Customer dress characteristics that influenced promptness of service were well-groomed hair, clothing of high-quality fabric, high-quality accessories, and high-quality purses.

RESEARCH ABOUT WHY NORM VIOLATIONS ARE LIKELY TO BE RECOGNIZED

Recall from Chapter 1 that power refers to the ability to change a belief, attitude, or behavior of an individual. The possession of power has important consequences for controlling social interactions. A higher status in a social hierarchy is associated with greater power. Some individuals may depend on recognizing the norm violations of others as a method for increasing their own status and power.

Adolescents who tease, bully, or ridicule their classmates perform a socialization function by recognizing norm violations (Wooten, 2006). Such adolescents use ridicule to control and humiliate norm violators, as entertainment for witnesses, and as a demonstration of their power. Witnesses reward the bully with laughter and approval, elevating his or her status among peers. The rewards for bullies and costs to violators maintain a system in which norm violation is actively monitored and conformity to norms is ensured.

In a law review article, Fisk (2006) discussed the issue of power in the workplace as demonstrated in workplace dress and appearance regulations. "An employer that announces a mandatory dress code and then cannot enforce it loses control over the workplace in a way that it would perceive as quite serious" (p. 6). The orderly power structure of a workplace is disrupted if employees refuse to comply with a workplace dress code. Willful violation of a dress code is a declaration by employees that the employer does not have the power to demand conformity.

When an employer notices a violation and demands conformity, the issue is one of power and control, not just enforcement of dress norms. Although an individually chosen style of dress can signal an individual's status, the same style of dress explicitly required by a dress code signals the employer's higher status and power and the employee's subordinate position. Dress and appearance codes in the workplace are avenues for demonstration of social power. Dress and appearance codes are commonly justified on the basis of an employer's right or power to display the chosen corporate image. When an employer has the power to establish and enforce an explicit dress code, violations will be recognized because "to have somebody really out of context destroys the illusion that a company chooses to create for its public" (Fisk, 2006, p. 15).

SUMMARY

This chapter looked at some research investigating variables related to recognition of norm violations. Among the research studies were studies about status positions, self-monitoring, fashion involvement, fashion innovativeness, and fashion opinion leadership, all of which affect who is likely to recognize norm violations. Norm violations that are visible, egregious, or blatant are more likely to be recognized than those that are covert. Norm violations are more likely to be recognized during periods of changing fashions, when publicity is heightened. As a new fashion becomes well known, commonly seen, and familiar, recognition of the fashion as a norm violation declines. Norm violations are more likely to be recognized in environments with explicit or implicit dress codes. Finally, individuals may use recognition of norm violation as a method for adding to their status and power.

KEY TERMS AND CONCEPTS

bellwether stores

bipolar adjectives

exemplars

fashion research

innovative communicators

materialism

replicate

screening

shock advertising

spaces

spatial visualization

structural design

trends

types

Zeitgeist

SUGGESTED READINGS

1. Auty, S., & Elliott, R. (1998). Fashion involvement, self-monitoring and the meaning of brands. *Journal of Product and Brand Management, 7*(2), 109–123.

2. Kim, M., & Lennon, S. J. (2005). The effects of customers' dress on salesperson's service in large-sized clothing specialty stores. *Clothing and Textiles Research Journal, 23*(2), 78–87.

3. Workman, J. E., & Studak, C. M. (2006). Fashion consumers and fashion problem recognition style. *International Journal of Consumer Studies, 30*(1), 75–84.

Research Activity 8.1 Literature Analysis

Purpose: To analyze research literature related to the *recognition* of violations of appearance norms, identifying the purpose, research method, and results.

Procedure:

1. Describe the characteristics of a research article.

2. Use the Google Scholar (http://scholar.google.com/) search engine or an academic database (EBSCO, ERIC, SocIndex) to locate one research article related to the recognition of violations of appearance

norms. For example, you might use the key words *dress norms violation recognition* or *appearance standard violation recognition* to search for research articles.

3. Print a copy of the research article.
4. Highlight and label the purpose of the study, the research method used, the results of the study related to its purpose, and the violations of appearance norm(s) studied.
5. Submit your work to your instructor.

Research Activity 8.2 *Bellwether Clothing Stores*

Purpose: To observe a sample of students to determine the proportion that exceeds the prevailing dress norms on your campus.

Procedure:
1. Review the definition of a bellwether clothing store.
2. Locate the website for a bellwether clothing store and view clothing of the current season. Explain what characteristics make the store a bellwether store.
3. View the store's merchandise for the current season and identify two clothing items that exceed the boundaries of prevailing social norms on your campus.
4. Choose a site in which you can observe people pass by slowly.
5. Set a time limit and record the number of people you observed; identify the percentage of the people you observed who wore the clothing items (or similar ones) that you identified in your bellwether clothing store research.
6. Summarize the conclusions about dress norms that you can make from your data and submit your work to your instructor.

Chapter Nine

Reports of Norm Violations: Spreading the Word

FROM THE HEADLINES

Question: A Human Resources manager for a certified public accountant (CPA) firm questioned whether male employees could be prohibited from wearing earrings. "Last week I noticed one of our junior CPAs, a male, wearing an earring, and I asked him to remove it. He responded that to require him to remove his earring while allowing females to wear earrings is discriminatory and I couldn't make him do it. Is he right?" (¶ 1).

Answer: The answer was provided by an employment law firm. "You may prohibit your male employees from wearing earrings if you wish" (¶ 2). Employers can have different dress codes for men and women provided that the codes are comparable. Employers can require men to have short hair but allow women to have long hair; require suits for men but allow women to wear skirts and dresses; prohibit men from wearing earrings but permit women to do so. If both men and women are asked to adhere to the same community standards, courts usually do not consider the dress or grooming code a problem.

Source: Can I make him take his earring off? (2006, September 18). *New Mexico Employment Law Letter, 12*(10). Retrieved October 11, 2006, from http://www.lexisnexis.com

This news article illustrates how a human resource (HR) manager reported a norm violation. Initially, the manager confronted the employee himself with a verbal report of a norm violation. Subsequently, the report appeared in a print source—an employment law letter—when the manager wrote for reassurance that the policy allowed him to require males to remove their earrings. Why do some employers prohibit males from wearing earrings at work? What motivated the HR manager to write for advice

FIGURE 9.1 THE FOURTH
STEP IN THE PROCESS OF SOCIAL
CONTROL INVOLVES REPORTS OF
NORM VIOLATIONS. PEOPLE
SPREAD INFORMATION ABOUT
DRESS NORM VIOLATIONS
THROUGH BOTH PRINT AND ORAL
CHANNELS.

about the employee dress code? What norm violation was reported in the question asked by the HR manager and the answer printed in the employment law newsletter? What effect did the type of firm (CPA) have on definition of the norm violation? Would this norm violation have been similarly defined in another workplace context? In this chapter, you will read about both print and oral mechanisms for spreading information about norm violations, which is the fourth step of the process of social control (Figure 9.1).

QUESTIONS TO ANSWER AS YOU READ

1. How do I recognize mechanisms for reporting norm violations?
2. What is the nature of print sources of reports of norm violations?
3. What is the nature of oral means of reporting norm violations?

PRINT SOURCES OF NORM VIOLATION REPORTS

Print sources of reports of norm violations from the popular press include newspapers and magazines. The **popular press** refers to readily available printed material easily understood by all people regardless of education or class. The popular press reflects the culture and society of which it is a part (Belk & Pollay, 1985). In doing so, the popular press operates as a mechanism for reports of norm violations whether available via the Internet or as hard copy. Other print sources of reports of norm violations include newsletters and reviews of litigation associated with employer dress codes.

Newspapers

One of the functions of reports of norm violations is to identify norm violators and expose their deviance. This function can be accomplished through several mechanisms that are essential parts of the newspaper—letters to the editor, letters to advice columnists, cartoons and comic strips, and human interest stories.

Letters to the Editor
Letters to the editor may be regarded as reports of norm violations. Letters to newspaper editors are a mechanism for feedback from readers who want to

express their personal opinion about some event or issue—political, social, and even personal problems and topics (Schultz, 2000). "Readership research shows that in all newspapers that carry them, the letters to the editor are widely read and highly valued" (Raeymaeckers, 2005, p. 200).

According to Wahl-Jorgensen (1999), letters to the editor are where the pros and cons of some issue are contrasted or where readers respond to the content of the newspaper from an individual position. Many letters are responses to an article or editorial (Figure 9.2). Letters that respond to what has been published in the paper are more likely to be selected (Raeymaeckers, 2005). For example, a reader wrote a letter to the editor reacting to a front page news story of a judge who sentenced a man to seven days in jail for wearing an obscene T-shirt in the courtroom. The letter writer agreed the T-shirt was inappropriate (confirmed the norm violation) but suggested a more reasonable solution would have been to reschedule the man's day in court (Moake, 2003).

Letters about personal problems are published as long as the problem is socially relevant (Raeymaeckers, 2005). For example, two readers wrote letters to the editor objecting strongly to publication of a photograph of a convicted murderer wearing his military uniform. The letter writers believed the photograph dishonored the military uniform; they expected to see the man in convict's clothing (Fiquette, 1994). The norm violation reported was that the convict's dress was not consistent with his status.

Not all topical discussions subside naturally. Sometimes the editors announce there will be no more letters published on a particular topic. One example was

> the wide public debate about headscarves worn by Muslim girls in the school environment. This topic, which had political as well as social and cultural relevance, generated a constant flood of letters in every editorial office. The topic remained prominent for a long time on the letter agenda and was showing no sign of dying down. At a certain point, several editors announced that the debate was to be concluded since no new arguments had been put forward. (Raeymaeckers, 2005, pp. 207–208)

Judge made the wrong decision

To the Editor:

In many ways I agree with Franklin County Judge Loren for finding that the T-shirt a 20-year-old Williamson County man wore to court was inappropriate.

I, too, find it inappropriate for a man in a robe to decide the fate of alleged criminals. But, we have a document in this country called the Constitution, with an amendment that guarantees the right of free speech and expression.

Defendant John Paul Hutson may have thought he was being cute and thumbing his nose at the legal system. Don't get me wrong, I believe responsibility comes before rights. I believe the judge lowered himself to the level of an immature individual to prove he could do it. Even though judges rule their courtrooms, the First Amendment overrules them.

Has it occurred to anyone in Franklin County that the ACLU is probably already on the way to defend Hutson? And they should be.

If an "artist" can express himself by putting an American flag on the floor as a doormat and get away with it, why can't a person wear a shirt with a double-meaning phrase on it? After all, filth is in the mind of the beholder.

It would have been a more reasonable solution to send Hutson away and reschedule his day in court than to put him in jail for seven days because of the shirt he chose to wear.

FIGURE 9.2 LETTERS TO THE EDITOR CONTRAST THE PROS AND CONS OF SOME ISSUE OR ALLOW READERS TO RESPOND TO THE CONTENT OF THE NEWSPAPER. THIS READER IS RESPONDING TO A DRESS ISSUE AND EXPRESSING A SUPPORTIVE VIEW OF THE PERSON'S CHOICE OF T-SHIRT.

Because it takes time and effort to write a letter to the editor, it can be assumed that the letter reflects a reader's strong concern about a topic (Dupre & Mackey, 2001). A study comparing published and unpublished letters found that letters about local, controversial issues were more likely to be published (Renfro, 1979). Letters to the editor offer insight into a community's social and cultural norms as expressed by writers (Sotillo & Starace-Nastasi, 1999). "Letters to a newspaper are not intended to be representative measures of public opinion; rather, they are measures representing public opinion" (Dupre & Mackey, 2001, p. 8).

Letters to Advice Columnists

Letters to advice columnists provide another mechanism for reporting violations of norms. Individuals seem to need reassurance about norms and sanctions associated with violations of norms. Are the norm violations similar to what other individuals would punish or reward in similar situations? Advice columns keep readers informed about the normative order—what the norms are, to whom they apply, and in what situations. For example, a wife wrote to an advice columnist to inquire whether her husband, who was sitting around in his undershorts when neighbors dropped by, should have put on some trousers. Her husband said that since *nothing showed*, he did not need to apologize ("He Should Have," 1994). The advice columnist supported the wife's report of a norm violation in her response that the husband should have put on some pants.

Advice columns are a component of almost every major U.S. newspaper (Hendley, 1977). Both the structure and content of advice columns are deliberate choices of an editorial staff. The question-and-answer structure encourages the belief that the columns address actual problems that readers might encounter (Currie, 2001). Questions are framed using the first person singular *I*. The letter writer is most often anonymous; initials or nicknames are used, for example, *Love is Blue* in California. The appeal of advice columns can be partially attributed to the ability of the question-and-answer format to assign authorship of questions to an individual who represents a typical reader, which calls up feelings of both intimacy and membership in a social world. This feeling is reinforced by locating the letter writer in a social situation that could be anywhere.

Specific questions are not treated in terms of the letter writer's individual existence, but rather as questions dealing with membership in the larger social world (Currie, 2001). Indeed, writers may include in their letters some reference to their normality. Normative prescriptions arise through the identification of norm violations and characterizing the questions as ones that are universal, natural, and normal. The focus on the reader with a personal and specific problem is shifted to a social and universal resolution through the response of the columnist. Advice columns allow letter writers to report norm violations and ask questions about culturally sensitive topics (cross-dressing) without fear of social stigmatization.

The question-and-answer structure encourages readers to assume that a specific individual has written a letter and influences readers to compare themselves to the norms addressed in the questions. Reader interest in the questions rather than the answers is evidence of the ability of the letters to define the bounds of normality (Currie, 2001). The result of comparison reading is that readers measure their own behavior against the normality specified by the questions and/or answers. It is possible, of course, for readers to reject or contradict the views offered. But rejecting or contradicting the views offered in favor of relying on their own experience would require readers to consider themselves outside the boundaries of normality created by the column. When norm violations are reported via letters to advice columnists, the mechanism is in place for the columns to establish boundaries of normal behavior.

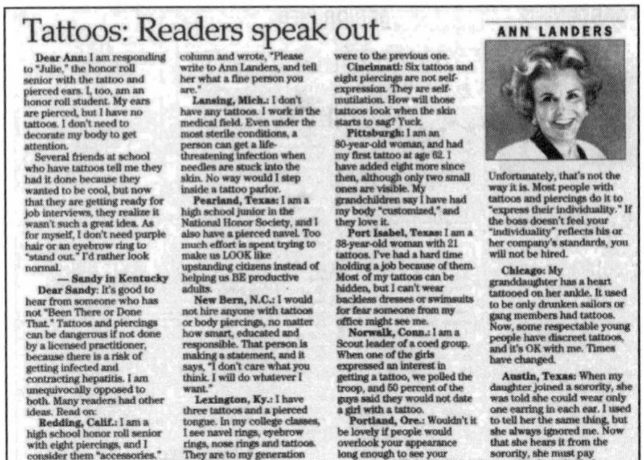

Because of their enormous audience, letters to advice columnists are important mechanisms for reporting norm violations. During the 1960s and 1970s, Ann Landers and Abigail Van Buren together were the two most widely syndicated newspaper advice columnists in the world, with a combined readership of over 150 million (Castro, Moritz, & Nash, 1981) (Figure 9.3). Landers received from 1,000 to 2,000 letters every day in the early 1990s (Buckley, 1995; Kogan, 1996), while Van Buren received 25,000 letters every week in the early 1980s (Castro, Moritz, & Nash, 1981). Landers' column appeared in more than 1,200 newspapers with an estimated 90 million readers daily in the early 1990s (Buckley, 1995; Matthews, 1993) while Van Buren's column was syndicated in around 1,000 newspapers and reported to have a daily readership of 65 million (Hendley, 1977).

Eppie Lederer, otherwise known as Ann Landers, died on June 22, 2002, at age 83. In writing of Landers' death, Cohen (2003) stated: "historians of the

FIGURE 9.3 THE DRESS NORM VIOLATION REPORTED IN THIS ADVICE COLUMN IS TATTOOS, AND THE LETTER WRITERS EXPRESS BOTH PRO AND CON VIEWS, MIRRORING THE VARIETY OF VIEWS ON THIS TOPIC IN THE LARGER SOCIETY.

future will read her columns not as advice but as anthropology, a compendium of the conventional wisdom of mid-century America" (¶ 10). Landers' column was considered to be America's bulletin board (Kogan, 1996). "I think that 200 years from now, if an anthropologist really wants to know what life in these United States—all of the United States—was like, all he or she might have to do is read every one of Ann Landers' columns" (Swanson, 2003, ¶ 19).

At the time of her death, Landers' column appeared in 1,200 newspapers with 90 million readers daily ("Former Lounge Singer," 2005). "Dear Abby" appears in 1,400 newspapers worldwide and is read by more than 100 million people, 70 percent female/30 percent male, 80 percent between the ages of 18 and 49 (Eila, 2005).

Cartoons and Comic Strips

Cartoons have been around for more than a century as components of daily newspapers (Berger, 1973). **Cartoons** (pictorial designs that include caricatures) are single-panel drawings and **comic strips** are sequential multiple-panel drawings.

The comics are the most widely read pages of the newspaper, are read equally by all classes of society, and in many cases are the main reason people buy newspapers (Reitberger & Fuchs, 1971). According to Berger, "any medium that has the continued attention of hundreds of millions of people deserves serious attention and study" (p. 15).

Because of their daily appearance and serial character, comic strips represent a "national diary, a running record of who we are and what we think" (Daviss, 1987, p. 181). Cartoons and comic strips provide entertainment, but also information about life (Berger, 1973). "Comic strips are complex stimulus patterns in which a variety of positive and negative values are expressed through the characters and situations depicted" (Spiegelman, Terwilliger, & Fearing, 1953, p. 189).

Saenger (1955) suggested that cartoons present a stereotypic view of American culture. Cartoons "present a packaged incident to the reader, peopled by stereotyped caricatures of men and women" (Morrison, 1982, p. 2037). Cartoons are effective in transmitting stereotypes partly because of their quick message quality (Hess & Mariner, 1975). Cartoonists use a technique called a *tab of identity* to allow readers to easily categorize stereotypic characters (Hess & Mariner, 1975).

A **tab of identity** is a symbol, a portrayal of eccentric characteristics of a subject (Streicher, 1965). "For example, the character Uncle Sam is easily recognized by tabs of identity: he wears striped trousers with straps under his boots, a star-spangled vest under a cut-away coat, and a top hat" (Workman & Freeburg, 1997, p. 392). As a symbol, Uncle Sam stands for something else—the United States. The identity tab can reinforce outdated stereotypic concepts (Hess & Mariner, 1975). Clothing and appearance are logical choices for identity tabs because of their visual salience.

Paoletti (1981) focused on cartoons as a source of information about clothing of a particular historical period. "By studying the clothing of men and women, old and young, people of all classes and professions as they appear in cartoons and by noticing correlations between styles of dress and personality traits, the historian can reconstruct the language of fashion as it was used generations ago" (p. 50). Cartoons express a society's beliefs, values, and opinions, as well as negative feelings about things considered unpleasant or unacceptable. A humorous situation depicted in a cartoon shows an unusual or unexpected violation of a group norm or unexpected conformity to it.

Successful cartoons contain words, symbols, settings, and ideas that are easily recognized by the reader. Likewise, the target of the joke must be easily identifiable, perhaps exaggerated or presented in an incongruous manner.

In U.S. culture, where fashion changes rapidly and with extensive publicity, part of the evaluation process seems to be ridiculing new fashions via their appearance in cartoons (Paoletti, 1981). During times of especially dramatic fashion changes (the extremely large, long, and sagging pants worn by teenagers in the early to mid-2000s), cartoons are a graphic record of public outrage or amusement (Figure 9.4). By comparing the normal portion of cartoons with the distorted target of the joke, the changing boundaries of popular tastes can be traced; for example, cartoons about women wearing trousers became less frequent as the public grew more used to the sight. Paoletti gave

FIGURE 9.4 THE TARGET OF THE JOKE IN THIS CARTOON IS BAGGY JEANS.

an example from cartoons in the 1880s and 1890s: A man in a cartoon wearing cuffed trousers was likely to be the target of the joke because cuffs were new and still not accepted by the general public.

Cartoons are deceptively simple, but the underlying message may be complicated (Paoletti, 1981). Information about the clothing worn may be related to (a) public awareness, (b) popular interest or concern, (c) contemporary perceptions, (d) contemporary associations, or (e) popular values and opinions. Documenting the frequency of cartoons on a specific topic (the length of skirts or the prevalence of shoulder pads) is one way to track the fluctuation of public interest. Analyzing cartoon characters' clothing is a way to understand the symbolic meaning of dress, because clothing is often used to depict dominant character traits.

Human Interest Stories

The focus of **human interest stories** is not factual presentation of breaking news, but rather presentation of information which is of *human interest* (Tuchman, 1973). Reports of social problems (norm violations) are the essence of human interest stories, which are important to newspapers in attracting readers (Johnson, 1989). Human interest stories present particular issues as problems, particular outcomes as desirable, and particular strategies as appropriate—a process called **framing** (Mulcahy, 1995). Through framing, news stories can typify a particular issue or event as a norm violation.

Components of human interest stories that can be used to report norm violations include the content, visuals or graphics accompanying the story, and the headline. The content of a human interest story includes amount and type of information—for example, demographic characteristics of individuals being reported about, quotes from experts, or statistics. Headlines can be used to capture readers' attention, to typify problems, and to shape perceptions. Visuals or graphics can be used to depict race, age group, social class, gender, and other characteristics. A given situation can be defined as a problem in many ways (Hilgartner & Bosk, 1988).

Claims making refers to the process whereby individuals (physicians, educators, reporters) call attention to a situation and try to change it (Best, 1989). Claims making is like reporting norm violations (Figure 9.5). Human interest stories do not merely restate

FIGURE 9.5 IN THIS HUMAN INTEREST STORY, THE ISSUE IS THE USE OF TOO-THIN MODELS ON DESIGNER RUNWAYS.

Spanish fasion show rejects too-thin models

MADRID, Spain — Spain's top fashion show has turned away a slew of models on grounds they are too skinny — an unprecedented swipe at body images blamed for encouraging eating disorders among young people.

Organizers of the pageant, known as the Pasarela Cibeles, used a mathematical formula to calculate the models' body mass index — a measure of their weight in relation to their height — and 30 percent of the women flunked, said the Association of Fashion Designers of Spain.

The association said Friday it wanted models at the show running from Sept. 18-22 to project "an image of beauty and health" and shun a gaunt, emaciated look.

The decision was made as part of a voluntary agreement

with the Madrid regional government, said Jesus del Pozo, a designer who is part of the association, said Thursday.

Last year's show, also called Madrid Fashion Week, drew protests from medical associations and women's advocacy groups because some of the models were positively bone-thin.

This time the Madrid regional government decided to intervene and pressure organizers to hire fuller-figured women as role models for young girls obsessed with being thin and prone to starving themselves into sickness, said Concha Guerra, deputy finance minister of the regional administration.

Fashion shows, Guerra said, "are mirrors for many young women."

—The Associated Press

claims, but through the process of framing, actively translate and transform claims into reports of norm violations.

Magazines

Magazines, despite their limited repertoire and repetitive messages, appeal to readers because readers seem compelled to search for what it means to be normal (Currie, 1997). Magazines are an important medium for shaping cultural ideals about appearance (Cusumano & Thompson, 1997; Levine, Smolak, & Hayden, 1994). "A **cultural ideal** is a kind of shorthand summary of aesthetic values. Because an ideal represents a set of values, it can also be seen as a goal, though often unstated" (Eicher, Evenson, & Lutz, 2000, p. 309). The repeated media images of thin females and muscular males make these idealized body shapes seem to be the norm, even though they do not reflect the norm of the U.S. population (Thompson, Coovert, & Stormer, 1999).

Magazine content includes editorial topics, recurrent features, and advertisements. Advertisements constitute about half of the total magazine space of fashion and beauty magazines. Indeed, advertisements are the major source of glossy imagery that makes reading these magazines visually pleasurable (Currie, 1997). Fashion magazines are called **glossy magazines** because they are printed on slick paper. The visual imagery used in advertisements has more impact than words because it is easier for readers to understand (Dyer, 1982) (Figure 9.6).

In U.S. culture, the content of the feminine gender role is influenced by written material, specifically women's magazines. These magazines inform women about what they should and should not wear, how and how not to apply their makeup and arrange their hair, and what are acceptable and unacceptable attitudes and behaviors. Women's magazines link meanings of femininity to everyday activities and beliefs (Smith, 1990). Adolescent magazines, in particular, socialize their readers about the feminine gender role by using messages that emphasize physical beauty (Evans, Rutberg, Sather, & Turner, 1991). A recent survey of adolescent girls revealed that 69 percent reported magazine pictures influenced their idea of the perfect body shape, and 47 percent claimed that the pictures influenced them to want to diet to lose weight (Field, Cheung, Wolf, Herzog, Gortmaker, & Colditz, 1999).

Readers from various backgrounds tend to view the stereotypical, dominant magazine images of femininity as true depictions (Currie, 1997). Many

FIGURE 9.6 HOW WOULD YOU EXPRESS IN WORDS WHAT THIS PHOTOGRAPH IS COMMUNICATING VISUALLY?

readers compare themselves to the magazine images, although they freely acknowledge that the magazines set unrealistic beauty standards. Readers' comparisons with magazine images can make them feel they are in violation of the norm. Magazines attempt to help readers come closer to the norm by providing advice about how to deal with problem areas (big hips, small bust, thick waistline, short legs). The reality of a culture that emphasizes good looks for women reinforces the power that magazine messages have for readers. Readers may criticize the magazines' use of beautiful models with perfect bodies, but they seldom challenge the cultural mandate for women to look good (Currie, 1997).

Law Review Articles

Law review articles are sources of reports of norm violations that resulted in litigation. A law review article typically takes one issue, for example, workplace equality for women, and presents a compilation of court cases related to the issue. The cases are analyzed to draw conclusions and make recommendations about the state of the issue.

Bartlett (1994) wrote a review of cases related to workplace equality for the purpose of drawing conclusions and making recommendations about the influence of community norms on dress and appearance standards in the workplace. Widely accepted norms are the basis for many dress and appearance requirements instituted by employers.

Even in the absence of mandatory dress and appearance codes, expectations about dress and appearance exist. Acquired during the process of socialization within a particular culture, the expectations are deeply ingrained and constitute the basis for beliefs about what is normal and acceptable. Bartlett (1994) questioned whether it is possible or desirable to evaluate workplace dress and appearance rules without taking norms into account. What individuals express through their dress is dependent on the cultural codes that give meaning to the expressions. Because meanings are socially constructed, abolishing employer dress and appearance requirements will not allow individuals to express themselves unconstrained by sanctions (the inability to obtain or retain a certain job).

At the hiring stage, employers can exclude applicants who appear to violate appearance norms, especially with respect to characteristics that are difficult or impossible to change (facial features, body build, posture). "Although it is impossible to determine with any reliability how much appearance matters in hiring decisions, there is reason to believe that many job applicants who would be constrained by dress and appearance standards on the job are never hired in the first place" (Bartlett, 1994, p. 2551) (Figure 9.7).

Oral traditions of dress and appearance prevail in some workplaces, making written codes unnecessary. For example, one source was reported as saying, "Leaving the second button on your suit jacket unbuttoned was an unspoken law until I broke it" (Bartlett, 1994, p. 2551). However, many businesses rely on written dress codes to preclude any misunderstanding about dress and appearance expectations. Dress norm violations need to be examined in light of workplace conditions, societal conditions, and cultural norms that give them meaning.

FIGURE 9.7 THE MAN WITH THE MAGAZINE MAY BE INTERVIEWING FOR A CREATIVE JOB, SUCH AS GRAPHIC ARTIST. HIS ATTIRE WOULD BE INAPPROPRIATE FOR INTERVIEWING FOR SOME JOBS.

FIGURE 9.8 BOTH POSITIVE COMMUNICATIONS (CONVERSATIONS WITH FRIENDS) AND NEGATIVE COMMUNICATIONS (GOSSIP) ARE EVERYDAY OCCURRENCES THROUGH WHICH ORAL REPORTS OF NORM VIOLATIONS ARE TRANSMITTED.

ORAL SOURCES OF NORM VIOLATION REPORTS

Reports of norm violations may be made verbally to violators, friends, relatives, or authorities. Oral means of reporting dress norm violations include conversations among peers and gossip.

Conversations Among Peers

Because of the trust and intimacy characteristic of friendships, an important cultural context for reports of norm violations is conversations among peers. "Appearance conversations direct attention to appearance-related issues, reinforce the value and importance of appearance to close friends, and promote the construction of appearance ideals" (Jones, Vigfusdottir, & Lee, 2004, p. 324). Conversations with friends provide the everyday context for paying attention to and interpreting information about dress (Figure 9.8). Conversations are likely to contain critical comments about dress. Such criticism can reinforce the value of appearance to peers

and highlight specific desirable appearance attributes, the absence of which is presumably the basis of the criticism—a report of a norm violation. Report of a norm violation via criticism can potentially contribute to individuals' internalization of society's appearance norms.

Not all conversations among peers take place among friends. Some interactions involve negative communication such as teasing, ridicule, insults, and sarcasm. In essence, reports of norm violations through negative communication can take three forms (Wooten, 2006, p. 191):

1. A peer is told why he or she is unacceptable ("You don't belong, because . . . "). Individuals who report such norm violations to their peers gain "status and power by consuming material objects and belittling those without them" (p. 192). For example, a young male adolescent with limited financial resources was ridiculed because he wore tight, high-water (too short) pants.

2. A peer is told what he or she needs to do or stop doing in order to be accepted ("You can belong, if . . . "). An obvious knowledge deficiency needs to be corrected; the individual "only needs to learn social norms and demonstrate commitment to them" (p. 193). For example, mixing competing brands in one outfit (pants and shirt) violated one group's norm.

3. A peer is rebuked for violating role expectations and encouraged to demonstrate commitment to group norms ("Act like you belong!"). Such rebukes "reinforce norms by calling attention to violations and highlighting acceptable excuses for them" (p. 194). For example, when a student wore khaki pants and a polo shirt to high school, his peers asked if he had a job interview.

Through negative communication, adolescents "apply cultural categories and principles to make sense and make fun of consumption practices that violate salient norms" (Wooten, 2006, p. 196). Information about the social consequences of nonconformity is conveyed via such remarks.

Gossip

Gossip is defined as evaluative (positive or negative) casual conversation about an absent third person (Foster, 2004; Kuttler, Parker, & La Greca, 2002). Gossip is not merely *idle chatter* (the common definition) but small talk with social functions (Rosnow, 1977). Gossip is an oral method by which norm violations are reported. Dunbar, Duncan, and Marriott (1997) estimated that approximately 65 percent of communication centers around social topics, also referred to as gossip. Gossip is a cultural universal (Stirling, 1956).

According to Foster (2004), there are four social functions of gossip: (a) information—when individuals disseminate information to others about someone who is absent, (b) entertainment—when individuals gossip or tell stories for pleasure, (c) friendship—building friendships by sharing gossip, thereby establishing boundaries to distinguish *insiders* from *outsiders,* and (d) influence—control of group norms to restrict unconventional behavior and maintain conformity. These functions are based on the assumption that gossip is a means of communicating information and strengthening group sanctions, thereby increasing group solidarity (Stirling, 1956).

Positive gossip conveys information about socially approved behavior, while negative gossip is a consequence of socially inappropriate behavior (Levin, Mody-Desbareau, & Arluke, 1988). Gossip functions within the process of social control by being a method of reporting appropriate as well as inappropriate behavior. Although gossip may be positive, the general consensus is that gossip is negative (Turner, Mazur, Wendel, & Winslow, 2003). According to Nevo and Nevo (1993), individuals gossip about others' achievements, physical appearance, and personal lives (Figure 9.9). In addition, people read gossip columns or biographies of famous people (Levin, Mody-Desbareau, & Arluke, 1988; Nevo & Nevo, 1993).

One function of gossip is to enforce conformity to group norms by allowing norms to be stated and reaffirmed (Suls, 1977). Gossip also serves as a warning that a person's behavior may become the topic of gossip if he or she violates group norms. As always, one assumption is that individuals in a social group agree on the norms for desirable and undesirable behavior. Gossip is

FIGURE 9.9 NEGATIVE GOSSIP IS A CONSEQUENCE OF SOCIALLY INAPPROPRIATE BEHAVIOR. THE GROUP OF FRIENDS IN THIS CARTOON IS TALKING ABOUT THE EX-GIRLFRIEND OF ONE OF THEM IN A NEGATIVE WAY.

REPORTS OF NORM
VIOLATIONS:
SPREADING
THE WORD

one of the strongest sanctions found in groups (Stirling, 1956). Maintaining the favorable opinion of other group members is important to individual group members.

Ostracism (isolation) from a group is one of the greatest fears of individuals and is a strong sanction against nonconformity. Members who violate the traditional standards of the group, unless such violations are accepted and form new behavior standards for the group, become group outcasts or deviants. Through the mechanism of gossip, traditional standards of morals, ethics, customs, and mores are upheld (Stirling, 1956). Threat of public disapproval as expressed in gossip compels many individuals to conform to the cultural rules of society.

Sometimes gossiping is initiated to learn what behaviors, achievements, or transgressions are acceptable or reasonable. In other words, gossip can be used to clarify ambiguous areas of behavior about which group members have little consensus. Group members may discuss the merits of a new fashion such as *skinny jeans* and how the jeans looked on someone who was wearing them. Gossip can be used to gather information in order to make comparisons between oneself and others (Suls, 1977). Such comparisons allow individuals to evaluate their own appearance, achievements, and abilities. Because gossip is thirdhand and unreliable, the recipient of gossip may need to share it with others to see whether they think it represents reliable information.

The **tendency to gossip** is a psychological trait that affects whether individuals will choose to talk or not talk about an absent third person (Nevo & Nevo, 1993). Individuals with people-oriented occupations (service, art, business) show a greater tendency to gossip (Nevo & Nevo, 1993). For example, these statements from the Tendency to Gossip Questionnaire (Nevo, Nevo, & Derech-Zehavi, 1994) reflect interests of those with careers in the fashion industry (a people-oriented occupation): "I like talking to friends about other people's clothes, When I come back from a party or some other event, I tend to talk about my impressions of the personal appearance of others who were there, [and] I like talking with a friend about the personal appearance of other people" (pp. 191–192).

"Children gossip practically from the time they can talk and can begin to recognize others" (Fine, 1977, p. 181). Gossip is a main feature of young children's conversations; tattling, which is common in childhood, is a form of gossip. Children's gossip has four components:

1. A content-socialization component—transfer of information which has a socializing effect
2. A normative or evaluative component—gossip that contains (explicitly or implicitly) some perspective on the behavior being described; gossip is one of the major methods by which norms are stated and reaffirmed
3. An interpersonal/social structural component—the reputational and impression-management functions of gossip are particularly powerful among children because the esteem of one's peer group is of great importance
4. An ability/competence component—by learning how to gossip effectively, a child can learn the rules for proper appearance or behavior

Gossip acts as a mechanism to regulate conformity to norms (Fine, 1977). Preadolescents and early adolescents are quick to notice and comment on violation of norms. One direct threat to an individual's reputation is gossip, so protecting against negative gossip may be a key task for preadolescents and early adolescents.

SUMMARY

In this chapter, we examined mechanisms for spreading information about norm violations. One of the functions of reports of norm violations is to identify norm violators and publicize their deviance. We looked at several specific mechanisms through which this function can be accomplished: letters to the editor, letters to advice columnists, human interest stories, cartoons and comic strips, magazines, reviews of litigation associated with employer dress codes, conversations among peers, and gossip.

KEY TERMS AND CONCEPTS

cartoons

claims making

comic strips

cultural ideal

framing

glossy magazines

gossip	ostracism
human interest stories	popular press
letters to advice columnists	tab of identity
letters to the editor	tendency to gossip

Suggested Readings

1. Kuttler, A. F., Parker, J. G., & La Greca, A. M. (2002). Developmental and gender differences in preadolescents' judgments of the veracity of gossip. *Merrill-Palmer Quarterly, 48*, 105–132.
2. Nevo, O. & Nevo, B. (1993). Gossip and counseling: The tendency to gossip and its relation to vocational interests. *Counseling Psychology Quarterly, 6*, 229–239.
3. Schultz, T. (2000). Mass media and the concept of interactivity: An exploratory study of online forums and reader e-mail. *Media, Culture and Society, 22*(2), 205–221.

Research Activity 9.1: Gossip and Dress

Purpose: To identify reports of dress norm violations in a gossip column.

Procedure:

1. Review the definition of gossip.
2. Locate and log on to a gossip column website. Example websites include Liz Smith (http://www.nypost.com/gossip/liz/liz.htm) and Miss No-Aphid Ladybug (http://www.kidsregen.org/gossip/flash/1002.swf).
3. Locate and print an article that reports a dress norm violation.
4. Highlight and label the report of the dress norm violation.
5. Submit your article to your instructor.

Purpose: To identify a comic strip portrayal of a dress norm violation.

Procedure:

1. Log on to the Google search engine (http://google.com).

2. Enter the key words *comic strips and cartoons* enclosed in quotation marks ("comic strips and cartoons").

3. Locate and print a comic strip related to a dress norm violation. For example, you might click on Momma@comics.com

4. Explain the dress norm violation reported in the comic strip or cartoon.

5. Submit your work to your instructor.

Chapter Ten

READING AND TALKING ABOUT NORM VIOLATIONS

FROM THE HEADLINES

A body modification artist has invented a way to implant jewelry under human skin. The process, called subdermal implants, is a form of three-dimensional body modification. The risky surgical procedure creates a raised area on the skin in a shape of the artist's choosing, for example, stars, hearts, or ridges. Inexperienced practitioners can cause damage to the nerve and lymphatic system. Incorrectly done implants can require surgical correction or skin grafts and can result in permanent disfigurement. Most medical professionals object to the procedure on ethical grounds. Under rules of the American Medical Association, "modifying the body toward societal ideals is considered ethical, but any modification away from those ideals is unethical and comes with potentially stiff penalties" (¶ 21).

Source: Norton, Q. (2006, March 8). Body artists customize your flesh. Retrieved October 11, 2006, from www.Wired.com

This news story reported on an egregious norm violation—subdermal implants. The American Medical Association (AMA) reported research regarding the consequences of incorrectly performed implants and warned of sanctions that could be levied against those who participated in such unethical procedures. The AMA considered societal ideals in deciding which practices are ethical and unethical. What are the risks associated with subdermal implants, an example of radical body modification? Why would someone decide to get a subdermal implant? Subdermal implants have been described as ritualistic scarification. What does that mean? In this chapter you will read research about both written and oral reports of norm violations.

This chapter builds on Chapter 9 by presenting research related to mechanisms for spreading information about norm violations. The methods and

TABLE 10.1 SUMMARY OF RESEARCH METHODS AND TOOLS RELATED TO REPORTS OF NORM VIOLATIONS

RESEARCH METHOD	TOOL(S)	AUTHOR(S)	YEAR	ARTICLE TITLE
Qualitative	Content analysis worksheet	Ballentine & Ogle	2005	The making and unmaking of body problems in *Seventeen* magazine, 1992–2003
Quantitative	Questionnaire	Baumeister et al.	2004	Gossip as cultural learning
Quantitative	Content analysis worksheet	Byrd-Bredbenner & Murray	2003	A comparison of the anthropometric measurements of idealized female body images in media directed to men, women, and mixed gender audiences
Qualitative	Content analysis worksheet	Damhorst	1991	Gender and appearance in daily comic strips
Theoretical	Literature analysis	Foster	2004	Research on gossip: Taxonomy, methods, and future directions
Qualitative	Content analysis worksheet	Freeburg & Workman	in press	A method to identify and validate social norms related to dress
Qualitative	Content analysis worksheet	Glascock & Preston-Schreck	2004	Gender and racial stereotypes in daily newspaper comics: A time-honored tradition
Quantitative	Questionnaire	Jones et al.	2004	Body image and the appearance culture among adolescent girls and boys: An examination of friend conversations, peer criticism, appearance magazines, and the internalization of appearance ideals
Theoretical	Literature analysis	Kamer & Keller	2003	Give me $5 chips, a jack and coke—hold the cleavage: A look at employee appearance issues in the gaming industry
Quantitative	Interview worksheet	Kuttler et al.	2002	Developmental and gender differences in preadolescents' judgments of the veracity of gossip

tools used in each research study are summarized in Table 10.1. Researchers have studied print sources of reports, including letters to advice columnists, cartoons, comic strips, human interest stories, magazines, and law reviews. Other researchers have concentrated on oral methods by which norm violations are reported, that is, conversations among peers and gossip.

QUESTIONS TO ANSWER AS YOU READ

1. How do researchers look at reports of norm violations?
2. What is the nature of research dealing with reports of norm violations?

RESEARCH METHOD	TOOL(S)	AUTHOR(S)	YEAR	ARTICLE TITLE
Qualitative	Content analysis worksheet	O'Neal	1997	Clothes to kill for: An analysis of primary and secondary claims-making in print media
Qualitative	Content analysis worksheet	Paoletti	1985	Ridicule and role models as factors in American men's fashion change, 1880–1910
Quantitative	Questionnaire	Parekh & Schmidt	2003	In pursuit of an identity—fashion marketing and the development of eating disorders
Qualitative	Content analysis worksheet	Pitts	1999	Body modification, self-mutilation, and agency in media accounts of a subculture
Quantitative	Questionnaire	Taylor	2005	Gossip as an interpersonal communication phenomenon
Qualitative	Interview worksheet	Wooten	2006	From labeling possessions to possessing labels: Ridicule and socialization among adolescents
Mixed methods	Literature and content analysis worksheets	Workman & Freeburg	1997	A method to identify occupational stereotypes

3. How do I analyze a research article for methods used to study reports of norm violations?

ANALYZING PRINT REPORTS OF NORM VIOLATIONS

As noted in Chapter 9, two functions of reports of norm violations are to tell people about the norm violation and label the norm violator. Newspapers are an important source of information for researchers studying reports of norm violations. Magazines and reviews of litigation surrounding disputed employer dress codes constitute other print sources for these reports. Norm violations that resulted in litigation are reported in law review articles.

Newspapers

Three of the newspaper features discussed in Chapter 9—letters to advice columnists, cartoons and comic strips, and human interest stories—lend themselves to analysis by researchers studying norm violations.

Letters to Advice Columnists

When asked which items in the newspaper they read, 57 percent of women listed personal advice columns—the highest percentage for any category for either sex (Bogart, 1984). Cartoons, comics, and graphics were popular choices as well. Newspapers are read at least occasionally by almost 90 percent of Americans, and 66 percent read a newspaper on any given day. Nearly 80 percent of readers reported looking at every page in the newspaper, including advice columns.

Excerpts from a few letters to advice columnists may help to clarify how these letters can be reports of norm violations (Freeburg & Workman, in press). Women wrote letters to advice columnists in which they threatened to sue stylists because the stylist cut their hair so short, it made them look like men. Indeed, a writer reported that she had sued a stylist and won by using before and after pictures. A writer criticized a woman who took her grandson to a barber for a real boy's haircut when the boy's parents were on vacation. The writer reported her son had long beautiful curls until age six. A writer reported birthday parties held in beauty salons during which young girls had their hair styled, after which each child was photographed in a glamorous pose.

A man reported that his girlfriend's mustache looked terrible and he wished she would bleach or remove it. A woman with facial and chest hair reported she only wore turtlenecks or blouses buttoned up to the neck. Another woman reported that she was taught by her mother that hairy legs were unsightly, but her husband did not want her to shave her legs. She reported that she felt she could not wear shorts or short dresses with hairy legs.

A mother reported that her daughter had a brownish birthmark on her face. Strangers asked about the birthmark and suggested her daughter have surgery. A woman reported that an automobile accident took her from pretty to hideous in seconds. She reported that people made her feel like a freak. She reported that plastic surgery made her look and feel normal again.

Women reported threatening divorce because their husbands would not bathe every day. Office workers reported a co-worker who showered only once a week and wore heavy perfume the rest of the week, resulting in offensive body odor.

A mother reported her daughter appeared normal except her fingernails were so long (6 inches) she looked like a freak. The mother suffered embarrassment and shame because of her daughter's appearance.

Because advice columns have enormous worldwide audiences, their influence as a mechanism for reporting norm violations is widespread. Letters to advice columnists keep readers informed about what the dress norms are for various situations by printing reports of norm violations.

Cabe, Walker, and Williams (1999) commented that newspaper advice columns are useful teaching tools. They contrasted **case studies** that typically describe behaviors and characteristics of individuals or groups with **case problems** that are scenarios to be analyzed and possibly resolved through discussion. Newspaper advice columns represent case problems. Information needed for case problem solution often is not overtly stated or may be absent. Thus, readers are required to derive inferences, make reasonable assumptions, and/or find additional information.

Cartoons and Comic Strips

Paoletti (1985) investigated the adoption of the business suit by American men. In the 1880s the appearance of a well-dressed man was that of the "Perfect Gentleman": "inconspicuous to the casual observer, but perfect in its attention to quality, fit, and correctness" (p. 121). The modern business suit (sack-type coat and trousers of the same material) was accepted for office wear in the 1880s and 1890s and then adapted for various activities, from sports to formal parties.

Paoletti analyzed the content of 256 cartoons taken from three magazines published between 1880 and 1910 as a means of conveying ridicule or criticism of older styles of men's clothing. The analysis showed that cartoons ridiculing men's dress were most common in the 1880s; the men in the cartoons were depicted as unattractive, unmanly, effeminate, and wearing the styles associated with the Perfect Gentleman (even after 1900, when these styles were hardly ever worn). Paoletti concluded that ridicule of these styles, particularly in the 1880s, expressed disapproval of the styles.

FIGURE 10.1 THE *DUDE*.

One caricature uncovered was the *Dude,* a stereotype of the well-dressed Perfect Gentleman (Figure 10.1). The Dude's caricature featured identity tabs of monocle, stiff collar, and cane; thus, the stereotypic figure was easily categorized as a sartorial fool, an example to be avoided. The name *Dude* probably originated from the slang expression *duden-kop,* or blockhead. Anecdotal evidence suggested that the label was hard to avoid and that well-dressed men reacted negatively to being called a dude. For example, one man sued another man for libel for calling him a dude. Paoletti encouraged further research into the Dude and other sartorial fools as a means of understanding how negative images such as these function in fashion change.

Glascock and Preston-Schreck (2004) analyzed 50 comic strips from four daily newspapers appearing during one month beginning in March 2002. Because of the appeal of comic strips to readers of all ages and demographics and because they appear in newspapers across the nation, the authors expected that depictions in comic strips would reflect stereotypical attitudes and beliefs held by readers. The comic strip characters were coded by gender, age, role, race, body shape, job, marital status, parental status, dress (average, provocative), and location.

Male characters appeared more than twice as often as female characters. Female characters were more than twice as likely to appear in the context of the home as male characters, who were more likely to appear at work. Male characters were more often portrayed as overweight compared with female characters. Female characters were more likely to be married and also more likely to be shown with children than male characters. Most characters were not provocatively dressed, but female characters were more likely to be provocatively dressed than male characters. Female characters were more likely to be involved in domestic activities such as child care, preparing or serving food, and performing household chores. One masculine stereotype detected was of "beer drinking, sports watching, couch potato men" (p. 428). Of all human cartoon characters, only 3 percent were minorities (actual percentage of minorities in the U.S. population is 25 percent).

Workman and Freeburg (1997) identified clothing and appearance cues used by cartoonists to allow readers to easily identify and categorize members of an occupational group—automobile salespeople. Further, they identified clothing and appearance cues associated with personal traits. To begin the analysis, the authors reviewed terms used in the popular press to describe the stereotypic appearance of automobile salespeople. Identity tabs used in the popular press to denote automobile salespeople included plaid clothing items, ties, white shoes, white belts, jackets, man, smoker, and loud, ugly clothing.

Forty nationally syndicated cartoons were content-analyzed to identify clothing and appearance variables used as identity tabs to denote automobile salespeople. The following identity tabs were found: balding, overweight, white men, tie, jacket/pants, plaid fabric, white shoes, and white belt (Figure 10.2). The cartoons were divided into two groups: those with some reference to dishonesty and those without a reference to dishonesty. Plaid clothing items were more likely to be found in the cartoons with references to dishonesty, leading to the conclusion that plaid clothing was used to depict the personal trait of dishonesty.

"Everything about the car business has changed, Jim—except my jacket."

FIGURE 10.2 CARTOONS DEPICT OCCUPATIONAL STEREO-TYPES THROUGH CLOTHING AND APPEARANCE VARIABLES USED AS IDENTITY TABS. SOME COMPONENTS OF THE OCCUPATIONAL STEREOTYPE ASSOCIATED WITH THE AUTOMOBILE SALESPERSON ARE DEPICTED IN THIS CARTOON.

Damhorst (1991) analyzed 1,045 cartoons and comic strips from 1951, 1953, and 1987 as a way of understanding the role and purpose of appearance in U.S. culture. "While one cartoonist gives his or her personal interpretation of the surrounding world, the many cartoonists that fill the funny pages with their work together give a larger, more diversified view of society" (p. 59). The cartoons and comic strips content-analyzed were those in which dress was essential to understanding the joke or in which dress was part of the verbal content of the script. Themes discovered included (a) concern with appearance, (b) opting out of norms, (c) bad taste, (d) faux pas, (e) help with dress, (f) marital conflict, (g) nonmarital conflict, (h) functional dress, (i) disguise, (j) costumes and silly dress, (k) cross-dressing, (l) caretakers, and (m) shoppers.

Male characters were more likely than females to willfully violate dress and attractiveness norms (Damhorst, 1991). Male characters were more likely to exhibit bad taste in dress and were depicted as clueless about normative combinations of aesthetic elements. Men were depicted as more often critiquing and ridiculing others' appearances. Female characters were often depicted as the principal caretakers of clothing, as shopping agents for self and family, and as enjoying shopping. Some differences were apparent between the decades studied; most noticeably, in 1987 cartoons and comic strips, men were depicted as more likely to be independent in managing their appearance and more likely to conform to gender-appropriate dress norms than in the 1950s.

Human Interest Stories

A **claim** is a demand by one party to another that something has to be done about some alleged situation (Spector & Kitsuse, 1977). Claims of social problems (what this text refers to as reports of norm violations) are the material of human interest stories (Johnson, 1989).

O'Neal (1997) analyzed 62 news articles for descriptions of victims and perpetrators of clothing-related violence and the clothing involved—that is, reports of norm violations. Popular items of clothing that became the target of thieves included jackets, jewelry, baseball caps, coats, and athletic shoes. Important attributes of these items (which were fashionable at the time) were brand names, sports team logos, leather, fur, gold, bright colors, and flashy styles. These attributes would qualify the items as status symbols.

A **claims maker** was defined as someone reporting a situation (reporting a norm violation) and demanding that something be done. Claims makers included "teenagers, parents of victims, survivors of personal larceny, elementary and secondary school officials, law enforcement personnel, politicians, university professors, psychiatrists, grassroots organizations . . . . and the American Civil Liberties Union" (p. 340). Reasons for the norm violation were explained in terms of the societal context of youth violence and illicit drugs, violence as a means to obtain material possessions, and emulation of gangs and gang symbols (expressed through colors, styles, brand-name merchandise, and modes of wearing clothes). The norm violation was associated with a particular ethnic and age group through use of stereotypic slang and images.

Pitts (1999) analyzed a sample of 35 human interest stories reporting on body modification and published between 1993 and 1998. Nearly all of the articles discussed the shocking, disturbing nature of nonmainstream, radical body modification. **Radical body modification** includes invasive, permanent, or non-normative forms such as scarification and branding. As discussed in the "From the Headlines" story at the beginning of this chapter, body modifiers create bodies that deviate from well-established bodily norms (Figure 10.3).

The most recurrent issue raised in the articles (17 of 35) was radical body modification as a sign of mental illness because it was labeled as self-mutilation. Reported testimony of medical and mental health experts lent authority to the claim of radical body modification as norm violation. In this case, the alleged situation was a norm violation by body modifiers.

The claim that radical body modification was a sign of mental illness gained credibility because of authorities, authoritative language, biased interests, and publicity (Pitts, 1999). The qualifications of the authorities included their scholarship (authors of books or articles), employment

FIGURE 10.3 RADICAL BODY MODIFICATION INCLUDES SUBDERMAL IMPLANTS. THE RESULTING LOOK IS VIEWED AS A DRESS NORM VIOLATION BY SOME PEOPLE AND THE PROCEDURE AS A HEALTH THREAT BY THE MEDICAL PROFESSION.

(experience treating body-related disorders), and/or education (psychologists, psychiatrists). The language used to describe body modifiers included such terms as self-mutilation, anger, counseling, anxiety, self-injury, and suffering. Body modification was associated with other norm violations, especially those associated with a lack of control (drug addiction, bulimia, and crime). Body modification was depicted as more of a problem for females than for males.

Pitts (1999) noted that "a subculture's mode or style of communicating, expressing problems or articulating knowledge can take forms outside established practices and institutions" (p. 293). The human interest stories operated as a medium to label radical body modification as a norm violation and to stigmatize body modifiers.

Magazines

"Societal factors have a powerful impact on the development and maintenance of body image through creation of an appearance culture that values, reinforces, and models cultural ideals of beauty and body shape" (Jones, Vigfusdottir, & Lee, 2004, p. 324). The popular press is a key element of an appearance culture. Text and images in the popular press influence appearance norms and affect perceptions of the self when individuals internalize cultural ideals for appearance.

Internalized appearance ideals are personal goals and standards against which the self and others are compared. Internalization of appearance ideals encourages individuals to interpret the text and images in the popular press as reports of ideal cultural norms and, implicitly then, reports of norm violations by the majority of readers who presumably do not measure up to the ideal norm. For example, girls who frequently read fashion magazines (compared to those who did not) were two to three times more likely to diet because of having read a magazine article and to report that the content of magazines influenced their ideas of ideal body shape (Field, Cheung, Wolf, Herzog, Gortmaker, & Colditz, 1999). Dieting was a response to violation of an ideal weight norm as reported in the magazines. Although the real norm for the U.S. population is not reflected in the images, the repetitive nature of images of thin females and muscular males make these idealized bodies appear to be the norm.

Research has found that magazines are an important source of information about social norms and cultural expectations for behavior (Hohlstein,

FIGURE 10.4 TEEN
MAGAZINES, WITH THEIR EMPHA-
SIS ON CONCERN WITH APPEAR-
ANCE, ARE INFLUENTIAL IN
SHAPING ADOLESCENT GIRLS'
IDEAS OF GENDER-APPROPRIATE
APPEARANCE AND BEHAVIOR.
SEVENTEEN MAGAZINE OFTEN
SERVES AS A SOCIALIZATION
AGENT FOR ADOLESCENT GIRLS.

Smith & Atlas, 1998). Ballentine and Ogle (2005) explored the content of *Seventeen*, a fashion and beauty magazine targeted to girls aged 12 to 24 (Figure 10.4). *Seventeen* has 14.45 million readers in the United States; one of every two female teens and one of every five women aged 18 to 24 read *Seventeen* (*Seventeen*, n.d.). As socialization agents, magazines play a key role in transmitting cultural body ideals. In particular, teen magazines, with their emphasis on concern with appearance, are influential in shaping adolescent girls' ideas of gender-appropriate appearance and behavior.

Two overarching themes were discovered in the content of *Seventeen*: (a) the making of body problems and (b) the unmaking of body problems (Ballentine & Ogle, 2005). The making of body problems is what this text refers to as reports of norm violations. Ballentine and Ogle found that the magazine presented a narrow view of ideal body characteristics—that is, the ideal body was described as "smooth, trim, toned, tight, long, lean, strong, young, sexy, healthy, clean, and free of odor and certain types of hair" (p. 290). Bodies that violated this ideal norm were labeled problems to be avoided and despised.

Mechanisms for dealing with the problems were controlling the body through fashion, cosmetics, diets, exercise, and surgery, as well as resisting the thin ideal. For example, some articles presented advice on how to dress to accentuate positive attributes and camouflage flaws. Ballantine and Ogle concluded that the content of *Seventeen* perpetuated the ideology of a **malleable body** (subject to transformation) and promoted the slim body as virtuous and disciplined. Marketing images in magazines can be viewed as reports of ideal norms for women, and by contrast, norm violations by the majority of females. They present an ideal standard of beauty, including thinness. In reality, over 64 percent of the U.S. population is overweight and about 30 percent are obese (American Obesity Association, 2002).

Parekh and Schmidt (2003) used an electronic questionnaire to investigate the influence of fashion marketing on eating disorders among young women. The questionnaires were completed by a sample of young women with eating disorders and by a control group of young women without eating disorders. According to Parekh and Schmidt, females' need to diet and lose weight is linked to media glamorization of thinness and a perceived link between being thin and being successful. Respondents with eating disorders reported the disorder had started when they went on a diet to lose a few pounds.

Respondents with eating disorders believed the most important thing in their lives was achieving thinness; they did not like to shop because the clothes they tried on made them look fat. Only 50 percent of respondents without an eating disorder had dieted in the last five years, but all respondents reported constant awareness of their body shape in everything they did.

When asked what made them think about their body shape, respondents listed worry about putting on weight, peer pressure, looking through women's magazines, watching television, low levels of confidence and self-esteem, men, and unhappiness with their current body shape (Parekh & Schmidt, 2003). When asked to name potential benefits of achieving their ideal body shape, respondents listed confidence, happiness, higher self-esteem, less paranoia about boyfriend looking at other girls, not comparing self to other women, being more attractive to men, wearing nicer clothes, feeling more comfortable in clothes, and feeling healthier.

Respondents listed what Parekh and Schmidt (2003) termed the four P's as motivations for clothes shopping: peer group pressures, physical pressures, product influences, and promotional influences. **Peer group pressures** referred to such things as copying friends and being influenced by observing what other girls were wearing. Physical pressures related to buying what flattered their shape and buying clothes that felt comfortable in relation to the size of their body. Product influences included the latest trends, garment quality, and price. Promotional influences listed were what fashion models wear and window displays. "All but one respondent regarded their body shape as one of the most important things in their life and as a key determinant of acceptance in society" (p. 235). In other words, they believed social acceptance depended on how thin they were (Figure 10.5). The authors concluded that respondents' (both those with and those without eating disorders) self-image and dieting habits were influenced by fashion marketing images—images

FIGURE 10.5 SOME PEOPLE WILL GO TO GREAT LENGTHS TO ACHIEVE THEIR "IDEAL" FIGURE.

that show narrowly restricted body shapes and sizes—and by implication designate other shapes and sizes as violations of the norm.

Byrd-Bredbenner and Murray (2003) compared the measurements of idealized female body images in *Playboy* magazine, Miss America Pageant winners, and fashion models with young women in general from the decade of the 1920s to the 1990s. Height and weight data for 631 fashion models were collected primarily from catalogs provided by modeling agencies. In all decades, fashion models had the highest mean height, while young women in general had the lowest mean height. In each decade from the 1960s onward, young women in general were heavier than all other groups.

Mean body mass index (BMI) for young women in general was higher than for all groups in every decade except the 1920s. Across the decades, all groups experienced a decrease in mean BMI except young women in general, which experienced an increase. The mean BMI of fashion models decreased because their height increased while their weight stayed the same. The authors concluded that the idealized women tended to be several inches taller and many pounds lighter than young women in general, with many of the idealized women meeting the criteria for underweight (Figure 10.6). The authors expressed concern about how the contrast between idealized female body sizes reported in the media and those of young women in general affects expectations women have for themselves.

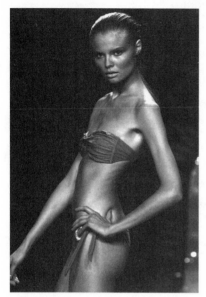

FIGURE 10.6 THE CONTRAST BETWEEN IDEALIZED FEMALE BODY SIZES AND THOSE OF YOUNG WOMEN CAN TAKE A TOLL ON WOMEN'S SELF ESTEEM.

FIGURE 10.7 DRESS NORM VIOLATIONS CAN BE A REASON FOR FIRING AN EMPLOYEE. IN THIS HUMAN INTEREST STORY, HAVING AN UNKNOTTED TIE WAS STATED AS A REASON FOR TERMINATION.

Unknotted tie cost career
New Windsor, NY (AP) – A former fire marshal says his unknotted tie unraveled his career.
John O'Brien Sr. said he was fired from the New York City Fire Bureau after he walked into a meeting with his tie undone.
O'Brien said May 1997 meeting was informal, and added that he was on his way to investigate a fire scene at the time.
"I was busy running around," O'Brien said this week. "I had my tie on, but it wasn't tied. No one brought this up at the meeting."
He was fired on Dec. 19. The union is appealing under the state Civil Practice Law. The department declined to comment on his firing.

Law Review Articles

Formal reports of norm violations may be stated when employees are dismissed and may later be reported in the text of lawsuits resulting from dismissal or in law review articles. Some of these formal reports are noted in the article by Kamer and Keller (2003) reviewing employee appearance issues in the gaming industry.

Hiring and Firing Decisions

Personnel decisions such as hiring and retention may be based on employees' personal appearance, dress, and grooming (Kamer & Keller, 2003) (Figure 10.7). "As a general rule, employers can lawfully issue and enforce personal appearance standards that regulate employees' dress, grooming habits, and hygiene while at work" (p. 335). Appearance policies can be gender-specific if they are based on social norms, enforced equally for both genders, and cause no undue burden for one sex. For example, an employee was reported for a norm violation of an appearance policy that required employees to cover their tattoos. The employee was terminated for refusing to cover a controversial tattoo. Other reports of norm violations gleaned from the text of court cases included policies prohibiting dreadlocks or cornrow hairstyles.

Appearance Policies

Reports of norm violations become obvious when perusing reports of policies requiring certain *looks:* Hooter girl waitresses, geisha girl cocktail server costumes, or a Bicentennial outfit (Kamer & Keller, 2003). Individuals who are reported for violating the norm of gender-role stereotypic appearances may be denied promotions. For example, a woman was denied a partnership in an accounting firm because she was reported as being too *macho*. The woman was told that her chances of being selected as a partner would improve if she would walk, talk, and dress more femininely, wear makeup, style her hair, and wear jewelry. Another woman was reported for violating the appearance norm for cocktail waitresses by refusing to wear sexually suggestive clothing; subsequently, she was terminated from her position. Kamer and Keller recommended that employers should carefully investigate an employee's objection to an appearance policy rather than immediately terminate the employee after a report of violation of a dress policy.

Bartlett (1994) gave abundant examples of judges rationalizing employer dress and appearance requirements based on community norms. Judges tend to uphold dress and appearance standards considered to have an inconsequential impact on employees, or that affect men and women in a similar manner, or that are necessary to an employer's lawful business purposes. Litigation results when an employer's report of a norm violation is challenged by an employee.

Dress requirements for women are often different from those for men. Women may be required to wear skirts of a certain length or be prohibited from wearing pantsuits. Women may be required to wear high-heeled shoes, to conform to different weight criteria than men, or to wear makeup. For example, a ticket agent was reported for violating company norms by failing to wear foundation and lipstick and subsequently was fired. Women may be fired if they are reported for violating the feminine norm of a hairless face. An audiovisual technician was fired from her hotel job because of unladylike facial hair. Women may be reported for wearing their hair in a way that may offend customers—for example, a company policy prohibited employees from wearing all-braided hairstyles.

Women may be required to wear sexually provocative clothing. For example, a waitress was transferred from the cocktail lounge to a less lucrative coffee shop assignment because her refusal to wear sexually suggestive clothing was reported to management. Conversely, women may be required to minimize their sexuality and reported for violating the norm when they do not. For example, a female employee was terminated after she was reported numerous times for wearing her hair down and wearing excessive makeup in violation of a dress code.

Men are also subjected to dress and appearance rules and reported when they violate the rules. For example, men may be required to wear ties, keep their hair short, or be prohibited from wearing women's jewelry (Bartlett, 1994). One company's policy stated that male employees were prohibited from wearing facial jewelry, including earrings. A transsexual was reported for violating a company norm by wearing excessively feminine attire, including a strand of pink pearls. He was terminated as a result of refusing to comply with the rules.

"The law shapes, and is shaped by, community norms" (Bartlett, 1994, p. 2546). Dress and appearance norms are widespread even in the absence of mandatory workplace dress and appearance codes. These norms are sometimes attributed to prevalent media images and to cultural assumptions and values. Acquired in the process of growing up within a particular culture, the norms are deeply entrenched. The norms become the basis for employers and employees to determine what is normal and acceptable. Violations of the norms are readily recognized and reported, sometimes in a formal written report that results in sanctions for the deviant employee.

ANALYZING ORAL REPORTS OF NORM VIOLATIONS

Both appearance conversations among peers and gossip function to highlight appearance-related issues, reaffirm the importance of appearance, and encourage formation of particular appearance ideals. During adolescence, peer criticism about appearance is inevitable (Eder, Evans, & Parker, 1995). Research has established a link between critical comments about appearance and negative body image for females from the elementary through college years (Thompson, Coovert, & Stormer, 1999). Critical comments about appearance are, in essence, reports of norm violations because they call attention to an appearance norm, the violation of which is presumably the basis of the criticism (Figure 10.8).

FIGURE 10.8 DURING ADOLESCENCE, PEER CRITICISM ABOUT APPEARANCE IS INEVITABLE.

Conversations Among Peers

Jones, Vigfusdottir, and Lee (2004) administered a questionnaire to 433 girls and 347 boys in grades 7 through 10 to investigate relationships among appearance magazine exposure, appearance conversations with friends, peer appearance criticism, body mass index (BMI), internalization of appearance ideals, and body image dissatisfaction. Students listed their favorite magazines, how frequently they read them, and how often they try to do the things suggested in the magazines. Students responded to items about appearance conversations with friends and peer appearance criticism.

Compared with males, females read more appearance magazines, reported more appearance conversations, endorsed greater internalization of appearance ideals, and were more dissatisfied with their bodies (Jones, Vigfusdottir, & Lee, 2004). For males, body dissatisfaction was not related to magazine exposure, but was related to appearance conversations with friends, peer appearance criticism, and BMI. Peer appearance criticism had the strongest relationship with body dissatisfaction for males.

Peer experiences, both positive/neutral (appearance conversations with friends) and negative (peer appearance criticism), were related to appearance internalization and body image satisfaction for both males and females. Students who more frequently engaged in conversations about appearance with friends were more likely to indicate greater internalization that, in turn, was related to greater feelings of body dissatisfaction (more so for females than for males). Heavier body weights and shapes are norm violations for both adolescent males and females, but deviation from the ideal, especially for females, serves to enhance the appeal of the ideal appearance. Among females, BMI was linked to body dissatisfaction and internalization.

There were gender differences in exposure to appearance magazines. Females had greater exposure because there are more magazines targeted to young females. For females, appearance magazines were linked to appearance conversations with friends. Magazines supplied topics for conversation that were personalized with friends. The interpersonal context of appearance conversations with friends was linked to internalization and body image satisfaction (Jones, Vigfusdottir, & Lee, 2004).

Wooten (2006) looked at the role of negative peer communication, specifically ridicule, as a means of reporting norm violations. **Ridicule** was defined as the "act of making fun of some aspect of another" (p. 188). Adolescents who violate norms are subject to ridicule by their peers. Ridicule serves a purpose in the process of social control by drawing attention to norm violations not only for the violator, but also for witnesses. Wooten analyzed interviews of 43 young adults aged 18 to 23 about adolescent experiences as targets, observers, and perpetrators of ridicule about clothing.

Wooten's (2006) analysis showed that young adults remembered adolescents using mean-spirited remarks to belittle and ostracize those who did not fit into the group. Ridicule was used as a means to report norm violations as well as to convey and reinforce group norms. For example, someone who was a knowledgeable source used ridicule to teach someone else how various brands, styles, and shopping outlets were perceived by the in crowd. Ridicule was used as a means to discourage norm violations by accusing others of acting like members of an avoidance group (nerds, punks). One interviewee remembered being ridiculed about some shoes (fake Jordans, plastic shoes) that his mother bought for him at Kmart. Another interviewee remembered the ridicule he endured about buying and wearing a pair of Hakeem Olajuwon sneakers from Payless when others were wearing Nike Air Jordans.

Gossip

Westen (1996) commented that gossip is a national growth industry: there are over 40 newspaper columns, dozens of magazines, 50 television talk shows, three major tabloids, electronic mail (E-mail), chat rooms, and word of mouth. Gossip serves an important social function by communicating a group's moral code. It is a way to let people know the limits on personal behavior without directly confronting them (Figure 10.9). Gossip is a way to report when people have crossed the boundary of appropriate behavior by violating a norm.

Foster (2004) reviewed gossip research, including definitions of gossip, functions of gossip, and methods by which data are collected. Gossip is a cultural universal; most societies have explicit sanctions against gossip. Ethical condemnation of gossip involves its violation of rules of privacy, as well as the misinformation gossip can convey. "An inclination to gossip covertly, anonymously, or vicariously betrays an awareness of the violation of privacy norms" (p. 79). Foster commented that "we all know what gossip is, but defining, identifying, and measuring it is a complex enterprise for practical investigation" (p. 80). Some common terms used to denote gossip are *idle talk, chitchat, girl talk, shop talk, shooting the breeze, chewing the fat,* and *socializing.* There are four social functions of gossip: information, entertainment, friendship, and influence.

Research methods used to study gossip included qualitative data collection methods as well as quantitative data collection methods. **Qualitative data collection methods** included participant observation, audiotaping and videotaping conversations followed by coding the frequency and **valence** (negative/positive) of gossiping behavior, and **eavesdropping** (listening to private conversations) in public places. **Quantitative data collection methods** included questionnaire studies and experimental research designs.

Kuttler, Parker, and La Greca (2002) interviewed 193 boys and 191 girls in third, fourth, fifth, and sixth grades. The researchers presented children with vignettes of two children having a conversation about an absent third child. The conversation involved failing a test, skipping school, not inviting someone to a birthday party, or someone being poor at sports. The majority of both boys and girls correctly labeled as gossip conversations about others who were not present and expressed disapproval of the gossiper's behavior. The authors concluded that the children were aware of cultural norms against gossip.

Children displayed skepticism regarding the reliability of information obtained from listening to gossip, although the skepticism seemed to decline slightly with age. If the vignette suggested that the gossiper might have been

FIGURE 10.9 TWO WOMEN GOSSIPING WITH EACH OTHER.

misinformed, children rated the gossiper's intent as misunderstanding rather than malicious. However, there was a tendency for children to assume that gossipers who conveyed false information did so intentionally and inferred jealous or self-serving motives.

Baumeister, Zhang, and Vohs (2004) studied 58 students in undergraduate psychology classes to gain insight into whether gossip might serve a valuable function for cultural learning. Students filled out two questionnaires: The first asked the participant to report the most interesting piece of gossip he or she had heard; the second asked various questions about the gossip reported (why, who, how many, did you tell others about it, what did you learn from it, etc.). Most of the gossip (85 percent) concerned people known to a participant; 15 percent concerned strangers, celebrities, and family members. About half of the gossip was passed on to others; on average, participants told two others, and 28 percent told more than three people.

About half of the participants reported negative emotions associated with the gossip, while only 15 percent reported strictly positive emotions. The worse people felt about hearing the gossip, the more they indicated they learned from it. Over half (64 percent) indicated that they had learned something from the gossip that was useful to them in their own lives. The information learned was usually expressed as general guidelines about how to function effectively in society. Because negative emotions stimulate retrospective analysis, the results supported a link between experiencing a negative emotion and learning a lesson. The authors concluded that the cultural learning function of gossip deserves a prominent place in the theory of gossip. Gossip can be viewed as an extension of observational learning; individuals can learn about social and cultural life by hearing reports about the conformity and deviance of others.

Taylor (2005) conducted two studies in order to validate Foster's (2004) Gossip Functions Questionnaire. The 24-item Gossip Functions Questionnaire purports to measure four reasons why people gossip: information, entertainment, friendship, and influence. Taylor discovered three types of gossip: trivial gossip, influential gossip, and behavioral guidance gossip. Taylor hypothesized that scores on the Gossip Functions Questionnaire would be related to scores on measures of indirect interpersonal aggression, Machiavellianism, and tendency to gossip. **Indirect interpersonal aggression** was defined as "a predisposition to harm other people without engaging in face-to-face interaction" and was measured by a 10-item scale (Beatty, Valencic, Rudd, & Dobos,

1999, p. 105). **Machiavellianism** refers to the degree to which a person manipulates and deceives others in order to get the response he or she wants (Christie & Geis, 1970) and was measured by a 10-item scale (Allsopp, Eysenck, & Eysenck, 1991). The Tendency to Gossip Questionnaire is a 20-item measure that has been found to be negatively related to liking, trust, and expertise of the source of the gossip. Previous research found that individuals who are feminine have a higher tendency to gossip than individuals who are more masculine (Kuttler et al., 2002; Nevo, Nevo, & Derech-Zehavi, 1994; Nevo & Nevo, 1993).

Individuals who scored high in indirect interpersonal aggression scored higher on the Gossip Functions questionnaire, indicating that they may use gossip as a means of indirectly attacking another person (Taylor, 2005). Individuals who scored high on Machiavellianism also scored high on the Gossip Functions questionnaire, indicating they may use gossip as a way of manipulating others to do what they want. Individuals who scored high on the Tendency to Gossip Questionnaire also scored high on the Gossip Functions questionnaire, indicating that those who have a tendency to gossip likely use the functions of gossip when interacting with others. Taylor speculated that individuals who are high in self-monitoring may have the ability to use gossip appropriately and positively.

SUMMARY

This chapter presented research that looked at mechanisms for reporting norm violations. Research included print sources of reports such as letters to advice columnists, cartoons and comic strips, human interest stories, magazines, and law review articles discussing dress and appearance codes in the workplace. Conversations and gossip were presented as oral methods by which norm violations are reported.

case studies	malleable body
case problems	peer group pressures
claim	qualitative data collection methods
claims maker	quantitative data collection methods
eavesdropping	radical body modification
indirect interpersonal aggression	ridicule
Machiavellianism	valence

SUGGESTED READINGS

1. Ballentine, L. W., & Ogle, J. P. (2005). The making and unmaking of body problems in *Seventeen* magazine, 1992–2003. *Family and Consumer Sciences Research Journal, 33*(4), 281–307.

2. Bartlett, K. T. (1994). Only girls wear barrettes: Dress and appearance standards, community norms, and workplace equality. *Michigan Law Review, 92*(8), 2541–2582.

3. Byrd-Bredbenner, C., & Murray, J. (2003). A comparison of the anthropometric measurements of idealized female body images in media directed to men, women, and mixed gender audiences. *Topics in Clinical Nutrition, 18*(2), 117–129.

Research Activity 10.1 *Literature Analysis*

Purpose: To analyze research literature related to *reports* of appearance norm violations, identifying the purpose, research method, and results.

Procedure:

1. Describe the characteristics of a research article.

2. Use the Google Scholar (http://scholar.google.com/) search engine or an academic database (EBSCO, ERIC, SocIndex) to locate one research article related to reports of appearance norm violations. For example, you might use the key words *reports of dress norm violations* or *reports of appearance standard violations* to search for research articles.

3. Print a copy of the research article.

4. Highlight and label the purpose of the study, the research method used, the results of the study related to its purpose, and report of appearance norm violation(s) studied.

5. Submit your work to your instructor.

Research Activity 10.2 *Making and Unmaking Body Problems*

Purpose: To analyze teen magazines for content that *makes* and *unmakes* body problems.

Procedure:

1. Review Ballentine and Ogle's (2005) analysis of how magazines make and unmake body problems.

2. Locate an online teen magazine. One example is the online version of *Teen* magazine (http://www.teenmag.com/).

3. Locate and print two articles that would support Ballentine and Ogle's analysis.

4. Compare and contrast the sections of each article that *make* body problems and that *unmake* body problems.

5. Submit your work to your instructor.

Chapter Eleven

RESPONSE TO NORM VIOLATION: SANCTIONS

FROM THE HEADLINES
A student wore a Marilyn Manson T-shirt at the Tater Days Festival in Benton, Kentucky. The T-shirt had a picture of the controversial singer printed on it along with a six-word phrase from his song "White Trash." The phrase contains an obscenity and the word *God*. Tater Day is a family-oriented festival and many of those in attendance are children with and without the presence of their parents. Three mothers with children complained to a police officer about the offensive language on the shirt. After refusing to change the shirt, the student was cited for harassment. In upholding the conviction, the judge wrote "However, by wearing a T-shirt displaying one particular phrase from a song, [the student] is essentially repeating the same lyric over and over. This, in the court's opinion, is what creates a separately identifiable conduct which separates it from constitutionally protected free speech" (p. 13). The student was fined $250.00 plus court costs.

Source: Conviction upheld in Manson T-shirt case. (1999, April 8).
Daily Egyptian, p. 13.

This story reports on the sanctions that resulted from a norm violation—complaints, a request to change, a citation for harassment, an appearance in court, and a fine. The process of social control is evident in this situation—the dress norm concerns decency and regard for others, especially women and children. The student violated the norm by wearing a T-shirt with an obscene slogan to a family-oriented event. Mothers with children noticed the violation and reported the violation to an authority—a police officer. The police officer levied a sanction—a citation for harassment, and a judge enforced the sanction by fining the student.

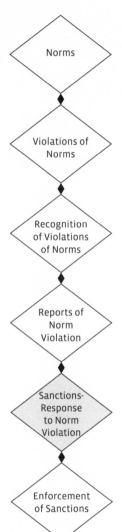

What sanctions were extended to the student as a result of the norm violation? Was the student in the introductory scenario male or female? Why do you think so? How effective were the sanctions?

The fifth step in the process of social control entails a response (a reaction) to a norm violation (Figure 11.1). The response often takes the form of sanctions, which are rewards or punishments that affect conformity to norms (Kendall, 2007). In this chapter, we will examine the seven aspects of sanctions and their variations: retribution, source, formality, obtrusiveness, magnitude, severity, and pervasiveness.

QUESTIONS TO ANSWER AS YOU READ

1. What are some specific sanctions against dress norm violations?
2. What are the aspects and variations of sanctions against dress norm violations?
3. How are the aspects and variations of sanctions against dress norm violations interrelated?

ASPECTS AND VARIATIONS OF SANCTIONS

Because the purpose of sanctions is to ensure conformity, sanctions operate to reward conformity and punish norm violations (Figure 11.2). The sanctioned person and observers of sanctions learn to avoid sanctions by conforming to the violated norm. In the "From the Headlines" article, the student who wore a T-shirt with an obscene phrase was reported to a police officer who cited the student for harassment ("Conviction Upheld," 1999). As a result, the student was fined $250 plus court costs. Presumably, the arrest and fine motivated the student to avoid violating the norm again.

Every sanction has seven aspects; each aspect has variations (Table 11.1). Each sanction varies in the aspects of retribution, source, formality, obtrusiveness, magnitude, severity, and pervasiveness. All of the aspects are interrelated (Blake & Davis, 1964; Gibbs, 1981; Hunt & Colander, 2005; Kendall, 2007; Schwartz & Ewald, 1968; Smelser, 1973; Workman & Freeburg, 2000a).

RETRIBUTION

Retribution refers to the distribution of rewards for correct behavior and punishment for transgressions, or incorrect behavior. Rewards are sanctions at the positive end of a continuum of retribution—for example, being rewarded with a letter jacket for outstanding athletic performance. Letter jackets are symbols of accomplishment, discipline, and commitment (Hill, 2006). A student wears a letter jacket because it is a badge of honor—it shows what he or she has accomplished (Gorrell, 2006).

FIGURE 11.2 THE PURPOSE OF SANCTIONS IS TO ENSURE CONFORMITY. THE PERSON WEARING THE COWBOY BOOTS IS BEING SANCTIONED BY RIDICULE FOR NOT CONFORMING TO THE NORM.

In the annual Best Dressed Police Department competition, the Bluffton, Indiana, Police Department was named the Best Dressed Law Enforcement Department ("Bluffton Police Ranked," 2004). The National Association of Uniform Manufacturers and Distributors (NAUMD) sponsors the award, which is designed to recognize departments' uniforms as judged on overall appearance, neatness, projection of authority, practicality, and adherence to uniform regulations.

Graduation is a ceremony in which rewards (diplomas) are distributed for correct behavior (fulfilling the requirements for a degree). Graduation gowns have a long history of academic symbolism (O'Neill, 2006). For example, the mortarboard (rectangular hat) was introduced in the 1200s to symbolize a campus quadrangle. The hood (fabric draped down the back of a graduation

TABLE 11.1 ASPECTS OF SANCTIONS AND THEIR VARIATIONS

ASPECTS	VARIATIONS	CONTINUUM OR CATEGORIES
Retribution	Positive.........Negative	Continuum
Source	Internal/External	Categories
Formality	Formal.........Informal	Continuum
Obtrusiveness	Obtrusive.........Unobtrusive	Continuum
Magnitude	Extreme.........Moderate	Continuum
Severity	Severe.........Mild	Continuum
Pervasiveness	Extensive.........Restricted	Continuum

robe) is usually lined in silk; the color of the lining is a symbol of the school from which the wearer earned a degree. The color of the outside trim represents the student's field of study. The level of the degree (bachelor's, master's, or doctorate) is indicated by the presence of a hood, the width of the trim on the hood, and length of the hood.

Punishment

Punishment is a sanction near the negative end of a continuum of retribution—for example, suspension from school for protesting a school dress code. Twenty-four students were suspended from school for three days when they staged a protest on the street in front of their school (Neufeld, 2005). Two 13-year-old brothers were not allowed to display Confederate flag symbols in their school (Stewart, 2006). Other students threatened the boys after hearing of the boys' protests involving Confederate flag symbols. The parents were informed they were prohibited from being on school grounds except to pick up or drop off the boys. The parents then withdrew their sons from school and home-schooled them; they also planned to file a lawsuit on behalf of their sons.

Recall from Chapter 10 that ridicule is the act of making fun of some aspect of another individual's behavior or appearance. Ridicule is a negative sanction that is "ubiquitous in modern North American culture, appearing in movies, advertisements, and television shows, often aimed at teenagers, who learn that it is *uncool* to wear certain clothes or display certain behaviors" (Janes & Olson, 2000, p. 474). Ridicule can affect adolescents' consumer behavior and brand consciousness ("Teen Ridicule Shapes," 2006). Ridicule is one means of communicating the consumption norms and values of peer groups. Observing or experiencing ridicule influences adolescents' purchase, use, and discard of possessions. Adolescents learn from ridicule what brands, styles, and stores to avoid if they want their peers to accept them.

Another type of negative sanction is use of nicknames. A **nickname** is a made-up name for somebody that is usually based on a conspicuous characteristic of the person involved. Unkind nicknames are names given to a person in contempt or derision. A 13-year-old girl wrote to an advice columnist about a special nickname given to her by her aunt (Van Buren, 2006b). Her aunt thought it was cute and funny to call her "Chubster," but the girl was self-conscious about her weight, and her feelings were hurt by the name.

Name-calling is verbal abuse that takes the form of calling someone abusive, disgraceful, or shameful names. Negative sanctions in the form of name-calling are common in the school environment. A student dropped out of high school because he was humiliated by students' teasing about his physical problems, which included a limp and a hunched back (Ellis, 2006). He wore a body cast from neck to legs because of surgery for scoliosis, which led some students to call him Frankenstein due to the stiff way he walked with his arms slightly extended. The Duchess of York, Sarah Ferguson, has been called the Princess of Pork because of her weight (Summerfield, 2006).

Another negative sanction common in the school environment is **teasing,** which is making fun of somebody, either playfully or maliciously. Teasing usually begins around the age of four or five, when children become aware of their differences (Brazelton, 2006). Children use binary categories to make sense of these differences: big/small, weak/strong, pretty/ugly, better/worse. Teasing is a way of expressing awareness of these differences and an effort to understand what they mean. Children learn from the judgments that adults make about differences that pretty is better than ugly, or that strong is better than weak.

One of the first differences children recognize is gender. Parents wrote to a parenting expert about their four-year-old boy, who liked to pretend he was a girl (Byron, 2006). The parents were concerned about how to protect him from teasing by his peers. The expert stated that children may see gender as an interchangeable state that can be reflected in their dress and that childhood is the only time when a child can express himself or herself without the restrictions of social convention, judgment, and censure.

Very near to the negative end of the retribution continuum is termination from a job. One manager wrote to a syndicated columnist concerning an employee who printed a make-your-own T-shirt with his negative opinion of the manager on the back and the phrase *free speech* on the front (Curry, 2006). The manager wanted to know if he could fire the employee for wearing the shirt to work. The columnist suggested that if the T-shirt disrupted the work of others and if that disruptive activity could be documented with concrete evidence, then it was possible that the manager could terminate him.

Punishment arouses complex emotions in people, not all of which are unsympathetic to the sanctioned individual or the deviant behavior. For example, a woman was fired from her job as a hospital receptionist because she refused to remove her lip ring, a 14-gauge hoop (Carleo-Evangelist, 2006). She was given three options: remove the hoop, replace the hoop with something transparent, or transfer to another job in the company. Her dilemma was published in the newspaper, providing her a certain notoriety. Many other body piercers were sympathetic to her plight and to her belief in body piercing. The woman claimed to be a member of the Church of Body Modification and contended that piercing was a spiritual act because of the control it gave her over her body.

Nonreward

Nonreward falls about midway on a continuum of retribution. Nonreward is punitive, but it is a milder sanction than punishment because it does not deprive individuals of something they already have (for example, loss of freedom because of a jail sentence) but rather of something they would have liked to have had (such as being hired for a job) (Figure 11.3). An acute sense

FIGURE 11.3 THE OLDER SISTER IN THE CARTOON WAS EXPECTING AN APPROVING RESPONSE, WHICH SHE DID NOT GET.

of deprivation may be experienced by one who is not rewarded. For example, a business intern who dressed in "a metallic crop-top cami, a floaty sheer chiffon tiered skirt, strappy stiletto sandals, lots and lots of bangle bracelets, and enough stringed beads to be the envy of any fortune teller" may be surprised and disappointed when she is not offered a job at the firm where she interned ("Clothing Etiquette," 2006, ¶ 1).

Because of its apparent mildness, and because it involves inaction rather than action, the role of nonreward as a control mechanism in the regulation of dress may be overlooked. Nonreward has certain advantages over punishment; it does not glamorize the sanctioned person and does not advertise the particular behavior that led to the sanction. For example, offensive T-shirts are banned in most schools. When offensive T-shirts are confiscated or turned inside out, students are deprived of the attention that might come from wearing the T-shirt (Shapira, 2006). Indeed, one student remarked, "I think most girls and boys get the T-shirts because they're funny and they draw attention to you" (¶ 8). Some school officials require students to exchange the offensive shirt for a school T-shirt.

Source

The **source** of a sanction refers to its origin, that is, whether it comes from an internal or external source.

Internal Sanctions

Internal sanctions occur when individuals rely on an inner sense of what is right and wrong to govern their actions. During socialization, some norms are internalized; that is, the norms become part of an individual's motivational system. When an individual is committed to the norms as being legitimate (he or she has internalized the norms), he or she conforms because of internal sanctions—feelings of guilt or discomfort when a norm is violated. For example, internalizing the value of purity can motivate young women to wear modest clothing, and thus external sanctions and reactions from others are not necessary (Flynn, 2006). Modest dress for Christian women can include such actions as wearing shirts that do not reveal the midriff, but this dress choice does not make the same visual statement as a Muslim *hijab* (head covering) worn with loose-fitting clothes that cover the arms and legs.

Internal sanctions can vary along the continuum of retribution from reward to punishment. Negative internal sanctions include depression, dissatisfaction with appearance, embarrassment, guilt, humiliation, sadness, shame, and fear of gossip. For example, a married father wrote to an advice columnist about his fetish for cross-dressing (Tesher, 2006). He wrote that he felt guilty and wished that his secret life did not exist. One woman related that she hated herself for being fat (Anderson, 2006a). She had painful memories of split jeans, tight shoes, constricting rings on her fingers, fatigue, and the struggle to pull on pants. She commented that she did not want to go anywhere or see anyone; she felt like crawling into a hole and covering herself up. "Almost everyone who has carried extra pounds knows the feelings of shame and guilt that accompany extra body fat in a culture obsessively focused on being slim" (Anderson, 2006a, ¶ 9).

Positive internal sanctions include contentment, psychological comfort, pride, self-acceptance, self-esteem, self-respect, and self-satisfaction. For example, one woman commented that her beauty pageant experience helped build her self-esteem (Simmons, 2006). Indeed, some parents believe child beauty pageants help children develop poise, confidence, social skills, and good grooming (Casstevens, 2006). Likewise, a survey of women's shoe shopping habits revealed that 58 percent felt that wearing a special pair of shoes actually boosted their self-esteem ("Mervyns' Study Reveals," 2006).

External Sanctions

External sanctions occur when members of society attempt to enforce norms for others. External sanctions can be negative or positive. Relatively mild negative external sanctions include an amused look, criticism, disapproval, frowns, gossip, insults, jokes, laughter, sarcasm, teasing, and rejection (Figure 11.4). "Since fatness is seen as a lifestyle choice rather than a genetic condition, many people tell themselves that it is OK to laugh at the overweight" (D'Souza, 2006, ¶ 8). Strangers even yell insults at fat people; for example, a woman asked a fat person, "Are you going to get something to eat?"

FIGURE 11.4 EXTERNAL SANCTIONS ARE ATTEMPTS TO ENFORCE NORMS FOR OTHERS.

More severe negative external sanctions include arrest, avoidance, coercion, divorce, fines, harassment, ostracism, ridicule, and threats. One example of a negative external sanction was a proposed law to make it a criminal offense to wear baggy pants that exposed underwear ("Dallas Council Examines," 2006). "I think it's disrespectful, it's dishonorable, and it's disgusting . . . when grown men walk about the city with pants below their buttocks" remarked a city resident (p. 2A). In Virginia, the Senate decided not to consider a bill that proposed to fine individuals who wore pants so low their underwear was exposed. The student described in "From the Headlines" who wore the T-shirt with the offensive slogan was subjected to external sanctions in the form of complaints, citation for harassment, and fines.

Desirable violations (like those associated with being an innovative fashion designer) may be controlled by positive external sanctions such as compliments, respect, and social acceptance. For example, fashion designers may be the recipients of compliments, respect, and acceptance for a new collection ("Young Charm," 2006). The designer Sonia Rykiel received a positive review of a recent spring collection with such compliments as "infectiously fun" and "Oh, the finale: It was pure Rykiel tongue-in-cheek chic."

More intense positive external sanctions include praise, admiration, and awards (being named to a best-dressed list, winning a beauty contest). Publicity given such awards conveys acceptable standards to the general public. Vanity Fair's Annual Best-Dressed List merits worldwide attention with positive external sanctions (Collins, 2006). In one recent list, Kate Moss received the highest number of votes in the women's category, followed by Her Majesty Queen Rania of Jordan. George Clooney was named the best-dressed man because he "is that rare Hollywood hunk who understands that real men wear real black-tie" (¶ 4). U.S. Secretary of State Condoleezza Rice was named to the best-dressed list for her "immaculately groomed and formidably dignified" but audacious fashion sense—"not to mention her black knee-high dominatrix boots" ("Rice's 'Renegade' Fashion Sense," 2006, ¶ 5).

FORMALITY

Formality refers to the condition of being formal, that is, the degree to which behavior is governed by rules or established methods. Behavior regarding dress is sometimes controlled by formal sanctions.

Formal Sanctions

A formal sanction is one that is verbally authenticated, either through written or oral means. Formal sanctions can be anywhere on the positive-negative continuum of retribution—rewards, nonrewards, or punishments. For example, positive formal sanctions include awards, honors, and citations. The Miss America pageant awards thousands of dollars in scholarship money, clothes, jewelry, cosmetics, the use of an automobile, and fitness center privileges (Simmons, 2006). For at least a year, Miss America rides on floats in parades and presides over honorary events across the country. The visibility can result in lucrative job offers for some pageant winners.

Negative formal sanctions include trials, jail sentences, and termination of employment. For example, a teacher's aide was warned that if she continued to wear a visible religious symbol she would be suspended (Zirkel, 2004). The school's employee handbook specified that employees should not display any religious emblems, dress, or insignia including jewelry. A one-year suspension was the negative formal sanction for the first violation and a permanent suspension for the second violation. When the employee wore a cross in a visible manner, her supervisor requested that she remove or conceal the cross. Subsequently, the employee was suspended because she refused to remove or conceal the cross.

Formal sanctions typically involve not only changes in the attitudes and responses of others toward the sanctioned individual, but some concrete and drastic change in life chances as well. A person may be expelled from school, fired from a job, or ostracized from a group. For example, one member of a divided school board distributed T-shirts that were regarded as offensive to victims of a hazing incident (Carlson, 2006). Adults who wore the offensive T-shirts to a school event were asked to change shirts or to turn the T-shirt inside out; if they failed to comply and refused to leave, they were subject to arrest. The school board discussed whether to remove the official from office or to censure him publicly.

Informal Sanctions

Informal sanctions are seemingly trivial or unimportant, but enable people to informally control some of their own as well as others' behavior regarding dress. Informal sanctions include raised eyebrows, jokes, a disapproving glance, or laughter (Figure 11.5). The unobtrusive operation of informal sanctions fulfills an important function—regulating dress in a relatively painless manner while reducing the need for formal measures. A player entered

FIGURE 11.5 THE VALUE PLACED ON COMPLYING WITH INFORMAL SANCTIONS IS IMPLICIT HERE.

the Astrodome clubhouse (home to the Houston, Texas, major league base-ball team) wearing a neon-blue suit with neon-blue alligator shoes. Another player remarked, just loud enough for the first player to hear, "Thousands of alligators in Florida and Derek finds the blue one" (Lopez, 2006, ¶ 1). The message, conveyed in the form of a joke, was subtle and humorous.

Sensitivity to public opinion may be interpreted not simply as a desire for social approval, but as sensitivity to signs of possible sanctions. Depending on such factors as sociocultural background, personality, and intelligence, people understand to varying degrees that informal sanctions such as a reprimand or criticism are hints of possibly more formal sanctions to follow (Blake & Davis, 1964). For example, one manager wrote that he had an ongoing con-cern with an employee's body odor causing unpleasant working conditions for his colleagues (*Body Odour Problem*, 2006). The man had been approached informally five times about the problem and had received two verbal warn-ings, but there had been no improvement. With disciplinary action outstand-ing against him, it was clear he was not interested in changing and would not cooperate—leading to possible formal disciplinary action for his general at-titude and behavior. If proper procedures were followed, they would result in the employee's termination.

Likewise, most schools have a progressive discipline plan to address dress code violations (Franklin, 2006), but many students do not seem to under-stand the increasing formality of the sanctions associated with violations. The discipline plan usually begins with an informal sanction—a simple request to replace the offending item or turn it inside out; a second offense might result in another informal sanction—a verbal reprimand. As the violations continue, sanctions become progressively more formal, including parent contact, loss of privileges, demerits, after-school detention, in-school suspension, out-of-school suspension, and expulsion—usually the last intervention for persistent student violations of the dress code (Workman, Freeburg, & Lentz-Hees, 2004).

OBTRUSIVENESS

Obtrusiveness refers to the degree to which a sanction is obvious. An obtru-sive sanction is conspicuous, blatant, or explicit. The annual release of Black-well's Worst-Dressed List receives worldwide attention (Grogan, 2006). The sarcastic remarks that accompany the selections are obtrusive negative external sanctions. For example, Blackwell described one woman as looking like a painted pumpkin on a pogo stick and said about another that her bag-lady rags looked depressingly decayed.

An unobtrusive sanction is inconspicuous or implicit. Avoidance is an unobtrusive sanction. While avoidance can hurt, it sometimes serves a constructive purpose (Anderson, 2006b). Avoidance can be a signal that a relationship is over or that the avoided person's behavior has been inappropriate. Bad breath or body odor can result in avoidance behavior on the part of others. A dentist reported one of the worst cases of bad breath he ever treated involved a famous nightclub singer who noticed that patrons backed up when she belted out a song ("Have You Met," 2006). Likewise, body odor can cause social anguish, as one person confirmed who wrote to a physician for advice because not a day went by without someone moving away from him (Graedon & Graedon, 2006). Body odor is a taboo subject (Curtis, 2006). Curtis wondered why a teacher, who was nicknamed BO Brown, smelled so bad and why no one mentioned it to the teacher.

MAGNITUDE

Magnitude refers to the total consequences that can be measured as the result of sanctions. A sanction with consequences of extreme magnitude affects all aspects of life (Figure 11.6). An external sanction of extreme magnitude is arrest and incarceration. For example, a man in his sixties revealed to his

FIGURE 11.6 THE DRESS NORM VIOLATION REPORTED IN THIS ARTICLE ENDED IN MURDER.

Two arrested in killings of cross-dresser, two others

HUMBOLDT, Neb. (AP) — A woman who posed as a man and dated women was found shot to death with two other people two weeks after residents of this rural area learned her true identity.

Two men accused of sexually assaulting Teena Brandon were arrested for investigation of murder. But authorities refused to say if the slayings were the result of the assault charges or Brandon's cross-dressing double life.

Friends said Brandon, 21, had posed for two months as a man named Brandon Teena and had told various stories of having an incomplete sex-change operation or of being a hermaphrodite.

"She said she felt like a man inside but she was a female outside," said Michelle Lotter, a friend of Brandon's and sister of one of the

men arrested.

The bodies of Brandon, Lisa Lambert, 23, and an Iowa man whose name was not released were found Friday in a farmhouse about three miles south of Humboldt, a southeast Nebraska town of 1,000 residents.

John Lotter, 22, and Marvin Nissen, 21, both of Falls City, were arrested for investigation of murder and held in the county jail. They also have been charged with kidnapping and sexually assaulting Brandon on Christmas Day, said Richardson County Attorney Douglas Merz.

Authorities had been investigating the kidnapping and assault allegations but did not issue an arrest warrant on them until after the bodies were found, Merz said Saturday.

Brandon had lived with Lambert for about three months.

friends that he had been a cross-dresser since boyhood (Van Buren, 2006a). His former friends now avoid him, and he is socially isolated. The magnitude of impact on his life was considerable, because social interaction has been shown to be important to health and longevity. One study concluded that such "inexpensive, time-honored steps as eating sensibly, spending time with friends and family, and exercising regularly" are ways to extend life expectancy ("Older and Better," 2006, p. A8).

A sanction with consequences of moderate magnitude is one that has limited impact on a person's life. A principal cut four students' hair on the first day of classes because they were in violation of the school dress code, which specified that hair could not be longer than the shirt collar (E. P. Garza, 2006). The boys were given a choice of three sanctions: in-school suspension for the rest of the day, leave school and get a haircut, or have the principal cut their hair. The sanction was of moderate magnitude because hair will grow back.

SEVERITY

Severity refers to the degree of strictness, harshness, intensity, or cruelty of a sanction. A mild sanction is a trivial, weak, or minor reward or punishment. For example, supervisors requested a flight attendant to quit wearing a small American flag pin because it violated the airline's dress code ("Flight Attendant," 1998). Being asked to remove an item of dress is a mild sanction because the item can be put back when the sanctioner is not present or when the flight attendant is not at work. A single female wrote to *Advice Diva* (http://www.advicediva.com/) about not feeling fashionably ready for the holiday season (Solomon, 2006). She wrote that she had a closet full of matronly pantsuits but did not think the everyday norm would be appropriate for special occasions. *Advice Diva* applied a mild sanction when she advised the woman to bag up the pantsuits, list them on eBay (an online resale venue), and find some classic clothes that did not scream "call me Aunt Hilda."

A severe sanction is a strict, harsh, intense, cruel, or stern sanction. Several severe sanctions occurred when a man underwent a sex change operation (Mortenson, 2006). After 26 years of marriage and with two grown children, the man told his wife he felt like a female inside. He took female hormones and began living as a woman outside of work. When he told his employer, he was fired. When he found another job with health insurance that covered the $20,000 cost of sexual reassignment, he decided to have the sex change operation. In the multiyear process, s/he was ridiculed and rejected and risked everything (marriage, relationships with children, friends, employment opportunities).

PERVASIVENESS: QUANTITY, DURATION, NUMBER OF SANCTIONERS

Pervasiveness refers to how widespread sanctions are in terms of the number of sanctions, how long the sanctions last, and how many people are involved in administering the sanctions. Some violations of dress norms are considered inconsequential, resulting in restricted pervasiveness—that is, limited temporary sanctions applied by only a few people. For example, pack rats or hoarders (those who cannot seem to relinquish useless possessions) may experience shame, guilt, embarrassment, and fear that others will find out about their habits (Verel, 2006). One man reported that he found clothes that fit buried under a bunch of useless clothes that he had not been able to relinquish. In the extreme, the propensity to hoard is a psychological disorder that has roots in obsessive-compulsive disorder but on a lesser scale may be related to frugality (thriftiness). One pack rat commented that he did not want others judging him for his collection. Most of the sanctions were internal and of restricted pervasiveness because hoarders made a special effort to keep their behavior secret except for perhaps family members or close friends.

Some violations of dress norms result in extensive pervasiveness—that is, multiple sanctions from more than one source operating against a person over an extended period of time (Figure 11.7). For example, obese people are frequently the target of remarks from family, friends, and even strangers. An overweight teenager had been ridiculed by more than 15 neighborhood boys and girls over a period of three years ("Teen Takes Overdose," 1997). The boys and girls called her "fatty" and "smelly," threw her clothes in the garbage, and threw butter at her house while shouting abusive phrases about lard and fat. To escape the taunting and abuse, the teenager took a fatal overdose.

FIGURE 11.7 IN THIS LETTER TO AN ADVICE COLUMNIST, THE LETTER WRITER HAS EXPERIENCED MANY SANCTIONS THROUGHOUT HER LIFE.

Here's the Skinny Large Reader Wants Respect

Dear Ann: You recently published yet another letter from someone who griped about sitting next to a fat person on a plane. I know all about the problem because I AM that fat person. Does the thin complainer know I am embarrassed that I am in his way, and avoid traveling because of it? I am not fat on purpose, nor do I stay fat just to irritate people on planes.

I was fat at age 5, and when I was 8, my mother put me on diet pills. All my father's relatives are large people, but my mother was pretty and slim, and she didn't know what to make of a fat child. When my younger sister turned out to be a fat child, too, the problems compounded. We were constantly told by our parents that no one would ever love us if we didn't lose weight. They talked about our weight to others in front of us. I was teased mercilessly at school, and never had a social life as a teenager.

I have joined TOPS (Take Off Pounds Sensibly) and Weight Watchers, tried every fad diet and food exchange program you can name, taken expensive and dangerous drugs, and exercised until I dropped from exhaustion. I spent $4,000 on a liquid diet, which took two years to repay on my credit cards. I have lost (and gained) hundreds of pounds, and have had my thyroid checked repeatedly. I am genetically predisposed to be big, and it's a source of grief daily for me that plane seats, restaurant booths, amusement park rides, movie theater seats, furniture and even cars are designed for smaller people.

I eat moderately, avoid junk food, do not binge, and swim twice a week, take the stairs instead of the elevator, and park my car far away so I have to walk further. I am not lazy, nor am I a glutton. I rarely travel by plane because I cannot afford the wider first class seats, nor can I pay for two tickets in coach. I board early and pray that no one will have to sit next to me because I know I'm a problem. If someone is seated next to me, I make it a point to hug the window, turning as far as I can—sometimes almost sideways—to make that person more comfortable.

Smaller people should try to be more understanding and thank God every time they can buy clothes off the rack and slip into any seat, anywhere. And please, never tell a large woman, "But you have such a pretty face."
—Any Girl, Any City

Dear Friend: You are not "any" girl. You are a sensitive woman who has written an extremely moving letter that a great many overweight people will relate to. Thank you for educating millions of readers today. Because you took the time to write, countless people will be more compassionate about the large individuals they encounter in their daily lives.

INTERRELATEDNESS OF ASPECTS

People motivate others to conform to rules by sanctioning their behavior and motivate themselves to conform by sanctioning their own behavior as well. Sanctions applied to violations of dress norms vary in retribution from positive to negative, in source from internal to external, in formality from informal to formal, in obtrusiveness from conspicuous to inconspicuous, in magnitude from moderate to extreme, in severity from mild to severe, and in pervasiveness from restricted to extensive sanctions and few to many sanctioners. Some external sanctions are positive; most are negative. Some internal sanctions are positive; more are negative.

TABLE 11.2 EXAMPLES OF SANCTIONS: RESPONSES TO REPORTS OF VIOLATIONS OF NORMS REGARDING DRESS

Accusations	Distress	Questions
Advice	Divorce	Raised eyebrows
Amused look	Embarrassment	Regret
Anger	Fear	Rejection
Arrest	Feeling like a slob	Remarks
Assumptions	Furious	Ridicule
Avoidance	Humiliation	Self-acceptance
Compliments	Inhibitions	Self-consciousness
Concern	Insults	Shame
Confusion	Jokes	Shock
Congratulations	Lawsuits	Stares
Criticism	Leering	Suggestions
Curse	Mental exam	Surprise
Depression	Name-calling	Suspicions
Disappointment	Nicknames	Teasing
Disapproval	Panic	Threats
Discipline	Pride	Warnings
Disgust	Punishment	Worry

Choose any one sanction and examine its interrelated aspects—for example, teasing (Table 11.2). Teasing is most often negative, external, informal, obtrusive, moderate in magnitude, mild, and can involve an isolated incident or many incidents as well as a single teaser or many teasers.

Contrast the following two incidents of teasing. Legg (2006) described attending a bridal shower with relatives who teased her about how she was dressed. Legg noted that fashion had been her obsession since childhood, when she played dress-up and spent hours reading fashion magazines. Her family, however, regarded her as a fashion outcast. The first two relatives she encountered at the shower gave her a lengthy, silent stare-down and then started laughing. Legg described how her relatives were dressed. "Both were wearing tapered jeans, straight from 1993, and oversized blouses that had seen many a child's spit-up and drool. Both also had hair big enough to block out the sun. Stylish they weren't, but I love them anyway" (p. F12). Other relatives scrutinized her, but the bride-to-be complimented her choice of outfit. "Finally, there will be another woman in this family who will recognize the inappropriateness of sharing clothes with your husband! A woman who will understand that shapeless flannel button-ups and men's Levi's aren't ever an acceptable substitute for the little black dress" (p. F12). Legg commented that her family often wondered how she could possibly be related to them and that she wondered that, too.

The second incident retraces the history of a 19-year-old prisoner convicted of plotting to kill at least 20 students, 3 teachers, and an administrator at his school. Upon meeting the prisoner, the interviewer noted that "The white prison uniform seems to swallow the slight 5-foot-3 frame" of the prisoner (Horswell, 2006, p. 1). The student had been shunned, ostracized, and teased at school because of his heavy metal Goth attire and sexual orientation. He was a member of a group of students who considered themselves outcasts. Like other members of the group, his dress was flamboyant and Goth—black clothing, black nail polish, dog collars, and chains. Being different from the other school cliques drew adverse attention. He told of being humiliated, degraded, relentlessly harassed, called names, shoved, pushed and tripped. During elementary school, he longed to be a member of the group that he later planned to kill, but the elite group shunned him. Group members did not verbally abuse him at first, but they would quit talking whenever he appeared. If members of the group agreed to go some place, they would neglect to tell him. If he tried to sit by them, they would declare the seat was saved for someone else.

The two incidents of teasing contrast sharply in the interrelatedness of aspects and variations of sanctions. In the first incident, well-loved family members teased one of their own who deviated from the family norm. The sanctions were negative, from an external source (her relatives), informal, obtrusive, moderate in magnitude, and mild. The teasing was good-natured, although pervasive because many members of her family teased her over many years with many different sanctions (laughing, staring, jokes, advice, and remarks). The second incident detailed severe teasing that escalated to bullying (verbal abuse such as name-calling, shunning, and relentless harassment; and physical abuse such as tripping, shoving, and pushing) that was of extensive pervasiveness (as many as 20 classmates over many years with many different sanctions). The sanctions were negative, from an external source (his classmates), informal, obtrusive, and of extreme magnitude. The boy was sentenced to four years in prison for conspiracy to murder those he accused of tormenting him—a sanction of extreme magnitude that will affect him for the rest of his life.

SUMMARY

Sanctions regulate conformity to the normative order for dress with varying degrees of effectiveness. If pervasiveness and severity of sanctions imposed upon violators are related to seriousness of violation, then we can assume immodest exposure of the body and cross-dressing are serious violations because many severe sanctions from multiple sources are applied for these violations. Individuals conform to some norms because they internalize an emotional commitment to the norms. Individuals conform to other norms only after assessing the sanctions associated with violating the norm.

KEY TERMS AND CONCEPTS

formality	pervasiveness
magnitude	retribution
name-calling	severity
nickname	source
obtrusiveness	teasing

SUGGESTED READINGS

1. Abeil, E., & Gecas, V. (1997, March). Guilt, shame, and family socialization. *Journal of Family Issues, 18*(2), 99–123.
2. Ohbuchi, K., Tamura, T., Quiciley, B., Tedeschi, J., Madi, N., Bond, M., & Mummendey, A. (2004). Anger, blame, and dimensions of perceived

norm violations: Culture, gender, and relationships. *Journal of Applied Social Psychology, 34*(8), 1587–1603.

Research Activity 11.1 *Fat Sanctions*

Purpose: To identify and characterize sanctions experienced by fat people.

Procedure:

1. Review the aspects of sanctions and how they vary.
2. Locate a web resource that is a source of information about a support group for fat people. One example is the *National Association for the Advancement of Fat Acceptance* (NAAFA) (http://www.naafa.org).
3. Print a recent article from a support group newsletter and highlight the sanctions experienced by fat people.
4. Highlight and label the sanctions reported in the article according to the aspects of sanctions and their variations.
5. Submit your work to your instructor.

Research Activity 11.2 *Childhood Teasing*

Purpose: To identify and characterize the effects of teasing on children.

Procedure:

1. Review the aspects of sanctions and how they vary.
2. Use the Google Scholar (http://scholar.google.com) search engine to locate and print an article that discusses the effects of teasing on children. Example key words include *teasing children* and *childhood teasing*.
3. Highlight and label the teasing (a sanction) reported in the article according to the aspects of sanctions and their variations.
4. Submit your work to your instructor.

Chapter Twelve

SANCTIONS IN VARIOUS SETTINGS

FROM THE HEADLINES

Results from a survey of 100 senior executives found that "a person's dress at work influences his or her chances of earning a promotion" (¶ 1). Twenty-five percent responded that style of dress significantly influenced promotion chances; 55 percent reported the influence as somewhat; and 20 percent said that dress did not influence advancement decisions. The executive director of OfficeTeam, a staffing service for highly skilled administrative professionals that developed the survey, commented that "a polished appearance lends credibility and may help employers envision the staff member in a role with greater responsibility" (¶ 4). Employers do not look solely at dress when selecting candidates for promotion, but dress is a contributing factor. The study suggested asking four questions when making decisions about what to wear to work: "(1) Would managers at my company wear this? (2) Does it give me confidence? (3) Is it clean and in good condition? (4) Is it comfortable?" (¶ 8).

Source: 'Clothing' in on the promotion: Attire affects potential for advancement, say most executives polled. (2007, January 27). *Canada News Wire.* Retrieved February 9, 2007, from http://www.lexisnexis.com

A staffing firm conducted a study to determine implicit sanctions for violating dress norms—specifically, how inappropriate dress affected an employee's chances of promotion. One hundred senior executives responded to the survey. On the basis of their responses, the researchers concluded that an employee's dress contributes to decisions about whether he or she is a suitable candidate for promotion. Is this a typical response to the violation of a norm? Do employers have the right to use dress at work as a component of their decisions for promoting employees? To what extent should dress influence advancement decisions? How does a polished appearance

TABLE 12.1 SUMMARY OF RESEARCH METHODS AND TOOLS RELATED TO SANCTIONS

RESEARCH METHOD	TOOL(S)	AUTHOR(S)	YEAR	ARTICLE TITLE
Qualitative	Interview worksheet	Crozier & Dimmock	1999	Name-calling and nicknames in a sample of primary school children
Qualitative	Narrative worksheet	Crozier	2002	Donkeys and dragons: Recollections of schoolteachers' nicknames
Quantitative	Questionnaire	Crozier & Skliopidou	2002	Adult recollections of name-calling at school
Law review	Literature analysis	Fisk	2006	Privacy, power, and humiliation at work: Re-examining appearance regulation as an invasion of privacy
Quantitative	Questionnaire and scale	Hayden-Wade et al.	2005	Prevalence, characteristics, and correlates of teasing experiences among overweight children vs. non-overweight peers
Quantitative	Questionnaire	Keery et al.	2005	The impact of appearance-related teasing by family members
Qualitative	Interview worksheet	Khosropour & Walsh	2001	That's not teasing–that's bullying: A study of fifth graders' conceptualization of bullying and teasing
Qualitative	Case study worksheets	Leary et al.	2003	Teasing, rejection, and violence: Case studies of the school shootings
Quantitative	Questionnaire	Mclaren et al.	2004	Positive and negative body-related comments and their relationship with body dissatisfaction in middle-aged women

contribute to employers' perceptions of an employee's credibility and ability to handle greater responsibility?

This chapter examines research about use of sanctions in three common settings: the family, the school, and the workplace. The methods and tools used in each research study are summarized in Table 12.1. Sanctions are powerful means of social control. The intent of sanctions is to enforce compliance with norms for correct behavior, attitudes, and appearance. Sanctions are used to penalize deviations from norms or reward compliance with norms. Sanctions can take many forms—for example, name-calling, nicknames, teasing, and ridicule. The interrelatedness of the aspects and variations of sanctions (see Table 11.1) contributes to their broad range of form.

RESEARCH METHOD	TOOL(S)	AUTHOR(S)	YEAR	ARTICLE TITLE
Qualitative	Narrative worksheet	Pelican et al.	2005	The power of others to shape our identity: Body image, physical abilities, and body weight
Mixed methods	Questionnaire, case study and inter-view worksheets	Persad & Lukas	2002	"No hijab is permitted here": A study of the experiences of Muslim women wearing hijab applying for work in the manufacturing, sales, and service sectors
Qualitative	Case study worksheets	Renteln	2004	Visual religious symbols and the law
Quantitative	Scale	Roth et al.	2002	The relationship between memories for childhood teasing and anxiety and depression in adulthood
Qualitative	Interview worksheet	Sissem & Maria	2007	The stigmatization of women of size
Quantitative	Questionnaire	Whitney & Smith	1993	A survey of the nature and extent of bullying in junior/middle and secondary schools
Qualitative	Interview worksheet	Wooten	2006	From labeling possessions to possessing labels: Ridicule and socialization among adolescents
Qualitative	Content analysis worksheet	Workman, Freeburg, & Lentz-Hees	2004	Sanctions connected to dress code violations in secondary school handbooks

QUESTIONS TO ANSWER AS YOU READ

1. How do researchers study sanctions against dress norm violations?
2. How does research reveal the interrelatedness of the aspects and variations of sanctions?
3. What methods are used to conduct research related to sanctions against dress norm violations?
4. What tools are used to collect data for research related to sanctions?

SANCTIONS WITHIN THE FAMILY

The socialization process is dependent on communication between generations, especially within a family unit. As **socialization agents,** parents/guardians are the earliest and potentially most influential in transmitting society's values and norms. In the course of socialization within the family, positive external sanctions such as praise and compliments (Figure 12.1), as well as negative internal sanctions such as guilt and shame, help keep children in conformity with standards of morality, propriety, and competence (Abell & Gecas, 1997). **Shame** is a negative self-evaluation that occurs when an individual perceives he or she is deficient, unacceptable, or incompetent compared to an established norm. **Guilt** is a negative self-evaluation that occurs when an individual behaves in a manner that is in conflict with his or her understanding of and commitment to social norms.

FIGURE 12.1 POSITIVE EXTERNAL SANCTIONS SUCH AS PRAISE AND COMPLIMENTS HELP CHILDREN CONFORM TO STANDARDS OF MORALITY, PROPRIETY, AND COMPETENCE.

Appearance-Related Teasing

Parents may use various means to induce feelings of shame or guilt in a child—for example, teasing. Teasing refers to both verbal and/or nonverbal behaviors that are humorous and playful on one level but may be annoying to the target child on another level (Vessey, Duffy, O'Sullivan, & Swanson, 2003). Teasing can take the form of sarcasm, insults, mockery, ridicule, making fun of, belittling, or malicious remarks in an attempt to provoke compliance to a norm.

One aspect of socialization within the family deals with the cultural principle of **acceptable and ideal appearance** as represented by weight/height ratio or body mass index (BMI). Appearance-related teasing can have long-term effects on body image, depression, and eating disturbances. Keery, Boutelle, van den Berg, and Thompson (2005) evaluated the prevalence and effects of teasing by family members on body dissatisfaction, eating disturbances, and psychological functioning.

Interpersonal relationships with family members have been identified as potential risk factors for body image and eating disturbance—in particular, teasing about appearance (Keery et al., 2005) (Figure 12.2). Self-report data were collected from 372 middle school girls. Twenty-three percent of the girls reported appearance-related teasing by a parent; 12 percent were teased by a parent about being overweight; 19 percent reported appearance-related or weight teasing by fathers, 13 percent by mothers; and 29 percent by siblings. Teasing by mothers was a predictor of depression (a negative internal sanction). Teasing by fathers was a predictor of body dissatisfaction, social comparison, thin-ideal internalization, restriction, bulimic behaviors, self-esteem, and depression.

Frequency of teasing was related to body dissatisfaction, social comparison, thin-ideal internalization, restriction, bulimic behaviors, self-esteem, and perfectionism (Keery et al., 2005). Approximately one-fourth of middle school girls were teased about their appearance by a parent and approximately one-third were teased about their appearance by at least one of their siblings. The highest level of appearance-related teasing came from siblings, followed by fathers and then mothers. An older brother was the most frequent source of teasing by siblings. Appearance-related teasing is not a harmless behavior. Teasing by fathers was particularly deleterious. Outcomes were worse for girls who were teased by a larger percentage of family members.

Positive and Negative Comments

Mclaren, Kuh, Hardy, and Gauvin (2004) looked at the effect of positive and negative body-related comments (external sanctions) on body satisfaction in middle-aged women. **Body satisfaction** was defined as individual's satisfaction with specific physical features, weight, and/or shape (internal sanction). The sample consisted of 898 54-year-old women from the Medical Research Council National Survey of Health and Development. The women completed the Body Esteem Scale for Adolescents and Adults and answered two pairs of questions (once phrased negatively and once phrased positively): Does your husband or partner make negative (positive) comments about your body weight or shape? When you were growing up did people make negative (positive) comments or tease you about your body weight or shape? Those who reported comments while growing up indicated the source of the comments.

More than 50 percent of the women reported positive comments and about 25 percent reported negative comments from their partners (Mclaren et al, 2004). Positive comments while growing up were reported by just over

DEAR ABBY: I am a 13-year-old who weighs 140 pounds and stands 5 feet tall. I feel self-conscious about my body, and hate it when people make comments about my weight.

My brother constantly calls me "fattie" and other rude names. For example, if I turn down an offer for ice cream in front of him, he'll say something like, "Wow! That's a miracle!"

His behavior really hurts, and although I've talked to my parents about it, they haven't done anything to stop him.

I feel ready to work on losing weight, but don't know where to begin. Is there anything I can say to my brother to shut him up? I'll make good use of any suggestions you have.
—**TIRED OF FEELING FAT IN WASHINGTON STATE**

DEAR FEELING FAT: Speak to your parents about your desire to adopt healthier eating habits, and ask them to make an appointment with your doctor so you can begin an approved program of diet and exercise.

Next, tell them again how hurtful and humiliating your brother's negative comments are. He may think they're funny, and he needs to be told otherwise. Ridicule never helped anyone solve a problem. Show them this letter and tell them who wrote it. I wish you the best of luck.

FIGURE 12.2 TEASING ABOUT APPEARANCE BY FAMILY MEMBERS HAS BEEN IDENTIFIED AS A POTENTIAL RISK FACTOR FOR BODY IMAGE AND EATING DISTURBANCE. THIS "DEAR ABBY" LETTER AND THE REPLY ILLUSTRATE HOW HURTFUL SUCH BEHAVIOR CAN BE.

25 percent of the women, the most common source being mothers. About 33 percent of the women reported negative comments while growing up, with the most common source being children at school. Body-related negative comments recalled from childhood had a negative effect on midlife body esteem. Positive comments by a partner could not reverse the harmful effects of the early negative comments. Positive or negative comments by partners had a greater effect on the body esteem of thinner women and of women who recalled positive body-related comments from their childhood. Heavier women reported more negative comments and thinner women reported more positive comments from partners. The authors concluded that "This is not particularly surprising, since thinness in women is considered to be more attractive than fatness in contemporary society, and presumably body-related compliments and criticism will correspond to this societal preference" (p. 270).

Pelican et al. (2005) used personal interviews and focus groups to study the "profound and potentially lifelong influence that other people can have on how individuals feel about their own body and their physical abilities" (p. 56). Many participants reported damaging experiences such as embarrassment and ridicule—for example, a man who would get sick to his stomach when it was time to go to school because his peers had teased him about being short. His physiological reaction constituted a severe internal sanction. A woman reported that her father commented on her getting fat when she went to college ("Wow, you really got fat . . . I didn't know that you gained the freshman 40," p. 68). Others felt strengthened by praise and support—for example, a tall woman said her parents had emphasized that she should stand up straight and be proud of her height. In addition to peers and parents, other particularly influential people included coaches, teachers, spouses, and physicians. Most of the sanctions related to body size and shape, with more women than men recalling these experiences. One woman recalled being called "Big Red," and a man mentioned that he was often asked if he bought his suits at a tent and awning store.

SANCTIONS WITHIN THE SCHOOL

Within the school environment, sanctions are used by peers to control conformity to peer group norms. Students may also use sanctions to express dissatisfaction with the power structure of the school environment. In addition, teachers and administrators use sanctions as a means of socializing students with regard to society's norms and values.

Sanctions by Students Against Peers

Researchers investigating sanctions used within the school have used both qualitative and quantitative research methods. Sanctions investigated include name-calling, nicknames, teasing, bullying, and ridicule, among others.

Name-calling, nicknames, teasing, and ridicule usually involve repeated exposure over time to negative actions on the part of one or more other people (Olweus, 1997).

Name-calling and Nicknames

Crozier and Dimmock (1999) interviewed nine- and ten-year-old children about name-calling and nicknames. The children's experience with name-calling was predominantly negative. The most common content of nicknames referred to physical appearance in a hurtful way, in particular, weight ("skinny bones," "fatty"), height ("daddy long legs"), nose ("rubber nose"), teeth ("piano teeth"), hair ("nesthead"), freckles ("spotty"), or warts ("wartman"). More than 20 percent of the children experienced nasty comments and unkind nicknames on a daily basis (extensive, negative sanctions). Children described the experience of being called names as hurtful, making them unhappy or upset. Nicknames, name-calling, and other forms of verbal harassment were most frequently targeted toward students who were different in some way—for example, in physical appearance, size, or weight.

Individuals who are targets of informal sanctions such as name-calling, nicknames, positive and negative remarks, teasing, and ridicule are different from their peers in appearance, personality, ability, ethnicity, or some other conspicuous category (Sweeting & West, 2001). For example, "recipients of chronic teasing are likely to be smaller, weaker, uncoordinated, less attractive, or obese" (Vessey et al., 2003, p. 3). Such individuals are vulnerable to sanctions because they deviate from some social norm, such as appearance or ability norms (Siann, Callaghan, Lockhart, & Rawson, 1993). There seems to be a particular lack of tolerance in our society for individuals who look different (Gerrard, 1991).

Crozier and Skliopidou (2002) surveyed adults regarding their recollections of name-calling and nicknames during their school years. Half of the items in an established bullying and victimization scale referred to being called horrible names, being laughed at, and being teased (Austin & Joseph, 1996), yet name-calling and nicknames have attracted little research attention.

Verbal sanctions can take the form of name-calling (calling someone abusive, disgraceful, or shameful names) and assigning unkind nicknames (Crozier & Skliopidou, 2002). Unkind nicknames are names given to a person in contempt or derision. More than half of the adults surveyed remembered being called hurtful names, a severe sanction from external sources. Name-calling peaked between the ages of eight and twelve years. The most common content of names referred to physical appearance.

However, Crozier and Skliopidou (2002) acknowledged that their analysis underestimated the names referring to appearance ("midget," "freckles") because appearance provided the basis for other categories of names (famous person, animals, or objects). For example, famous persons included Twiggy (a 1960s fashion model known for her anorexic look), Barbra Streisand (a late twentieth to early twenty-first century singer known for her prominent nose), and Santa (a mythical Christmas visitor known for his rotund appearance). Objects such as matchsticks and toothpicks (used to denote thinness) and animals such as elephants and whales (known for their large size) were also used to refer to physical characteristics.

A substantial proportion of the participants reported they had been the target of hurtful names or nicknames. They reported largely negative feelings caused by name-calling, such as anger, embarrassment, shame, and unhappiness (negative internal sanctions). Some adults reported that the effects of name-calling lasted into adulthood.

Teasing and Bullying

Khosropour and Walsh (2001) interviewed 40 fifth-grade boys and girls from four schools to determine how they perceived and described problems with teasing and bullying that they experienced or witnessed in their schools. Children did not think teasing was joking or playful behavior but considered teasing to be verbal aggression—the most common type of bullying. When asked what children do or say to make other children feel bad, every child interviewed mentioned some form of verbal aggression, such as name-calling; laughing at others' appearance, race, academic, or athletic abilities; cursing at them; or spreading rumors about them. Children recalled such names as geek, shrimp, wimp, fruitcake, dork, square head, and nerd.

Teasing remarks about another's appearance included remarks about size (too big, too fat, too skinny, too tall, or too short), attractiveness (ugly, smell bad, or had funny teeth), and the way a child dressed (dressed weird, had Barney or Tweetie Bird characters on their clothes, or wore old clothes with holes). When asked to describe the type of child who is targeted for teasing, children said the targets of teasing did not look like everyone else—for example, they wore eyeglasses or bad clothes. These findings suggest that teasing is viewed as an extreme and extensively pervasive sanction (Figure 12.3).

FIGURE 12.3 TEASING HAPPENS FREQUENTLY AMONG YOUNG CHILDREN.

Whitney and Smith (1993) assessed bullying in school by distributing questionnaires to more than 6,000 students in 17 junior/middle and 7 secondary schools. The questionnaire contained a definition of bullying and 25 single or multiple-choice questions to which students responded by circling one or more relevant answers. The definition of **bullying** contained the following concepts: when children say nasty things to a child; when a child is hit, kicked, threatened, locked inside a room, or sent nasty notes; when no one ever talks to the child; or when a child is teased repeatedly in a nasty way. Most of the bullying reported took the form of name-calling, with 50 percent of junior and middle school students, and 62 percent of secondary students being called names. While informal, these sanctions were negative, obtrusive, of severe magnitude, and extensive in their variation.

Roth, Coles, and Heimberg (2002) explored the relationship between memories for childhood teasing and anxiety and depression in adulthood. The authors developed a Teasing Questionnaire (TQ) to measure the degree to which people recalled having been teased about 20 different topics during childhood. Teasing was defined as verbal taunts about appearance, personality, or behavior. Items in the Teasing Questionnaire related to appearance included being ugly or unattractive, weight, height, aspects of appearance (dress, glasses, hair color), and ethnic or cultural differences (skin color or wearing special items of clothing such as a head covering). Males and females did not differ on scores on the TQ.

Consistent with previous research that has shown physical appearance is the most common topic of teasing, both males and females endorsed appearance-related items most strongly. Females most frequently recalled being teased about their weight, height, and aspects of their appearance such as the way they dressed or their hair color. Males most frequently recalled being teased

FIGURE 12.4 SOME YOUNG BOYS ARE MADE FUN OF FOR THE WAY THEY WEAR THEIR HAIR.

about aspects of their appearance such as the way they dressed and their hair color, their weight, and about excelling at school or being brainy (Figure 12.4). There was a relationship between teasing during childhood and the experience of both depression and anxiety as adults. Teasing is an external sanction that results in internal sanctions for the individual being teased. These internal sanctions can be severe and extensive.

Hayden-Wade, Stein, Ghaderi, Saelens, Zabinski, and Wilfley (2005) investigated the prevalence, nature, sources, and psychosocial correlates of teasing among 70 overweight and 86 nonoverweight children aged 10 to 14. Children filled out a pencil-and-paper questionnaire; overweight children were at a fitness camp and nonoverweight children at a demographically similar school. In addition, overweight children were interviewed. Teasing history was measured by using the 11-item Perception of Teasing Scale (POTS) and the 9-item Appearance Teasing Inventory (ATI). The ATI contains items covering physical attributes about which children were teased or criticized and disparaging nicknames they were called, and detailed the frequency (from rarely to very often), duration (in years), perpetrators (family, peers, other adults), and emotional impact of the teasing (from not at all upset to extremely upset).

Among the overweight children (when compared with the nonoverweight children), appearance-related teasing was more prevalent (especially about weight), frequent, and upsetting, involved disparaging nicknames focused more on weight rather than less stigmatized aspects of appearance, and was more often perpetrated by peers in general rather than a specific peer (Hayden-Wade et al., 2005). The overweight children had experienced many **contemptuous** nicknames (expressing a lack of respect for someone considered to be worthless, inferior, or undeserving of respect) related to body fat ("fatso," "chubbs"), body parts ("lard legs," "blubber-butt," "fat-ass"), overweight characters ("Santa Claus," "Porky"), and large animals or objects ("whale," "Titanic"). Most nicknames among the nonoverweight sample related to underweight status ("stickman") or non-weight-related aspects of appearance ("tomato head," "shorty"). Among all children, teasing was related to more weight concerns, more loneliness, more negative self-perception of physical appearance, higher preference for sedentary/isolative activities, and lower preference for active/social activities.

Thus, these sanctions had several interrelated aspects. Overweight children had been teased by a variety of sources, including teachers, friends, parents, and other family members, but reported the most common source of teasing was peers. The authors speculated that teasing overweight peers may be a common and socially approved part of youth culture. The youth peer group may consider it acceptable and normative to tease about overweight, whereas teasing about other issues would not be so widely approved.

Leary, Kowalski, Smith, and Phillips (2003) examined case studies of 15 school shootings to determine the possible role of teasing and rejection in school violence. "Among adolescents, rejection tends to occur in one of three forms—teasing, ostracism, and romantic rejection" (p. 203). Disliked and unpopular individuals may be bullied, taunted, and maliciously teased. People who are the victims of bullying and teasing receive a clear message that the perpetrators do not like, value, or accept them. Bullying and teasing typically occur in the presence of other people, thereby providing an element of public humiliation as well. Interpersonal rejection was clearly indicated in most of the 15 shootings. In at least 12 of the 15 incidents, the perpetrators had been subject to a pattern of malicious teasing or bullying—for example, teased about their weight or appearance, maliciously taunted and humiliated (regularly called a nerd, dweeb, faggot), or otherwise picked on.

Many cases involved ongoing ostracism that left the perpetrator on the periphery of the school's social life (Leary et al., 2003). In many of the incidents, the victims included those individuals who had teased, bullied, or rejected the shooter. Social rejection was involved in most cases of school violence. Several of the perpetrators explicitly explained their actions as a response to being mistreated by other students. The painful feelings of shame that often result from rejection may provoke anger and aggression, in much the same way that physical pain can make people angry. Most of the shooters had experienced an unusually high amount of bullying or ostracism that was particularly relentless, humiliating, and cruel. Victims of malicious teasing and bullying experience internal sanctions as well as the external sanctions—for example, anger, shame, humiliation, depression, anxiety, and low self-esteem.

Ridicule

Wooten (2006) investigated ridicule as one means of communicating consumption norms and values among adolescents. Wooten used purposive sampling to recruit young people for interviews. **Purposive sampling** refers to choosing participants who have experienced the event of interest (adolescent shopping behavior) because they are ideally suited to shed light on the event. Participants were young enough to recall their adolescent experiences but old enough to be candid about discussing them with an adult interviewer.

Participants recalled mean-spirited **barbs** (hurtful remarks) used to put down and exclude those who did not fit in with the group (Wooten, 2006). For example, one participant mentioned how classmates made cruel jokes about a boy whose family was poor and who always wore tight pants that were too short. The classmates who taunted the boy "gained status and power by consuming material objects and belittling those without them" (p. 192). Some participants recalled being taunted about being immature or having overprotective parents because their strict parents refused to purchase provocative styles or pay inflated prices.

Being independent is high on the list of status characteristics for adolescents. Independence and dependence are cultural principles by which individuals are divided into groups. Name-calling was based on cultural categories such as *momma's boy* or *baby*. Many participants responded to ridicule by conforming to group norms. For example, one student replaced his unpopular white sneakers with acceptable black ones after his peers laughed at his choice of colors.

Many participants said they sought greater control over their clothing purchases. They were eager to do their own shopping because they had suffered the consequences of parents' choices. One student recalled coming home from school and crying because his classmates made fun of a shirt he wore to school. His mother had purchased an inexpensive alternative to the popular brand. The student looked to his peers for input to replace his parents' influence. The participants commented that they tried to comply with group norms, but their efforts to conform were complicated by parental restrictions, budgetary limits, and changing fashions. One young man considered back-to-school shopping as an opportunity to correct mistakes from the previous year. When group norms are tied to fashion trends, complying with the norms is made difficult by the speed at which fashion changes. Participants acknowledged middle school as marking the onset and peak of ridicule about possessions and the emergence of fashion awareness, brand consciousness, and interest in shopping.

Wooten (2006) concluded that observing or experiencing ridicule influenced adolescents' purchase, use, and discard of possessions. Both targets and observers of ridicule learned which social categories were perceived as avoidance groups and which objects were associated with the avoidance groups. Adolescents learned from ridicule what brands, styles, and stores to avoid if they wanted their peers to accept them. Participants mentioned feelings of inadequacy and concerns about belonging as reasons why they complied with the norms they once violated.

Jeer pressure was a term coined by Janes and Olson (2000) to refer to the pressure felt by witnesses of ridicule to behave in conventional ways. Ridicule and teasing are methods by which individuals establish or maintain power and control over another person by intentionally embarrassing the person (Sharkey, 1997). **Embarrassment** refers to becoming or causing somebody to become painfully self-conscious, ashamed, humiliated, or ill at ease. Ridicule is humiliating because others are enjoying a joke at the expense of the person being ridiculed. It is a universal human need to be liked by others and to fear rejection. It seems socially acceptable among teenagers to ridicule their peers. Insulting someone else may result in negative perceptions (rude, hostile), while ridiculing someone else may result in positive perceptions (witty, clever).

Sanctions Against Teachers and Administrators

Crozier (2002) examined the characteristics of students' nicknames for teachers. "Name-calling and coining hurtful nicknames usually reflect an imbalance of power, where the weaker are called names by the stronger" (p. 133). However, students who are in a weaker power position may use derogatory nicknames for teachers within a small peer group, where the teacher cannot hear, suggesting an unobtrusive sanction against the teacher. Crozier analyzed university students' recollections of nicknames given their teachers. Most teachers with nicknames were viewed negatively. The nicknames expressed dislike or contempt or were attempts to get even with the teacher. Teachers who had the most hurtful nicknames were less admired, less popular, less respected, and more disliked.

The most frequent category for nicknames was some distinctive feature of physical appearance, for example, baldness, protruding eyes, large mole, double chin, hanging jowls, or being overweight. Physical features also provided the basis for choosing a nickname that reflected a well-known character or

FIGURE 12.5 NICKNAMES ARE OFTEN GIVEN TO TEACHERS WHO ARE DISLIKED. THESE COMMENTS ABOUT TEACHERS ARE MADE IN A SECRETIVE FASHION.

person—Father Christmas (white beard and hair) or Hitler (moustache). Students used the nicknames in a secretive fashion, although some teachers were aware of their nicknames (Figure 12.5).

Sanctions Against Students

Norms for student appearance as well as sanctions for dress code violations are published in school handbooks. **Dress code violations** are violations of norms for student appearance. A content analysis of 155 student handbooks uncovered 26 sanctions (Workman, Freeburg, & Lentz-Hees, 2004) (Table 12.2).

Each of the sanctions represented more than one variation of the aspects, demonstrating the interrelatedness of the aspects of sanctions. All 26 sanctions originated from an external source, were formal in nature with the exception of verbal reprimand, and represented various forms of punishment. Twenty-one sanctions were obtrusive; 22 were moderate in magnitude; 16 were mild in severity; 13 were pervasive (multiple sanctioners, multiple sanctions, prolonged duration); and 13 were nonpervasive (single sanctioner, single sanction, short time frame). There were no internal or reward-oriented sanctions and only one informal sanction. The obtrusiveness of the sanctions suggested the desire to make the offending student an example to avoid and in this way communicate to others the consequences of inappropriate dress.

T A B L E 1 2 . 2 SANCTIONS IN STUDENT HANDBOOKS

After-school detention	Parental supervision
Alternative school	Rearranging class schedule
Alternative work	Referral to law enforcement
Demerits	Removal from class
Disciplinary probation	Review committee
Expulsion	Saturday school
Friday reports	School counseling services
Good record keeping	School service
In-school suspension	Student behavior contract
Loss of privileges	Student court
Out-of-school suspension	Student interview
Overnight dismissal	Temporary suspension from a single class
Parent contact	Verbal reprimand

Sanctions Within the Workplace

Creating a company image is important to many organizations, but the methods by which the image is created can lead to practical and legal problems (King, Winchester, & Sherwyn, 2006). Dress and appearance policies can result in negative sanctions against a company in the form of grievances, lawsuits, and negative publicity. For example, Abercrombie & Fitch paid millions of dollars to settle lawsuits based on the argument that its appearance-based hiring practices discriminated against women and minorities.

Sanctions Associated with Appearance Regulation

In a law review, Fisk (2006) examined appearance regulation at work as an invasion of privacy by analyzing case studies. "Workplace rules that deny fundamental aspects of personal autonomy are (in many states) and should be actionable invasions of privacy. Perhaps nowhere is the invasion more keenly felt than when an employer demands, under penalty of forfeiting one's livelihood, that one dress or alter one's physical appearance in a way that one finds offensive, degrading, inappropriate, or alien" (p. 1) (Figure 12.6). "Being told you'll be fired unless you attend a business meeting on Wall Street wearing a pin-striped suit has a whole different connotation than reluctantly choosing to wear one because you know you'll raise eyebrows if you don't" (p. 16).

FIGURE 12.6 WORKPLACE RULES THAT DENY PERSONAL AUTONOMY ARE FREQUENTLY VIEWED AS AN INVASION OF PRIVACY. THIS IS ESPECIALLY TRUE WHEN AN EMPLOYER DEMANDS, UNDER PENALTY OF TERMINATION, THAT AN EMPLOYEE DRESS IN AN INAPPROPRIATE WAY.

A school instituted a dress code for all staff requiring male staff to wear khaki slacks and a collared shirt (Fisk, 2006). An electrician protested the requirement to wear khaki slacks on the basis of his working conditions (outdoors, no air-conditioning) and his physical condition (he had a medical condition that caused him to perspire profusely). He remarked: "If I have to wear khaki pants, inside of an hour I'll look like I wet myself. The students will laugh, and I'm just not willing to be humiliated" (p. 5). The man resigned rather than be humiliated when the employer would not accommodate his request.

Other sanctions associated with workplace appearance include being passed over for promotion or partnership. For example, a female accountant was denied a partnership because she did not wear makeup, style her hair, or wear jewelry; in other words, she was not feminine enough (Fisk, 2006).

Sanctions Associated with Visible Religious Symbols

Renteln (2004) scrutinized the contexts in which litigation has centered on visual religious symbols, including those that individuals wear. Visual religious symbols tend to arouse anxiety or fear in others not belonging to the religion symbolized. "Individuals who wish to stand out for their commitment to their religious communities are often subject to serious sanctions such as expulsion from school, termination of employment, and social ridicule" (p. 1574). The workplace is one context in which religious symbols have caused controversy. Workplace dress and appearance policies often prohibit employees from wearing religious symbols required by their faiths. One case study detailed a fast food restaurant's no-facial hair policy that prevented a Sikh candidate from being hired as a manager. After a successful interview, he explained that he would not shave off his beard because it was one of the five symbols required by his religion. He was not offered the position. Likewise, a man who applied for a position as a chauffeur was not offered the job because he would not cut off dreadlocks that were required by his Rastafarian religion.

FIGURE 12.7 WOMEN WHO WEAR *HIJAB* ARE OFTEN TREATED RUDELY IN THE WORKPLACE.

Several hotels and airlines claimed cornrow hairstyles would frighten guests or were inconsistent with their corporate image and threatened to terminate women who wore the braided styles (Renteln, 2004). The four most common justifications for not allowing particular dress were aesthetics, public health, public safety, and solidarity. In the majority of cases, courts upheld dress code policies although evidence of any threat of harm to society was lacking.

Persad and Lukas (2002) examined employment discrimination experienced by Muslim women who wear the *hijab*. Among other methods, data were collected using survey research with Muslim women and in-person field tests at job sites. Ninety percent of the Muslim women who participated in the survey responded that a prospective employer had said something to them regarding their wearing of *hijab* and 40 percent were told they must take off their *hijab* if they wanted a job.

Results from the field tests revealed that applicants without *hijab* were treated in a courteous manner, while applicants with *hijab* were treated in a dismissive and rude manner (Figure 12.7). Sometimes applicants with *hijab* were told there were no application forms or there were no jobs available, but applicants without *hijab* (at the same site) were given an application form to fill out and allowed to apply for a job. Results showed that women who wore *hijab* experienced negative sanctions in the workplace, for example, they were "denied jobs, told they must remove their *hijab,* harassed in the workplace and fired from jobs" (Persad & Lukas, 2002, p. 3).

Sanctions Associated with Weight

Sissem and Maria (2007) interviewed 16 women of size of various racial and ethnic backgrounds to assess weight as an appearance norm violation and associated labels. People who do not match normative expectations of the body encounter sanctions, such as **taunting** (provoking, ridiculing, or teasing in a hurtful or mocking way) or name-calling. The women interviewed by Sissem and Maria believed the societal stereotypes that existed about women of size included unattractive, lazy, incompetent, and second-class citizen. One woman suspected that because of her weight she was written off as having a lack of energy at her job; the employer said they needed someone with more energy. Another woman experienced consequences of the stereotype of incompetence—she was called lazy, stupid, and incapable of doing many things. Women of size are discriminated against in employment situations when employers screen applicants for their ability to represent the organization's image.

The respondents interviewed by Sissem and Maria (2007) described their perceptions of peoples' impressions of them with adjectives such as sloppy, dirty, ugly, disgusting, and unkempt, all of which suggest sanctions of extensive pervasiveness. One woman remarked about perceptions of women of size: "I think some think they're dirty, that they are not clean and that they dress however they feel; they don't dress to look presentable, sloppily" (pp. 10–11). Another woman commented on informal sanctions:

> I think society is repulsed by obese people. . . . This disgust is displayed in numerous ways. For instance, go to the grocery store sometime as a fat person and watch the people watch you. God forbid you should buy something they consider fattening. The dirty looks will fly. (p. 11)

A third woman commented, "Either people look at you and make fun of you or they look right through you and don't even notice that you're there.

I've noticed a lot of cruelty behind a lot of things that people do or say or make fun of" (p. 1 3). Common and frequent names mentioned by these women were "fat cow," "fat slob," "fatso," "Baby Huey," and "fat pig." Respondents stated that the negative names made them "hate themselves" or feel "disgusting and ashamed" (p. 14).

SUMMARY

In this chapter, we have seen how sanctions are powerful means of social control. Sanctions are used within common socialization contexts such as the family, the school, and the workplace with the intent to encourage compliance with norms for correct behavior, attitudes, and appearance. Within these socialization contexts, negative sanctions are used to punish violations of norms and positive sanctions are used to reward compliance with norms. Sanctions include name-calling, nicknames, teasing, ridicule, detention, suspension, expulsion, or termination from a job. Sanctions can take many other forms in addition to those addressed in this chapter because the aspects of sanctions and their variations are interrelated.

KEY TERMS AND CONCEPTS

acceptable/ideal appearance	guilt
barbs	jeer pressure
body satisfaction	purposive sampling
bullying	shame
contemptuous	socialization agents
dress code violations	taunting
embarrassment	

1. Hayden-Wade, H. A., Stein, R. I., Ghaderi, A., Saelens, B. E., Zabinski, M. F., & Wilfley, D. E. (2005). Prevalence, characteristics, and correlates of teasing experiences among overweight children vs. non-overweight peers. *Obesity Research, 13*(8), 1381–1392.

2. Sissem, P., & Maria, D. (2007). The stigmatization of women of size. Retrieved February 1, 2007, from http://www.misu.nodak.edu/research/Stigma.pdf

3. Wooten, D. B. (2006). From labeling possessions to possessing labels: Ridicule and socialization among adolescents. *Journal of Consumer Research, 33*, 188–198.

Research Activity 12.1 Literature Analysis

Purpose: To analyze research literature related to sanctions as a response to appearance norm violations, identifying the purpose, research method, and results.

Procedure:

1. Describe the characteristics of a research article.

2. Use the Google Scholar (http://scholar.google.com/) search engine or an academic database (EBSCO, ERIC, SocIndex) to locate one research article related to sanctions as a response to appearance norm violations. For example, you might use the key words *dress norm violations sanctions* or *sanctions for appearance standard violations* to search for research articles.

3. Print a copy of the research article.

4. Highlight and label the purpose of the study, the research method used, the results of the study related to its purpose, and sanctions for appearance norm violation studied.

5. Submit your work to your instructor.

Purpose: To analyze personal experiences expressed through stories to understand sanctions associated with middle school memories.

Procedure:

1. Review the definition of dress.
2. Select three males and three females of about the same age (college age or older) who will agree to be interviewed by you.
3. Interview each individual by asking the following questions:
   a. Were you teased as a child in middle school (grades 6, 7, and 8)?
   b. About what topics were you teased? Prompt each individual by giving the following examples: appearance, personality, behavior.
   c. What is a specific example of the topic about which you were teased and that you remember the most clearly?
4. Summarize your findings in a word table (see example below) to determine the number and type associated with dress. Also include the differences according to the gender of the interviewee.
5. Submit the results to your instructor.

Table: Middle School Memories of Teasing

Question	Males	Females
Percent teased		
Teasing topics		
Most memorable example		

Chapter Thirteen

ENFORCEMENT OF SANCTIONS

FROM THE HEADLINES

A school committee of students, parents, teachers, and administrators was charged with looking at dress code changes and policy enforcement changes for the 2006–2007 school year. Last year flip-flops, defined as "flat rubber sole held on the foot by a strap slipped between the big toe and the toe next to it," (p. 1) were banned, but the rule was not enforced. Administrators admit it is difficult to monitor students at each middle and high school, where most violations occur. The most frequent dress code violation for girls has been wearing flip-flops; for boys, wearing pants several sizes too big, allowing their underwear to show at the waistband. A principal remarked "If you have to walk with your hands on your pants to keep them up, that's my definition of too big" (p. 1). Sanctions for dress code violations include parental notification and/or change of attire for the first offense, detention for a second offense, in-school suspension for a third offense, and out-of-school suspension for four or more violations. One student expressed concern about teachers' uneven enforcement of dress codes and suggested sanctions be related to losing exam exemptions, not suspension. "Dressing appropriately sets an environment for learning and prepares students for the workplace, say those pushing for tougher enforcement" (p. 1).

Source: Brown, M. (2006, March 10). Dressing rite. *The Tampa Tribune*, p. 1.
Retrieved January 12, 2007, from http://www.lexisnexis.com

This story illustrates the difficulties inherent in enforcing sanctions in a secondary school context. In secondary schools, school administrators are charged with the responsibility for ensuring that disciplinary measures are enforced. However, administrators recognize how difficult it is to monitor student dress. Teachers contribute to the problem by unequal enforcement. Students try to escape detection by avoiding teachers who are likely to notice and report norm violations.

Who other than teachers and administrators enforces sanctions? In what other contexts are sanctions enforced? What are the components of the physical environment in the scenario described in the article? How does the relationship between the enforcer and the violator of dress norms influence development of the dress code policy? Which other contexts besides the school might influence dress code policy development, particularly the guidelines related to effective enforcement of the policy? How? Why? In this chapter you will read about enforcement of sanctions in various contexts and learn why the effectiveness of sanctions depends on enforcement.

This chapter will examine the sixth step in the process of social control—enforcement of sanctions (Figure 13.1). Aspects and variations of norms, aspects of norm violations, recognition of norm violations, reports of norm violations, and the nature of sanctions interact to affect enforcement. Recall from Chapter 1 that enforcement of sanctions refers to the ability to require compliance with a norm. For example, teachers and principals have the responsibility for enforcement of dress norms in public schools, as illustrated in the "From the Headlines" article.

QUESTIONS TO ANSWER AS YOU READ

1. How is the enforcement of sanctions influenced by the process of social control?
2. How do various social contexts enforce sanctions against norm violations?
3. What are some examples of effectiveness and ineffectiveness related to enforcement of sanctions?
4. How is the enforcement of sanctions from various contexts interrelated?

ENFORCEMENT OF SANCTIONS AND THE PROCESS OF SOCIAL CONTROL

All societies have methods for social control of their members. One means of social control is to enforce sanctions as a way to encourage compliance with norms. Every step in the process of social control that precedes enforcement affects enforcement of sanctions.

Enforcement of a sanction depends on the aspects and variations of the norm for which an individual is being sanctioned. Recall from Chapter 3 that norms vary in salience, content, authority, origination, realism, acceptance, properties, application, transmission, and in the sanctions associated with violation of the norm. Each variation of a norm introduces variation in enforcement of sanctions associated with violation of a norm. Each variation expresses the relative extent, amount, intensity, or level of some aspect of a norm, especially when compared with other norms.

Enforcement of sanctions is influenced by the reason for the norm violation. Recall from Chapter 5 that violations of norms occur for a number of reasons: geographic locality, faulty transmission of expectations, degree of socialization, values and motives, physical conditions, environmental conditions, demands on resources, temporal incompatibilities between statuses, the normative system itself, and internalization.

The nature of norm recognition influences enforcement of sanctions. Recall from Chapter 7 that recognition of norm violations varied according to who, what, when, where, and why. Among the factors affecting *who* was most likely to recognize dress norm violations were status, sensitivity to aesthetic rules, self-monitoring, fashion interest, fashion knowledgeability, fashion involvement, fashion innovativeness, and fashion opinion leadership. Factors affecting *what* norm violations were most likely to be recognized included visibility, egregiousness, and incongruity. A factor affecting *when* norm violations were most likely to be recognized was the stage of the fashion cycle. Factors affecting *where* norm violations were most likely to be recognized were places with explicit and implicit dress codes. Factors affecting *why* particular norm violations were likely to be recognized were unpredictability and uncertainty. The interrelationships among these factors add to the complexity of enforcing sanctions.

Recall from Chapter 9 that one of the functions of reports of norm violations is to identify norm violators and expose their deviance. This function can be accomplished through several print and oral mechanisms, including letters to the editor, letters to advice columnists, comic strips or cartoons, human interest stories, magazine advertisements, newsletters, reviews of litigation associated with employer dress codes, conversations among peers, and gossip. Reports of a norm violation vary in several ways—to whom it is reported, how readily it identifies norm violators, how extensively it publicizes their deviance, and the means by which it is reported. All of the ways in which reports vary interact to affect enforcement of sanctions.

TABLE 13.1 OVERVIEW OF SOCIAL INTERACTION CONTEXT

CONTEXT	COMPONENTS
Physical environment	• Material artifacts • Geographic location • Setting
Social environment	• Characteristics of enforcer: statuses and roles • Characteristics of violator: statuses and roles • Relationship between enforcer and violator: power, prestige, and privilege • Occasion • Circumstances
Temporal environment	• Past experience of enforcer and violator • Present experience of enforcer and violator • Future experience of enforcer and violator

Each of the aspects and variations of sanctions can affect enforcement of sanctions. Recall from Chapter 11 that every sanction has seven aspects and each aspect of a sanction has variations. Each sanction varies in the aspects of retribution, source, formality, obtrusiveness, magnitude, severity, and pervasiveness. Again, all the aspects are interrelated.

FIGURE 13.2 THE ENFORCEMENT OF SANCTIONS MIGHT BE INFLUENCED BY A FORMAL PHYSICAL ENVIRONMENT SUCH AS THE GRAND HOTEL PICTURED HERE.

CONTEXT OF A SOCIAL INTERACTION

The context of a social interaction influences enforcement of sanctions. All norms are created, enforced, or changed through social interaction. The context of any given social interaction can be characterized by its (a) physical environment, (b) social environment, and (c) temporal environment (Table 13.1).

The **physical environment** refers to the surroundings, that is, the immediate environment including the **setting** (the place in which the event takes place) and material artifacts such as dress (Figure 13.2). The physical environment also refers to the distant environment of a geographic locality (country, region, city).

The **social environment** refers to the people who are present—each person with his or her statuses (gender, age, occupation) and associated roles. The status and role relationships among the people present are influenced by their power, prestige, and privilege. The occasion and the circumstances are also part of the social environment. The **occasion** refers to an important or special event such as a social function, a sports competition, eating at a restaurant, a wedding, a funeral, a baptism, attending church, and so forth. **Circumstances** are the conditions that affect what happens or how somebody reacts in a particular situation and include nonmaterial culture—that is, society's norms, values, beliefs, and abstract concepts.

The **temporal environment** refers to events that have taken place in the past (occurred in a previous time), in the present (currently happening) and in the future (events that have not yet happened). Experiences from the past shape current thinking and behavior, and also influence future reactions to events that are currently happening (Figure 13.3).

FIGURE 13.3 THE ENFORCEMENT OF SANCTIONS AT THE WEDDING PICTURED HERE WOULD BE INFLUENCED BY THE CUSTOMS AND TRADITIONS OF THE PAST AS WELL AS THE FADS AND FASHIONS OF THE PRESENT.

In order to clarify how enforcement of sanctions operates within the context of social interaction, we'll examine examples from several different social interaction contexts in greater detail. This chapter is organized around the following contexts: family, school, workplace, religion, government (judicial system, legislative system), and community (restaurants, clubs, retail stores, public buildings). Although the contexts will be discussed separately, in actuality there is significant interaction between and among them.

ENFORCEMENT WITHIN THE FAMILY CONTEXT

The family provides the earliest and most influential social interaction context. Enforcement of sanctions within the family depends, in part, on the parents' or guardians' philosophy of child-rearing and discipline (Figure 13.4).

In this context, families may enforce, or choose not to enforce, norms for gender-appropriate dress and behavior. Past generations believed that deviance from gender norms for dress and behavior was largely the result of dysfunctional families. Sanctions against sissy boys and tomboy girls were enforced as means of ensuring conformity in gender expression (P. L. Brown,

FIGURE 13.4 THE FAMILY CONTEXT, INCLUDING THE PHILOSOPHY OF CHILD-REARING AND DISCIPLINE, INFLUENCES THE ENFORCEMENT OF SANCTIONS.

2006). **Sissy** is an offensive term referring to a boy who does not exhibit stereotypical masculinity. **Tomboy** refers to a girl who dresses or behaves in a way regarded as boyish, especially a girl who enjoys rough, boisterous play. **Transgender** is a term that refers to those who do not conform to traditional notions of gender expression. One parent of a transgendered child recalled how therapists urged her to put her son in psychoanalysis and in hypermasculine activities such as karate. She and her husband became gender cops. They believed they could never leave him alone and needed to monitor his every action.

As gender-identity rights receive increased support, some families are changing their tactics (P. L. Brown, 2006). Instead of enforcing sanctions against transgender behavior, a growing number of young parents are supporting their children who display an inclination to dress like the opposite sex. Supportive attitudes are easier to find in areas of the country known for social tolerance, like San Francisco. One characteristic of tolerant communities is that they support transgender behaviors.

Some pediatricians advise parents and guardians to let transgendered children be *who they are* to nurture a sense of security and self-esteem (P. L. Brown, 2006). However, teachers blame parents/guardians for allowing their children to attend school dressed in clothing of the other gender and for the difficulties presented by accommodating these children in school. A principal remarked that allowing a child to express gender differences would be very difficult to accommodate in an elementary school. "I'm not sure it's worth the damage it could cause the child, with all the prejudices and parents possibly protesting. I'm not sure a child that age is ready to make that kind of decision" (p. 1).

Parents and guardians are looking for advice about whether they should allow cross-dressing in public or how to protect a transgendered child from other children's cruelty (P. L. Brown, 2006). The prospect of kindergarten children attending school dressed as the other gender has inspired a philosophical debate among professionals over how best to advise families. Which is better for families—to support the child or to guide the child toward accepting his or her biological gender? In theory, the former course of action nurtures a sense of security and self-esteem; the latter course provides emotional, psychological, and physical security by protecting the child from potential abuse, humiliation, and isolation (Table 13.2).

CONTEXT/COMPONENTS	EXAMPLES
Physical environment	
• Setting	• Home
• Material artifacts	• Dress
• Geographic location	• U.S.
Social environment	
• Characteristics of enforcer	
▪ Statuses	▪ Parent/guardian
▪ Roles	▪ Responsibility for ensuring physical, emotional, spiritual, and psychological security of children
• Characteristics of violator	
▪ Statuses	▪ Transgendered child
▪ Roles	▪ Gender
• Relationship between enforcer and violator	
▪ Power	▪ Parent
▪ Prestige	▪ Parent
▪ Privileges	▪ Parent
• Occasion	• Social life in general
• Circumstances	• Gender norms for dress; stereotypes associated with cross-dressers
Temporal environment	
• Past	
▪ Enforcer	▪ Parents enforced sanctions related to gender norms for dress: sent violator to psychoanalysis and behavior modification
▪ Violator	▪ Expressed preference for dressing as other gender
• Present	
▪ Enforcer	▪ Insists on enforcement of sanctions or supports child's violation
▪ Violator	▪ Expressed preference for dressing as other gender
• Future	
▪ Enforcer	▪ Will continue to enforce sanctions until the child has left home?
▪ Violator	▪ Will continue to cross-dress? Will conform to norms for gender-appropriate dress?

ENFORCEMENT WITHIN THE SCHOOL CONTEXT

One of the most difficult problems facing high school administrators and teachers is determining how to consistently enforce sanctions in a way that encourages compliance with the dress code policy. Discipline is the practice of ensuring that students obey rules by teaching them to do so and punishing them if they do not comply.

FIGURE 13.5 THE
AUTHORITY OF SCHOOL OFFICIALS
TO ENFORCE SANCTIONS AGAINST
WEARING PROHIBITED ITEMS HAS
BEEN UPHELD IN THE COURTS
WHEN IT RELATES TO CONCERNS
ABOUT HEALTH, SAFETY, GANG
AFFILIATION, OR DISRUPTIONS TO
THE EDUCATIONAL PROCESS.

The most commonly used arguments in legal challenges to enforcement of sanctions for violations of school dress codes involve freedom of speech and freedom of religion ("Attire Must Express," 2007). Dress code policies often include regulations about body modifications, such as where and when body piercings can be displayed. Although it is possible for body piercing to communicate a religious, political, cultural, or sociological message, the more common reason for body piercing is individual expression. "Body piercings are not considered expressive conduct protected by the First Amendment unless the student intends for them to convey a particular message" (¶ 2).

A student's request for a court order that would allow her to display body piercings on her tongue, nasal septum, lip, navel, and chest at school was denied ("Attire Must Express," 2007). The school's dress code allowed students to wear pierced jewelry only in their ears. On the first day of school, a school administrator enforced the sanctions specified by the dress code by sending the student home after she refused to remove the body piercings. When the student violated the dress code a second time, sanctions of a disciplinary referral and four days of lunch detention were enforced. School officials had authority to enforce sanctions supporting the ban on wearing pierced body jewelry due to concerns related to health, safety, gang affiliation, or disruptions to the educational process (Figure 13.5). Attorneys recommended that religious beliefs requiring a student to wear pierced jewelry be accommodated with a process for requesting a religious exemption to enforcement of the sanction.

ENFORCEMENT WITHIN THE WORKPLACE CONTEXT

Recall from Chapter 3 that dress codes in the workplace are defended on the basis of the role of employees as representatives of the business. Employee dress affects not only the public's impression of the business, but also workplace morale. Enforcement of sanctions in the workplace is based on rational authority.

Inappropriate workplace dress can result in sanctions as mild as raised eyebrows or as severe as termination. Recruiters can enforce sanctions by making decisions about whether or not to hire a job candidate. For example, a woman interviewed for a job at a law firm dressed in a modest turquoise suit. She was not hired because the interviewer, on the basis of the eye-popping color of the suit, believed the woman did not seem serious enough and questioned her ability to make sensible decisions (Marshall, 2006). Another woman came to an interview wearing a short skirt and a low-cut blouse. She was hired because of her outgoing personality, but she had to make a special effort to overcome that initial first impression and be taken seriously.

When fulfilling job requirements in the workplace, employers can enforce sanctions by using reprimands. For example, in a simulated work environment—moot court—a law student wore a green pantsuit to make a legal argument in front of a panel of judges. One of the female judges on the panel criticized the student's choice of attire and said that she should have worn a skirt. Inappropriate dress can indicate arrogance, a lack of sensitivity to office culture, or a lack of experience (Figure 13.6). Regardless of the reason, people in a position of authority can enforce sanctions to encourage compliance with appropriate workplace attire.

FIGURE 13.6 WHEN FULFILLING JOB REQUIREMENTS IN THE WORKPLACE, EMPLOYERS CAN ENFORCE SANCTIONS FOR INAPPROPRIATE DRESS BY USING REPRIMANDS AND STRONGER TECHNIQUES. IN THIS CARTOON, DAGWOOD IS ABOUT TO FIND OUT HOW MR. DITHERS WILL REACT.

One woman related that she recently learned she was not approved for venture capital funding six years ago for a company she was building because she came to a meeting wearing a top that was considered too revealing (Smith, 2006b). Not being approved for funding is an unobtrusive sanction enforced by financiers who have the power to approve or disapprove requests for financial support. The woman was sensitized to the issue of appropriate dress in the workplace and now advises women entering the workforce to dress conservatively. Low-cut necklines are inappropriate because, in addition to being distracting to others, they do not send appropriate messages about the personal characteristics of the wearer—for example, credible, professional, serious, sensible, and reliable.

Recall from Chapter 3 that religion encourages social cohesion, maintains norms, provides emotional support, validates a group's beliefs and values, and transmits the religious heritage to the next generation (Hunt & Colander, 2005). Generally, religious groups have traditional authority to enforce sanctions for norms related to moral standards, including modesty.

Dress is an outward expression of how people view themselves. Many clergy as well as laypeople express their religious views by the way they dress. "Church leaders have endorsed modesty in dress as a Christian virtue for both women and men" (Rowbotham, 2006). There are two kinds of immodesty in dress: (a) sexually provocative dress—intended to arouse other people sexually, and (b) ostentatious dress—a vulgar display of wealth and success designed to impress people.

The High School Prom

A parochial school is a private school affiliated with a church that provides children with a general education as well as religious instruction. In parochial schools, the high school prom is an event that brings issues of modesty and immodesty to the forefront. The prom has been canceled at a number of high schools across the United States and replaced with alternate end-of-high-school celebrations. At one Catholic high school (KMHS), the prom was canceled because "[e]ach year the prom culture becomes more exaggerated, more expensive, more emotionally traumatic . . . . KMHS is willing to sponsor a prom, but not an orgy" (Belz, 2006, p. 102).

As with their future weddings, girls in the United States are taught explicitly or implicitly to anticipate the prom as a major event. Studies show that girls spend anywhere from $300 to $3,000 on the event (Belz, 2006), in a display of wealth designed to impress other people. Cancellation of the prom is a severe sanction enforced by authorities within the context of a religious educational environment to ensure that students do not engage in vulgar displays of wealth and success.

At another religion-affiliated high school, the prom was not canceled, but students' dresses were scrutinized by staff for modesty (Andersen, 2007). Many girls feel self-conscious and uncomfortable (internal sanctions) wearing revealing styles, but school officials use their authority to also enforce external sanctions to ensure modesty. One conservative dress code required girls' dresses to fall no lower than four finger-widths from the hollow of the neck, backs could be no lower than the shoulder blades, side and back slits could not come past a girl's fingertips when her arm was fully extended at her side, and midriffs needed to be fully covered.

One student thought she had found a modest dress, but school staff did not agree—they pinned a white cloth across her chest because the neckline on her dress was considered too low to be modest (Andersen, 2007). A second girl had napkinlike cloths pinned to her straps because the V-neck on her dress was too low. A third girl had the back of her dress pinned because it was an open-backed dress. A fourth girl who was well-endowed needed multiple pinnings of cloth to cover exposed skin.

A teacher said one year she was directed to remove tulle from the prom decorations and tuck it in girls' dresses where too much skin or cleavage was revealed. Tulle is a thin, stiff, net fabric of silk, nylon, or rayon that is used

FIGURE 13.7 STUDENTS IN PROM ATTIRE.

on ballet costumes, on evening dresses, and for veils. Another year, she was told to buy several yards of white broadcloth to be cut and pinned where needed. Broadcloth is a fine, closely woven cloth of wool, cotton, or silk with a shiny finish, used for clothing. School officials used their authority to enforce sanctions to ensure that immodest dress in the form of sexually provocative dress was not an issue at the prom (Figure 13.7).

Modesty

Modest dress focuses attention on substance rather than image (Cosco, 2006). According to a book of Catholic teachings, "purity requires modesty . . . modesty protects the intimate center of the person. It means refusing to unveil what should remain hidden" (¶ 9). However, the form of modest dress varies from one religion to another. To indicate religious belief, Orthodox Jewish women may wear long skirts, long-sleeved shirts, and avoid V-necked tops, and Muslim women may wear a *hijab*. Sanctions against use of these religious symbols would be contrary to the basic American values of freedom of religion and individualism.

However, in other countries, some Muslim women have experienced discrimination because of their religious dress (Monsen, 2006). In some European countries, government policies have restricted the wearing of religious garb in schools, offices, and other public places in an attempt to encourage

Muslims to blend in with their non-Muslim neighbors. One Muslim woman, born and raised in the United States, began wearing the *hijab* in the mid-1990s. Many of her relatives, including her parents, objected and tried to talk her out of it. She noted that she feels an obligation to smile or otherwise be friendly and approachable to non-Muslims so that they do not feel uneasy with her when they notice the *hijab*.

Bob Jones University, a Christian college and seminary, has banned all Abercrombie & Fitch and Hollister clothing because the retailer has "shown an unusual degree of antagonism to the name of Christ and an unusual display of wickedness in their promotions" (Bob Jones University, 2007). As a means of sanctioning the retailer, the university prohibits students from wearing, carrying, or displaying articles with the retailer's logos even if the logos are covered or masked. Other dress-related regulations for men include traditional, conservative hairstyles and no tattoos or body piercings. For women, tops must be long enough to cover the midriff, sleeves are required, necklines may come no lower than four fingers below the collarbone and skirts must cover at least the bottom of the knee.

ENFORCEMENT WITHIN THE GOVERNMENT CONTEXT

The context of government encompasses the legislative and judicial branches of the government at the local, state, and federal levels. At all these levels, there are laws concerning dress with associated sanctions. Underlying enforcement of the sanctions is the rational authority of the government.

In Utah, it is a misdemeanor to give a tattoo to anyone under the age of 18 without a parent's consent ("Tattoo Rules," 2006). However, the law appeared to be ignored and one legislator feels the sanctions need to be more severe. A bill introduced in the legislature would increase the severity of sanctions for unapproved tattooing of minors from a class C misdemeanor (3 months in jail; $750 fine) to a class B (6 months in jail; $1,000 fine). The ban on tattooing minors without parental consent is the only state law on the subject of tattoos. Health and safety regulations dealing with tattooing and body piercing exist at the local level, where boards of health have instituted them. For example, one county board of health has 13 pages of regulations that set out a protocol of cleanliness and inspection designed to fight the serious, even fatal, diseases that could be spread by sloppy body illustrators.

A city council debated requiring merchants to provide warning tags for furs ("Beverly Hills Considers," 1999). The tags would have read "Consumer notice: This product is made with fur from animals that may have been killed by electrocution, gassing, neck breaking, poisoning, clubbing, stomping or drowning and may have been trapped in steel-jaw leg-hold traps" (p. A6). The tags undoubtedly would be an effective sanction resulting in loss of sales to retailers.

In Idaho, a bill was introduced in the legislature that would impose more severe sanctions on gang members (Henderson, 2006). The bill specifically mentions gang fashions and tattoos as ways to identify gang members. Once identified as gang members, offenders could have as much as two years' extra time added on to their sentences. However, gang fashions sometimes become mainstream fashions, setting up first-time offenders to serve more time because they were wearing the wrong clothes at the wrong time.

In Massachusetts, a group of city councilors discussed a possible district-wide dress code in Boston city schools (Viser, 2006). Currently, each school in Boston has its own dress code. The councilors want to establish a standard dress code that prohibits hats, exposed midriffs, and pants with belt lines worn below the waist. One option is mandated uniforms, an easy policy to enforce and a relatively inexpensive alternative for parents. The city council does not have the authority to dictate a citywide dress code, but a resolution would pressure the School Committee, whose budget must be approved by the council. The superintendent did not believe a new policy was needed, but agreed there could be better enforcement of the current dress code.

ENFORCEMENT WITHIN THE COMMUNITY CONTEXT

The anonymous and impersonal nature of living in a densely populated society decreases the effectiveness of enforcing some sanctions (gossip and ridicule) except among friendship and kinship groups (Tischler, 2004). Informal sanctions are especially effective in encouraging conformity in smaller and personally important social groups, such as a close-knit family or a small community. The process of social control capitalizes on anticipation of evaluation by anonymous others—that is, public opinion. In a community context, many of the people present during any given social interaction will be strangers. Nevertheless, their evaluation of an individual's behavior carries weight.

Strangers may enforce sanctions ranging from mild (raised eyebrows, unsolicited advice, rude questions, remarks, laughter) to severe (calling the police) against inappropriate dress.

Public Nudity

Recently, a board of city officials discussed an antinudity ordinance introduced in response to a clothing-optional movement launched by local teenagers ("Vermont Town Skips Ordinance," 2006). Vermont has no state law against nudity, but at least eight local communities have ordinances that ban nudity. The public nature of naked teens in the heart of downtown Brattleboro raised a few eyebrows. One nudist told the town board the issue was freedom, an act of celebration of the history and traditional values as a place where people are allowed to be nude. A resident disagreed, stating that nudity was inappropriate behavior for downtown. The town manager said the town's image was tarnished by the uproar. "We have been the brunt of phone calls from all over the world. The media has made this into nothing less than a circus" (¶ 13).

A 75-year-old man called the Pekin nudist had been arrested at least a dozen times over a span of about twenty years ("Pekin Nudist," 1998). His neighbors complained to the police about him being outside in the nude. The man obviously was not concerned with what people would think, and formal sanctions, even though enforced, were not effective in deterring him from violating the norm of being covered in public.

Cross-Dressing

A woman wrote to an advice columnist in response to a column on cross-dressing (Landers, 1999). She reported that while cleaning out her dead husband's workshop, she found evidence that he had been a secret transvestite. She commented that she could not talk to anyone about this because her husband was prominent in the community, and she did not want to tarnish his good name. She would not let her children help clean out their father's things and remarked that she would rather die than have it known he had this weird side to him. The imagined opinions of community members and the fear of gossip were effective in keeping the norm violation secret both before and after the husband's death.

Golf Club and Restaurant Dress Codes

The Parks Commission of Brockton, Massachusetts, unanimously approved a new dress code requiring collared shirts and banning golfers from wearing jeans, cutoff shorts, T-shirts, sweatshirts, sweatpants, and boots (Schworm, 2006). Some players described the proposed dress code as too highbrow for a blue-collar town. Club and city officials responded that the stricter dress requirements would restore a modicum of decorum to a genteel game known as a model of propriety. Some golfers said the dress code confirmed the sport's snobbish, stuffy stereotypes. Others said proper golf attire shows respect for a storied, time-honored game with a long tradition (Figure 13.8). The course's golf pro remarked that players should not play golf dressed like construction workers with paint or plaster all over their clothes; some golfers had been hitting the links in clothes better suited for pickup basketball. Most golfers have been obliging, but a defiant few have refused to comply with the new dress code: one golfer wore jeans four times before officials refused to let him play.

FIGURE 13.8 MEN IN GOLF ATTIRE.

A group of co-workers visited a restaurant after work to see the recently renovated bar area, a place they frequented before its remodeling. When they arrived at the restaurant, they discovered there were new rules for patrons' appearance in the form of a dress code (Chase, 2006). The dress code specified that jeans, T-shirts, shorts, and sandals were not recommended. Several people in the group were in violation of the dress code. Their violation was unintentional, because they were unaware of the new dress requirements. The manager, who was dressed in a tuxedo, did not use the power of his position to enforce the dress code by refusing them entrance. However, one co-worker commented that their dress code violation was sanctioned through their seating assignment, which caused physical discomfort: "[A]t our corner booth, my feet were dangling a few inches above the floor, which temporarily cut off the flow of blood to my legs" (¶ 4).

After they were seated, the female waiter continued the sanctioning process by her attitude; she was "less than thrilled to serve [them] and didn't even flinch when she accidentally stabbed [one customer] with her fingernail" (¶ 7). The co-workers' response to the sanctions was covert (subtle) as they otherwise tried to conform to the new customs of a favorite restaurant. If and when they return to the restaurant, what do you predict they will wear? Will the sanctions be effective in enforcing the dress code?

Effectiveness of Sanctions

The ability to enforce a sanction determines its effectiveness. Effectiveness is defined as achieving a desired end result, in this case, conformity to a given norm. The "notion of effectiveness is vague to the point of defying a precise definition (let alone measurement)" (Gibbs, 1981, p. 166). It is difficult to provide evidence that enforcement of a given sanction promoted conformity to a particular norm.

Sanctions of various types (fines, detention, suspension) may be imposed on norm violators. Enforcement of the sanction (payment of the fine imposed, serving detention, serving in-school or out-of-school suspension) may be interpreted as paying for the violation.

FIGURE 13.9 Covering up an inappropriate T-shirt slogan with a jacket is an example of covert deviance.

Through the process of socialization, individuals learn what social norms are, learn to identify norm violations, become aware of how norm violations are reported, and learn to administer sanctions and respond appropriately to sanctions. Because of socialization, it is generally assumed that members of a society will respond to sanctions or the threat of sanctions by conforming. However, individuals actually respond to enforcement in two ways: conformity or deviance. Both conformity and deviance can be overt (directly observable; done openly and without any attempt at concealment) or covert (not intended to be known, seen, or found out) (Figure 13.9).

Conformity Response

Recall the man who was sentenced to seven days in jail for contempt of court for wearing an obscene T-shirt (Muir, 2003a). When he was released, he was interviewed by a local reporter (Muir, 2003c). The man stated that he learned a lesson from the experience—there are certain things you should not wear to court. He said that although he still has the shirt, he is not sure when, or if, he will wear it again. In commenting on the incident, the reporter acknowledged that many people have learned through experience that life's lessons sometimes come with a price attached (Muir, 2003b).

Sometimes the lessons involve sanctions such as money; other times, more severe sanctions are involved such as seven days in jail, loss of a week's wages, and a criminal record. Muir (2003b) pointed out that the judge had the authority to enforce the sanctions and provided a definition of **contempt of court:** "conduct calculated to embarrass, hinder or obstruct the court in its administration of justice or to derogate from its authority or dignity, thereby bringing administration of law into disrepute" (p. A4).

Deviance Response

Theoretically, violators resume their previous life in society or in school after paying for the violation. However, remedial training may be needed to enable the individual to assume a normal and acceptable place in society. Training can be an appropriate and effective response to violations, whether the violation was deliberate or due to ignorance of the norm. Recall from an earlier chapter the student who was convicted of harassment and fined $250 for wearing a Marilyn Manson T-shirt to a local festival. The student might have benefited from training because she was apparently not deterred by the fine. She was quoted as saying she planned to attend the festival the next year, had not decided what T-shirt she would wear, but she would make sure it made a statement (*Conviction Upheld*, 1999).

Because of the socialization process, individuals ought to anticipate there will be sanctions associated with dress norm violations. The threat of sanctions should act as an incentive to encourage conformity to dress norms. Indeed, at least one high school student decided it was time for a change in attitude and wardrobe after school officials warned students there would be stricter enforcement of the dress code in the upcoming school year (Fortin, 2006). The student had grown accustomed to weekly reprimands for violating the school dress code by wearing blouses that were too low-cut and shirts that exposed her midriff. As a result of increasing complaints from parents and school board members about inappropriately dressed students, school officials decided to intensify enforcement of sanctions for violations of the dress code.

Individuals must believe that sanctions actually will be a consequence for norm violations. Apparently, some students did not believe there would be any sanctions for their norm violations because 23 students were sanctioned for dress code violations during the first three weeks of school. A verbal warning was the initial sanction but subsequent violations incurred more severe sanctions, ranging from after-school detention to a one-day suspension. The principal remarked: "Usually the progressive consequences plan sends a message to the students, and they quickly abide by the rules" (Fortin, 2006, p. G1).

Sanctions operate on the basis of individuals' expectations, and when the expectations are not fulfilled, sanctions lose their power to encourage conformity (Tischler, 2004). To maintain their credibility and authority, school officials followed through with their warning of consequences.

ENFORCEMENT OF SANCTIONS AND CONTRADICTORY SUPPORT

Enforcement of sanctions is affected by whether there is any contradictory support. Every society develops supports to help individuals resist pressure to conform as well as to help them conform (Blake & Davis, 1964). School dress code policies are often challenged by parents as well as by the students. For example, after more than 100 parents challenged many details of a dress code, a school board modified it (Mathias, 2006). Parents telephoned and emailed the superintendent, criticized the board, and threatened to sue. There was standing room only at the school board meeting during which the dress code was discussed. Parents were vocal; the school board president often had to use the gavel to silence them when they interrupted someone who was speaking. Without parental support, it is difficult for school officials to enforce sanctions for dress code violations.

Sanctions are not so precisely synchronized (coordinated) with changing situations that it is always beneficial for individuals to respond by conforming. The process of social control is partially self-correcting in that a negative sanction enforced by one individual may be countered by a positive sanction enforced by another individual. Social approval and prescription of a behavior may exist in one context; disapproval and proscription of the identical behavior in another context. For example, a woman wrote to an advice columnist about negative reactions to her tattoos (Landers, 1998). She stated that people asked her stupid questions such as if the tattoos were real or if it hurt when she had them done. She remarked that not a single day went by without someone making a snide remark or asking a stupid question. Recall the research by Irwin (2003), who found that tattoo collectors received positive reinforcement from their friends who were also tattoo collectors. But in mainstream society, they received many negative sanctions.

SUMMARY

It should be clear that enforcement of sanctions is complex. It is difficult to predict whether a particular sanction will promote conformity to a given norm. This chapter has illustrated how the process of social control can be used to examine which sanctions are likely to be enforced. The influence of the social interaction context on enforcement of sanctions was clarified by giving examples of how norms are created, enforced, and changed through social interaction. Examples have revealed how characteristics of a norm, nature of a norm violation, recognition of a norm violation, report of a norm violation, and the nature of sanctions interact to affect the enforcement of sanctions.

KEY TERMS AND CONCEPTS

circumstances	sissy
contempt of court	social environment
occasion	temporal environment
physical environment	tomboy
setting	transgender

SUGGESTED READINGS

1. Nielsen, J. M., Walden, G., & Kunkel, C. A. (2000). Gendered heteronormativity: Empirical illustrations in everyday life. *Sociological Quarterly, 41*(2), 283–296.

2. Pitts, V. (1999). Body modification, self-mutilation, and agency in media accounts of a subculture. *Body & Society, 5,* 291–304.

3. Jones, D. C., Vigfusdottir, T. H., & Lee, Y. (2004). Body image and the appearance culture among adolescent girls and boys: An examination of friend conversations, peer criticism, appearance magazines, and the

internalization of appearance ideals. *Journal of Adolescent Research, 19*(3), 323–339.

Research Activity 13.1 Enforcing Court Attire Rules

Purpose: To identify and characterize who is responsible for enforcing sanctions for violations of rules of proper attire for court.

Procedure:
1. Review the concept of the social interaction context.
2. Use the Google (http://google.com) search engine to locate and print an article that details the rules for proper attire for a court appearance and the sanctions for not complying with the rules. For example, you may use the key words *court dress rules, enforcement,* or *sanctions.*
3. Highlight and label the rules, sanctions, and who is responsible for enforcing the rules.
4. Submit your work to your instructor.

Research Activity 13.2 Enforcing Workplace Dress Codes

Purpose: To identify and characterize who is responsible for enforcing sanctions for violations of dress code rules at work.

Procedure:
1. Review the concept of the social interaction context.
2. Use the Google (http://google.com) search engine to locate and print an article that details the dress code guidelines for work. For example, you might use the key word *employee dress codes* to search for articles.
3. Highlight and label the rules, sanctions, and who is responsible for enforcing the rules.
4. Submit your work to your instructor.

Chapter Fourteen
_____

RESEARCH ABOUT
ENFORCEMENT OF SANCTIONS

FROM THE HEADLINES

"The body . . . à la Elle Macpherson . . . or the mannequin dummy in the shop window—which measurements best represent real people?" (¶ 1). A group of experts held a workshop on body shapes and sizes to answer that question. The World Engineering Anthropometry Resource (WEAR) group analyzes data on the human body. Clothing sizing is the most common use of the data, but "the data helps designers, engineers, and companies fit clothing, furniture, technology, and buildings for people" (¶ 4). The group collects data in 10 countries from 3-dimensional body scans and adjusts it for varying weights, sizes, and ages. Clients include The Gap, which uses the data for clothing sizing, and the U.S. Air Force, which uses the data for military body armor.

Nearly 90 percent of 5,000 survey respondents found shopping for clothing difficult. In particular, finding dresses that fit was the biggest problem followed by differing sizes according to style and brand. Tall women found it especially difficult to buy women's clothing and sometimes resorted to menswear; petite women sometimes shopped in the children's department. "Shopping has become time-consuming for women who have to try on everything . . . to find something to wear" (¶ 14). The data have potential to help designers develop clothing sizes that match trends in body sizes.

Source: Cardy, T. (2007, January 29). Body experts to discuss people's measurements. AAP Newsfeed. Retrieved April 6, 2007, from http://www.lexisnexis.com

This news story addresses the power of certain societal structures to enforce sanctions. For example, a group of experts met to discuss sizing data—data that will be used to determine standardized clothing sizes. Consumers whose body measurements do not fall within the normative standards may feel they are being sanctioned because of their size. Enforcement of sanctions is illustrated in the results of a shopper survey showing that only about 10 percent of people have no complaints about standardized sizing.

To which body modifications and/or body supplements does enforcement of the sanctions relate? Why? What other research methods could be used to study enforcement of the sanctions studied by the WEAR group? In this chapter, you will read about different methods of enforcing sanctions as well as gain an understanding of the forces that operate to enforce sanctions.

This chapter examines research related to body modifications and body supplements that encompasses the whole process of social control, ending with enforcement of sanctions (see Figure 13.1). The methods and tools used in each research study are summarized in Table 14.1. We will see how norms,

TABLE 14.1 SUMMARY OF RESEARCH METHODS AND TOOLS RELATED TO ENFORCEMENT OF RESPONSE TO NORM VIOLATION

RESEARCH METHOD	TOOL(S)	AUTHOR(S)	YEAR	ARTICLE TITLE
Qualitative	Interview worksheet	Elliott & Leonard	2004	Peer pressure and poverty: Exploring fashion brands and consumption symbolism among children of the "British poor"
Qualitative	Interview worksheet	Fuller & Groce	1991	Obese women's responses to appearance norms
Qualitative	Interview worksheet	Gagne & McGaughey	2002	Designing women: Cultural hegemony and the exercise of power among women who have undergone elective mammoplasty
Qualitative	Observation worksheet	Garot & Katz	2003	Provocative looks: Gang appearance and dress codes in an inner-city alternative school
Qualitative	Interview worksheet	Heckert	2003	Mixed blessings: Women and blonde hair
Qualitative	Interview worksheet Observation	Huisman & Hondagneu-Sotelo	2005	Dress matters: Change and continuity in the dress practices of Bosnian Muslim refugee women
Qualitative	Interview worksheet	Hurd	2000	Older women's body image and embodied experience: An exploration
Mixed methods	Survey and interview worksheet	Ross & Harradine	2004	I'm not wearing that! Branding and young children
Qualitative	Interview worksheet	Wooten	2006	From labeling possessions to possessing labels: Ridicule and socialization among adolescents

norm violations, recognition of norm violations, reports of norm violations, and sanctions interact to affect enforcement. Some concrete examples of the ways in which social control actually works as revealed in academic research studies will illustrate these concepts. As you read these research studies, look for the steps in the process of social control: norms, violation of norms, recognition of violation, report of violation, response to violation, and enforcement of response.

Attempts to enforce sanctions in everyday life are revealed in a number of ways:

▼ Feelings of pressure to conform
   a. **Peer pressure**, that is, social pressure on somebody to adopt a particular type of behavior, dress, or attitude in order to be accepted as part of a group
   b. Internalization, that is, acceptance of the beliefs, values, and attitudes of others. Recall from Chapter 5 that internalization results in a norm becoming part of an individual's motivational system so that the individual feels internal pressure to conform.
▼ Efforts by violators to comply with the norm (dieting, cosmetic surgery, dyeing hair)
▼ Complaints about enforcement or nonenforcement (by students, school officials, parents, or others)
▼ Active efforts to resist enforcement (shift priorities, redefine the norm)
▼ **Complacency**—that is, self-satisfied response, usually without thinking and without awareness of possible consequences (ignore attempts to enforce sanctions).

QUESTIONS TO ANSWER AS YOU READ

1. How does the enforcement of sanctions relate to the process of social control?
2. What is the nature of research related to the enforcement of sanctions?
3. What research methods are used to investigate the enforcement of sanctions?

4. What tools are used to collect data for research about the enforcement of sanctions?

BODY MODIFICATIONS

Dress as we have defined it includes body modifications as well as body supplements. Recall from Chapter 1 that body modifications are alterations to the body itself and that the modifications can be temporary (weight loss, age), semipermanent (hair color), or permanent (breast augmentation) (Eicher, Evenson, & Lutz, 2000). Efforts to enforce sanctions related to the normative body can encourage individuals to undertake temporary, semipermanent, and/or permanent modifications of the body.

TEMPORARY MODIFICATIONS

Temporary modifications such as weight and age are alterations that change over time and the life span.

Temporary Modification: Weight Loss

Obesity is nonconformity with societal expectations, and thus is a norm violation (Fuller & Groce, 1991). Indeed, some definitions of obesity refer to *normal* weight by defining obesity as weighing a certain percentage more than normal (20 percent above the normal weight set up by medical and/or insurance height/weight tables). In a variety of ways, obese women are negatively defined by their weight, are judged as responsible for their obesity, and deterred from social interaction with those of normal weight. Obese women experience sanctions such as finger-pointing, shame, and ridicule.

Fuller and Groce (1991) interviewed 15 obese women using open-ended questions to allow the women to use their own words to describe their experiences as obese women. All of the women had experienced negative sanctions during childhood related to their obesity, such as being teased, ridiculed, criticized, rebuked, ostracized, alienated, called names, and given nicknames. The women felt upset, angry, resentful, frustrated, lonely, and stigmatized. The power of the social control process (Table 14.2) was reflected in the fact that these

TABLE 14.2 THE PROCESS OF SOCIAL CONTROL: OBESITY

SOCIAL CONTROL PROCESS STEP	EXAMPLES*
1. Norm	Normal weight for height
2. Violation of norm	Weighing 20% more than normal weight for height
3. Recognition of violation of norm	Who: parents, peers, medical professionals, insurance executives What: salient, visible When: interacting with family members, visit to doctor, meeting with insurance agent, encountering people in everyday life Where: home, school, work Why: fear, uncertainty
4. Reports of norm violation	Oral method: conversation and gossip
5. Sanctions	Childhood: ostracized, alienated, given nicknames, teased Adulthood: finger-pointing, shame, ridicule
6. Enforcement of sanction(s)	Internalization of appearance standards External pressure to conform

*Examples are derived from Fuller and Groce (1991).

women had internalized cultural appearance norms and were also subjected to the external sanctions of significant others.

Excess weight is the most salient physical characteristic of obese women, and violation of the appearance norm is immediately apparent to others. Some of the women indicated that they were not consciously aware of how large they were until they saw a reflection in a mirror or a picture of themselves (Fuller & Groce, 1991). Some of the women expressed low self-esteem by describing themselves as overweight, ugly, guilty, depressed, or stupid; these women still tried to conform to the norm by dieting. Some of the women expressed high self-esteem by noting that they felt good about themselves; these women described themselves as obese. Their self-esteem came from their educational and professional accomplishments.

Fuller and Groce (1991) stated that as children, these women "were ostracized and alienated simply because their developing bodies were of a different size and shape from what in our culture the majority of people define as 'normal'" (p. 172). However, attempts to enforce the negative sanctions did not result in consistent responses across respondents. The women who internalized most strongly the appearance norms from which they deviated had negative self-images and low self-esteem. By contrast, the women who had dissociated themselves from cultural standards of appearance found satisfaction through activities and accomplishments and had positive self-images and high self-esteem. These two groups represent **acquiescence** (compliance or conformity) and **resistance** to (refusal to accept) enforcement of sanctions associated with cultural definitions of normal appearance.

Temporary Modification: Age

Hurd (2000) interviewed 22 women aged 61 to 92 regarding their perceptions and feelings about their aging bodies. Because beauty is seen as synonymous with youthfulness and thinness in U.S. society, older women are challenged to construct and maintain positive evaluations of the self (Figure 14.1). The women in the study showed signs of internalization of ageist beauty norms even though they said that health was more important than physical attractiveness and that aging was natural.

Little is known about how older women cope with the aging process and its effects on body image (perceptions of and feelings about their bodies), embodied experiences (their lived experiences in their bodies), or the relationship between identity and body image (Hurd, 2000). **Embodied** refers to giving a tangible or visible form to something abstract, such as a personal or social identity. Older women are at a disadvantage in efforts to conform to cultural standards of physical attractiveness because of the cultural beauty ideal and because of a double standard of aging: physical signs of aging are judged more harshly in women than in men.

Body image has been defined as "a multidimensional self-attitude toward one's body, particularly its size, shape, and aesthetics" (Cash, Ancis, & Strachan, 1997, p. 433). Body image includes a perceptual component—how we perceive our bodies—and an attitudinal component—how we feel about our bodies (Slade, 1994). According to Slade, body image is created by interaction among an individual's personal history, attitudes and feelings regarding body weight and shape, cultural and social norms, and psychological and biological factors. Because of the interaction of these factors, a

FIGURE 14.1 OLDER WOMEN ARE CHALLENGED TO CONSTRUCT AND MAINTAIN POSITIVE SELF-EVALUATIONS, BECAUSE BEAUTY IS SEEN AS SYNONYMOUS WITH YOUTHFULNESS AND THINNESS. THE ADS FOR THESE PRODUCTS SHOW THE PROCESS OF SOCIAL CONTROL.

woman's body image changes throughout her life span. With declining health and physical abilities, older women might value physical function more than physical attractiveness. Some research indicates that appearance continues to be important to older women, although not as important as it was when they were younger.

Weight is one issue that concerns women of all ages. It is normal for women to gain weight as they age (Chirsler & Ghiz, 1993), so it is reasonable to assume that older women will be concerned about weight gain. Indeed, in a longitudinal study (a study encompassing a number of years) of elderly people, women's second greatest concern, following memory loss, was change in body weight (Rodin, Silberstein, & Striegel-Moore, 1984). Elderly men did not express concern with weight changes.

Hurd (2000) examined how older women cope with the inevitable weight gain experienced by most older women, along with the difficulty of losing weight, particularly as functional abilities and activity levels decline. The realities of an aging body are evidenced by sagging skin, wrinkles, increased fat deposits, loss of elasticity, and declining physical abilities. When older women internalize the cultural norms of physical attractiveness, it becomes a challenge to maintain positive body-image and self-esteem.

The women Hurd interviewed had internalized the cultural beauty norm, as evidenced by their descriptions of an older woman's body as well as descriptions of their own bodies: "ugly," "sagging," "yuck," "a disaster," and "awful." The women discounted the possibility of aging bodies as attractive and/or desirable and expressed feelings of dissatisfaction and loss with their physical selves. Many of the women (82 percent) accepted the loss of physical beauty as unavoidable, part of a natural aging process, and outside of their control. Most of the women expressed negative attitudes toward their appearance, but stressed the importance of being healthy and independent, the triviality of emphasizing appearance, and the importance of good health over physical attractiveness. Many of the older women expressed a sense of loss about what their aging bodies could do—for example, loss of health, mobility, and energy.

The women noted that current fashions and fashion models represented extreme and unattractive role models for younger women, but that they themselves were not influenced by cultural norms for weight and fashion trends (Hurd, 2000). Weight gain was the cause of much self-criticism and monitoring. Many of the women had internalized cultural beliefs that weight gain and fatness indicate moral failure or lack of discipline and that weight, in contrast to wrinkles and sagging body parts, was due to personal choices and responsibility. All of the women interviewed expressed concern about their weight—wanting to lose weight and/or trying to maintain current or past weight. They expressed negative sentiments about their weight and most indicated they had dieted.

Resistance to enforcement of sanctions was evidenced by a shift in priorities so that health (freedom from disease, chronic illness, and declining energy) and function were considered more important than physical attractiveness (Hurd, 2000). Some women noted that healthy people were attractive people, indicating that physical attractiveness may be redefined in later life. The women acknowledged the inevitability of the natural life cycle and the changes that accompany the aging process. The contradiction between older women's stated rejection of cultural beauty norms and their negative body images raises the question: If older women do not aspire to cultural beauty norms, why are their body images not more positive?

SEMIPERMANENT AND PERMANENT MODIFICATIONS

Semipermanent and permanent modifications include hair color and elective mammoplasty.

Semipermanent Modification: Hair Color

Heckert (2003) interviewed naturally blonde women to determine their experiences with being blonde. Only 16 percent of U.S. females are born naturally blonde (Loftus, 2000) and only 5 percent remain naturally blonde as adults (Synott, 1987). Brown hair is the norm.

Heckert (2003) described blonde women as both positive and negative deviants. **Positive deviance** was described as a violation of the norm in "behaviors or conditions that both overconform to the norms and are positively appraised" (p. 47). **Negative deviance** was defined as a violation of the norm in "behaviors or conditions that underconform, or fail to conform, to normative expectations and subsequently receive negative evaluations" (p. 47). Blonde women are positive deviants because they receive positive evaluations for exceeding normative appearance expectations; however, they are also negative deviants because they receive negative evaluations and negative treatment (Figure 14.2).

Heckert (2003) asked 20 blonde women about: their experiences of being blonde as a child, adolescent, and adult; blonde stereotypes; positive and negative aspects of being blonde; cultural definition of attractiveness of hair; reactions of men and women to blonde hair; positive and negative consequences of blonde hair; commonality with other blonde women; and their overall reaction to blonde hair. Heckert concluded that blondes have a cultural advantage in relation to definitions of attractiveness because blonde hair has long been a beauty standard in Western culture. Blonde women are disproportionately represented in appearance-based occupations such as models, actresses, and other entertainers.

FIGURE 14.2 BLONDE WOMEN ARE POSITIVE DEVIANTS BECAUSE THEY EXCEED NORMATIVE APPEARANCE EXPECTATIONS, ALTHOUGH THERE ARE ALSO NEGATIVE SANCTIONS ASSOCIATED WITH BEING BLONDE.

Positive attention and positive treatment were common experiences for the blonde women Heckert interviewed. Cultural stereotypes applied to blonde women included innocence (depicted as angels, saints, princesses, or fairies), sexy/fun ("blondes have more fun," "blonde bombshell"), easy ("sex kitten"), and dumb ("dumb blonde," "ditzy blonde"). The women described strategies they used to cope with the stereotype of the dumb blonde. For example, they ignored the remarks or returned the joke, acted out the role of the dumb blonde, overcompensated or concealed any characteristics associated with the label of dumb blonde, fought back by attempting to demonstrate their intelligence through subtle or confrontational means, and became a member of the dominant group (by dyeing or cutting their hair or wearing glasses). Blonde women felt that their relationships with other women were negatively affected by jealousy of their attractiveness and hair color.

Permanent Modification: Elective Mammoplasty

Gagne and McGaughey (2002) conducted in-depth, semistructured interviews with 15 women who had undergone **elective mammoplasty** (breast augmentation, breast reduction, or corrective surgery on the breasts). All of the women wanted to achieve a level of normalcy. Their understanding of the norm came from a variety of sources, including ideals generated by the media and fashion, their own observations of other women, and their own perceptions of men's observations of themselves and other women (Figure 14.3).

Perceptions of physical abnormality, combined with a self-concept that did

FIGURE 14.3 WOMEN WHO UNDERGO ELECTIVE MAMMOPLASTY DO SO TO HAVE A NORMAL APPEARANCE. THIS WOMAN USED IMPLANTS TO CHANGE HER APPEARANCE TO FOLLOW THE NORM.

not include physical abnormalities, motivated the women to seek elective mammoplasty. Some of the women were very distressed about their appearance. "I was always a flat-chested, redheaded, freckle-faced kid and was teased a lot about being flat" (Gagne & McGaughey, p. 822). Age was also a motivational factor. Every woman interviewed had a self-concept or an idealized self that was not represented by her body—for example, "I had several people say to me, . . . you're not fat. You just have big boobs. They make you look matronly" (p. 822).

Cosmetic surgery was perceived as a means of establishing congruency between the body and mind or developing an embodied self that was comfortable. One woman explained that before her surgery, people would stare or *talk to* her breasts. She said that since her surgery people pay attention to her and not a part of her body. Women explained that undergoing mammoplasty was important because it prompted people to treat them in the way they perceived themselves. With more positive reactions from others, their self-confidence increased, and many said they felt liberated.

Because one's body affects the reactions one receives from others, changing one's body to fit ideals of attractiveness has the potential to improve social opportunities. Some women were ignored by men while their friends received more attention. Having men pay attention to them was one way they could be seen in the manner they desired, achieve the reactions they desired, and measure their desirability.

Surgically altering their appearance had improved their lives: "I work for a very image-conscious company. They want you to look a certain way, talk a certain way, dress a certain way . . . they hire very attractive people. . . . Once you get hired on, they look at what you wear, your nails, your hair, how you speak, how you come off. Because they have an image they want to project" (Gagne & McGaughey, p. 824). Another woman explained, "I am conscious of the way I look. I hold a public job, and as I get older, I have to look good because you're in competition with these pretty young things" (p. 824). After mammoplasty, these women felt they commanded greater respect and were better able to compete in a job market that favored youth.

The main difference between mammoplasty and using clothing or bras to disguise or enhance breasts was that breast surgery was a more permanent choice. Permanence gave women more fashion options and greater control over their clothing choices. These women had internalized society's standards of beauty.

The embodied self these women chose to construct was based on a norm that is inherently ageist—a look that signified youthful sexual vitality. The practice of cosmetic surgery perpetuates racism and classism as well as ageism because only a minority—generally white, economically privileged women—have the means to have surgery and because the ideal of feminine beauty is essentially a white standard.

All of the women emphasized that they did not feel coerced, cajoled, or otherwise forced to have surgery. Cosmetic surgery was seen as a beauty secret employed by women with the means to pay for it. In most cases, family members and partners tried to convince the women not to have surgery. The women thought of cosmetic surgery as a normal part of the culture and technology of beauty in the United States.

Social factors influenced the women's ideas about beauty and their decision to have surgery. The media, particularly women's magazines, provided the most obvious messages about what it means to be beautiful and desirable. The influence of the media was apparent in the narratives of the women interviewed. Referring to *Cosmopolitan* magazine, one woman remarked that she was sure that, subconsciously, the images influenced her decision to have bigger breasts. Perhaps more encompassing than print media is the impact that movies and television programs have on women's ideas of the social adequacy of their bodies. Even when they knew the images of women in the media were not representative of the way those women would look without surgery, body doubles, and alterations to photography, the women still compared themselves to what they perceived as the ideal and sought ways to embody it.

The fashion industry played a role in women's initial dissatisfaction with, and subsequent appreciation of, their bodies and breasts. The fashion industry, like the media, is geared toward making profits. To do so, it mass-produces clothing for what is perceived as normal-sized humans so the maximum number of sales will result. For women, the norm of fashion is thin and proportionate and women who are overweight, tall, big-boned, or whose hips are wider or narrower than their bust sizes find it difficult to dress fashionably or even to find clothing that fits properly. And in not being able to find fashions that fit, many women blame themselves for not disciplining their bodies. Through sizing, the fashion industry sets a norm for women's bodies.

Most of the women talked about how their too small or too large breasts made it impossible to wear certain styles. Before their surgeries, women used bras to maximize, minimize, or otherwise alter the shape and size of their breasts. Moreover, they used techniques to draw attention to or away from their breasts or toward other parts of their bodies that they thought were more attractive. One woman, who thought her breasts were too small, tended to wear crop-top T-shirts and, as she referred to it, "big hair" in an effort to draw the viewer's eyes upward toward her face or downward toward her abdomen, which she thought was attractive. Whether they thought their breasts were too small, too large, too saggy, or too deformed, all of the women interviewed wore oversize blouses, T-shirts, and sweatshirts to disguise their breasts, but none thought that clothing offered an acceptable solution to their problem.

After their surgeries, most women changed their wardrobes, partly to accommodate the changed proportions of their bodies but also to include items they had longed to wear but felt they could not. One woman who had breast augmentation said, "I pretty much changed my wardrobe. I wore the tighter tops, the tank tops . . . I really went for the cleavage look tops . . . more form fitting" (Gagne & McGaughey, p. 831). A woman who had breast reduction surgery said, "It's just been wonderful for me. I feel I can buy a shirt and it buttons" (p. 831).

Enforcement of the cultural norm of beauty was exercised less in one-on-one interactions wherein a significant other expressed dissatisfaction with a specific woman's beauty than with women's internalization of the norm. In making the decision to have cosmetic surgery, women were more often influenced by other women than by men. Knowing someone who actually had surgery, or was about to do so, made mammoplasty seem less radical and more like a reasonable solution to a problem over which they had only temporary control (with padded bras and Wonderbras).

The **hegemonic gaze** is a sense that individual women have that everyone is looking at them and the discomfort they feel if they fail to meet the cultural beauty norm. After surgery, these women were liberated from the gaze because they conformed to societal expectations.

BODY SUPPLEMENTS

Dress includes body supplements as well as body modifications (Eicher, Evenson, & Lutz, 2000). Efforts to enforce sanctions related to normative body supplements can be found in many contexts in everyday life. Recall from Chapter 1 that body supplements are items placed on the body. This can be done by

- ▼ wrapping the item around the body (belts, headscarves)
- ▼ suspending the item from the body (sunglasses)
- ▼ wearing preshaped items (athletic shoes)
- ▼ inserting the items into the body (piercing jewelry)
- ▼ clipping the item to the body (hair clips)
- ▼ adhering the item to the body (temporary tattoos)
- ▼ holding or carrying the item (backpacks, purses)

Dress almost always has ambiguous meanings; indeed, ambiguity is an important element of the messages sent by fashion. **Ambiguity** refers to a message that can be understood in more than one way; it is not clear which meaning is intended (Figure 14.4). Incorrect interpretation of a fashion message is always a possibility because the aesthetic code is a combination of aesthetic rules, social rules, and cultural customs regarding dress.

F I G U R E 1 4 . 4 Dress
sends ambiguous messages—
messages that can be understood in more than one way,
like the clothing chosen by
this man.

Enforcement of Dress Norms in a School Context

Ambiguity can cause confusion or uncertainty. Garot and Katz (2003) stated that, in a school context, the uncertainty caused by ambiguous dress meanings is revealed in

- ▼ efforts to keep school regulations current with changing styles
- ▼ inconsistency in enforcing rules
- ▼ conformity with the letter but not the spirit of the rules
- ▼ the use of dress to deliberately cause a reaction in others
- ▼ the use of dress to demonstrate group affiliation
- ▼ a deliberate failure to understand the meaning of dress symbols in spite of knowing that misinterpretation is likely to injure somebody physically, mentally, or morally
- ▼ the presumption that the meanings of dress are completely clear
- ▼ the fact that the meanings of dress are context-dependent

Enforcement by Peers

Wooten (2006) used semistructured interviews with 43 young adults (aged 18–23 years) to examine the use of ridicule as a means of communicating and enforcing consumption norms and values among adolescents in a school context. (For additional information about this study, refer to Chapters 10 and 12.) Peer pressure as expressed in ridicule was used to belittle and exclude those who did not fit in with the group. Adolescents responded to ridicule in several ways: (a) doing nothing about stigmatized objects, (b) concealing stigmatized objects, (c) more closely watching what their peers wore, (d) seeking safe havens, (e) defending unpopular choices, or (f) adopting popular objects. For example, some adolescents who continued wearing unpopular brands of clothing attempted to defend their unpopular choices and sought out others who shared their preferences.

Other adolescents tried to conceal the stigmatized objects (by turning their shirts inside-out) or began watching their peers more closely to determine the norm. Others conformed by adopting the popular objects but sometimes found their efforts thwarted by parental restrictions, monetary limits, and changing fashions. Those who could not afford to purchase the popular objects endured the consequences of wearing unpopular items, and some actually changed schools to find a safe haven from the ridicule.

Wooten (2006) concluded that observing or experiencing ridicule influenced adolescents' purchase, use, and discard of possessions. Both targets of ridicule and bystanders learned which items (brands, styles, and stores) were associated with **avoidance groups** (groups to stay away from). Targets of ridicule learned the norms of **aspirational groups** (groups of which one would like to become a member) and the social costs of nonconformity. Feelings of inadequacy and concerns about belonging were reasons they chose to conform to the norms.

Attitudes Toward Branded Athletic Shoes
Elliott and Leonard (2004) examined attitudes toward fashion brands of athletic shoes and their symbolic meanings among a sample of 30 children aged 8 to 12 years from poor homes. The children had stereotypes about the owners of athletic shoes; if the shoes were an expensive brand, the children believed the owner was young and rich; if the shoes were inexpensive, unbranded shoes, the children believed the owner was old and poor. If a child wore branded athletic shoes, he or she was believed to be popular and to fit in with peers; indeed, these beliefs were so strong that the children preferred to talk to someone wearing branded athletic shoes. Attempts to enforce sanctions

were revealed in the peer pressure children felt to wear the athletic shoes their friends wore, partly to make friends and fit in and partly to avoid the teasing experienced by those wearing unbranded shoes (Figure 14.5).

Probably the strongest influence on children is their peer group (Pilgrim & Lawrence, 2001). Peer group influence starts as early as six years old (McNeal, 1987). Peer group influence becomes more important during adolescence, when youths become aware of their peers' favorite products and consider those preferences when making their own consumer choices, especially choices about symbolic consumer products such as dress.

Children feared that their peers would refuse to be friends with them, or would bully them, if they did not fit in with the group by wearing the same fashionable brand of athletic shoes. Almost all of the children interviewed said they owned branded athletic shoes—some worn until ripped and frayed. One interviewee remarked "my best friends wear [athletic shoes] that I like" (Elliott & Leonard, 2004, p. 355). Peer pressure seemed to convince many of the children that they needed branded athletic shoes to fit in with their friends and the popular children at school.

Sanctions included harassing someone with manky (dirty, greasy, or otherwise unpleasant) athletic shoes and the threat of being beaten up because of not being a member of the *in crowd*—a group one could not join without the appropriate footwear (Elliott & Leonard, 2004). Most of the children were either the victims or the potential perpetrators of bullying. One boy said he

FIGURE 14.5 HERE BASKETBALL PLAYER LEBRON JAMES ADVERTISES NIKE SHOES.

would be unwilling to let someone in *granny shoes* join in his football game. Some of the children seemed to want to wear branded athletic shoes as a defense mechanism. One girl said she did not believe that anyone should have to wear branded athletic shoes, but she wore them to prevent other children from picking on her.

Most of the children interviewed had experienced the pressure to wear fashionable clothing. Children seemed to be targeted for bullying based on their clothing and financial situation, and many of the children chose their footwear accordingly. Many of the children said they would not talk to someone, and they would be embarrassed to be seen with someone, who was wearing unfashionable shoes.

Children wanted to own the branded athletic shoes their peers did in order to have equal status in the eyes of their friends (Elliott & Leonard, 2004). The children who owned branded athletic shoes had referent power, as revealed by the admiration of their peers and attempts of others to imitate them. The symbolic meaning of branded athletic shoes appeared to be that of a fashionable and popular person. The children felt that, by wearing branded athletic shoes, they were saying that they were fashionable, popular, and equal to their peers.

Brand-Name Awareness

Ross and Harradine (2004) investigated children's awareness of brand names. One objective was to determine the degree of brand awareness within different age groups. "But ultimately the playground also remains the prime location for brand awareness to be seen in. Advertisers know this all too well. If you have the wrong type of training shoes then you are excluded . . . The thing about kids is, yes, they are keen to be individuals, but there is nothing worse than not being the right type of individual who is included in the group" (Novakovich, 1999, pp. 8–9). Brand awareness is the ability to identify the brand under different conditions and included brand recognition and brand recall (Keller, 1998). Brand recognition required an individual to correctly identify a brand as being previously seen or heard. Brand recall required the ability to retrieve the brand from memory when provided with a cue (Keller, 1998).

Children become aware of brands at an early age; all of the five- and six-year-old children were aware of branded sportswear and claimed to have been aware for a long time (Ross & Harradine, 2004). Compared with younger age groups, 9- to 11-year-old children had a more sophisticated level of awareness. For example, they said they could tell the difference between counterfeit brands and the real thing. The children agreed that they would rather have a counterfeit product that looked like the real brand than a product that was unbranded. The children said that if they wore a less prestigious brand their peers might laugh at them or leave them out. The children believed that well-known brands made them feel cool, older, and provided conformity with their peer groups so they wouldn't be left out.

Although they were influenced by their peers, particularly popular peers, the children believed that brands helped them stand out from the crowd and be different (Ross & Harradine, 2004) (Figure 14.6). Individuality was achieved, however, within fairly narrow constraints (wearing a different version of an acceptable brand). Some children were motivated by the need to belong, while others saw the brand as a status symbol. The children said that people were more likely to notice branded garments than branded footwear, and therefore branded garments were more important. The older age groups mentioned the need to conform or for others to recognize the brand as key factors in their clothing choices.

"Put on your sandals, Otis! Your lights are detracting from the Star of Bethlehem!"

FIGURE 14.6 CHILDREN RECEIVE PEER PRESSURE TO WEAR FASHIONABLE ITEMS LIKE SHOES THAT LIGHT UP WHEN THE WEARER MOVES.

ENFORCEMENT OF DRESS NORMS BY SCHOOL OFFICIALS

By enforcing dress codes, school officials are trying to prohibit an embodied way of being (Garot & Katz, 2003). The constantly evolving character of student appearance shows that it is a central youth concern. By devoting as much time, energy, and thought to their dress as they do, students implicitly declare the significance of subtle details that adults do not even observe. The variety and innovativeness of student appearance make enforcement of dress codes a matter of scrutinizing the body from top (caps, hats, and hairstyles) to bottom (footwear) and of regulating the appearance of everything from ears to derrieres.

The students observed by Garot and Katz seemed interested in drawing attention to every part of the body that can be changed: hair, face, eyebrows, nose, lips, tongue, ears, rear ends, abdomen, breasts, chests, shoulders, legs, and feet. The problem for school authorities is that the creative appearance derives from youth culture, which evolves and celebrates a self-regulating logic not dependent on school concerns. Some of the employees interviewed by Garot and Katz argued that the rules should be more detailed and thorough and more consistently enforced. However, even if rules for every detail of student dress could be stated explicitly and enforced, it would not deter a student who is trying to create an identity.

The dress code and its enforcement were common sources of conversation among school employees, who rarely knew what student dress signified. They instinctively responded with fear when they unexpectedly met a student who looked defiant. To overcome that fear, school employees exerted their authority by enforcing rules about dress in an attempt to have something tangible to regulate. One point of discussion among school employees was the issue of power and the notion that young people must obey their elders and must obey the rules.

Students received an introduction to the dress code rules at orientation. An administrator went over the rules, which consisted primarily of prohibited items, especially items that might be perceived as indicating gang affiliation (no colored shoe strings, no sagging pants, no hats or earrings, no sports logo on shirts, no BK or CK tennis shoes, no sunglasses, no belts with letters or colors). During orientation, the administrator read the list of prohibited items.

Sometimes, principals announced dress code rules over the public address system or teachers announced the rules to their classes. Sometimes the rules were treated as superficial both by students and school employees. In such cases, signs and announcements concerning the dress code might be dismissed, making it clear that the rules did not apply or were not important.

On occasion, enforcement of a dress code emerged out of current interactions; for example, if a student was acting rebellious or obstinate, then the dress code might become an issue. In this way, enforcement of the dress code could be used to try to suppress disorderly behavior or convert it into more acceptable conduct.

Everyone was involved in enforcement of dress code rules at most schools: teachers and administrators, students, parents, and any adults present. Some students seemed to enjoy using the rules to reprimand other students. Enforcement of the dress code implied character traits of the enforcer in terms of their feelings, sensibility, kindness, or meanness. Despite all the strategies used by school authorities, students violated the dress code on a daily basis. There were many opportunities for enforcement, or for making exceptions.

When teachers, staff, and administrators do not enforce the rules, nonenforcement will be noted by their peers and by other students.

Dress codes affect the culture of the school when rules are enforced, when exceptions are granted, and when uncertainties are debated. Uncertainties are a recurrent part of dress code enforcement. Uncertainties emerge in part because the dress code must try to keep up with the evolution of youth styles. Because styles that reveal gang affiliations constantly change, dress codes also need to change. Because rules change frequently and are frequently overlooked, many students share the uncertainties associated with enforcement.

For students, details of dress are ways of eliciting a response from others, and in turn, of creating a self that responds to others' responses. Students may have their peers in mind, not school authorities and school rules, when they choose their dress. One constant with adolescents is the creative use of appearance. "At times it appears that the enforcement of dress codes can incite student antagonism towards school, but the social realities of dress are more complex than simple 'blame-the-authorities' perspectives may suggest" (Garot & Katz, 2003, p. 422).

ENFORCEMENT OF DRESS NORMS AMONG REFUGEE WOMEN

Huisman and Hondagneu-Sotelo (2005) examined "the ways in which Bosnian Muslim refugee women used agency to negotiate meanings of dress within specific temporal and structural-historical contexts" (p. 45). Agency was defined as the action, medium, or means by which something was accomplished. Data were collected between 2000 and 2002 as part of an ethnographic case study of a Bosnian Muslim settlement in Vermont. Findings were based on extensive participant observations and in-depth interviews with 14 women.

In Bosnia, Muslim women were accustomed to wearing relatively elaborate, carefully cultivated styles for hair, dress, and makeup; the effect produced was *emphasized femininity*. In Vermont, as refugees, they gradually adopted some local dress practices such as jeans, less elaborate makeup, and more casual clothing for everyday wear, but they remained ambivalent and critical of norms for women's dress in the United States. Some refugees adhered to their original dress norms, and some adopted new gendered dress norms. Participants were confronted with new audiences, an increased range of permissible dress options, and dramatic changes in the structure of their everyday lives. They understood changes in dress as symbols of freedom and autonomy; but they still enjoyed dressing up for special occasions, and they were critical of women whom they perceived as going too far in adopting casual styles (Huisman & Hondagneu-Sotelo, 2005).

While there was selective adoption of casual, simple dress in Vermont, there was also resistance to these dress norms. Resisting U.S. dress norms was a means for Bosnian Muslim refugee women to communicate, through their dress practices, a group identity to others, and to create that identity for themselves.

Dress communicates via a nonverbal language, the meanings of which change over time and space. The meanings of dress do not always translate easily from one location to another. Individuals who travel to another location may interpret the dress they see there through the dress language of their homeland and the recent past. Over time, however, immigrants may adopt new gendered dress practices in response to the changed context. Through repeated interactions with new audiences, dress norms from the past may be challenged or modified (Huisman & Hondagneu-Sotelo, 2005).

Dress practices are rooted in history and culture, but they are actively enforced in social interaction. Dress code enforcers used social sanctions as a means to enforce and perpetuate women's dress codes (Huisman & Hondagneu-Sotelo, 2005). **Dress code enforcers** were usually older women who used mild forms of disapproval and shame. These people had great influence in Bosnia and in the United States. The strict standards of Westernized, feminine dress were enforced by older (but not elderly) women. As the women aged and gained status, they exercised power over other women through gossip and social disapproval—key mechanisms of social control in women's clothing conformity. As one woman noted, "People watched to see how you looked, what you were wearing, how you were dressed, you know. Every day, they looked at everything" (Huisman & Hondagneu-Sotelo, 2005, p. 56). Dress code enforcers encouraged and monitored feminine dress standards. Deviation from impeccably groomed feminine dress resulted in sanctions of public staring and humiliation. When asked what the consequences were for women who violated the dress norms, one woman laughed and said that others would think she was crazy.

Another means of actively enforcing gendered dress norms were **internalized mechanisms** of self-discipline. Dress norms were enforced not only by the threat of punishment from peers and code enforcers, but also by deeply internalized beliefs held by individual women as revealed in both self-discipline and self-surveillance. The **panoptic** (all-inclusive) view was internalized and became part of an individual's self-appraisal. Individuals monitor their dress through a "disciplinary gaze that they direct upon themselves" (Danaher, Schirato, & Webb, 2000, p. 57).

Historically, the state used coercion to encourage people to claim a Yugoslav secular identity over a religious or ethnic/national identity (Huisman & Hondagneu-Sotelo, 2005). Muslims, more than Christians, were the targets of this campaign, and Muslim women were singled out. Overt state efforts encouraged modern Western dress and sanctioned and punished women for wearing Muslim dress. According to Dragnich (1954), "in some Moslem areas, the women were compelled to throw off the veil by being threatened with arrest. In others, they were bribed by making scarce textiles for suit or coat available at a low cost, and sometimes the services of a tailor were thrown in as part of the bargain" (p. 54).

FIGURE 14.7 MUSLIM WOMEN ARE FREQUENTLY CONFLICTED OVER THE DECISION TO COMMUNICATE A SECULAR, RELIGIOUS, OR ETHNIC/NATIONAL IDENTITY.

Women reported that in Bosnia, they never left the house without wearing heels, makeup, and carefully pressed clothes (Huisman & Hondagneu-Sotelo, 2005). This attentiveness to dress was necessary for any public appearance (Figure 14.7). With the exception of some elderly women, who wore long skirts and headscarves, nylons and heels were required for women in all public settings. Wearing heels, nylons, makeup, the latest Western European styles, and dyed, coiffed hair were symbols of modernity and femininity. Hair, especially, became a symbol of modernity, femininity, and national identity.

Women's dress practices were attributable to habit, repetition, and enforcement by dress code enforcers (Huisman & Hondagneu-Sotelo, 2005). With the passage of time, Bosnian women became more aware of and reflective about changes to their dress practices brought about by the changed context and the introduction of new routines in their daily lives. Dress practices began to be challenged as women were exposed to new meanings of dress, to a wider range of dress options, and to new competing audiences and dress code enforcers.

While Bosnian dress code enforcers continued to exert authority, the Bosnian women encountered greater anonymity in the United States than they did in their homeland, they had less time to spend on personal adornment, and they were subjected to new dress code enforcers, namely their Vermont co-workers, who exerted counterpressure. Competing dress code enforcers pulled in different directions, but Bosnian Muslim dress standards of the past were still influential (Huisman & Hondagneu-Sotelo, 2005).

SUMMARY

In this chapter we looked at research that illustrated the entire process of social control. Within these research studies, the steps in the process of social control were evident: norms, violation of norms, recognition of violation, report of violation, response to violation, and enforcement of response. In particular, we saw how attempts to enforce sanctions were revealed in feelings of pressure to conform caused by peer pressure or internalization, efforts to comply with the norm, complaints about enforcement or nonenforcement, efforts to resist enforcement, and complacency.

KEY TERMS AND CONCEPTS

acquiescence	embodied
ambiguity	hegemonic gaze
aspirational groups	internalized mechanisms
avoidance groups	negative deviance
body image	panoptic view
complacency	peer pressure
dress code enforcers	positive deviance
elective mammoplasty	resistance

SUGGESTED READINGS

1. Heckert, D. M., & Best, A. (1997). Ugly duckling to swan: Labeling theory and the stigmatization of red hair. *Symbolic Interactionism, 20,* 365–384.
2. Slade, P. D. (1994). What is body image? *Behavior Research and Theory, 32*(5), 497–502.

3. Synott, A. (1987). Shame and glory: A sociology of hair. *British Journal of Sociology, 38,* 381–413.

Research Activity 14.1 *Literature Analysis*

Purpose: To analyze research literature related to the enforcement of sanctions for appearance norm violations, identifying the purpose, research method, and results.

Procedure:

1. Describe the characteristics of a research article.
2. Use the Google Scholar (http://scholar.google.com/) search engine or an academic database (EBSCO, ERIC, SocIndex) to locate one research article related to the enforcement of sanctions for appearance norm violations. For example, you might use the key words *enforcement of dress norm violation sanctions* or *enforcement of sanctions for appearance standard violations* to search for research articles.
3. Print a copy of the research article.
4. Highlight and label the purpose of the study, the research method used, the results of the study related to its purpose, and enforcement of sanctions for the appearance norm violation studied.
5. Submit your work to your instructor.

Research Activity 14.2 *Contexts of Dress Code Enforcement*

Purpose: To identify and characterize who is responsible for enforcing sanctions for violations of dress code rules in different contexts.

Procedure:

1. Use the Google (http://google.com) search engine to search the key words *enforcement of dress rules* enclosed in quotation marks.
2. Identify and list five contexts in which articles about dress codes are found, for example, schools, cruise lines, specific occupations.
3. Print out articles from three different contexts and compare how dress rules are enforced by highlighting key points in each article and making notations in the margins.
4. Submit your work to your instructor.

Purpose: To analyze high school student handbooks, specifically rules regarding student dress.

Procedure:

1. Use the Google (http://google.com) search engine to search the key words *high school student handbook dress codes* enclosed in quotation marks.

2. Print out dress codes from 10 different high schools and the sanctions for not complying with the rules.

3. Create a chart listing prohibited items, required items, sanctions for violations of the dress code, and who is responsible for enforcement.

4. Submit your work to your instructor.

References

Abell, E., & Gecas, V. (1997). Guilt, shame, and family socialization. *Journal of Family Issues, 18*(2), 99–123.

Abercrombie and Fitch. (2006, November 11). Message posted to www.offtheshelf.com

Adam, A. (2001). Big girls' blouses: Learning to live with polyester. In A. Guy, E. Green, and M. Banim (Eds.), *Through the wardrobe: Women's relationships with their clothes* (pp. 39–52). Oxford: Berg.

Adkins, L. (1995). *Gendered work: Sexuality, family, and the labour market.* Buckingham, UK: Open University Press.

Adler, P. A., & Adler, P. (1994). *Constructions of deviance: Social power, context, and interaction.* Belmont, CA: Wadsworth.

Alexander, G. (2006, September 29). Parent says teachers need dress code, too. *The Clovis Independent.* Retrieved November 16, 2006, from http://www.lexisnexis.com

Allsopp, J., Eysenck, H. J., & Eysenck, S. B. G. (1991). Machiavellianism as a component in psychoticism and extraversion. *Personality and Individual Differences, 12,* 29–41.

American Anthropological Association. (2001). What is anthropology? Retrieved September 7, 2006, from http://www.asanet.org/anthbroc.htm

American Obesity Association. (2002). *Obesity in the U.S.* Retrieved August 21, 2006, from http://www.obesity.org/

American Sociological Association. (2005). Retrieved September 6, 2006, from http://www.asanet.org/

Americans with Disabilities. (2007). Retrieved January 2, 2007, from http://www.usdoj.gov/kidspage/crt/disable.htm, p. 13.

Andersen, E. (2007, February 2). The modesty squad. *Lincoln Journal Star,* p. 1. Retrieved March 14, 2007, from http://www.lexisnexis.com

Anderson, V. (2006a, January 4). Our fight with fat; shame on you; overcoming the guilt of being overweight can take a lifetime. *The Atlanta Journal-Constitution.* Retrieved January 1, 2007, from http://www.lexisnexis.com

Anderson, V. (2006b, October 3). The art of avoidance. *The Atlanta Journal-Constitution.* Retrieved January 2, 2007, from http://www.lexisnexis.com

Appearance standards. (2006). Stowe Mountain Resort. Retrieved November 16, 2006, from http://www.stowe.com/employment/index/jobs_appearance/

Are dress codes a drag? (2005, September 30). *Current Events.* Retrieved May 15, 2006, from www.weeklyreader.com/ce

Armstrong, M. L. (1996). You pierced what? *Journal of School Nursing, 22,* 236–238.

Armstrong, M. L., & Kelly, L. (2001). Tattooing, body piercing, and branding are on the rise: Perspectives for school nurses. *Journal of School Nursing, 17,* 12–23.

Armstrong, M. L., Ekmark, E., & Brooks, B. (1995). Body piercing: Promoting informed decision making. *Journal of School Nursing, 112,* 20–25.

Armstrong, M. L., Roberts, A. E., Owen, D. C., & Koch, J. R. (2004). Contemporary college students and body piercing. *Journal of Adolescent Health, 35,* 58–61.

Arnett, J. (1992). Reckless behavior in adolescence: A developmental perspective. *Developmental Review, 12,* 339–373.

Arnett, J. (2000). Emerging adulthood: A theory of development from the late teens through the twenties. *American Psychologist, 55,* 469–480.

Arnett, J. J. (2001). Conceptions of the transition to adulthood: Perspectives from adolescence through midlife. *Journal of Adult Development, 8*(2), 133–143.

Arthur, L. (1997). Role salience, role embracement, and the symbolic self-completion of sorority pledges. *Sociological Inquiry, 67*(3), 364–379.

Asimov, N. (2006, April 22). Carpenter nailed for working in the buff. *The San Francisco Chronicle.* Retrieved December 13, 2006, from http://www.lexisnexis.com

Atherton, L. (1964). Cattleman and cowboys: Fact and fancy. In M.S. Kennedy (Ed.), *Cowboys and cattlemen: Fact and fancy* (pp. 3–26). New York: Hastings House.

Attire must express message to merit protection. (2007, February 1). *School Law Bulletin, 10*(10). Retrieved March 7, 2007, from http://www.lexisnexis.com

Austin, S., & Joseph, S. (1996). Assessment of bully/victim problems in 8 to 11 year olds. *British Journal of Educational Psychology, 66,* 447–456.

Auty, S., & Elliott, R. (1998). Fashion involvement, self-monitoring and the meaning of brands. *Journal of Product & Brand Management, 7*(2), 109–123.

Awosika, M. (2006, February 23). Mixed-media messages: Peer and media influence add to the pressure in the lives of teenage and preteen girls. *Sarasota Herald-Tribune,* p. E1. Retrieved December 21, 2006, from http://www.lexisnexis.com

Bachmann, K. (2006, June 17). Custom and ritual played role on wedding day. *Timmins Daily Press.* Retrieved December 11, 2006, at http://www.lexisnexis.com

Baker, R. A., & Mannion, B. (2006, August 2). Chalk up arrest for fashion police. *The Post-Standard,* p. B3. Retrieved January 11, 2007, from http://www.lexisnexis.com

Ballentine, L. W., & Ogle, J. P. (2005). The making and unmaking of body problems in *Seventeen* magazine, 1992–2003. *Family and Consumer Sciences Research Journal, 33*(4), 281–307.

Bandura, A. (1969). Social learning and the shaping of children's judgments. *Journal of Personality and Social Psychology, 11,* 275–283.

Banks, T. (2006, February 17). Dressed to Kilgour. *The Evening Standard,* p. 25. Retrieved January 18, 2007, from http://www.lexisnexis.com

Barney, K. (2006, March 21). Kate's fur faux pas; experts criticize the mink hat worn by William's girlfriend as 'totally out of touch.' *The Evening Standard*. Retrieved December 13, 2006, from http://www.lexisnexis.com

Bartlett, K. T. (1994). Only girls wear barrettes: Dress and appearance standards, community norms, and workplace equality. *Michigan Law Review, 92*(8), 2541–2582.

Bass, D. (2006, June 8). Tips for getting fitted. *St. Louis Post-Dispatch*. Retrieved January 18, 2007, from http://www.lexisnexis.com

Baumeister, R. F., Zhang, L., & Vohs, K. D. (2004). Gossip as cultural learning. *Review of General Psychology, 8*(2), 111–121.

Beatty, M. J., Valencic, K. M., Rudd, J. E., & Dobos, J. A. (1999). A "dark side" of communication avoidance: Indirect verbal aggressiveness. *Communication Research Reports, 16*, 103–109.

Beaudoin, J., & Drevitch, G. (1998, May 11–17). Schools under fire. *Southern Illinoisan* React [insert], p. 4.

Belk, R., & Pollay, R. (1985). Images of ourselves: The good life in twentieth century advertising. *Journal of Consumer Research, 11*, 887–897.

Bell-Price, S. (2006). *Vivienne Westwood (born 1941) and the postmodern legacy of punk style*. Retrieved December 15, 2006, from http://www.metmuseum.org/toah/hd/vivw/hd_vivw.htm

Belz, L. (2006, April). Out of control proms. *TeenVogue*, pp. 102–104. Retrieved January 5, 2007, from http://www.lexisnexis.com

Bem, S. L. (1974). The measurement of psychological androgyny. *Journal of Consulting and Clinical Psychology, 42*, 151–156.

Bennett, A. (2006). Punk's not dead: The continuing significance of punk rock for an older generation of fans. *Sociology, 40*(2), 219–235.

Benson, S. (2004, Spring/Summer). Clothing, grooming, and social acceptability: Part 2. *Future Reflections*. Retrieved January 4, 2007, from http://www.nfb.org

Bentley, R. (2006, April 23). High school prom season. *The Atlanta Journal-Constitution*, p. J1. Retrieved January 5, 2007, from http://www.lexisnexis.com

Berger, A. (1973). *The comic-stripped American*. New York: Walker.

Berghom, J. L. (2006, October 13). Employee dress code analyzed. *The News & Advance*. Retrieved December 12, 2006, from http://www.lexisnexis.com

Best, J. (1989). Secondary claims-making: Claims about threats to children on the network news. *Perspectives on Social Problems, 1*, 259–282.

Best, J. W., & Kahn, J. V. (2006). *Research in education* (10th ed.). Boston: Allyn and Bacon.

Beverly Hills considers warning tags for furs. (1999, February 4). *Southern Illinoisan*, p. A6.

Biography: Dame Vivienne Westwood. (2006). Retrieved December 15, 2006, from http://www.bbc.co.uk/arts/livingicons/bio10.shtml

Birkner, G. (2006, June 20). For black tie nights, the white jacket is back. *The New York Sun*, p. 13. Retrieved December 21, 2006, from http://www.lexisnexis.com

Blake, J., & Davis, K. (1964). Norms, values, and sanctions. In R. Faris (Ed.), *Handbook of modern sociology* (pp. 456–484). Chicago: Rand McNally.

Blakemore, J. E. (2003). Children's beliefs about violating gender norms: Boys shouldn't look like girls and girls shouldn't act like boys. *Sex Roles, 48*(9/10), 411–419.

Blakemore, J., & Russ, L. (1997). Preschool children's attitudes about deviations from gender-role behaviors. Paper presented at the Biennial Meeting of the Society for Research in Child Development (62nd, Washington, DC, April 3–6, 1997). ED 406 049.

Blip.tv and Conde Nast's *Glamour* team up as fashion police: Company lets anyone with a camera submit fashion dos & don'ts to Glamour.com (2006, October 4). *PR Newswire US.* Retrieved January 9, 2007 from http://www.lexisnexis.com

Bluffton police ranked as nation's best dressed law enforcement. (2004). Retrieved December 20, 2006, from http://ci.bluffton.in.us/police/news-bestdressed.htm

Blumer, H. (1969). *Symbolic interactionism: Perspective and method.* Englewood Cliffs, NJ: Prentice-Hall.

Bob Jones University. (2007, March 14). *Student expectations.* Retrieved March 14, 2007, from http://www.bju.edu/prospective/expect/dress.html

Bodi, S. (2002). How do we bridge the gap between what we teach and what they do? Some thoughts on the place of questions in the process of research. *Journal of Academic Librarianship, 28*(3), 109–114.

Body odour problem. (2006, May 9). *Personnel Today.* Retrieved January 2, 2007, from http://www.lexisnexis.com

Bogart, L. (1984). The public's use and perception of newspapers. *The Public Opinion Quarterly, 48*(4), 709–719.

Borcover, A. (2006, June 1). The other code we Yanks should watch. *Chicago Tribune.* Retrieved January 1, 2007, from http://www.lexisnexis.com

Bostrom, M. (2006, May 11). Inmates' guests dressed down; new rules call for appropriate, modest attire. *Star News.* Retrieved December 12, 2006, from http://www.lexisnexis.com

Brandt, L. J. (2003). On the value of an old dress code in the new millennium. *Archives of Internal Medicine, 163*, 1277–1281.

Brazelton, T. B. (2006, August 10). Replace reliance on teasing with openness to difference. *The Times Union.* Retrieved December 20, 2006, from http://www.lexisnexis.com

Bridge, B. (2006, December 6). Seeing red: Color blindness complicates everyday life—not to mention the holidays. *Bedford Times Mail.* Retrieved January 4, 2007, from http://www.tmnews.com

Brown, M. (2006, March 10). Dressing rite. *The Tampa Tribune,* p. 1. Retrieved January 12, 2007, from http://www.lexisnexis.com

Brown, P. L. (2006, December 2). Supporting boys or girls when the line isn't clear. *The New York Times.* Retrieved January 1, 2007, from http://www.nytimes.com

Brunner, L. (2006, November 21). Are women pressed to choose a hair-free life? *The Pitt News* via University Wire. Retrieved December 1, 2006, from http://www.lexisnexis.com

Buckley, C. (1995, December 4). You got a problem? *The New Yorker,* pp. 80–85.

Burger, T., & Finkel, D. (2002). Relationships between body modifications and very high-risk behavior in a college population. *College Student Journal, 36*(2), 203–213.

Burn, J. (2006). An experiment in white. *American Journal of Nursing, 106*(3), 64A–64C.

Buy early to beat First Communion shopping frenzy. (2006, December 5). *PR Newswire US.* Retrieved January 1, 2007, from http://www.lexisnexis.com

Byrd-Bredbenner, C., & Murray, J. (2003). A comparison of the anthropometric measurements of idealized female body images in media directed to men, women, and mixed gender audiences. *Topics in Clinical Nutrition, 18*(2), 117–129.

Byron, T. (2006, August 28). Our little boy often pretends to be a girl. Should we be worried? *The Times.* Retrieved January 1, 2007, from http://www.lexisnexis.com

Cabe, P. A., Walker, M. H., & Williams, M. (1999). Newspaper advice column letters as teaching cases for developmental psychology. *Teaching of Psychology, 26*(2), 128–130.

Calasibetta, C., & Tortora, P. (2003). *The Fairchild dictionary of fashion.* New York: Fairchild.

Can I make him take his earring off? (2006, September 18). *New Mexico Employment Law Letter, 12*(10). Retrieved October 11, 2006, from http://www.lexisnexis.com

Cardell, A. (1996). *Absolutely Queen Viv.* Retrieved December 15, 2006, from http://www.fashion-icon.com/blur/index.html

Cardy, T. (2007, January 29). Body experts to discuss people's measurements. AAP Newsfeed. Retrieved April 6, 2007, from http://www.lexisnexis.com

Carleo-Evangelist, J. (2006, August 10). A lost job and a case of faith. *The Times Union.* Retrieved November 16, 2006, from http://www.lexisnexis.com

Carlson, H. J. (2006, October 12). Hazing divides Byron. *Post-Bulletin.* Retrieved January 1, 2007, from http://www.lexisnexis.com

Carroll, L., & Anderson, R. (2002). Body piercing, tattooing, self-esteem and body investment in adolescent girls. *Adolescence, 37*(147), 627–637.

Carroll, S., Riffenburgh, R., Roberts, T., & Myhre, E. (2002). Tattoos and body piercings as indicators of adolescent risk-taking behaviors. *Pediatrics, 109*(6), 1021–1027.

Cash, T. F., Ancis, J. R., & Strachan, M. D. (1997). Gender attitudes, feminist identity, and body images among college women. *Sex Roles, 36*(7/8), 433–447.

Casstevens, D. (2006, October 9). More children stepping into beauty pageants, drawing controversy. *Fort Worth Star-Telegram.* Retrieved December 20, 2006, from http://www.lexisnexis.com

Castro, J., Moritz, M., & Nash, J. M. (1981, January 19). Advice for the lonely hearts. *Time,* pp. 56–57.

Cates, K. (2004, August 30). Local schools crack down on risqué fashion fads. *Southern Illinoisan,* p. A-1.

Ceglian, C. M., & Lyons, N. N. (2004). Gender type and comfort with cross-dressers. *Sex Roles, 50*(7/8), 539–546.

Ceniceros, S. (1998). Tattooing, body piercing, and Russian roulette. *Journal of Nervous and Mental Disease, 186,* 503.

Ceniceros, S., Brown, G., & Swartz, C. (1998). Tattoos, body piercing, and psychiatric disorders. *Southern Medical Journal, 91*(10), S52–S53.

Charen, M. (2005, December 10). A modest backlash against the trash culture. *Southern Illinoisan,* p. 4A.

Chase, K. J. (2006, December 15). Eating steak and sipping martinis with the in-crowd. *The Boston Globe.* Available from http://www.lexisnexis.com

Chin, E. (1996). Hemmed in and shut out: Urban minority kids, consumption, and social inequality in New Haven, Connecticut. In A. Marcus (Ed.), *Anthropology for a small planet: Culture and community in a global environment* (pp. 158–180). St. James, NY: Brandywine.

Chirsler, J. C., & Ghiz, L. (1993). Body image issues of older women. In N. D. Davis, B. Cole, & E. D. Rothblum (Eds.), *Faces of women and aging* (pp . 67–75). New York: Harrington Park.

Cho, K. (2006). Redesigning hospital gowns to enhance end users' satisfaction. *Family and Consumer Sciences Research Journal, 34*(4), 332–349.

Cholachatpinyo, A., Padgett, I., Crocker, M., & Fletcher, D. (2002). A conceptual model of the fashion process–part 1: The fashion transformation process model. *Journal of Fashion Marketing and Management, 6*(1), 11–23.

Christie, R., & Geis, F. L. (1970). *Studies in Machiavellianism.* New York: Academic Press.

Clandinin, D. J., & Connelly, F. M. (2000). *Narrative inquiry: Experience and story in qualitative research.* San Francisco, CA: Jossey-Bass.

Clothes of the nineties. Retrieved May 30, 2006, from www.inthe90s.com

Clothing etiquette—bad wardrobe decisions are a serious career mistake. (2006, August 29). *Yearbook of Experts News Release Wire.* Retrieved November 26, 2006, from http://www.lexisnexis.com

'Clothing' in on the promotion: Attire affects potential for advancement, say most executives polled. (2007, January 27). *Canada News Wire*. Retrieved February 9, 2007, from http://www.lexisnexis.com

Clothing the clergy. (1997, February 8). *Southern Illinoisan*, p. A7.

Cohen, M. (2000). A student profiling technique will not effectively deter juvenile violence in our schools. *New York Law School Journal of Human Rights, 17*, 298–340.

Cohen, R. (2003, January 2). Everyday ethics: A final good bye to Eppie Lederer. *Amarillo Globe News*. Retrieved February 3, 2004, from www.amarillonet.com/stories/010203/bel_ethics.shtm/

Collins, A. F. (2006, September). Vanity Fair presents the 67th annual international best-dressed list 2006. *Vanity Fair*. Retrieved December 20, 2006, from http://www.lexisnexis.com

Colls, R. (2004). 'Looking alright, feeling alright': Emotions, sizing, and the geographies of women's experiences of clothing consumption. *Social & Cultural Geography, 5*(4), 583–595.

Colls, R. (2006). Outsize/outside: Bodily bignesses and the emotional experiences of British women shopping for clothes. *Gender, Place, and Culture: A Journal of Feminist Geography, 13*(5), 529–545.

Colman, R., & Colman, A. (2004, June). Risk-taking. *Youth Studies Australia, 23*(2), p. 9.

Confederate shirts spark fashion fight. (2001, April 7). *Southern Illinoisan*, p. A9.

Connell, R. W. (1987). *Gender and power*. Cambridge: Polity Press.

Conviction upheld in Manson T-shirt case. (1999, April 8). *Daily Egyptian*, p. 13.

Copeland, D. (2006, November 19). Prom night with family. *The State*. Retrieved January 2, 2007, from http://www.lexisnexis.com

Cosco, K. (2006, December 12). Religious garb makes U. Massachusetts students discrimination targets. *Massachusetts Daily Collegian*. Retrieved March 14, 2007, from http://www.lexisnexis.com

Crane, D. (1999a). Diffusion models and fashion: A reassessment. *The Annals of the American Academy of Political and Social Science, 556*, 13–24.

Crane, D. (1999b). Fashion design and social change: Women designers and stylistic innovation. *Journal of American Culture, 22*(1), 61–68.

Critchell, S. (2006, January 30). Follow the rainbow: Museum exhibit examines the use of color in fashion. *The Associated Press*. Retrieved January 18, 2007, from http://www.lexisnexis.com

Crockett, D., & Wallendorf, M. (1998). Sociological perspectives on imposed school dress codes: Consumption as attempted suppression of class and group symbolism. *Journal of Macromarketing, 18*(2), 115–131.

Cross purposes: A short history of cross-dressing women. (2006, September). *Contemporary Women's Issues*. Retrieved December 4, 2006, from http://www.lexisnexis.com

Crow, K. (2006, October 11). Anything goes in fashion now, so should rules. *Plain Dealer*, p. E1. Retrieved January 18, 2007, from http://www.lexisnexis.com

Crowl, T. K., Kaminsky, S., & Podell, D. M. (1997). *Educational psychology*. Madison, WI: Brown & Benchmark.

Crozier, W. R. (2002). Donkeys and dragons: Recollections of schoolteachers' nicknames. *Educational Studies, 28*(2), 133–142.

Crozier, W. R., & Dimmock, P. S. (1999). Name-calling and nicknames in a sample of primary school children. *British Journal of Educational Psychology, 69*(4), 505–516.

Crozier, W. R., & Skliopidou, E. (2002). Adult recollections of name-calling at school. *Educational Psychology, 22*(1), 113–124.

Currie, D. (1997). Decoding femininity: Advertisements and their teenage readers. *Gender & Society, 11*(4), 453–477.

Currie, D. (2001). Dear Abby: Advice pages as a site for the operation of power. *Feminist Theory, 2*(3), 259–281.

Curry, L. (2006, July 17). An offensive T-shirt may not justify firing. *Anchorage Daily News.* Retrieved January 1, 2007, from http://www.lexisnexis.com

Curtis, J. (2006, April 21). Smell you later. *The Times Educational Supplement.* Retrieved January 2, 2007, from http://www.lexisnexis.com

Cusumano, D. L., & Thompson, J. K. (1997). Body image and body shape ideals in magazines: Exposure, awareness, and internalization. *Sex Roles, 37,* 701–721.

Dahl, D. W., Frankenberger, K. D., & Manchanda, R. V. (2003, September). Does it pay to shock? Reactions to shocking and nonshocking advertising content among university students. *Journal of Advertising Research,* 268–280.

Dallas council examines baggy pants problem. (2006, September 4). *Southern Illinoisan,* p. A2.

Damhorst, M. L. (1991). Gender and appearance in daily comic strips. *Dress, 18,* 59–67.

Danaher, G., Schirato, T., & Webb, J. (2000). *Understanding Foucault.* London: Sage.

Davis, F. (1994). *Fashion, culture, and identity.* Chicago, IL: The University of Chicago Press.

Davis, J. R. (2006). Growing up punk: Negotiating aging identity in a local music scene. *Symbolic Interaction, 29*(1), 63–69.

Daviss, B. (1987). World of funnies is "Warped with fancy, woofed with dreams." *Smithsonian, 18*(8), 180–195.

de Kretser, L. (2006, December 8). Red alert for poor Laura—three others in her frock. *The New York Post,* p. 3. Retrieved January 11, 2007, from http://www.lexisnexis.com

de la Haye, A., & Dingwall, C. (1996). *Surfers, soulies, skinheads, and skaters: Subcultural style from the forties to the nineties.* Woodstock, NY: Overlook Press.

Deam, J. (2006, June 25). Sexy styles aimed at youngsters. *The Houston Chronicle,* p. 3. Retrieved December 21, 2006, from http://www.lexisnexis.com

DeBare, I. (2006, September 13). Difference between loser, dedicated worker is in eye of beholder. *The San Francisco Chronicle,* p. C1. Retrieved January 11, 2007, from http://www.lexisnexis.com

Deil-Amen, R. (2006). To teach or not to teach "social" skills: Comparing community colleges and private occupational colleges. *Teachers College Record, 108* (3), 397–421.

Dellinger, K. (2002). Wearing gender and sexuality "on your sleeve": Dress norms and the importance of occupational and organizational culture at work. *Gender Issues, 20*(1), 3–25.

Dellinger, K., & Williams, C. (1997). Makeup at work: Negotiating appearance rules in the workplace. *Gender & Society, 11*(2), 151–177.

DeMitchell, T. (2002). The duty to protect: Blackstone's doctrine of *in loco parentis:* A lens for viewing the sexual abuse of students. *Brigham Young University Education and Law Journal, 12*(1), 17–52.

Distinguishing scholarly journals from other periodicals. (2006). Retrieved October 4, 2006, from http://www.library.cornell.edu/olinuris/ref/research/skill20.html

Dodd, C. A., Clarke, I., & Kirkup, M. H. (1998). Camera observations of customer behaviour in fashion retailing: Methodological propositions. *International Journal of Retail & Distribution Management, 26*(8), 311–317.

Do-Dots. (2007, January 2). Retrieved January 2, 2007, from http://www.abledata.com

Donais, B. (2006). Every workplace has a culture. Excerpt from *Workplaces That Work: A Guide to*

Conflict Management in Union and Non-Union Work Environments. Aurora: Canada Law Book. Retrieved January 30, 2007, from www.mediate.com/articles/donaisB3.cfm

Doniach, A. (2006, December 28). Saucy 'cops' don't work shoe leather; Fashion police for PETA pull in easy prey with fishnet stockings. *The Commercial Appeal,* p. B7. Retrieved January 5, 2007, from http://www.lexisnexis.com

Dragnich, A. B. (1954). *Tito's promised land: Yugoslavia.* New Brunswick, NJ: Rutgers University Press.

A dress code for wedding guests. (2006, December 18). Scripps Howard News Service. Retrieved January 1, 2007, from http://www.lexisnexis.com

D'Souza, B. (2006, June 21). Why fat jokes aren't funny. *USA Today.* Retrieved January 1, 2007, from http://www.lexisnexis.com

Dunbar, R., Duncan, N., & Marriott, A. (1997). Human conversational behavior. *Human Nature, 8,* 231–246.

Dupre, M. E., & Mackey, D. A. (2001). Crime in the public mind: Letters to the editor as a measure of crime salience. *Journal of Criminal Justice and Popular Culture, 8*(1), 1–24.

Dyer, G. (1982). *Advertising as communication.* London: Methuen.

Eckert, C., & Stacey, M. (2001). Designing in the context of fashion—Designing the fashion context. In P. H. Lloyd & H. C. M. Christiaans (Eds.), *Designing in Context: Proceedings of the 5th Design Thinking Research Symposium* (pp. 113–129). Delft, Netherlands: Delft University Press.

Eckert, C., & Stacey, M. (2003). Adaptation of sources of inspiration in knitwear design. *Creativity Research Journal, 15*(4), 355–384.

Eckert, P. (1989). *Jocks and burnouts: Social categories and identity in the high school.* New York: Teachers college.

Eder, D., Evans, C., & Parker, S. (1995). *School talk: Gender and adolescent culture.* New Brunswick, NJ: Rutgers University Press.

Eger, A. (2006, October 6). Schools fight back against gangs. *Tulsa World.* Retrieved December 9, 2006, from http://www.ebscohost.com

Eicher, J. B. (2000). The anthropology of dress. *Dress, 27,* 59–70.

Eicher, J., Evenson, S., & Lutz, H. (2000). *The visible self.* New York: Fairchild.

Eicher, J., & Roach-Higgins, M. (1992). Definition and classification of dress: Implications for analysis of gender roles. In R. Barnes & J. Eicher (Eds.), *Dress and gender* (pp. 8–28). Providence, RI: Berg.

Eila, L. (2005, November 1). *Speak to Dear Abby Live During First-Ever Radio Broadcast.* Retrieved August 17, 2006, from http://www.uexpress.com/dearabby/dar_press_release.html

Elliott, R. (1994). Exploring the symbolic meaning of brands. *British Journal of Management, 5,* s13–s19.

Elliott, R., & Leonard, C. (2004). Peer pressure and poverty: Exploring fashion brands and consumption symbolism among children of the 'British poor.' *Journal of Consumer Behavior, 3*(4), 347–359.

Ellis, A. D. (2006, November 25). Adult student's story offers lesson for life. *Fresno Bee.* Retrieved December 20, 2006, from http://www.lexisnexis.com

Elmore, C. (2006, June 29). Venus' foe: All fashion but no show. *Palm Beach Post,* p. C8. Retrieved January 17, 2007, from http://www.lexisnexis.com

Erikson, E. (1997). *The life cycle completed.* New York: Norton.

Estimates of personal power. (1980). Plymouth, MN: Management Renewal Associates.

Etiquette and local customs in New York City. (2006, December 29). Retrieved January 1, 2007, from http://www.citidex.com/342.htm

Evans, E. D., Rutberg, J., Sather, C., & Turner, C. (1991). Content analysis of contemporary teen magazines for adolescent females. *Youth & Society, 23*, 99–120.

Faludi, S. (1999). *Stiffed: The betrayal of the American man.* New York: William Morrow and Company.

Family Dollar recalls "Creepy Cape" costumes due to flammability hazard. (2006, October 31). Retrieved November 17, 2006, from http://www.cpsc.gov/cpscpub/prerel/prhtml07/07021. html

Fashion police. (2006, November 30). Retrieved January 8, 2007, from http://en.wikipedia.org/ wiki/Fashion_police

Fashion survey reveals that executives prefer business casual. (2006, September 6). *PR Newswire US.* Retrieved December 13, 2006, from http://www.lexisnexis.com

Faux pas. (2006, October 17). Retrieved January 8, 2007, from http://en.wikipedia.org/wiki/ Faux_pas

Ferguson, P. (2006, November 16). Teen talk: Teens get bunched up over school dress code. *The Oregonian,* p. 14. Retrieved November 30, 2006, from http://www.lexisnexis.com

Field, A. E., Cheung, L., Wolf, A. M., Herzog, D. B., Gortmaker, S. L., & Colditz, G. A. (1999). Exposure to the mass media and weight concerns among girls. *Pediatrics, 103*(3), 36.

Fine, G. (1977). Social components of children's gossip. *Journal of Communication, 22*(1), 181–185.

Fiore, A., Lee, S-E., Kunz, G., & Campbell, J. R. (2001). Relationships between optimum stimulation level and willingness to use mass customization options. *Journal of Fashion Marketing & Management, 5*(2), 99–107.

Fiquette, L. (1994, August 14). What belongs on page one? *St. Louis Post-Dispatch,* p. A2.

Fisk, C. L. (2006). Privacy, power, and humiliation at work: Re-examining appearance regulation as an invasion of privacy. *Duke Law School Working Paper Series.* Retrieved January 26, 2007, from http://lsr.nellco.org/duke/fs/papers/40

5 tips to look younger longer. (2006, November 16). Retrieved January 2, 2007, from http://www. chickadvisor.com, p. 15.

Flight attendant told to remove American flag pin. (1998, July 4). *Southern Illinoisan,* p. A11.

Flynn, E. E. (2006, June 24). The promise of purity. *The Austin American-Statesman,* p. A1. Retrieved January 1, 2007, from www.lexisnexis.com

Former lounge singer and Sunday school teacher to succeed Ann Landers. (2005, April 20). Retrieved August 17, 2006, from http://www.siouxcityjournal.com/articles/2005/04/20/ news_living/local/d0cfd114214365ba86256d5f001187b5.prt

Fortin, C. A. (2006, September 17). Dress code gets stricter. *The Baltimore Sun,* p. G1. Retrieved March 15, 2007, from http://www.lexisnexis.com

Foster, E. K. (2004). Research on gossip: Taxonomy, methods, and future directions. *Review of General Psychology, 8*(2), 78–99.

Four in ten Toronto workers bundle up to beat A/C. (2006, August 23). *The Globe and Mail,* p. C3. Retrieved January 6, 2007, from http://www.lexisnexis.com

Franklin, H. (2006, February 22). Board OKs revised dress policy: Schools must come up with a discipline plan for violations. *Columbus Ledger-Enquirer.* Retrieved January 1, 2007, from http://www.lexisnexis.com

Frederick, C., & Bradley, K. (2000). A different kind of normal? Psychological and motivational characteristics of young adult tattooers and body piercers. *North American Journal of Psychology, 2*(2), 380–394.

Freeburg, E. W., & Workman, J. E. (2000, November 8–11). *An empirical test of norms related to appearance.* Research presented at International Textile and Apparel Association Annual Meeting, Cincinnati, OH.

Freeburg, B. W., & Workman, J. E. (in press). A method to identify and validate social norms related to dress. *Clothing and Textiles Research Journal.*

Freeburg, E. W., Workman, J. E., & Lee, S. H. (2001, November 9–13). A cross-cultural comparison of norms related to appearance. Oral research presentation at International Textile and Apparel Association Annual Meeting, Kansas City, MO.

Freeburg, E. W., Workman, J. E., & Lentz-Hees, E. (2004). Rationale for student dress codes: A review of school handbooks. *Journal of Family and Consumer Sciences, 96*(1), 77–82.

Freitas, A., Kaiser, S., Chandler, J., Hall, C., Kim, J., & Hammidi, T. (1997). Appearance management as border construction: Least favorite clothing, group distancing, and identity . . . not! *Sociological Inquiry, 67*(3), 323–335.

Frings, G. (1999). *Fashion from concept to consumer* (3d edition). Englewood Cliffs, NJ: Prentice-Hall.

Fuller, M. L., & Groce, S. B. (1991). Obese women's responses to appearance norms. *Free Inquiry in Creative Sociology, 19*(2), 167–174.

Gabay, S. (2006, November 14). An indie influence in fashion. *Daily Bruin.* Retrieved January 17, 2007, from http://dailybruin.com/news/articles.asp?id=38908

Gagne, P., & McGaughey, D. (2002). Designing women: Cultural hegemony and the exercise of power among women who have undergone elective mammoplasty. *Gender & Society, 16*(6), 814–838.

Garot, R., & Katz, J. (2003). Provocative looks: Gang appearance and dress codes in an inner-city alternative school. *Ethnography, 4,* 421–454.

Garza, A. (2006, October 14). Students suspended for violating dress code. *Corpus Christi Caller-Times,* p. B2. Retrieved November 16, 2006, from http://www.lexisnexis.com

Garza, E. P. (2006, August 23). Making the cut: Scissors-wielding principal enforces dress code. *Valley Morning Star.* Retrieved November 16, 2006, from http://www.lexisnexis.com

Gelpi, G. (2006, July 6). Rules might relax, setting shirttails free. *The Augusta Chronicle.* Retrieved December 12, 2006, from http://www.lexisnexis.com

Gerrard, J. M. (1991). The teasing syndrome in facially deformed children. *Australian and New Zealand Journal of Family Therapy, 12,* 147–154.

Gibbs, J. (1981). *Norms, deviance, and social control: Conceptual matters.* New York: Elsevier.

Givhan, R. (2006, January 27). Skirting: The issue. *The Washington Post,* p. C02.

Glanz, J. (2006). *Fundamentals of educational research.* Norwood, MA: Christopher-Gordon.

Glascock, J., & Preston-Schreck, C. (2004). Gender and racial stereotypes in daily newspaper comics: A time-honored tradition. *Sex Roles, 51*(7/8), 423–431.

Glentzer, M. (2006, November 26). Common-sense chic; vow to be dowdy no more. *The Houston Chronicle,* p. 4. Retrieved January 1, 2007, from http://www.lexisnexis.com

Goldsmith, R. (2000). Characteristics of the heavy user of fashionable clothing. *Journal of Marketing Theory and Practice, 8*(4), 1–9.

Goldsmith, R. (2002). Some personality traits of frequent clothing buyers. *Journal of Fashion Marketing and Management, 6*(3), 303–316.

Goldstein, J. (2006, July 13). Sikh employee unwilling poster boy for Transit Authority dress code. *The New York Sun,* p. 4. Retrieved December 1, 2006, from http://www.lexisnexis.com

Gorrell, M. (2006, November 30). Regarding letter jackets, store is no new kid on block. *The Salt Lake Tribune.* Retrieved December 21, 2006, from http://www.lexisnexis.com

Gostomski, C., & Kennedy, S. (2006, November 26). Casino wants servers with big, uh, personalities. *Morning Call*. Retrieved December 1, 2006, from http://www.lexisnexis.com

Gothic fashion. (2006). Retrieved December 15, 2006, from http://www.answers.com/topic/gothic-fashion

Graedon, J., & Graedon, T. (2006, December 13). *Buffalo News*. Retrieved January 2, 2007, from http://www.lexisnexis.com

Green, L. (2006, October 8). Has chic become sickly? *St. Petersburg Times*. Retrieved November 30, 2006, from http://www.lexisnexis.com

Grief, J., & Hewitt, W. (1999). Tattooing and body piercing. *Clinical Nursing Research, 8*(4), 368–385.

Grogan, L. (2006, January 11). Fashion fiascos for 2005. *Sacramento Bee*. Retrieved December 20, 2006, from http://www.lexisnexis.com

Gunter, T., & McDowell, B. (2004). Body piercing: Issues in adolescent health. *Journal for Specialists in Pediatric Nursing, 9*(2), 67–69.

Gustafson, K. L. (2006, May 13). Mourning attire: At funerals, don't show off, show respect. *The Times Union*, p. D1. Retrieved January 17, 2007, from http://www.lexisnexis.com

Hahn, H. (1988). The politics of physical differences: Disability and discrimination. *Journal of Social Issues, 44*(1), 39–47.

Hajewski, D. (2006, August 1). Back-to-school crunch: Average family will spend more than $500, analysts predict. *The Milwaukee Journal Sentinel*. Retrieved January 17, 2007, from http://www.lexisnexis.com

Hall, A., & Berardino, L. (2006). Teaching professional behaviors: Differences in the perceptions of faculty, students, and employers. *Journal of Business Ethics, 63*(4), 407–415.

Hancock, N. (2006, July 10). Fashion faux pas: What's wrong with this picture? Retrieved January 15, 2007, from http://usmagazine/fashion_faux_pas_whats_wrong_with_this_picture

Hansen, K. T. (2004). The world in dress: Anthropological perspectives on clothing, fashion, and culture. *Annual Review of Anthropology, 33*, 369–392.

Harris, M. (2006, October 7). Glamour recruits fashion police: Website welcomes faux pas postings. *The Vancouver Sun*, p. F7. Retrieved January 19, 2007, from http://www.lexisnexis.com

Hauser, K. (2004). A garment in the dock: Or, how the FBI illuminated the prehistory of a pair of denim jeans. *Journal of Material Culture, 9*(3), 293–313.

Have you met the bad breath doc? (2006, June 21). *PR Newswire US*. Retrieved January 2, 2007, from http://www.lexisnexis.com

Hawley, J. (2005). The commercialization of Old Order Amish quilts: Enduring and changing cultural meanings. *Clothing and Textiles Research Journal, 23*(3), 102–114.

Hayden-Wade, H. A., Stein, R. I., Ghaderi, A., Saelens, B. E., Zabinski, M. F., & Wilfley, D. E. (2005). Prevalence, characteristics, and correlates of teasing experiences among overweight children vs. non-overweight peers. *Obesity Research, 13*(8), 1381–1392.

He should have put on some pants. (1994, August 10). *Southern Illinoisan*, p. C4.

Hebdige, D. (1979). *Subculture: The meaning of style*. New York: Routledge.

Heckert, D. M. (2003). Mixed blessings: Women and blonde hair. *Free Inquiry in Creative Sociology, 31*(1), 47–72.

Heckman, J., & Lochner, L. (2000). Rethinking education and training policy: Understanding the sources of skill formation in a modern economy. In S. Danziger & J. Waldfogel (Eds.), *Securing the future: Investing in children from birth to college* (pp. 47–86). New York: Russell Sage Foundation.

Hegland, J. (1999). Drag queens, transvestites, transsexuals: Stepping across the accepted boundaries of gender. In M. L. Damhorst, K. A. Miller, & S. O. Michelman (Eds.), *The meanings of dress* (pp. 193–205). New York: Fairchild.

Heinberg, L. J., Thompson, J. D., & Stormer, S. (1995). Development and validation of the Sociocultural Attitudes Towards Appearance Questionnaire. *International Journal of Eating Disorders, 17*, 81–89.

Heins, M. (2006). Gender identity. *Parent Kids Right*. Retrieved December 15, 2006, from http://www.parentkidsright.com

Heller, K. (2006, October 23). Models are so thin, designers so dense. *Philadelphia Inquirer*. Retrieved November 30, 2006, from http://www.lexisnexis.com

Hemmings, A. (2002). Youth culture of hostility: Discourses of money, respect, and difference. *Qualitative Studies in Education, 15*(3), 291–307.

Henderson, T. (2006, February 7). Crime doesn't pay (and neither do baggy pants). *Lewiston Morning Tribune*, p. A6. Retrieved January 17, 2007, from http://www.lexisnexis.com

Hendley, W. C. (1977). Dear Abby, Miss Lonelyhearts, and the eighteenth century: The origins of the newspaper advice column. *Journal of Popular Culture, 11*, 345–352.

Henry, B. (2006, May 18). Bonnie Henry: 'disABLED Divaz' ready for the runway. *Arizona Daily Star*. Retrieved December 8, 2006, from http://www.charityadvantage.com

Hess, A., & Mariner, D. (1975). On the sociology of crime cartoons. *International Journal of Criminology and Penology, 3*, 253–265.

Hicks, P. H., Hall, V. A., & Westbrook, D. L. (2006). Reasonable dress and grooming requirements survive court scrutiny. *Gaming Law Review, 10*(4), 342–346.

Hilgartner, S. & Bosk, C. L. (1988). The rise and fall of social problems: A public arenas model. *American Journal of Sociology, 94*, 53–78.

Hill, J. W. (2006, December 3). Program snaps letter jackets on athletes. *Arkansas Democrat-Gazette*. Retrieved December 21, 2006, from http://www.lexisnexis.com

Hill, R. L. (2005, August 17). Case clothed: Austin students wearing what they're told. *Austin American-Statesman* (Texas). Retrieved December 3, 2005, from http://www.lexisnexis.com

Hirano, K. (2004, October 22). Lolipop Goth. *Women's Wear Daily, 188*(86), pp. 62–64.

Hirschfeld, S. (2005, March 22). National poll shows public opinion sharply divided on regulating appearance—from appearance to tattoos—in the workplace. Retrieved October 31, 2006, from http://www.hrmguide.com/diversity/appearance-at-work.htm

Hirschman, E., & Adcock, W. (1978). An examination of innovative communicators, opinion leaders, and innovators for men's fashion apparel. In H. Keith Hunt (Ed.), *Advances in consumer research* (pp. 303–314). Ann Arbor, MI: Association for Consumer Research.

Hirschman, E. C., & Holbrook, M. B. (1982). Hedonic consumption: Emerging concepts, methods, and propositions. *Journal of Marketing, 46*, 92–101.

Hodkinson, P. (2002). *Goth: Identity, Style, and Subculture*. In J. B. Eicher (Ed.), Dress, Body, and Culture Series. Oxford: Berg.

Hohlstein, L. A., Smith, G. T., & Atlas, J. G. (1998). An application of expectancy theory to eating disorders: Development and validation of measures of eating and dieting expectancies. *Psychological Assessment, 10*, 49–58.

Holbeche, L. (2006, September 19). The soft skills are the hardest of all. *Personnel Today*, p. 18.

Holme, P. (2005). Modeling the dynamics of youth subculture. *Journal of Artificial Societies & Social Simulation, 8*(3), 43–54.

Hood, M. (2006, March 12). Appearances matter: Shoppers who are well-dressed get better service, study confirms. *The Columbus Dispatch*. Retrieved February 14, 2007, from http://www.lexisnexis.com

Horswell, C. (2006, March 26). Schools learn bullying can plant seed for tragedy. *The Houston Chronicle*, p. 1. Retrieved January 12, 2007, from http://www.lexisnexis.com

Houweling, L. (2004). Image, function, and style: A history of the nursing uniform. *American Journal of Nursing, 104*(4), 40–48.

Hsuan, A., & Melton, K. (2006, November 7). Schools become stricter on clothes that send signal. *The Sunday Oregonian*, p. B1. Retrieved January 4, 2007, from http://www.lexisnexis.com

Huber, S. J. (2003). The white coat ceremony: A contemporary medical ritual. *Journal of Medical Ethics, 29*(6), 364–366.

Huisman, K., & Hondagneu-Sotelo, P. (2005). Dress matters: Change and continuity in the dress practices of Bosnian Muslim refugee women. *Gender & Society, 19*, 44–65.

Hunt, E. F., & Colander, D. C. (2005). *Social science: An introduction to the study of society* (12th Ed.). Boston: Pearson.

Hurd, L. C. (2000). Older women's body image and embodied experience: An exploration. *Journal of Women & Aging, 12*(3/4), 77–97.

Huun, K., & Kaiser, S. B. (2001). The emergence of modern infantwear, 1896–1962: Traditional white dresses succumb to fashion's gender obsession. *Clothing and Textiles Research Journal, 19*(3), 103–119.

Indie rock. (2007, January 16). Retrieved January 17, 2007, from en.wikipedia.org/wiki/Indie_rock

Irwin, K. (2001). Legitimating the first tattoo: Moral passage through informal interaction. *Symbolic Interaction, 24*(1), 49–73.

Irwin, K. (2003). Saints and sinners: Elite tattoo collectors and tattooists as positive and negative deviants. *Sociological Spectrum, 23*, 27–57.

Israelsen, S. (2006, January 18). A dress designer at age 7. *Deseret Morning News*. Retrieved January 12, 2007, from http://www.lexisnexis.com

It's official wearing miniskirts no longer a crime in South Korea. (2006, November 4). *Global News Wire*. Retrieved January 11, 2007, from http://www.lexisnexis.com

Janes, L. M., & Olson, J. M. (2000). Jeer pressure: The behavioral effects of observing ridicule of others. *Personality and Social Psychology Bulletin, 26*(4), 474–485.

Johnson, J. M. (1989). Horror stories and the construction of child abuse. In J. Best (Ed.), *Images of issues*, pp. 5–20. New York: Aldine de Gruyter.

Jones, C. (2006, August 24). Back to school shopping season. *Las Vegas Review-Journal*, p. D7. Retrieved January 17, 2007, from http://www.lexisnexis.com

Jones, D. C., & Crawford, J. K. (2006). The peer appearance culture during adolescence: Gender and body mass variations. *Journal of Youth and Adolescence, 2*, 257–269.

Jones, D. C., Vigfusdottir, T. H., & Lee, Y. (2004). Body image and the appearance culture among adolescent girls and boys: An examination of friend conversations, peer criticism, appearance magazines, and the internalization of appearance ideals. *Journal of Adolescent Research, 19*(3), 323–339.

Judges to lawyers: Dress up or stay out. (2006, August 21). *The Associated Press State & Local Wire*. Retrieved December 12, 2006, from http://www.lexisnexis.com

Junkin, B. S. (2006, July 14). Keeping in step by following rules for buying, wearing. *Plain Dealer* (Cleveland), p. E2. Retrieved January 18, 2007, from http://www.lexisnexis.com

Kaiser, S. B. (1997). *The social psychology of clothing: Symbolic appearances in context* (2nd ed. revised). New York: Fairchild.

Kaiser, S. B. (1993). Linking the social psychology of dress to culture: A contextual perspective. In S. Lennon & L. Burns (Eds.), *The social science of dress: New directions* (pp. 39–47). Monument, CO: International Textile & Apparel Association.

Kamer, G. J., & Keller, E. A. (2003). Give me $5 chips, a jack and coke–hold the cleavage: A look at employee appearance issues in the gaming industry. *Gaming Law Review, 7*(5), 335–346.

Kanzler, M. H., & Gorsulowsky, D. C. (2002). Patients' attitudes regarding physical characteristics of medical care providers in dermatologic practices. *Archives of Dermatology, 138,* 463–466.

Kate Moss named top British model. (2006, November 2). Agence France Press—English. Retrieved November 30, 2006, from http://www.lexisnexis.com

Keery, H., Boutelle, K., van den Berg, P., & Thompson, J. K. (2005). The impact of appearance-related teasing by family members. *Journal of Adolescent Health, 37,* 120–127.

Kelleher, J. S. (2006, June 6). Pregnant cops' trial begins. *Newsday.* Retrieved January 5, 2007, from http://www.lexisnexis.com

Keller, K. (1998). *Strategic Brand Management.* Upper Saddle River, NJ: Prentice Hall.

Kelly, D., Pomerantz, S., & Currie, D. (2005). Skater girlhood and emphasized femininity: 'You can't land an ollie properly in heels.' *Gender and Education, 17*(3), 229–248.

Kendall, D. E. (2007). *Sociology in our times* (6th ed.). Belmont, CA: Wadsworth.

Khosropour, S. C., & Walsh, J. (2001, April). *That's not teasing—that's bullying: A study of fifth graders' conceptualization of bullying and teasing.* Paper presented at the Annual Meeting of the American Educational Research Association, Seattle, WA. ED 453 474

Kidd, L. K. (2006). A case study: Creating special occasion garments for young women with special needs. *Clothing and Textiles Research Journal, 24*(2), 161–172.

Kim, M., & Lennon, S. J. (2005). The effects of customers' dress on salesperson's service in large-sized clothing specialty stores. *Clothing and Textiles Research Journal, 23*(2), 78–87.

King, G. R., Winchester, J. D., & Sherwyn, D. (2006). You (don't) look marvelous: Considerations for employers regulating employee appearance. *Cornell Hotel and Restaurant Administration Quarterly, 47*(4), 359–368.

Kinnon, J. B. (2000, April). Pierced to death. *Ebony,* pp. 143–144, 146.

Kitsuse, J. (1972). Deviance, deviant behavior, and deviants: Some conceptual issues. In W. J. Filstead (Ed.), *An introduction to deviance* (pp. 233–243). Chicago: Markham.

Kitwana, B. (2002). *The Hip Hop generation: Young Blacks and the crisis in African American culture.* New York: Basic Books.

Koenig, H. G., McCullough, M. E., & Larson, D. B. (2001). *Handbook of religion and health.* London: Oxford University Press.

Koenig, L. M., & Carnes, M. (1999). Body piercing: Medical concerns with cutting-edge fashion. *Journal of General Internal Medicine, 14,* 379–385.

Kogan, R. (1996, May 29). Forty years of letters. *St. Louis Post-Dispatch,* p. 3–E.

Kuhlthau, C. (1993). *Seeking meaning: A process approach to library and information services.* Norwood, NJ: Ablex Publishing.

Kunkel, C., & Nielsen, J. M. (1998). Gender, residual deviance, and social control. *Deviant Behavior: An Interdisciplinary Journal, 19,* 339–360.

Kuntzman, G. (1999). It's been 40 years coming and now . . . Barbie's new, improved and tattooed. *New York Post, 4,* 61–62.

Kuttler, A. F., Parker, J. G., & La Greca, A. M. (2002). Developmental and gender differences in preadolescents' judgments of the veracity of gossip. *Merrill-Palmer Quarterly, 48*(2), 105–132.

Kwon, K-N., & Lee, J. (2003). Concerns about payment security of Internet purchases: A perspective on current on-line shoppers. *Clothing and Textiles Research Journal, 21*(4), 174–184.

Lamont, M., & Lareau, A. (1988). Cultural capital: Allusions, gaps and glissandos in recent theoretical developments. *Sociological Theory, 6,* 153–168.

Landers, A. (1998, August 23). Tattoos meant to draw attention. *Southern Illinoisan,* p. E2.

Landers, A. (1999, May 2). Dead husband's secret is torture. *Southern Illinoisan,* p. E2.

Lands' End [catalog]. (2006). Retrieved January 3, 2007, from http://www.landsend.com

Laue, C. (2006, May 28). Dress to express Omaha's indie rockers and fans roll against the mainstream fashion tide. *Omaha World-Herald,* p. E1. Retrieved January 11, 2007, from http://www.lexisnexis.com

Lawrence, B. (1996). Organizational age norms: Why is it so hard to know when you see one? *Gerontologist, 36*(2), 209–220.

Leary, M. R., Kowalski, R. M., Smith, L., & Phillips, S. (2003). Teasing, rejection, and violence: Case studies of the school shootings. *Aggressive Behavior, 29,* 202–214.

Leblanc, L. (1999). *Pretty in punk: Girls' gender resistance in a boys' subculture.* New Brunswick, NJ: Rutgers University Press.

Legg, K. (2006, April 16). Passion for fashion makes me the family outcast. *Charleston Gazette,* p. F12. Retrieved January 12, 2007, from http://www.lexisnexis.com

Lennon, S. J. (1999). Sex, dress, and power in the workplace: Star Trek, the Next Generation. In K. K. Johnson & S. J. Lennon (Eds.), *Appearance and power* (pp.103–126). New York, NY: Berg.

Levenson, E. (2006, January 13). Whoops! You can see my underwear. *The Times Educational Supplement,* p. 30. Retrieved January 11, 2007, from http://www.lexisnexis.com

Levin, J., Mody-Desbareau, A., & Arluke, A. (1988). The gossip tabloid as agent of social control. *Journalism Quarterly, 65,* 514–517.

Levine, M. P., Smolak, L., & Hayden, H. (1994). The relation of sociocultural factors to eating attitudes and behaviors among middle school girls. *Journal of Early Adolescence, 14,* 471–490.

Loftus, M. (2000). The roots of being blonde. *U.S. News & World Report, 128,* p. 52.

Loker, S., Cowie, L., Ashdown, S., & Lewis, V. D. (2004). Female consumers' reactions to body scanning. *Clothing and Textiles Research Journal, 22*(4), 151–160.

Loomis, S. (1988, October 16). Shopper's world: Hawaii's short-sleeve plumage. *The New York Times.* Retrieved January 4, 2007, from http://query.nytimes.com

Lopatto, D. (2003, March). The essential features of undergraduate research. *Council on Undergraduate Research Quarterly,* 139–142.

Lopatto, D. (2006, Winter). Undergraduate research as a catalyst for liberal learning. *Association of American Colleges and Universities Peer Review,* 22–25.

Lopez, J. P. (2006, March 28). With bags, some things irreplaceable. *The Houston Chronicle.* Retrieved January 2, 2007, from http://www.lexisnexis.com

Lutey, T. (2006, July 23). Tradition tops temperature: Heavy heirloom dresses worn with pride at Julyamsh ceremonies. *Spokesman Review* (Spokane, WA), p. B1. Retrieved January 1, 2007, from http://www.lexisnexis.com

Luther, M. (2006, May 24). Punk influence slight in fashions of today. *Plain Dealer,* p. E6. Retrieved January 19, 2007, from http://www.lexisnexis.com

Madden, D. (2006, October 14). Fashion flap vexes school. *Brattleboro Reformer.* Retrieved November 16, 2006, from http://www.lexisnexis.com

Man dressed as a woman is no threat in the ladies' restroom. (2006, August 18). *Chattanooga Times Free Press.* Retrieved December 14, 2006, from http://www.lexisnexis.com

Mansfield, S. (2006, May 14). Not your mother's prom. *The Washington Times,* p. D1. Retrieved January 5, 2007, from http://www.lexisnexis.com

Maragh, R. (2006, September 1). Why we clique. *Tulsa World* (Oklahoma), p. D1. Retrieved January 19, 2007, from http://www.lexisnexis.com

Maraghy, M. (2006, September 30). Sometimes, teachers have to become fashion police: There are students who leave home dressed OK, then change at school. *Florida Times-Union,* p. M1. Retrieved January 11, 2007, from http://www.lexisnexis.com

Marshall, S. (2006, January 16). Fashion faux pas: Some women learn the hard way what works. *Crain's New York Business,* p. 51. Retrieved January 6, 2007, from http://www.lexisnexis.com

Mathias, M. (2006, August 18). Easton Area relaxes parts of its new dress code after outcry from parents, students. *Morning Call,* p. B5. Retrieved January 1, 2007, from http://www.lexisnexis.com

Matthews, P. (Ed.). (1993). *Guinness Book of World Records.* New York: Bantam.

May, T. A. (2006, March 14). Appearance matters, even in IT. *Computerworld, 39*(11), pp. 22–23.

Mccahill, K. (2006, December 5). Resident dress code targets gangs: But apartment complex's rules prompt criticism. *Saint Paul Pioneer Press.* Retrieved December 9, 2006, from http://web.ebscohost.com

McCloud, C. (2006, August 24). School's in; hats off, boys and girls. *The Dominion Post.* Retrieved November 30, 2006, from http://www.lexisnexis.com

McCracken, G., & Roth, V. (1989). Does clothing have a code? Empirical findings and theoretical implications in the study of clothing as a means of communication. *International Journal of Research in Marketing, 6,* 13–33.

McDowell, K. (2006, December 17). Glamour Web Photo column: Some fashion advice is just too obvious. *The Dominion Post.* Retrieved January 1, 2007, from http://www.lexisnexis.com

McGee, J. (2006, October 14). T-shirt words: Harmless or provocative? *The Post and Courier,* p. B1. Retrieved January 4, 2007, from http://www.lexisnexis.com

McGee, M. (1979). *Human spatial abilities.* New York: Praeger.

Mclaren, L., Kuh, D., Hardy, R., & Gauvin, L. (2004). Positive and negative body-related comments and their relationship with body dissatisfaction in middle-aged women. *Psychology and Health, 19*(2), 261–272.

McNeal, J. (1987). *Children as consumers.* Lexington, MA: Lexington Books.

The media business: Advertising; Dot-com companies have built their brands by using more ads, in good taste or not. Often not. *The New York Times.* Retrieved January 1, 2007 from http://query.nytimes.com

Mehrabian, A., & Russell, J. A. (1974). *An approach to environmental psychology.* Cambridge, MA: MIT Press.

Meier, R. (1982). Perspectives on the concept of social control. In R. H. Turner & J. F. Short (Eds.), *Annual review of sociology* (pp. 35–55). Palo Alto, CA: Annual Reviews Inc.

Mervyns' study reveals a new pair of shoes can step up your self-confidence. (2006, March 8). *PR Newswire US.* Retrieved January 1, 2007, from http://www.lexisnexis.com

Metrosexual. (2007). Retrieved January 6, 2007, from http://en.wikipedia.org/wiki/Metrosexual

Miceli, M., & Castelfranchi, C. (2005). Anxiety as an "epistemic" emotion: An uncertainty theory of anxiety. *Anxiety, Stress, and Coping, 18*(4), 291–319.

Moake, D. (2003, June 17). Judge made the wrong decision. *Southern Illinoisan*, p. A4.

Monsen, L. (2006, November 30). Acceptance of religious garb in U.S. shows diversity, tolerance. Retrieved March 14, 2007, from http://www.lexisnexis.com

Moore, P. J. (2006, May 1). Responding to recent trends in dress and appearance. Retrieved November 18, 2006, from http://www.mccarter.com

Morrison, C. (1982, October 22). Cartoon coppers. *Police Review*, 2034–2037.

Morsch, L. (2006, September 11). 10 crimes of work fashion. CNN. Retrieved November 16, 2006, from http://www.lexisnexis.com

Mortenson, E. (2006, July 27). 'My name used to be Larry Deyo.' *The Oregonian*. Retrieved January 2, 2007, from http://www.lexisnexis.com

Mosley, S. (2006, September 8). Dos and don'ts still important even without hard fashion rules. *Copley News Service*. Retrieved January 18, 2007, from http://www.lexisnexis.com

Mui, Y. Q. (2006, March 18). The selling of 'trailer park chic.' *The Washington Post*, p. D1. Retrieved January 1, 2007, from http://www.lexisnexis.com

Muir, J. (2003a, June 12). Judge dresses down man over T-shirt. *Southern Illinoisan*, p. A1–A2.

Muir, J. (2003b, June 17). Shirt 'tale' doesn't fly with Franklin judge. *Southern Illinoisan*, p. A4.

Muir, J. (2003c, June 18). Man sent to jail for obscene T-shirt released. *Southern Illinoisan*, p. A1.

Mulcahy, A. (1995). Claims-making and the construction of legitimacy: Press coverage of the 1981 Northern Irish hunger strike. *Social Problems, 42*(4), 449–467.

Murray, B. (2006, November 20). How pop culture icons become religious-like figures. Retrieved November 20, 2006, from http://www.facsnet.org/issues/faith/selena.php

Murray, Plumb, & Murray. (2006, August). Hot child in the city. *Maine Employment Law Letter, 11*(12). Retrieved January 6, 2007, from http://www.lexisnexis.com

Nardi, E. (2006, April 8). Teens find ways to make prom priceless without breaking the bank. *The Associated Press State & Local Wire*. Retrieved January 5, 2007, from http://www.lexisnexis.com

National casual businesswear survey sparks debate: What is appropriate attire for the office? (2001, May 9). Retrieved May 25, 2006, from http://www.textile.texworld.com/informationcenter/News/2001/May/nw2001may09001.htm.

National School Boards Association. (1993). *Violence in the schools. How America's school boards are safeguarding your children.* Alexandria, VA.

Nenga, S. K. (2003). Social class and structures of feeling in women's childhood memories of clothing, food, and leisure. *Journal of Contemporary Ethnography, 32*(2), 167–199.

Neufeld, S. (2005, November 12). Protest is a lesson in conflict; Students suspended after walking out. *The Baltimore Sun*. Retrieved December 3, 2005, from http://www.lexisnexis.com

Nevo, O., & Nevo, B. (1993). Gossip and counseling: The tendency to gossip and its relation to vocational interests. *Counseling Psychology Quarterly, 6*, 229–239.

Nevo, O., Nevo, B., & Derech-Zehavi, A. (1994). The tendency to gossip as a psychological disposition: Constructing a measure and validating it. In B. F. Goodman & A. Ben-Ze'ev (Eds.), *Good gossip* (pp. 180–189, 191–192). Mahwah, NJ: Erlbaum.

Newman, B., & Newman, P. (1987). *Development through life: A psychosocial approach.* Chicago, IL: Dorsey Press.

Nickson, D., Warhurst, C., & Dutton, E. (2005). The importance of attitude and appearance in the service encounter in retail and hospitality. *Managing Service Quality, 15*(2), 195–208.

Nielsen, J. M., Walden, G., & Kunkel, C. A. (2000). Gendered heteronormativity: Empirical illustrations in everyday life. *Sociological Quarterly, 41*(2), 283–296.

Norton, Q. (2006, March 8). Body artists customize your flesh. Retrieved October 11, 2006, from http://www.Wired.com

Novakovich, M. (1999, November 3). The playground pound. *The Guardian*, pp. 8–9. Retrieved March 14, 2007, from http://www.guardian.co.uk

Nurses' attire shows no pride. (1997, August 25). *Southern Illinoisan*, p. B5.

Obesity research: Some people would give life or limb not to be fat. (2006, June 6). *Obesity, Fitness & Wellness Week*, p. 101. Retrieved January 18, 2007, from http://www.lexisnexis.com

O'Brien, M., Peyton, V., Mistry, R., Hruda, L., Jacobs, A., Caldera, Y., et al. (2000). Gender role cognition in three-year-old boys and girls. *Sex Roles, 42*, 1007–1025.

O'Cass, A. (2004). Fashion clothing consumption: Antecedents and consequences of fashion clothing involvement. *European Journal of Marketing, 38*(7), 869–882.

O'Cass, A. (2001). Consumer self-monitoring, materialism and involvement in fashion clothing. *Australasian Marketing Journal, 9*(1), 46–60.

Old Navy recalls children's clothing. (2004, June 9). *Southern Illinoisan*, p. D1.

Older and better. (2006, January 3). *The News & Observer*, p. A8. Retrieved January 1, 2007, from http://www.lexisnexis.com

Olweus, D. (1997). Bully/victim problems in school: Facts and intervention. *European Journal of Psychology of Education, 4*, 495–510.

O'Neal, G. (1997). Clothes to kill for: An analysis of primary and secondary claims-making in print media. *Sociological Inquiry, 67*(3), 336–349.

O'Neill, J. M. (2006, May 20). As students plan futures, schools plan graduation. *The Dallas Morning News*. Retrieved December 21, 2006, from http://www.lexisnexis.com

*O*Net Descriptors*. (2004). Retrieved December 18, 2006, from http://online.onetcenter.org/find/

Onquegbuzie, A., & Leech, N. L. (2005). On becoming a pragmatic researcher: The importance of combining quantitative and qualitative research methodologies. *International Journal of Social Research Methodology, 8*(5), 375–387.

Pacio, N. (2006, October 23). At his girlfriend's behest, rumpled tech worker gets advice for a new look. *San Jose Mercury News*. Retrieved January 4, 2007, from http://www.lexisnexis.com

Paoletti, J. (1981). Cartoons and the costume historian. *Dress, 7*, 47–51.

Paoletti, J. (1985). Ridicule and role models as factors in American men's fashion change, 1880–1910. *Costume, 19*, 121–134.

Paoletti, J. B., & Kregloh, C. L. (1989). The children's department. In C. B. Kidwell & V. Steele (Eds.), *Men and women: Dressing the part* (pp. 22–41). Washington, DC: Smithsonian Institution Press.

Parekh, F. S., & Schmidt, R. A. (2003). In pursuit of an identity—fashion marketing and the development of eating disorders. *British Food Journal, 105*(4/5), 230–238.

Parker, M. (2006, May 1). Prom chance to see young people in full bloom. *The Free Press*. Retrieved January 1, 2006, from http://www.lexisnexis.com

Pasciak, M. (2006, September 5). Schools say no to 3 fashion R's: Raunchy, revealing, and risqué. *Buffalo News*, p. A1. Retrieved January 1, 2007, from http://www.lexisnexis.com

Payne, B., Winakor, G., & Farrell-Beck, J. (1992). *The history of costume* (2nd ed.). New York: HarperCollins.

Pekin nudist found guilty. (1998, December 11). *Southern Illinoisan*, p. A5.

Pelican, S., Heede, F. V., Holmes, B., Melcher, L. M., Wardlaw, M. K., Raidl, M., et al. (2005). The power of others to shape our identity: Body image, physical abilities, and body weight. *Family and Consumer Sciences Research Journal, 34*(1), 56–79.

Peluchette, J. V., Karl, K., & Rust, K. (2006). Dressing to impress: Beliefs and attitudes regarding workplace dress. *Journal of Business and Psychology, 21*(1), 45–63.

Persad, J. V., & Lukas, S. (2002). *"No hijab is permitted here": A study of the experiences of Muslim women wearing hijab applying for work in the manufacturing, sales, and service sectors.* Toronto, ON: Canadian Heritage—Multiculturalism.

Personal appearance of employees. (2006). Available from https://www.hrpolicyanswers.com/xstore/product.php?productid=64&cat=0&page=1

Personality Plus. (2002, July 25). *Women's Wear Daily Lifestyle Monitor.* Article 261. Retrieved December 2004, from http://www.cottoninc.com/wwd/homepage.cfm

Pierce, B. (2003, Spring/Summer). Clothing, grooming, and social acceptability: Part 1. *Future Reflections.* Retrieved January 4, 2007, from http://www.nfb.org

Pilgrim, L., & Lawrence, D. (2001). Pester power is a destructive concept. *International Journal of Advertising and Marketing to Children, 3*(1), 11–22.

Pitts, L. (2005, Oct. 26). Is NBA dress code racist? Who cares? *Southern Illinoisan,* p. 4A.

Pitts, V. (1999). Body modification, self-mutilation, and agency in media accounts of a subculture. *Body & Society, 5,* 291–304.

Podsada, J. (2006, August 23). The brand-name game. *Hartford Courant,* p. E1. Retrieved January 18, 2007, from http://www.lexisnexis.com

Pomerantz, S., Currie, D., & Kelly, D. (2004). Sk8er girls: Skateboarders, girlhood and feminism in motion. *Women's Studies International Forum, 27,* 547–557.

Post, R., Appiah, K. A., Butler, J., Grey, T. C., & Siegel, R. B. (2001). Prejudicial appearances: The logic of American antidiscrimination law. Durham, NC: Duke University Press.

Price, J., & Zamkoff, B. (1996). *Grading techniques for fashion design.* New York: Fairchild.

Punk fashion. (2006). Retrieved December 15, 2006, from http://www.answers.com/topic/punk-fashion

Raeymaeckers, K. (2005). Letters to the editor: A feedback opportunity turned into a marketing tool. *European Journal of Communication, 20*(2), 199–221.

Rauh, G. (2006, October 23). Bay Area public schools embrace uniforms. *Inside Bay Area.* Retrieved January 3, 2007, from http://www.lexisnexis.com

Raven, B. H. (1992). A power interaction model of interpersonal influence: French and Raven thirty years later. *Journal of Social Behavior and Personality, 7,* 217–244.

Read, M. (2006, October 18). Tattoos, piercings slip into dress codes. *Associated Press Online.* Retrieved November 16, 2006, from http://www.lexisnexis.com

Reddington, H. (2004). The forgotten revolution of female punk musicians in the 1970s. *Peace Review, 16*(4), 439–444.

Reed, B. (2006, May 9). Redneck chic: Endearment or ridicule? *The Gazette.* Retrieved January 4, 2007, from http://www.lexisnexis.com

Reese, A. T. B., & Strauss, G. (2004, April 28). Prom costs how much? *USA Today,* p. 14. Retrieved January 2, 2007, from http://usatoday.com

Reglin, G. L., & Chisom, M. (1993). Self-perception and achievement of 10th grade urban African American males: Classroom instructional implications. *Journal of Research on Minority Affairs, 4*(1), 41–50.

Reitberger, R., & Fuchs, W. (1971). *Comics: Anatomy of a mass medium.* Boston: Little, Brown.

Renfro, P. (1979). Bias in selection in letters to the editor. *Journalism Quarterly, 56,* 822–826.

Renteln, A. D. (2004). Visual religious symbols and the law. *American Behavioral Scientist, 47,* 1573–1596.

Ribeiro, A. (1986). *Dress and morality.* New York: Holmes & Meier Publishers.

Rice's 'renegade' fashion sense gets her on best dressed list. (2006, July 31). *Agence France-Presse.* Retrieved December 20, 2006, from http://www.lexisnexis.com

Ridgley, J. (2006, September 21). New school year brings new changes to the school handbook. *The Prowler,* p. 1.

Roberts, T. (2006, September 3). Tommie's fashion talk. *Charleston Gazette,* p. F1. Retrieved January 18, 2007, from http://www.lexisnexis.com

Roberts, T. A., Auinger, P., & Ryan, S. A. (2004). Body piercing and high-risk behavior in adolescents. *Journal of Adolescent Health, 34,* 224–229.

Rodin, J., Silberstein, L., & Striegel-Moore, R. (1984). Women and weight: A normative discontent. *Nebraska Symposium on Motivation, 32,* 267–307.

Rosenbaum, J., Kariya, T., Settersten, R., & Maier, T. (1990). Market and network theories of the transition from high school to work: Their application to industrialized societies. *Annual Review of Sociology, 16,* 263–299.

Rosenberg, M. (1965). *Society and the adolescent self-image.* Princeton, NJ: Princeton University Press.

Rosnow, R. L. (1977). Gossip and marketplace psychology. *Journal of Communication,* 158–163.

Ross, J., & Harradine, R. (2004). I'm not wearing that! Branding and young children. *Journal of Fashion Marketing and Management, 8*(1), 11–26.

Roth, D. A., Coles, M. E., & Heimberg, R. G. (2002). The relationship between memories for childhood teasing and anxiety and depression in adulthood. *Anxiety Disorders, 16,* 149–164.

Rowbotham, J. (2002, October 28). Modesty is important, say Christian leaders. *Weekend Australian,* p. 9. Retrieved March 14, 2007, from http://www.lexisnexis.com

Rubinstein, R. (1995). *Dress codes: Meanings and messages in American culture.* Boulder, CO: Westview Press.

Rudd, N. A., & Lennon, S. J. (2000). Body image and appearance management behaviors in college women. *Clothing and Textiles Research Journal, 18*(3), 152–162.

Saenger, G. (1955). Male and female relations in the American comic strip. *Public Opinion Quarterly, 19*(2), 195–205.

Salas, R. (2006, February 16). Web search: On the red carpet. *Star Tribune,* p. E2. Retrieved January 11, 2007, from http://www.lexisnexis.com

Salerno, C. (2006, August 8). The heat is on; Flip-flops need to stop, work attire experts say. *Modesto Bee,* p. D1. Retrieved January 6, 2007, from http://www.lexisnexis.com

Salter, F., Grammer, K., & Rikowski, A. (2005). Sex differences in negotiating with powerful males. *Human Nature, 16*(3), 306–321.

San Francisco Museum of Modern Art. (1997). *A family guide for icons: Magnets of meaning* [Brochure]. San Francisco.

Scheff, T. J. (1984). *Being mentally ill: A sociological theory* (2d edition). New York: Aldine de Gruyter.

Schmidt, K. D. (2001). "Sacred farming" or "working out": The negotiated lives of conservative Mennonite farm women. *Frontiers: A Journal of Women's Studies, 22*(1), 79–102.

Schneider, S. M. (1996, March 20–22). *The bigger picture: Context in the research methods course.* Proceedings of the Tenth Annual Conference on Undergraduate Teaching of Psychology, Ellenville, NY. (ERIC Document Reproduction Service No. ED 405025)

Schultz, J. (2006, June 6). Martin lightens up dress code for summer. *Palm Beach Post,* p. B1. Retrieved January 6, 2007, from http://www.lexisnexis.com

Schultz, T. (2000). Mass media and the concept of interactivity: An exploratory study of online forums and reader e-mail. *Media, Culture and Society, 22*(2), 205–221.

Schwartz, B. M., & Ewald, R. H. (1968). *Culture and society.* New York: Ronald Press.

Schworm, P. (2006, March 27). Dress code in play at blue-collar course. *The Boston Globe,* p. B1. Retrieved January 6, 2007, from http://www.lexisnexis.com

Scott v. School Board of Alachua County. (2003). *West's Education Law Reporter,* 175, pp. 88–92.

Seventeen. (n.d.). Retrieved October 13, 2006, from http://www.hearst.com/magazines/

Shapira, I. (2006, September 26). Teens' T-shirts make educators squirm. *The Washington Post.* Retrieved October 4, 2006, from http://www.washingtonpost.com

Sharkey, W. F. (1997). Why would anyone want to intentionally embarrass me? In R. M. Kowalski (Ed.), *Aversive interpersonal behaviors,* pp. 57–90. New York: Plenum.

Shen, D., & Dickson, M. A. (2001). Consumers' acceptance of unethical clothing consumption activities: Influence of cultural identification, ethnicity, and Machiavellianism. *Clothing and Textiles Research Journal, 19*(2), 76–87.

Shepard, J. (2005). *Sociology* (9th ed.). Belmont, CA: Wadsworth.

Siann, G., Callaghan, M., Lockhart, R., & Rawson, L. (1993). Bullying: Teacher's views and school effects. *Educational Studies, 19,* 307–321.

Simmons, K. (2006, April 16). Lure of fame, fortune helps pageants last. *The Atlanta Journal-Constitution.* Retrieved December 20, 2006, from http://www.lexisnexis.com

Simpson, M. (2002). Meet the metrosexual. *Salon.* Retrieved January 1, 2007, from http://www.salon.com/ent/feature/2002/07/22/metrosexual/print.html

Singer, G. (2006, April 3). Dress codes a key component for companies looking to build their images. *Fort Lauderdale Sun-Sentinel.* Retrieved August 27, 2006, from http://web.ebscohost.com.proxy.lib.siu.edu/ehost/delivery?vid=18&hid=102&sid=2dc3df3

Sissem, P., & Maria, D. (2007). The stigmatization of women of size. Retrieved February 1, 2007, from http://www.misu.nodak.edu/research/Stigma.pdf

6th Cir. upholds Ky. middle school's strict student dress code; Legal expert calls the ruling a victory for 'common sense.' (2005, March 9). *Your School and the Law,* 35(5). Retrieved December 3, 2005, from http://www.lexisnexis.com

Skaggs, P. (2004, September). Observational research: Formalized curiosity. *The Technology Teacher,* 11–13.

Skinner, B. F. (1953). *Science and human behavior.* New York: Macmillan.

Slade, P. D. (1994). What is body image? *Behavior Research and Theory, 32*(5), 497–502.

Smelser, N. J. (Ed.). (1973). *Sociology: An introduction* (2nd Ed.). New York: John Wiley.

Smith, D. (1990). *Texts, facts, and femininity: Exploring the relations of ruling.* London: Routledge.

Smith, S. T. (2006a, April 18). A corsage and cummer-whats? A guys' guide to making the prom the best night of your life, too. *The News & Observer.* Retrieved January 5, 2007, from http://www.lexisnexis.com

Smith, S. T. (2006b, September 25). Taking the plunge: In the name of all that is decent, how low should you go? *The News & Observer,* p. C1. Retrieved March 14, 2007, from http://www.lexisnexis.com

Snead, E. (2003, June 1). The beauty of symmetry. *USA Weekend.* Retrieved December 8, 2006, from http://www.usaweekend.com/03_issues/030601/030601symmetry.html

Snyder, M. (1974). Self-monitoring of expressive behavior. *Journal of Personality and Social Psychology, 30,* 526–537.

Snyder, M. (1979). Self-monitoring processes. *Advances in Experimental Social Psychology, 12,* 86–128.

Solomon, M. (1996). *Consumer behavior,* 3rd ed., Englewood Cliffs, N.J: Prentice-Hall.

Solomon, T. (2006, December 6). Time for single gal to dump dowdy duds. *The Miami Herald.* Retrieved December 11, 2006, from http://www.lexisnexis.com

Sonner, A. (2006, April 15). Bartenders' makeup stays on, court rules. *Southern Illinoisan,* p. 5A.

Sotillo, S., & Starace-Nastasi, D. (1999). Political discourse of a working-class town. *Discourse and Society, 10,* 249–276.

South Carolina prisons director defends putting inmates in pink. (2007, August 21). *International Herald Tribune.* Retrieved October 18, 2007, from www.iht.com/articles/ap/2007/08/21/america/NA-GEN-US-Pink-Prisoners.php

Spector, M., & Kitsuse, J. (1977). *Constructing social problems.* Menlo Park, CA: Cummings Publishing Company.

Spicuzza, M. (2006, July 25). District may tell teachers what not to wear. *St. Petersburg Times.* Retrieved November 30, 2006, from http://www.lexisnexis.com

Spiegelman, M., Terwilliger, C., & Fearing, F. (1953). The content of comics: Goals and means to goals of comic strip characters. *Journal of Social Psychology, 37,* 189–203.

Spring into cotton—Runway trends. Retrieved May 30, 2006, from www.thefabricofourlives.com/StyleFile/SpringIntoCotton

Sproles, G., & Burns, L. (1994). *Changing appearances.* New York: Fairchild.

Stewart, R. (2006, November 11). Confederate flag dispute brings two Alvin teens home. *The Houston Chronicle.* Retrieved November 16, 2006, from http://www.lexisnexis.com

Stirling, R. B. (1956). Some psychological mechanisms operative in gossip. *Social Forces, 34,* 262–267.

Stirn, A. (2003). Body piercing: Medical consequences and psychological motivations. *Lancet, 361*(9364), 1205–1216.

Stohs-Krause, H. (2006, July 9). Birthday suit: The classic two piece is still going strong after 60 years. *Wisconsin State Journal.* Retrieved December 4, 2006, from http://www.lexisnexis.com

Streicher, L. (1965). David Low and the sociology of caricature. *Comparative Studies in Society and History, 8*(1), 1–23.

Suitor, J. J., & Carter, R. S. (1999). Jocks, nerds, babes and thugs: A research note on regional differences in adolescent gender norms. *Gender Issues, 17*(3), 87–101.

Suitor, J. J., & Reavis, R. (1995). Football, fast cars, and cheerleading: Adolescent gender norms, 1978–1989. *Adolescence, 30*(118), 265–272.

Sullivan, B. (2006, June 3). Short & sweet: Whether they're Bermudas, crops or gauchos, short pants are earning respectability in the workplace. *The Buffalo News,* p. C1.

Suls, J. M. (1977). Gossip as social comparison. *Journal of Communication, 27*(1), 164–168.

Summary report for fashion designers. (2004). Occupational Information Network O*NET On-Line. Retrieved December 14, 2006, from O*Net Descriptors at http://online.onetcenter.org/find/

Summerfield, R. (2006, May 30). What's in a nickname? *Times Colonist.* Retrieved December 20, 2006, from http://www.lexisnexis.com

Swanson, A. (2003, July 6). Born on the 4th of July. *Capitol Hill Blue.* Retrieved February 3, 2004, from www.capitolhillblue.com/artman/publish/article_2502.shtml#top

Sweeting, H., & West, P. (2001). Being different: Correlates of the experience of teasing and bullying at age 11. *Research Papers in Education, 16*(3), 225–246.

Synott, A. (1987). Shame and glory: A sociology of hair. *British Journal of Sociology, 38,* 381–413.

Szkrybalo, J., & Ruble, D. N. (1999). "God made me a girl": Sex-category constancy judgments and explanations revisited. *Developmental Psychology, 35*, 392–402.

Tanner, L. (2002, April 14). Despite TV image, patients want docs to be well-dressed, study says. The Associated Press State & Local Wire. Retrieved May 31, 2006, from http://www.lexisnexis.com.

Tattoo rules: Aesthetic sensibilities poor reason for legislation. (2006, January 28). *The Salt Lake City Tribune*, p. A14. Retrieved January 17, 2007, from http://www.lexisnexis.com

Taylor, E. M. (2005). Gossip as an interpersonal communication phenomenon. Unpublished master's thesis. Morgantown, WV: West Virginia University.

Teen ridicule shapes brand awareness. (2006, July 18). *United Press International*. Retrieved December 20, 2006, from http://www.lexisnexis.com

Teen takes overdose after years of taunts. (1997, October 2). *Southern Illinoisan*, p. A5.

The 10 commandments of style. (2006, May). *Gentlemen's Quarterly*, pp.164–171.

Tesher, E. (2006, November 30). Dad ashamed to be walking 'round in women's underwear. *Chicago Sun Times*. Retrieved January 1, 2007, from http://www.lexisnexis.com

Thomas, P. W. (2006). *1970s punk fashion history development*. Retrieved December 15, 2006, from http://www.fashion-era.com/punks_fashion_history1.htm

Thomas, S. (2006, June 29). Culture a driving factor behind body modification. *The Oracle via U-Wire*. Retrieved December 11, 2006, from http://www.lexisnexis.com

Thompson, C. & Haytko, D. (1997, June). Speaking of fashion: Consumers' uses of fashion discourses and the appropriation of countervailing cultural meanings. *Journal of Consumer Research, 23*, 15–42.

Thompson, J. K., Coovert, M. D., & Stormer, S. M. (1999). Body image, social comparison, and eating disturbance: A covariance structural modeling investigation, *International Journal of Eating Disorders, 26*(1), 43–51.

Thompson, M. J. (2000). Gender in magazine advertising: Skin sells best. *Clothing and Textiles Research Journal, 18(*3), 178–181.

Tischler, H. L. (2004). *Introduction to sociology*. Belmont, CA: Wadsworth.

Townsend, A. (2006, October 9). Dress to impress—or else; Area schools' stricter codes stress importance of appearance. *Cleveland Plain Dealer*. Retrieved November 16, 2006, from http://www.lexisnexis.com

Traud, L. (2006, April 5). Fashion police to report for new duty. *The Roanoke Times*, p. B7. Retrieved January 11, 2007, from http://www.lexisnexis.com

Troha, T. (2006, January 26). Crimes of fashion: County tries to upgrade looks. *Daily Press*. Retrieved January 6, 2007, from http://www.lexisnexis.com

Troller, S. (2006, August 12). Disruptive duds. *The Capital Times* (Madison, WI), p. A1. Retrieved January 1, 2007, from http://www.lexisnexis.com

T-shirt ban upheld. (2001, July 25). *Southern Illinoisan*, p. A7.

Tuchman, G. (1973). Making news by doing work: Routinizing the unexpected. *American Journal of Sociology, 79*, 110–131.

Turner, M. M., Mazur, M. A., Wendel, N., & Winslow, R. (2003). Relational ruin or social glue? The joint effect of relationship type and gossip valence on liking, trust, and expertise. *Communication Monographs, 70*, 129–141.

Vagnoni, A. (1999, February 8). Something about this advertising. *Advertising Age*. Retrieved November 30, 2006, from http://www.highbeam.com/doc/161_5388004.htm.

Van Buren, A. (2006a, September 1). Dear Abby. *Southern Illinoisan*, p. B6.

Van Buren, A. (2006b, October 10). Dear Abby. *Southern Illinoisan*, p. C2.

Vassallo, S. M. (2006, May 22). Commentary: How to dress for success. *Virginia Lawyers Weekly*. Retrieved December 13, 2006, from http://www.lexisnexis.com

Verdisco, B. (1999). Lions, tigers, and bears . . . oh my! *Discount Store News, 38*(18), 15.

Verel, D. (2006, September 6). Excess baggage: When our collecting instinct degenerates into cluttering or, worse, hoarding, there is a place for people to turn. *East Bay Express*. Retrieved January 1, 2007, from http://www.lexisnexis.com

Vermont town skips ordinance, lets Mother Nature chill teens' public nudity spree. (2006, September 6). *The Associated Press*. Retrieved December 13, 2006, from http://www.lexisnexis.com

Vessey, J. A., Duffy, M., O'Sullivan, P., & Swanson, M. (2003). Assessing teasing in school-age youth. *Issues in Comprehensive Pediatric Nursing, 26*, 1–11.

Via makes noise for punk show. (2006, April 28). *Design Week*, p. 5.

Viren, S. (2006, September 17). Houston schools try to balance dress codes, faith. *Houston Chronicle*. Retrieved November 30, 2006, from http://www.lexisnexis.com

Viser, M. (2006, September 27). City councilors may press for a school dress code. *The Boston Globe*, p. B1. Retrieved January 1, 2007, from http://www.lexisnexis.com

Vivienne Westwood latest fashion designer to go fur-free. (2006, October 2). The Humane Society of the United States. Retrieved December 15, 2006, from http://www.hsus.org

Volokh, A., & Snell, L. (1998, January). *School violence prevention: Strategies to keep schools safe*. Policy Study No. 234. Reason Public Policy Institute. Retrieved May 17, 2005, from http://www.reason.org/ps234.html

Waggoner, M. (2006, March 27). Mother accused of abducting children, then posing as their father. *The Associated Press State & Local Wire*. Retrieved December 12, 2006, from http://www.lexisnexis.com

Wahl-Jorgensen, K. (1999). Letters to the editor. *Peace Review, 11*(1), 53–59.

Walhof, R. (2000, December). Color. *The Braille Monitor*. Retrieved January 4, 2007, from http://www.nfb.org

Walker, R. (2006, February 12). Pelt appeal. *The New York Times*. Retrieved December 13, 2006, from http://www.lexisnexis.com

Was inadequate protective equipment a repeat violation? (2006, August 1). *Safety Compliance Letter*, issue 2468, p. 9. Retrieved December 9, 2006, from http://ebscohost.com

Weber, T. (2006, March 23). Cabdriver dress code debatable. *Bangor Daily News*. Retrieved December 12, 2006, from http://www.lexisnexis.com

Wedding dress. (2006, November 28). Retrieved December 4, 2006, from http://en.wikipedia.org/wiki/Wedding_dress

Weiss, T. (2006, October 12). Solving the 'proper interview attire' puzzle. Retrieved October 17, 2006, from http://www.msnbc.msn.com/id/15211788/

Welling, A. (2006, October 17). Smoking fading like fashion faux pas, ad campaign says. *Deseret Morning News*. Retrieved January 11, 2007, from http://www.lexisnexis.com

Wenegrat, B., Abrams, L., Castillo-Yee, E., & Romine, I. J. (1996). Social norm compliance as a signaling system. I. Studies of fitness-related attributions consequent on everyday norm violations. *Ethology and Sociobiology*, 17, 403–416.

West, N. (2006, April 23). Fashion, church cross paths each Sunday. *Herald & Review*. Retrieved December 1, 2006, from http://www.lexisnexis.com

Westen, R. (1996). The real slant on gossip. Retrieved October 13, 2006, from www.psychology-today.com

What not to wear: 128 suspended for violating school dress code. (2006, August 25). *South Bend Tribune*. Retrieved November 16, 2006, from http://www.lexisnexis.com

Wheatt, D. (2006, October 20). Why gray is the new black. *St. Petersburg Times*, p. 44. Retrieved January 4, 2007, from http://www.lexisnexis.com

White shoes after Labor Day remain a no-no. (2006, October 21). *The Times Union*. Retrieved December 1, 2006, from http://www.lexisnexis.com

White, T. (2006, July 31). Short change: Men's capris? Long shorts? Whatever you call them, the latest regional fashion fad may be the 'Baltimore short.' *The Baltimore Sun*, p. D1. Retrieved December 4, 2006, from http://www.lexisnexis.com

Whitney, I., & Smith, P. K. (1993). A survey of the nature and extent of bullying in junior/middle and secondary schools. *Educational Research, 35*(1), 3–25.

Wight, P. (2006, June 23). Dark image bothers local business owners. *Whittier Daily News*. Retrieved January 19, 2007, from http://www.lexisnexis.com

Willis, P. (1978). *Profane culture*. London: Routledge & Regan Paul.

Wilson, E. (2006b, January 5). The good, the bad, and the huh? *The New York Times*, p. G1. Retrieved December 20, 2006, from http://www.lexisnexis.com

Wilson, E. (2006a, August 6). I wore shorts to work and they all laughed. *The New York Times*, Section 9, p. 1. Retrieved January 6, 2007, from http://www.lexisnexis.com

Wilson, L. (2001). American cowboy dress: Function to fashion. *Dress, 28*, 40–52.

Wilson, L. E. (1991). "I was a pretty proud kid": An interpretation of differences in posed and un-posed photographs of Montana cowboys. *Clothing and Textiles Research Journal, 9*(3), 49–58.

Women prefer thin models. (2006, September 21). *Bath Chronicle*. Retrieved November 30, 2006, from http://www.lexisnexis.com

Wong, A. S. W., & Li, Y. (2004). Relationship between thermophysiological responses and psycho-logical thermal perception during exercise wearing aerobic wear. *Journal of Thermal Biology, 29*(7–8), 791–796.

Wood, D. B. (2006, May 5). Big night. Big plans. Big tab. Can the prom be tamed? *The Christian Science Monitor*, p. 1. Retrieved January 5, 2007, from http://www.lexisnexis.com

Wooten, D. B. (2006). From labeling possessions to possessing labels: Ridicule and socialization among adolescents. *Journal of Consumer Research, 33*, 188–198.

Workman, J. E. (2003). Alcohol promotional clothing items and alcohol use by underage con-sumers. *Family and Consumer Sciences Research Journal, 31*(3), 331–354.

Workman, J. E., Arseneau, N. E., & Ewell, C. J. (2004). Traits and behaviors assigned to an adoles-cent wearing an alcohol promotional T-Shirt. *Family and Consumer Sciences Research Journal, 33*(1), 62–80.

Workman, J. E., & Freeburg, B. W. (2006). Safety and security in a school environment: The role of dress code policies. *Journal of Family and Consumer Sciences, 98*(2), 19–24.

Workman, J. E., & Freeburg, E. W. (1996a). Consumer responses to fashion advertisements using models in wheelchairs: Is there a relationship to consumers' optimum stimulation level? *Family and Consumer Sciences Research Journal, 24*(3), 237–253.

Workman, J. E., & Freeburg, E. W. (1996b). The newspaper advice column as regulatory device for normative standards of dress. In C. M. Ladisch (Ed.), Proceedings of the International Textile and Apparel Association, Inc. [p. 55]. Monument, CO: ITAA.

Workman, J. E., & Freeburg, E. W. (1997). A method to identify occupational stereotypes. *Family and Consumer Sciences Research Journal*, 25(4), 390–411.

Workman, J. E., & Freeburg, E. W. (2000a). Part I: Expanding the definition of the normative order to include dress norms. *Clothing and Textiles Research Journal*, 18(1), 46–55.

Workman, J. E., & Freeburg, E. W. (2000b). Part II: Testing the expanded definition of the normative order. *Clothing and Textiles Research Journal*, 18(2), 90–99.

Workman, J. E., Freeburg, E. W., & Lentz-Hees, E. S. (2004). Sanctions connected to dress code violations in secondary school handbooks. *Journal of Family and Consumer Sciences*, 96(4), 40–46.

Workman, J. E., & Johnson, K. (1993). Cultural aesthetics and the social construction of gender. In S. Lennon and L. Burns (Eds.). *Social science aspects of dress: New directions*, pp. 93–109. Monument, CO: International Textile and Apparel Association.

Workman, J. E., & Lentz, E. S. (2000). Measurement specifications for manufacturers' prototype bodies. *Clothing and Textiles Research Journal*, 18(4), 251–259.

Workman, J. E., & Studak, C. M. (2005). *Stereotypes associated with design of plus-size apparel*. Research poster presentation at American Association of Family and Consumer Sciences annual meeting, June 23–26, 2005, Minneapolis, MN.

Workman, J. E., & Studak, C. M. (2006). Fashion consumers and fashion problem recognition style. *International Journal of Consumer Studies*, 30(1), 75–84.

Workman, J. E., & Studak, C. M. (2008). Use of the means/ends test to evaluate public school dress-code policies. *Educational Policy*, 22(2), 295–326.

World's oldest person dies in Ecuador at 116. (2006, December 12). Retrieved August 28, 2006, from www.msnbc.msn.com

Wu, W., & Workman, J. E. (1993). Restrictive forces in clothing design for large-size women. *American Home Economics Association Abstracts of Research*, Annual Meeting, p. 78.

Young charm. (2006, October 9). *Women's Wear Daily*. Retrieved January 1, 2007, from http://www.lexisnexis.com

Zirkel, P. A. (2004, December). Employees wearing religious attire. *Principal*, p. 10–11.

GLOSSARY

Note: Key terms and concepts appear in **bold.** Other terms of interest appear in *italic.*

acceptable/ideal appearance represented by weight/height ratio or body mass index (BMI)

achieved statuses obtained due to effort or choice such as educational and occupational statuses

acquiescence compliance or conformity

adolescence stage of development: early adolescence (ages 12 to 18) and late adolescence (ages 18 to 22)

aesthetic anxiety fears engendered by persons whose appearance deviates markedly from the usual

aesthetic code combination of aesthetic rules, social rules, and cultural customs regarding dress

aesthetic elements basic components used to create a visual design such as color, pattern, line, shape, form, texture, light

aesthetic rules principles of design that are used to manipulate the aesthetic elements during the design process

aesthetic skills attitude and appearance, categorized as soft skills

agency the action, medium, or means by which something is accomplished

ambiguity message that can be understood in more than one way and it is unclear which meaning is intended

anarchy rebellion or disorder

androgynous gender-type an individual who incorporates masculinity and femininity equally in his or her personality and behaviors

anthropology the study of humankind from a historical and comparative perspective

appearance management a process of identity expression

appearance perception process of observing and making evaluations or drawing inferences based on how people look

applied research conducted primarily to solve practical problems

artifact analysis study of things created by humans for a practical purpose and from a particular period

ascribed statuses assigned due to birth or other significant factors not under an individual's control, for example, gender and age

aspirational groups groups in which one would like to become a member

avant-garde ahead of the times

avoidance groups groups to stay away from

barbs hurtful remarks

basic research adds to an existing knowledge base in a field of study by building theories, or the broad generalizations that explain phenomena

bellwether store indicators of future developments or trends

bespoke tailoring men's custom-made garments such as suits and coats

binary gender system system divided into two distinct groups—male and female

bipolar adjectives presented with both the positive and negative ends of the scale

body image multidimensional self-attitude toward one's body, particularly its size, shape, and aesthetics

body modification changes made to the body itself

body piercing insertion of jewelry into openings made in the body

body satisfaction individual's satisfaction with specific physical features, weight, and/or shape

body supplements items positioned on the body

boundary challenges type of noncompliance

brand awareness ability to identify the brand under different conditions

brand recall ability to retrieve the brand from memory when provided with a cue

brand recognition correctly identify a brand as being previously seen or heard

broadcloth fine, closely woven cloth of wool, cotton, or silk with a shiny finish

bullying negative behavior toward another: saying nasty things or sending nasty notes; hitting, kicking, or threatening; avoiding conversation; or teasing someone in a repeated and nasty way

cartoon pictorial design that includes caricatures

case problems scenarios to be analyzed and possibly resolved through discussion

case studies describe behaviors and characteristics of individuals or groups

causal-comparative research another name for ex post facto research that includes analysis of data to identify potential causal connections between variables, factors, and/or constructs

cause and effect one variable is the direct result of a second variable

chaos rebellion or disorder

charismatic authority based on the exceptional characteristics of an individual

circumstances conditions that affect what happens or how somebody reacts in a particular situation; include nonmaterial culture, that is, society's norms, values, beliefs, and abstract concepts

claim demand by one party to another that something has to be done about some alleged situation

claims maker someone reporting a situation (reporting a norm violation) and demanding that something be done

claims making process whereby individuals call attention to a situation and try to change it

clique social group often formed on the basis of similar values and interests such as fashion, wealth, status, acceptance, or education

clothing generic term that refers to garments, especially outer or decorative clothing

clothing function use for which clothing is suited or designed

clothing image characteristic or distinctive impression created by the clothing

codes system of rules relating to one subject

coercive power based on negative sanctions, i.e., punishment results from failure to comply

comic strips sequential multiple-panel drawings

commodification process by which a product is developed for buying and selling

complacency self-satisfied response, usually without thinking and without awareness of possible consequences

condition variables with different values

conformity a process whereby individuals maintain or change their behavior to act in accordance with society's norms

confounding variables groups of characteristics that could influence research results and that can be equally distributed through randomization

connection power based on associations with influential or important persons

contempt of court conduct calculated to embarrass, hinder, or obstruct the court in its administration of justice or to derogate its authority or dignity, thereby bringing administration of law into disrepute

contemptuous expressing a lack of respect for someone considered to be worthless, inferior, or undeserving of respect

content analysis process in which narrative is summarized into categories—words, phrases, sentences, or themes

content of norms subject matter the norms address

context dependent operative norms as well as the saliency of norms depend on the situation

context of social interaction characterized by its (a) physical environment, (b) social environment, and (c) temporal environment

continuous variable within the numerical limits of the variable range, any value is possible

conventional culture artifacts and understandings shared by the majority of members of a society

core gender identity describes one's sense of belonging to one gender (and not the other) and valuing this

correlation coefficients calculated to identify the strength and direction of a linear relationship between two variables

correlational studies examine the degree of relationship between and among variables

covert not intended to be known, seen, or found out

cross-dressing occasions when a male puts on feminine dress or a female adopts masculine dress for whatever purpose or to whatever effect

cultural anthropology applies the comparative method and evolutionary perspective to human culture

cultural capital widely shared, high-status cultural signals (attitudes, preferences, formal knowledge, behaviors, goals, and credentials) used for social and cultural exclusion

cultural code shared cultural knowledge

cultural customs traditions associated with a particular society or subcultural group within a society

cultural diversity differences between and within societies

cultural icon someone who embodies abstract cultural ideas in a tangible and visible manner

cultural ideal shorthand summary of aesthetic values

cultural lag occurs when material culture changes faster than nonmaterial culture, thus creating a lag between the two cultural components

cultural universals customs and practices that are believed to exist in all known cultures

culture knowledge, language, values, customs, and material objects that are passed from person to person and from one generation to the next in a human group or society

culture change modification of norms at different periods of time

customs enduring norms; refer to situations in which people always dress in a particular way because of tradition

data information in the form of numbers (numerical), pictures (graphic), or words (narrative)

data reduction data are selected, focused, simplified, and transformed for manageability and understanding in terms of what is being studied

deferred delayed until a later time

degree of acceptance ranges from voluntary to mandatory

demand on resources incompatible claims on time, facilities, money, or energy

demographic variable individual characteristics such as gender, ethnicity, education, occupation, socioeconomic status, religious affiliation, and age

descriptive results describe a situation as it exists

deviance any behavior, belief, or condition that violates cultural norms

discipline practice of teaching and ensuring that individuals obey rules and punishing them for noncompliance

double standard of aging physical signs of aging are more harshly judged in women than in men

drag queen homosexual male who cross-dresses in the spirit of satire

dress assemblage of body modifications and/or supplements displayed by a person in communicating with other human beings

dress code enforcers older persons who use mild forms of disapproval and shame to enforce dress norms

dress code violations violations of norms for appearance

dress customs practices of dress that originate informally from tradition

dress norms acceptable ways to look in specific situations

Dude caricature, a stereotype of the well-dressed Perfect Gentleman

dysfunctional fails to perform the function that is normally expected

eavesdropping listening to private conversations

economic function production, distribution, and consumption of society's resources

educational function efforts, usually by more mature members of a society, to teach each new generation the beliefs, the way of life, the values, and some portion of the knowledge and skills of the group

effectiveness achieving a desired end result

effeminate male who is similar to or imitates the behavior, appearance, or speech traditionally associated with females

egregious violations bad, blatant, or ridiculous to an extraordinary degree

elective mammoplasty breast augmentation, breast reduction, or corrective surgery on the breasts

embarrassment becoming or causing somebody to become painfully self-conscious, ashamed, humiliated, or ill at ease

embodied giving a tangible or visible form to something abstract such as a personal or social identity

emerging adulthood late adolescence

emotional responses feelings such as anger, pride, shame, and embarrassment

emphasized femininity traditional femininity based on subordination to men and boys

enforcement of sanctions insist upon carrying out the sanction

environmental conditions ecological state such as the temperature, humidity, or precipitation

ethnocentrism tendency to interpret unfamiliar customs based on biases derived from one's own culture

ethnographic method based on field observation in combination with face-to-face interviews

etiquette norms legitimized by an authority on manners but generally regarded as voluntary

ex post facto research analyzing events that have already happened for the purpose of understanding differences between two or more groups

exemplars prime examples

exhibitionism deliberately behaving or dressing in a way that attracts attention

existential anxiety feeling of personal identification with another person

expert power based on possession of expertise, skill, and knowledge that gains the respect of others

explicit norms clearly delineated by law books, regulations, and codes

extensive pervasiveness multiple sanctions from more than one source operating against a person over an extended period of time

external sanctions occur when members of society attempt to enforce norms for others

extreme magnitude affects all aspects of life

fad fashion change characterized by a rapid rise in popularity followed quickly by an abrupt drop in popularity

fashion sociocultural phenomenon in which a preference is shared by a large number of people for a particular style that lasts for a relatively short time, and then is replaced by another style; the currently prevailing style of dress

fashion awareness recognition of fashion objects and their meanings

fashion career implies that someone is trained for and expects to work in a fashion-related occupation for his or her entire working life

fashion change changing aesthetic rules

fashion conscious awareness of current fashion

fashion faux pas fashion mistake

fashion innovativeness willingness to try new products relatively early in the product life cycle

fashion interest measured by the amount of time, energy, money, and personal commitment an individual expends in the pursuit of fashion

fashion involvement extent to which an individual views the activities surrounding fashion as a meaningful and engaging part of life

fashion knowledgeability amount of fashion information obtained and used by individuals

fashion maven somebody who is an expert or knowledgeable enthusiast in the field of fashion

fashion opinion leadership influencing others in purchase decisions, giving advice, and being an information source

fashion police imaginary police force that ensures people dress in accordance with fashion

fashion problem recognition tendency of some individuals to buy clothing simply because they *want* something new while other individuals shop primarily when they *need* something to replace what wears out or for a specific context

fashion research systematic approach to collecting data to answer a question or solve a problem related to fashion

fashion symbols a collection of signs that convey ideas or information in a particular context; created using an aesthetic code

faux pas violation of accepted, albeit unwritten, social rules or norms

feminine gender-type individuals who possess traits congruent with female gender-role expectations

fit models models used by apparel manufacturers to fit and size their styles

flexible norms allow leeway in conformity

folkways norms that allow a wide range of individual interpretation as long as certain boundaries are not exceeded

formal origination norms that derive from a political function

formal sanction verbally authenticated, either through written or oral means

formality condition of being formal; the degree to which behavior is governed by rules or established methods

frame transformation process whereby groups take a negative concept and try to turn it into something positive in order to create a sense of belonging and pride

framing a process used in human interest stories that present particular issues as problems, particular outcomes as desirable, and particular strategies as appropriate

frequency a count or the number of times a phenomenon occurs

frugality thriftiness

gang a group of young people who socialize and may engage in antisocial and delinquent behavior

gender psychological and cultural term, referring to an individual's subjective feelings of maleness or femaleness

gender constancy knowing that when a child dresses in the clothing of the other sex it does not change his or her gender

gender identity individual's subjective feelings of maleness or femaleness

gender norm violation doing the unexpected or not doing the expected for a given gender

gender norms rule or standard of behavior held for one sex or the other and shared by most members of society

gender role behaviors or characteristics that are attributed to one gender or another and are culturally determined

gender role socialization process by which members of society learn what males and females should or should not think, say, or do, and how they should or should not look

gender stability knowing that a child's gender was there when he or she was born and it will stay the same when he or she grows up

gender understanding knowing that gender is defined by genitals, not external appearance

glossy magazine fashion magazine printed on slick paper

goal end which an individual aims to accomplish

gossip evaluative (positive or negative) casual conversation about an absent third person

Goth style commonly includes black hair and clothes, horror-style makeup (white facial foundation, black eyeliner, and dark lipstick for both women and men), and symbols of death (crucifixes)

Goth-Loli style Goth but with an abundance of decorativeness, incorporating frills and layers

group made up of people sharing something in common such as interests, beliefs, or goals

group comparison research compares data from members of different groups who have been exposed to different treatments

guilt negative self-evaluation that occurs when an individual behaves in a manner that is in conflict with his or her understanding of and commitment to social norms

hangtag small paper or plastic slip attached to an item being sold that gives information about the item

hard skills technological, financial, legal, strategic and analytical skills, understanding business dynamics, ability to make effective decisions, and ability to use evidence and data as bases for decision making

hegemonic gaze sense that individual women have that everyone is looking at them and the discomfort they feel if they fail to meet the cultural beauty norm

heightened publicity period when extra attention is brought to acceptable and/or unacceptable fashion trends

historical research provides information about past events and conditions from primary or secondary sources

hoarders those who cannot seem to relinquish useless possessions

human interest stories not factual presentation of breaking news, but presentation of information which is of *human interest*

ideal norm norm that members of a society aspire to attain

identity who one is

ideology ideas or values

image symbolic aspects of a product including color, attractiveness, fashionability, and brand name

immediate taking place at once, without delay

immodesty in dress sexually provocative dress or ostentatious dress

implicit norms norms that are understood or implied without being stated

incongruous dress dress that is unsuitable, strange, or out of place in a particular setting or context

indefinite threat uncertainty about a possible danger; arouses anxiety

indie type of alternative rock music that is characterized by its reliance on independent record labels rather than major record labels

indirect interpersonal aggression predisposition to harm other people without engaging in face-to-face interaction

informal origination method by which norms develop unofficially

informal sanction seemingly trivial rewards and/or punishments that enable people to informally control some of their own as well as others' behavior regarding dress

information power based on possession of valuable information

innovative communicators among the first to buy and wear new fashions and also influence others to follow the fashion trend

intact group naturally occurring group such as students in classrooms, workers in a particular office, or members of a club

internal sanction occurs when individuals rely on an inner sense of what is right and wrong to govern their actions

internalization adoption of others' attitudes, beliefs, and values, either consciously or unconsciously

internalized appearance norms personal goal and standard against which one measures the self and others

internalized mechanisms beliefs held by individuals as revealed in both self-discipline and self-surveillance

interrelatedness of norms the interaction and interdependence of the ten aspects of norms and the variations of those aspects

interval variable based on equal units of measurement

jargon language that is used by a particular group, especially when the words and phrases are not understood or used by other people

jeer pressure pressure felt by witnesses of ridicule to behave in conventional ways

knowledge organized sets of principles and information with general relevancy

laissez-faire the practice of letting children do as they wish with no interference

laws norms that are formally defined and enforced by officials

legitimate power based on the position held; the higher the position, the more legitimate power attributed to a person

letters to advice columnist mechanism for reporting violations of norms

letters to the editor mechanism for feedback from readers who want to express their personal opinion about some event or issue

life chances likelihood of securing the good things in life, such as housing, education, good health, and food

lingo specialized set of terms requiring that it be learned like a language

location geographical locality

longitudinal study study encompassing a number of years

look appearance, style, or fashion, especially dress or hairstyle

lookism hiring decisions based on physical appearance

lower class (15 to 20 percent of the population) bottom of the economic ladder, have little education or occupational skills, often unemployed or underemployed in unskilled labor and service work

lower-middle class (25 to 30 percent of the population) have a high school education or some college; work in clerical and sales positions, are small-business semiprofessionals or farmers

Luddite anyone who opposes technological change

Machiavellianism the degree to which a person manipulates and deceives others in order to get the response he or she wants

magnitude total consequences that can be measured as the result of sanctions

mainstream culture artifacts and understandings shared by the majority of members of a society

malleable body subject to transformation

mandatory acceptance acceptance is required and enforced

manipulation of variables one group is exposed to one value of a variable (e.g., intensity, characteristic, treatment) while a second group is exposed to another value of the variable

manky dirty, greasy, or otherwise unpleasant

masculine gender-type an individual who possesses traits congruent with male gender-role expectations

mass media refers to television, radio, and newspapers in particular but generally includes all communications media that reach a sizeable audience

material culture tangible artifacts or products

materialism value that reflects the importance people attach to owning worldly possessions

mean the average number in a data set

means measures or methods adopted to reach a goal

median middle number in a data set; 50 percent of the data points are greater than this number and 50 percent are less than this number

metrosexual urban male who has a strong aesthetic sense and spends a substantial amount of time and money on his appearance

mild sanction trivial, weak, or minor reward or punishment

mixed methods research employs multiple methods, both qualitative and quantitative

moderate magnitude has limited impact on a person's life

mode most frequent number

modern business suit sack-type coat and trousers of the same material

mores strongly held norms that usually have a moral connotation and are based on the central values of the culture

motive that which causes an individual's action

mullet hairstyle that is long at the back and short at the front and sides

multidisciplinary multiple specialized subjects

name-calling form of verbal abuse that takes the form of calling someone abusive, disgraceful, or shameful names

narrative written or oral stories or other accounts of an event

narrative inquiry study of social behavior based on individuals' personal experiences, expressed through stories

negative deviance behaviors or conditions that underconform, or fail to conform, to normative expectations and subsequently receive negative evaluations

nickname made-up name for somebody usually based on a conspicuous characteristic of the person involved

nominal variable two or more values are assigned to categories; each value can be a member of only one category; all other members of the category have the same characteristic

nonidentity who one is not

nonmaterial culture abstract concepts, beliefs, and values

nonreward punitive, but a milder sanction than punishment because it does not deprive individuals of something they already have, only of something they would have liked to have had

norm clarity refers to whether the norm is explicit or implicit

normality what is customary, common, or ordinary

normative order consists of shared norms, that is, shared standards or rules which specify what human beings should or should not think, say, or do, and how human beings should or should not look under given circumstances

normative socialization theory assumes that one way individuals learn desirable behaviors in society is through a system of positive and negative reinforcements from others

normative system combination of related norms organized into a complex whole

obesity weighing 20 percent above the normal weight according to medical and/or insurance height/weight tables

obligation the behavior others expect from an individual in a particular status because of legal or moral duty

norm established rule of behavior or standard of conduct

observational research method used when information needed to answer a question is best obtained through direct observation *obtrusive sanction* conspicuous, blatant, or explicit

obtrusiveness the degree to which a sanction is obvious

occasion important or special event

occupational stereotype overgeneralized idea about the attributes and behaviors of individuals in occupational categories

operative norm norm in effect for a particular situation

opinion leader publicly recognized expert that people feel they can draw on if needed

ordinal variable two or more values are assigned to categories with ranking from lowest to highest

ostentatious dress clothing that is a vulgar display of wealth and success designed to impress people

ostracism isolation from a group

overt directly observable

oxymoron phrase in which two words of contradictory meaning are used together

pack rats hoarders

panoptic view all-inclusive view

parochial school private school affiliated with a church that provides children with a general education as well as religious instruction

peer group made up of social equals who interact socially on a regular basis

peer group pressures motivation for clothes shopping characterized by copying friends and/or being influenced by observing what other girls are wearing

peer pressure social pressure on somebody to adopt a particular type of behavior, dress, or attitude in order to be accepted as part of a group

peer reviewed experts in the same field as the author have reviewed the article and decided it was authoritative enough for publication

percentages proportion of the total

Perfect Gentleman inconspicuous to the casual observer, but his appearance is perfect in its attention to quality, fit, and correctness

personal identity attributes assigned to the self

personal well-being frame of mind that reflects comfort with existing conditions

pervasiveness how widespread sanctions are in terms of the number of sanctions, how long the sanctions last, and how many people are involved in administering the sanctions

phenomena observable facts, experiences, events, trends

physical condition bodily state over which an individual has no control such as age, body build, facial structure, or physical disability

physical environment surroundings, immediate environment including the setting and material artifacts

physical pressures buying clothes that flatter one's shape and/or feel comfortable in relation to body size

physical security freedom from harm to the bodily self

political function actions by the government on behalf of its citizens

popular periodical entertains readers, sells products, and promotes a viewpoint

popular press readily available printed material easily understood by all people regardless of education or class

poser wears the right clothes and carries a skateboard, but does not really skate

positive deviance behaviors or conditions that both overconform to the norms and are positively appraised

post hoc fallacy attributing cause and effect to a correlational relationship *pragmatic control* power over events

predictive control able to foresee what will happen or being able to predict a threat's occurrence and consequences

prestige an evaluation by others of a person's position in a status hierarchy

presumption acceptance that something is correct, without having proof of it

primary group made up of people who interact regularly face-to-face, including families or friendship groups, such as sororities

primary socialization those interactions through which a child initially learns a language, adopts basic cultural norms and values, behaves in terms of these norms and values, and forms a culturally appropriate social identity

primary source firsthand account of events that include original written, graphic, artifactual, or otherwise depicted sources of information

privilege a right or advantage enjoyed by a person or body of persons beyond the common advantages of other individuals

product influences latest trends, garment quality, and price

promotional influences what fashion models wear and retail windows display

psychological security freedom from perceived threats to personal well-being

public opinion certain attitudes and beliefs that are widespread among members of a society

punishment sanction at the negative end of a continuum of retribution

punk look clothing that has been destroyed and put back together, is worn inside out, or is unfinished or deteriorating

purposive sampling choosing participants who have experienced the event of interest because they are ideally suited to shed light on the event

qualitative data collection methods include participant observation, audio- and video-taping conversations, and eavesdropping

qualitative research provides descriptive results using words (rather than numbers)

quantitative data collection methods include questionnaire studies and experimental research designs

quantitative research provides data in the form of numbers, which are then subjected to statistical analyses

quasi-experimental research design intact groups are randomly assigned to conditions or treatments and data are collected

radical body modification invasive, permanent, or nonnormative forms such as scarification and branding

random assignment individuals have an equal chance of being assigned to any group

range calculated by subtracting the lowest number from the highest number

rational authority based on a conviction that a specific individual has a clearly defined right and duty to uphold rules in an impersonal manner

real norm norm that members of a society actually can attain

realism faithful portrayal of reality

reckless behavior non-socially approved acts where precautions could easily be taken, but are not, to avoid potentially negative consequences

recognition of violation become aware of a norm violation

referent power based on personal characteristics; individuals with high referent power are liked, admired, and imitated

religious function organized system of beliefs, practices, rituals, and symbols designed (a) to facilitate closeness to the sacred or transcendent (God, higher power, or ultimate truth/reality) and (b) to foster an understanding of one's relationship and responsibility to others in living together in community

replacement function necessity of replacing each of society's members when they die

replicate repeat a study

report of violation eyewitness testimonies

research systematic approach to collecting data in an effort to answer a question or solve a problem

research hypothesis way of stating a research question or research problem that includes predicting a relationship between two variables

research problem area of concern

research question asks what the researcher wants to learn from an investigation

research topic broad area of interest

residual deviance violation of unwritten, unarticulated but taken for granted rules that govern the mass of society in everyday life

resistance refusal to accept

response to norm violation a reaction to the violation

restricted pervasiveness limited temporary sanctions applied by only a few people

retribution distribution of rewards for correct behavior and punishment for transgressions, or incorrect behavior

reward sanction at the positive end of a continuum of retribution

reward power based on positive sanctions; compliance leads to rewards

ridicule act of making fun of some aspect of another

rights behaviors that an individual in a particular status is entitled to expect from others

rigid norms require exact conformity

risky behavior socially approved adventurous or thrill-seeking acts

rite of passage public ceremony that is used to validate changes in a person's status

role conflict occurs when the performance of a role in one status clashes with the performance of a role in another status

role strain takes place when roles associated with a single status are in opposition to one another

roles culturally defined rights and obligations attached to a status

salient conspicuous and attracts attention

sanction reward or punishment that affects conformity to norms

scholarly journals reports of original research

screening using clothing and appearance to assess a prospective employee for certain traits, then using these implied traits as a basis for a hiring decision

secondary group formally organized; often focused on specialized needs or goals of the members

secondary socialization processes by which individuals learn new statuses or roles

secondary sources accounts of events that are one or more levels removed from the primary source

self-corrective having the power to correct itself

self-monitoring degree to which individuals monitor and control their self-presentations in harmony with social cues

sensational periodicals publications that arouse curiosity and cater to popular superstitions

sensitivity to aesthetic rules responsiveness to aesthetic stimuli

setting the place where an event occurs

severe sanction strict, harsh, intense, cruel, or stern

severity the degree of strictness, harshness, intensity, or cruelty of a sanction

sex biological term; individuals are either male or female depending on their sex organs and genes

sexually provocative dress clothing intended to arouse other people sexually

shame negative self-evaluation; occurs when an individual perceives he or she is deficient, unacceptable, or incompetent compared to an established norm

shock advertising intentionally startles and offends its audience by deliberately violating norms for societal values and personal ideals

sissy offensive term referring to a boy who does not exhibit stereotypical masculinity

sized body quantifying the physical size of the body via a numerical clothing size

skateboarders individuals who demonstrate an interest in, and technical knowledge of, skateboarding

skater girl girl who is a member of the skateboarding culture

social class societal subgroups with similar origins, upbringing, education, and occupations and whose members share personal circumstances and experiences

social classes in United States upper class, upper-middle-class, lower-middle-class, working class, and lower class

social control mechanism to encourage compliance with norms

social control theory specifies a basic social process that is designed to maintain social order by encouraging compliance with norms

social environment people who are present—each person with his or her statuses and associated roles

social identity attributes assigned to others in order to categorize them as members of particular social groups

social learning theory considers that individuals learn desirable behaviors by imitating the actions and behaviors of those around them, who serve as role models

social power ability to bring about a change in the belief, attitude, or behavior of a person resulting from the action, or presence, of another person or group of persons

social roles highly standardized sets of expectations

social rule a norm that governs groups and situations

social skill a soft skill; refers to the way people in groups behave and interact

social stratification social divisions or hierarchy

socialization a process whereby individuals become aware of society's expectations and learn how they are expected to behave

socialization agents individuals, such as parents or guardians, who are influential in transmitting society's values and norms

society a large community of people tied together by geographical territory, traditions, institutions, nationality, and important cultural expectations

sociology study of social life, social change, and the social causes and consequences of human behavior

soft skills creativity, emotional intelligence, empathy, self-awareness, flexibility, resilience, social skills, ability to cope with ambiguity and paradox, and ability to communicate effectively

source origination of a sanction, that is, whether it comes from either an internal or external source

spaces boundaries within which creative interpretation of fashion can occur

spatial visualization ability to mentally manipulate an entire spatial configuration, to imagine the rotation of depicted objects, to imagine the folding and unfolding of flat patterns, and to imagine the relative changes of position of objects in space

special interest periodical provides specialized information to an audience in a particular occupation or trade

status person's position in a social hierarchy

standard deviation reflects the average difference of each number from the mean

status disparities unequal distribution of money, power, and prestige among the social classes

stereotypes oversimplified images used to categorize individuals based on appearance or behavior

structural design how garment parts are put together and work together

subculture distinctive lifestyles, values, norms, and beliefs of certain segments of the population within a society

substantive news or general interest periodicals provide general information to a broad audience of readers

survey research gathers data at one point in time from individuals who represent groups with specific characteristics

symbol a visible or tangible object that represents something else

symbolic interactionist theory focuses on interaction among individuals based on symbols that are used or understood by everyone in a particular group

symbolic life cycle emergence and change in the meanings of fashion symbols over time and among individuals

synchronized coordinated

tab of identity symbol or portrayal of eccentric characteristics of a subject

taboos norms that are associated with moral or ethical misconduct

tattoo permanent design made on skin by the process of pricking and ingraining indelible pigment

taunting provoking, ridiculing, or teasing in a hurtful or mocking way

teasing making fun of somebody, either playfully or maliciously

technical skills competency in design, setup, operation, and correction of malfunctions related to machines or technological systems

temporal environment events in the past, present, and future

temporal incompatibility between statuses time as a quality that renders something incompatible with something else

tendency to gossip psychological trait that affects whether individuals will choose to talk about an absent third person

theory a collection of evidence, hypotheses, or principles used to explain social behavior

tomboy girl who dresses or behaves in a boyish way and enjoys rough boisterous play

tools used to collect data

trade publication another name for special interest periodicals

traditional authority based on the time-honored status of ancient traditions and authorities

transgender not conforming to traditional notions of gender expression

transmission passed along through members of a society

transsexual someone who identifies himself or herself as a member of one sex but has the reproductive organs of the other sex

transvestite male who dresses in feminine attire and emulates the female form, but never forgets he is a male

trends a general tendency, movement, or direction of fashion change

true experimental research design groups are formed by randomly assigning individuals to different conditions or treatments

tulle thin, stiff, net fabric of silk, nylon, or rayon

types category of things whose members share some qualities, such as types of skirts or types of sleeves

unobtrusive sanction inconspicuous or implicit

upper class (about 1 to 3 percent of the population) wealthy, educated, have occupations related to politics, corporate ownership, or honorific positions in government and the arts

upper-middle class (10 to 15 percent of the population) affluent, successful business and professional people, with a college education

valence negative/positive continuum

values the accepted principles or standards of a society

vanity sizing practice in which manufacturers label garments one size smaller

variables factors having two or more values or distinguishable properties or characteristics

variance spread of the numbers in a data set around a specific number such as the mean

violation of norms disobedience or noncompliance with a norm; deviance

virtual ethnography conducting ethnographic studies on the Internet

voluntary acceptance may choose whether to abide by the norms

working class (25 to 30 percent of the population) adequate financial resources but little money available for luxuries, grade school or high school education, work in skilled and semiskilled manual labor, factories, and other blue-collar jobs

workplace culture system of shared understandings, beliefs, values, behaviors, and norms for workers in a particular workplace

youth subculture subdivision within a society with a distinctive lifestyle, values, norms, and beliefs that attract young people as members

Zeitgeist thought and feeling of a particular period of time

zoot suit man's suit, popular in the 1940s, with baggy high-waisted trousers tapering to a narrow hem and a long jacket heavily padded at the shoulders

INDEX

Culture (*continued*)
as shared, 11
transformation of, 12
transmission of, 8–9
Culture change, 105–6
Currie, D., 146, 150, 151, 152, 200, 201, 205, 206
Curry, I., 241
Curtis, J., 248
Customs, 65
Cusumano, D. L., 205

Dahl, D. W., 179, 187, 188
Damhorst, M. L., 216, 221
Danaher, G., 315
Data, 28
Davis, J. R., 131, 146, 147, 161
Davis, K., 7, 19, 52, 105, 156, 173, 238, 247, 292
Daviss, B., 202
Deam, J., 121
DeBare, I., 163
Deil-Amen, R., 78, 83
de Kretser, L., 169
de la Haye, A., 146
Dellinger, K., 78, 84–85
DeMitchell, T., 88
Derech-Zehavi, A., 33, 210, 233
Deviance, 17, 20, 104
negative, 302
positive, 302–3
Dickson, M. A., 10–11
Dimmock, P. S., 256, 261
Dingwall, C., 146
Disabled, 115–16
Dobos, J. A., 33, 232–33
Dodd, C. A., 29
Donais, B., 80
Doneger Group, 107
Doniach, A., 124
Dragnich, A. B., 315
Drag queen, 144–45
Dress, defined, xxii, 5
Dress code enforcers, 314, 315–16

Dress codes, 77–90, 160
golf club, 289
implicit, 171–72, 192–93
restaurant, 289–90
school, 67, 87–90, 133–34, 171, 191–92, 268, 282, 287, 292, 311–13
workplace, 59–60, 80–86, 113, 119, 160, 191, 194, 249, 283
Dress code violations, 268
Dress norms, 20
Drevitch, G., 67
D'Souza, B., 244
Duffy, M., 258
Dunbar, R., 209
Duncan, N., 209
Dupre, M. E., 200
Dutton, E., 80, 82

Eavesdropping, 231
Eckert, C., 179, 180, 182, 183
Eckert, P., 92
Eder, D., 229
Effeminate males, 109
Eger, A., 57
Eicher, J., 5, 29, 35, 92, 205, 298, 306
Eila, L., 202
Ekmark, E., 137
Elective mammoplasty, 303–6
Elliott, R., 162, 166, 179, 183, 184, 296, 308, 309, 310
Ellis, A. D., 241
Elmore, C., 167
Embarrassment, 267
Embodied experiences, 300
Emerging adulthood, 121, 122
Emphasized femininity, 151, 313
Enforcement of sanctions, 19, 275–93, 295–316
body modifications and, 298–306
body supplements and, 306–16
within the community context, 287–90
context of a social interaction, 278–79
effectiveness of, 290–92
within the family context, 279–81

Manchanda, R. V., 187, 188

Mannion, B., 170

Mansfield, S., 120

Maragh, R., 172

Maraghy, M., 171

Maria, D., 257, 271

Mariner, D., 202, 203

Marriott, A., 209

Marshall, S., 283

Mass media, norm violations and, 110

Material culture, 8
   technology's transformation of, 12

Materialism, 185

Mathias, M., 292

Mattek, Bethanie, 167

Mazur, M. A., 209

Medical Research Council National Survey of Health
      and Development, 259

Mehrabian, A., 36

Meier, R., 52, 74

Melton, K., 114

Metrosexual, 109

Miami Ink, 136

Miceli, M., 173, 174

Mistry, R., 142

Mixed methods research, 43–45

Mizrahi, Isaac, 58

Moake, D., 199

Modesty of dress, religious groups and, 285–86

Mody-Desbareau, A., 209

Monsen, L., 285

Mores, 66

Moritz, M., 201

Morrison, C., 202

Mortenson, E., 249

Mosley, S., 167

Moss, Kate, 63, 64

Motive, 113

Mui, Y. Q., 109

Muir, J., 103, 290, 291

Mulcahy, A., 204

Murray, Plumb, & Murray, 119

Murray, B., 64

Murray, J., 216, 226

Myhre, E., 138

Nardi, E., 120

Narrative inquiry, 41–42

Nash, J. M., 201

National School Boards Association, 87

Nenga, S. K., 131, 134, 135

Neufeld, S., 240

Nevo, B., 33, 209, 210, 233

Nevo, O., 33, 209, 210, 233

Newman, B., 122

Newman, P., 122

Newspaper reports of norm violations, 198–205
   analyzing, 217–23

Nicknames, 240, 259–60, 267–68
   contemptuous, 264

Nickson, D., 79, 80, 82

Nielsen, J. M., 91, 106, 131, 140, 141, 142

Nonmaterial culture, 8

Nonreward, 242–43

Normative order, 7

Normative socialization theory, 5, 114

Normative system, 123

Norms, 7, 18, 51–74, 77–100
   acceptance of, 66
   application of, 69–71
   aspects of, and their variations, 52–53, 54
   authority of, 62–64
   content of, 57–62
   identifying, 52–74
   interrelationship of, 73
   origination of, 64–65
   properties of, 67–68
   realistic, 65–66
   salience of, 53–57
   sanctions and, 72–73
   summary of qualitative research methods and
      tools, 78
   transmission of, 71–72

Norm violations, 18, 103–25, 129–52
   body modification, 135–39

PHOTO CREDITS

CHAPTER ONE:

Figure 1.1: © Blend Images/Alamy

Figure 1.2: © 1991 Lynn Johnston. Distributed by Universal Press Syndicate

Figure 1.3: Jupiterimages/Polka Dot/Alamy

Figure 1.4: © 1997 GarLanCo. Universal Press Syndicate

Figure 1.5: © Masterfile/Masterfile

Figure 1.6: © Darius Ramazani/zefa/Corbis

Figure 1.7: © CW Network/Courtesy Everett Collection

Figure 1.8: Courtesy of Jane E. Workman and Beth W. Freeburg

Figure 1.9: Photograph by William Claxton/Courtesy Demont Photo Management

CHAPTER TWO:

Figure 2.1: © Jose Luis Perez/Getty Images

Figure 2.2: Image courtesy of The Advertising Archives

Figure 2.3a: Courtesy of Sage Publications

Figure 2.3b: Courtesy of Time, Inc.

Figure 2.3c: Courtesy of Fairchild Publications, Inc.

Figure 2.3d: Courtesy of Condé Nast Publications Inc.

Figure 2.3e: Courtesy of The National Enquirer

Figure 2.4: AP Photo/Stephen J. Carrera

Figure 2.5: Courtesy of National Geographic

Figure 2.6: AP Photo/Jacqueline Roggenbrodt

Figure 2.7: Karen Kasmauski/National Geographic/Getty Images

CHAPTER THREE:

Figure 3.1: Courtesy of Jane E. Workman and Beth W. Freeburg

Figure 3.2: Geoff A. Howard/Alamy

Figure 3.3: © 2006. Scott Borgman, ZITS Partnership. Distributed by King Features Syndicate

Figure 3.4: AP Photo/Jim Cooper

Figure 3.5: Photodisc/Alamy

Figure 3.6: AP Photo/Jennifer Graylock

Figure 3.7: © 2007 Cathy Guisewite. Distributed by Universal Press Syndicate

Figure 3.8: Courtesy of Fairchild Publications, Inc.

Figure 3.9: AP Photo/Rusty Kennedy

Figure 3.10: © 2006 Baby Blues Partnership. Distributed by King Features Syndicate

CHAPTER FOUR:

Figure 4.1: Courtesy of Jane E. Workman and Beth W. Freeburg

Figure 4.2: © 1994 Lynn Johnston. Distributed by Universal Press Syndicate

Figure 4.3: AP Photo/Janet Hostetter

Figure 4.4: joSon Nicholas-lee/Getty Images

Figure 4.5: AAGAMIA/Getty Images

Figure 4.6: © ColorBlind Images/Blend Images/Corbis

Figure 4.7: © 2007 Cathy Guisewite. Distributed by Universal Press Syndicate

Figure 4.8: Altrendo/Getty Images

CHAPTER FIVE:

Figure 5.1: Courtesy of Jane E. Workman and Beth W. Freeburg

Figure 5.2: © 1996 by King Features Syndicate, Inc. World Rights Reserved

Figure 5.3: Digital Vision/Alamy

Figure 5.4: © Toby Melville/Reuters/Corbis

Figure 5.5: © 1994 by King Features Syndicate, Inc. World Rights Reserved

Figure 5.6: © Daniel Lainé/Corbis

Figure 5.7: AP Photo/University of Southern Mississippi, Steve Rouse

Figure 5.8: © 1997 by King Features Syndicate, Inc. World Rights reserved.

CHAPTER SIX:

Figure 6.1: © Heide Benser/zefa/Corbis

Figure 6.2: © Anderson Ross/Blend Images/Corbis

Figure 6.3: © Tyler Stableford/Stone Sub/Getty Images

Figure 6.4: © Ariel Skelley/Corbis

Figure 6.5: AP Photo/Dan Steinberg

Figure 6.6: © 1998 Lynn Johnston. Distributed by Universal Press Syndicate

Figure 6.7: © Camille Tokerud

Figure 6.8: © Janine Wiedel Photolibrary/Alamy

Figure 6.9: AP Photo/Charlie Neibergall

CHAPTER SEVEN:

Figure 7.1: Courtesy of Jane E. Workman and Beth W. Freeburg

Figure 7.3: Eyecandy Images Inc./Alamy

Figure 7.4: © 2007 Jupiterimages

Figure 7.5: © Doug Pensinger/Getty Images

Figure 7.6: Cartoonstock

Figure 7.7: Courtesy of Southern Illinoisan

Figure 7.8: Bob Daemmrich/PhotoEdit Inc.

Figure 7.9: © Piotr & Irena Kolasa/Alamy

CHAPTER EIGHT:

Figure 8.1: © Ted Soqui/Corbis

Figure 8.2: AP Photo/Jason DeCrow

Figure 8.3: AP Photo/Jennifer Graylock

Figure 8.4: © 1996 by King Features Syndicate, Inc. World Rights Reserved

Figure 8.5: AP Photo/Natacha Pisarenko

Figure 8.6: Bill Aron/PhotoEdit, Inc.

Figure 8.7: AP Photo/Alastair Grant

Figure 8.8: The Kobal Collection/ABC-TV/Danny Feld

CHAPTER NINE:

Figure 9.1: Courtesy of Jane E. Workman and Beth W. Freeburg

Figure 9.2: Courtesy of Southern Illinoisan

Figure 9.3: By permission of Esther P. Lederer Trust and Creators Syndicate, Inc.

Figure 9.4: © 1995 by King Features Syndicate, Inc. World Rights Reserved.

Figure 9.5: Courtesy of Southern Illinoisan

Figure 9.6: AP Photo/Stuart Ramson

Figure 9.7: © Peter Cade/Getty Images

Figure 9.8: © John Berry/Syracuse Newspapers/The Image Works

Figure 9.9: © 1997 Lynn Johnston. Distributed by Universal Press Syndicate

CHAPTER TEN:

Figure 10.1: Library of Congress

Figure 10.2: Cartoonbank

Figure 10.3: Kevin Winter/Getty Images

Figure 10.4: Courtesy of Seventeen

Figure 10.5: © 1992 Lynn Johnston/Distributed by Universal Press Syndicate

Figure 10.6: AP Photo/Diane Bondareff

Figure 10.7: Courtesy of Southern Illinoisan

Figure 10.8: © 1992 King Features Syndicate, Inc. World Rights Reserved

Figure 10.9: © Jupiterimages/Brand X/Alamy